Divine and
Human Action

WORKS BY THOMAS V. MORRIS

Understanding Identity Statements
The Logic of God Incarnate
Anselmian Explorations
Philosophy and the Christian Faith

Divine and Human Action

Essays in the
  Metaphysics of Theism

Edited by Thomas V. Morris

Cornell University Press

Ithaca and London

First published in 1988 by Cornell University Press.

International Standard Book Number (cloth) 0–8014–2197–7
International Standard Book Number (paper) 0–8014–9517–2
Library of Congress Catalog Card Number 88–47738

Printed in the United States of America

Librarians: Library of Congress cataloging information appears on the last page of the book.

The paper in this book is acid-free and meets the guidelines for permanence and durability of the Committee on Production Guidelines for Book Longevity of the Council on Library Resources.

Contents

Divine and
Human Action

Introduction

Thomas V. Morris

This is a book of new essays in the rapidly developing field of philo-sophical inquiry known as the philosophy of religion or, perhaps more specifically and appropriately, philosophical theology. It focuses on a vitally important but, in the past century or so, relatively neglected terrain within the province of theistic metaphysics.

In recent decades, most of the philosophical attention devoted to religion has been directed either to problems about the semantic status of religious language, a topic especially dominant during the fifties and sixties, or to questions concerning the epistemological credentials of religious belief. Much of the literature has been polemical in nature, consisting in pointed examinations of various arguments for or against taking certain standard religions utterances to convey true propositions about what there is. There have been, for example, extensive discus-sions of the positivist challenge to the cognitive meaningfulness of religious discourse, rigorous critiques, analyses, and defenses of tra-ditional arguments for the existence of God, and manifold investiga-tions into that cluster of fascinating issues often known simply as 'the problem of evil.' Along the way, there have been treatments of meta-physical matters endemic to classical theistic belief, but until very re-cently much of this metaphysical work has been rather narrowly delimited and also quite polemical in character. Critics have attacked the coherence or plausibility of a traditional conception of God, tar-geting one or more of the metaphysical attributes of deity, and other

1

philosophers have come to the defense, seeking to explicate the impugned feature of divinity in a logically consistent and intuitively plausible manner. Contemporary discussions of omnipotence, omniscience, the nature of divine eternity, and the modal status of God's goodness, for instance, often have exemplified this dynamic.[1]

So, within the range of recent philosophical work on religion, the consideration of metaphysical topics has been limited largely to such disputes over the necessary or defining attributes thought to be constitutive of the nature of God. Little else has been done by way of exploring the contours of theistic metaphysics. And because of this, some of the other discussions have suffered. A specific conception of God is, after all, most typically the capstone of an overall theistic world view. And a theistic world view is just that—a view of the *world*, and of the world's relation to God, as well as of the God to whom the world stands in relation. Some of the philosophical exchanges over the existence of God during the past few decades can seem a bit shallow or "thin" precisely because they do not take adequate account of the deeper metaphysical implications of theism. The debate over the existence of God is not just a disagreement over whether there is one more, admittedly important, item in the inventory of reality, but rather is a much deeper controversy with profound and far-reaching ramifications. Most of the essays in this book contribute toward making clearer what is at stake in this debate by laying out and examining some of the most important metaphysical elements of classical theism. But it is not the main purpose of this volume merely to contribute toward enriching the ongoing discussion of whether theism is true. We are at a point where the philosophically intriguing features of a thoroughly theistic world view can be appreciated in their own right as a proper topic of metaphysical research.

It was my intent, in commissioning the essays assembled here, to provide an example of the fruitfulness and extraordinary interest of careful and creative explorations into the metaphysics of theism. The authors invited were left free to choose their own subject matter, subject only to the proviso that they treat in some manner the theistic conception of God's relation to, and interaction with, the created realm, inclusive of physical objects and rational beings. In numerous ways, the resulting essays demonstrate the philosophical interest of theistic

---

[1]Examples of the contemporary discussions can be found in *The Concept of God*, ed. Thomas V. Morris (Oxford: Oxford University Press, 1987).

metaphysics. It is my hope that they will stimulate other scholars to investigate further the metaphysical resources of the theistic vision.

It is the shared assumption of these authors that religion, in particular the Judeo-Christian religious tradition, is not just a domain of poetry, imagery, mystical transport, moral directive, and noncognitive, existential self-understanding. Interacting especially with the philosophically developed tradition of Christian theology, they join the vast majority of the other leading contributors to contemporary philosophical theology in taking for granted *theological realism*, the cognitive stance presupposed by the classical theistic concern to direct our thoughts as well as our lives aright. It has been the intent of theologians throughout most of the history of the Christian faith to describe correctly, within our limits, certain important facts about God, human beings, and the rest of creation given in revelation and fundamental to the articulation of any distinctively Christian world view. In particular, reflective Christians throughout the centuries have understood their faith as providing key insights into, and resources for, the construction of a comprehensive metaphysics. The essays published here take seriously the import of this tradition in its historical self-presentation.

Of course, many intelligent and sensitive religious people have on occasion expressed doubts or misgivings of one sort or another about exercises in theistic metaphysics. Some devout theists have even been known to belittle such matters. Blaise Pascal, for example, once seemed to express this sort of attitude by saying: "Even if someone were convinced that the proportions between numbers are immaterial, eternal truths, depending on a first truth in which they subsist, called God, I should not consider that he had made much progress toward his salvation."[2] A great number of contemporary academic theologians, professors of theology in seminaries, divinity schools, and departments of religious studies, appear to have developed a highly negative attitude toward theistic metaphysics and, more generally, toward what I have called "theological realism." It is not that they share Pascal's worries about the evangelical impact or soteriological efficacy of such an enterprise; it is rather that they seem to have come to certain conclusions about the *intellectual* futility of these major features of traditional theology. For one thing, many prominent theologians seem to think that the philosophical work of David Hume and Immanuel Kant long ago

---

[2]Blaise Pascal, *Pensées*, trans. A. J. Krailsheimer (New York: Penguin Books, 1966), p. 169.

effectively proved the miraculous and the transcendent to be excluded from the reach of human cognition. But more important, they appear to have become convinced that the legacy of Hume and Kant, crystallized in the domineering pronouncements of the logical positivists, has foreclosed forever the possibility of intellectually respectable and epistemically productive metaphysical thinking in the realm of religion.

This is a highly regrettable state of affairs. Neither Hume, Kant, the Vienna circle of early positivists, nor their philosophical descendants have succeeded in accomplishing anything of the sort. All they have accomplished is the sociological feat of discouraging great numbers of well-meaning religious scholars from appreciating and pursuing a perfectly respectable, vitally important, and tremendously fruitful intellectual activity that should be firmly placed within the center of their sphere of interests. Of course, it is still possible to construct and adopt theories within the philosophy of language and in epistemology that, if true, would disallow the human grasp and expression of metaphysical truths about God and the world. However, none of these possible theories is self-evident, compelling, or even very plausible. In light of this, it is hard to see how anyone whose personal faith is rooted in the Judeo-Christian religious tradition, and who is aware of the metaphilosophical facts of the matter, could be tempted in the slightest to buy into any such impoverished philosophical perspective, vetoing as it would effective human reflection on ultimate matters. The authors of the essays published here reject the assumptions that prevent many academic theologians nowadays from following their tradition in seeking to elucidate the metaphysical implications of theistic belief.

Of course, there is no single, comprehensive theistic metaphysic universally agreed upon by theists in all its details. The core commitments of a theistic religious tradition do not self-evidently entail a metaphysically determinate, precise conception of God, of God's relation to the world, or of the structure of creation itself. Fundamental Christian convictions, for example, provide suggestions for and constraints on an acceptable, philosophically precise conception of deity. And the resultant range of acceptable conceptions in turn provides a limited spectrum of permissible accounts of a general theistic metaphysic. But at every stage, as in theory construction in the natural sciences, we face the phenomenon of underdetermination.

Metaphysics is no simple business in general, so the outlining of a distinctively theistic metaphysic should not be expected to be a simple or altogether straightforward matter. There is, for example, no simple decision procedure for adjudicating rival metaphysical positions. A complex of considerations must be brought to bear in order to generate any progress. But of course, it is precisely the complaint of many theologians and even of some philosophers who eschew work in this field that there is no solid progress in metaphysics. For it seems obvious that the fortunes of metaphysics have been quite different from those of the natural sciences. This, at least, is a frequently voiced complaint about metaphysical endeavors.

But contrary to what is often charged, the history of metaphysics is not at all bereft of progress. In metaphysics, progress involves laying out clear options, charting interconnections among views, and discovering exactly where the problems and strengths of various alternatives lie. And with the sorts of independent convictions theists bring to the task, even more positive forms of progress are possible. It is my hope that the various views presented here will contribute in important ways toward such progress in understanding the metaphysics of theism.

In "Divine Conservation and the Persistence of the World," Jonathan L. Kvanvig and Hugh J. McCann argue from the perspective of the doctrine of creation *ex nihilo* that the God who brings the world into existence must also be responsible, through the exercise of his power, for its persistence moment to moment. They offer a battery of metaphysical considerations against the view that, once created, things can continue to exist on their own thanks to a natural power of self-sustenance. Throughout, their arguments make clear the dramatic difference between a thoroughly theistic account of the world and the sort of quasi-deism that many people seem to assume will be required by any scientifically responsible world view that countenances the existence of a creator.

In "Divine Conservation, Secondary Causes, and Occasionalism," Philip L. Quinn continues this examination by laying out very carefully a theory of divine creation and conservation and defending it against the charge that it is incompatible with real secondary causation in nature. After formulating the theory, he surveys all the major views of causation to see how each of them would affect his account of the intimate dependency relation between the world and God.

Because of the extraordinary dependence of the world on God in the theistic vision of things, important theistic philosophers have denied any autonomous, independent, or even distinct causal powers to created objects. On such a view, standardly known as 'occasionalism,' God is not only the primary or first cause of every natural phenomenon, he is its only true cause. In "Medieval Aristotelianism and the Case against Secondary Causation in Nature," Alfred J. Freddoso begins to investigate the question of whether occasionalism, a view held by such philosophers as al-Ghazali, Gabriel Biel, Nicolas Malebranche, and George Berkeley, can provide theists with a plausible and satisfying philosophy of nature. Although it is not a view entailed by just any theistic doctrine of creation and conservation, it is one that has fascinated and attracted many philosophers of the past set on developing a theistic metaphysic that allots a properly exalted role to divine action in the drama of existence.

How to understand the metaphysics of creation *ex nihilo* has been a long-standing challenge for theistic philosophers. 'Divine exemplarism' is a view stemming from Augustine which sees the metaphysical possibilities of creation to be resident in a realm of divine ideas ontologically prior to any divine action that brings about *ex nihilo* the physical and spiritual realm of created substances. The recognition of such divine ideas as exemplars of created substances allows theists to explicate the element of intelligent and rational selection, the element of planning presumed to characterise divine creation. In "Individual Essence and the Creation," Linda Zagzebski argues for a view of individual essences consonant with this theory of divine exemplarism. Tackling some central issues in modal ontology, she provides a very interesting case in favor of a crucial component for any contemporary development of this important theory.

In "Two Accounts of Providence," Thomas P. Flint traces a classic theological dispute to its roots in action theory. His focus is on the two different accounts of divine providence provided by Thomism and Molinism, views derived respectively from the great medieval thinkers St. Thomas Aquinas and Luis de Molina. Flint shows how Thomism seems to involve a basically compatibilist conception of creaturely freedom, and how the distinctive features of Molinism result from combining a libertarian account of freedom with a strong conception of providence. It is Flint's aim to make clear how a resolution of the theological dispute will finally require resolving the underlying metaphysical disagreement it presupposes.

William E. Mann explores issues of divine omniscience, rationality, sovereignty, and simplicity in "God's Freedom, Human Freedom, and God's Responsibility for Sin." Explicating the controversial but captivating medieval doctrine of divine simplicity, Mann shows that if God's knowing is one and the same activity as his willing, then God's refraining from willing some state of affairs S is equivalent to his willing S not to be the case. The view that results presents all worldly events due to creaturely causes as *joint ventures* between those creatures and God.

In "The Place of Chance in a World Sustained by God," Peter van Inwagen seeks to identify the nature of divine action on the created universe, and to delineate the most general outlines of what can count as part of God's plan for the world. He broaches the topics of creation, sustenance, law, miracle, providential design, and chance along the way, and succeeds in adumbrating a very interesting perspective for further work on such a vital religious topic as the problem of understanding the presence of evil in our world.

Central to many theistic conceptions of God's providential ordering of worldly events has been the belief that God has direct and comprehensive knowledge of everything lying in the future of his creation's development. In "Freedom and Actuality," John Martin Fischer continues his ongoing work probing the traditional problem of logical compatibility between divine foreknowledge and creatively freedom that can arise from this belief about God and the world. This essay examines an interesting strategy for attempting to reconcile foreknowledge and freedom, and points out the costs it incurs when its implications for divine immutability, perfection, and creation are considered.

With William P. Alston's "Divine and Human Action," an essay independently but very appropriately homonymous with this book, we turn our attention to our conception of the Divine Agent himself. It is obvious that our conception of God as an agent is modeled on our understanding of agency in our own case. But God is thought by most traditional theists to be radically different in nature from any denizen of the physical universe. He is said, for example, to be immaterial, infinitely perfect, and timeless. When these differences are appreciated, we begin to wonder how we can apply any substantive concepts at all, such as the concept of agency, to both God and creatures in an even partially univocal sense. Seeking to solve this problem, Alston appropriates elements of a contemporary functionalist account of many psychological states that holds that identical, or nearly identical, types of psychological, intentional states can be instantiated by very different sorts of beings, in very different ways. Delimiting what some of the components of a divine psychological structure might be like, consistent with the divine nature, Alston lays out a position that will provide for a solid core of literal, univocal language about God as an agent, but that will allow ample room for a figurative and symbolic under-standing of much other religious discourse as well.

Both God and his free creatures, such as human beings, are stan-dardly thought of as moral agents. A thoroughgoing theism must ad-dress the issue of the relation between God and moral goodness. In "Being and Goodness," Eleonore Stump and Norman Kretzmann pres-ent and defend some of the distinctive features of Aquinas's meta-physical views relevant to this important issue. In the course of their clear and precise explication of his metaethical and normative positions relevant to the assessment of value in free actions, Stump and Kretz-mann present a fascinating explication of what a human action is, and exactly how it is to be evaluated. On Aquinas's view of being and goodness, God is "being itself" and "goodness itself." This provides a unique perspective for viewing the relation between God and mo-rality, one that Stump and Kretzmann argue avoids the well-known difficulties of alternative positions that have dominated more recent theological reflection on this issue. In addition to laying out the rele-vance of Aquinas's metaphysical views to this problem, the authors also spell out the ways in which they serve to restrict the range of admissable solutions to the problem of evil.

In "Divine Goodness and Divine Necessity," Keith E. Yandell takes a look at two interestingly different forms of theism that disagree on the modal status of God's existence. What he calls 'plain theism' holds that the existence of the divine agent is a contingent matter. 'Anselmian theism,' on the other hand, follows St. Anselm in thinking of God as a necessarily existent being. Focusing on a problem dramatically raised for Anselmian theism by the central Christian doctrine of the Incar-nation, Yandell works out a case for preferring plain theism. By the use of a distinctively Christian example, he explores in an interesting manner a problem that could be raised in different ways for the other major theistic religious traditions insofar as their philosophically de-veloped expressions might present the creator as a necessary being.

Theists believe that God acts in the world and that his action is rational. Rational action is action guided by knowledge. So, funda-mental to any theistic account of God's action in the world should be a conception of God's knowledge of the world. In "How Does God Know the Things He Knows?" George I. Mavrodes launches an original investigation of the nature of God's knowledge. Aquinas and others have thought it important to affirm that everything God knows, he knows directly and noninferentially. Mavrodes controverts this eminent tradition, exploring the contrary suggestion that God knows everything he knows by inference. He characterizes his efforts in behalf of this thesis as an essay in "speculative epistemology," although it has numerous interesting metaphysical implications, some of which he discusses, especially those touching on the idea of divine perfection.

I would like to thank all the contributors to this volume for their willingness to participate in such a joint venture. They have graciously acceded to numerous common conventions of scholarly format and style in order to give the book a measure of unified presentation. However, since linguistic usage and stylistic convention can at times express important differences in philosophical commitment and approach, individual authors have been allowed more elbow room in these matters than publishers often like to see. I thank Cornell University Press for its reasonable approach to these matters. And I especially want to express my gratitude to John Ackerman, whose ongoing editorial encouragement and good will have been very important in the development of this project.

The similarities and diversities among these essays mirror those to be found more generally in the field of contemporary philosophical theology. Drawing on and interacting with the best philosophical work on religious topics in past centuries and applying the best of contemporary techniques, all the leading contributors to the field now are beginning to seek a new depth of understanding and a new breadth of perspective on the metaphysical resources and commitments of classical theism. It is to assist in furthering this process in philosophical understanding that this book of essays is presented.

Part One

DIVINE CAUSALITY AND
THE NATURAL WORLD

1

Divine Conservation and the Persistence of the World

Jonathan L. Kvanvig and Hugh J. McCann

Theists hold that God is the creator of, among other things, the physical universe and all that it contains. But exactly how is the dependence of the world on divine creativity to be conceived? Two pictures of God's relation to the world dominate the thoughts of those who have considered this issue. On the first, God continually sustains the universe at every instant of its existence. Further, His sustenance of it is not merely an effect of some other or previous action; it is the direct result of His present involvement in the world. On the second picture, God is directly responsible only for bringing the universe into existence. Its sustenance, insofar as it is owing to God's action, is merely an indirect result of His initial creative act. What separates these two pictures is their respective answers to this question: Are the things God creates able to continue in existence without His direct support? On the first the answer is no, and on the second it is yes. We argue that the first position is the correct one. In so doing, we focus primarily on God's relationship to the concrete world of ordinary experience. The argument we give is, however, general enough to show that our question must receive the same answer for anything God creates, physical or not. Throughout, we shall assume that God did in fact create all things other than Himself that have real existence; our question concerns only His relationship to those things once they appear.

1 Preliminary Considerations

There are at least two ways of conceiving God's role as Creator that would motivate an affirmative answer to our question. The first is associated with certain forms of fundamentalism. On a literal interpretation, the Genesis account of creation presents it as being terminated by a period of rest on God's part. If "rest" is taken to signify the cessation of any creative activity by God, it would seem to follow that since the close of the Sixth Day, the universe has been able to sustain itself without the aid of any direct assistance from Him. The second conception is deist in nature. On this view God is conceived as a sort of cosmic engineer Who, in the beginning, created a world that operates according to certain immutable laws, including laws of conservation. Once the universe was in place, it was no longer necessary for God to be active in sustaining it, nor is it so today. He may, on some accounts, intervene periodically to cause certain adjustments or changes within the universe or its operations, but no continuous activity on God's part is needed simply to keep it in existence.

Although deistic accounts of creation usually appeal to immutable laws as the explanatory device that allows for God's inactivity, it is worth noting that a more Aristotelian conception of nature leads to a very similar view. Instead of claiming that laws, conceived as relations between types of events, explain how God need not be active, one might claim that in creating, God implants a capacity for self-sustenance in what He creates, and that it is the presence or operation of this capacity that absolves God from sustaining the world after His initial creative activity ceases. Indeed, a theory that exempts God from directly sustaining the universe by appealing to laws must ultimately ground the truth of those laws in the characteristics of the things whose behavior the laws describe, and so must in the end appeal to a self-sustaining capacity of the things God creates.

It would be naive to underestimate the prevalence of conceptions such as the above, especially in popular thinking about divine creativity. Nevertheless, it seems fair to say that they are, from the point of view of philosophical theology, unorthodox. The orthodox position would seem to be that the things God creates have no more capacity to continue in existence than to bring themselves to be, and hence that God must not only create the universe, but also conserve it in existence at every point in time after it appears.[1] Indeed, many thinkers have held an even stronger thesis: that it is in the end impossible to distinguish God's bringing things to be from His sustaining them in existence. According to this view, God must be as actively and directly involved in the latter as in the former, and His activity of sustaining the existence of the world is essentially the same as His activity of producing it.[2]

This latter thesis concerning divine conservation is sometimes called the "continuous creation" theory, and it is subject to more than one interpretation. As we view the matter, continuous creation should *not* be taken to imply a view that was held by Jonathan Edwards: that each of the things God creates somehow begins to exist *anew* at each moment of its duration.[3] Such a position would face insuperable difficulties,[4] and in any case it is not what most adherents of continuous creation theories have wished to hold. Rather, what is intended is a view according to which each instant of the existence of any of God's creatures is as radically contingent as any other, and equally in need of activity on His part to account for it. Furthermore, God's activity as Creator is held to be essentially the same no matter what instant of the being of the thing created is at stake. He does not engage in one type of action to produce a thing and another to sustain it. To speak of this as "continuous creation" is misleading in at least one respect—namely, that the word "creation" usually implies novelty on the part of the thing created. In the present context, however, this implication counts as no more than a terminological infelicity, and is not part of the view intended.

Thus construed, the doctrine of continuous creation has much to be said for it, and in what follows we offer at least a partial defense of it.

---

[1]See, for example, Augustine, *De Genesi ad litteram* 4:12; Thomas Aquinas, *Summa theologiae (ST)* I, Q. 104, A. 1; and René Descartes, *The Principles of Philosophy* in *The Philosophical Works of Descartes*, trans. Elizabeth S. Haldane and G.R.T. Ross, vol. 1 (New York: Dover, 1955), pp. 227–228. Scriptural bases for the view include Colossians 1:17 and Hebrews 1:3.

[2]Among others, Descartes, Berkeley, and Leibniz clearly endorse this view. See the citations on pp. 56–57 of Philip L. Quinn, "Divine Conservation, Continuous Creation, and Human Action," in *The Existence and Nature of God*, ed. Alfred J. Freddoso (Notre Dame, Ind.: University of Notre Dame Press, 1983), pp. 55–80.

[3]Jonathan Edwards, *Works*, vol. 3, ed. C. A. Holbrook (New Haven: Yale University Press, 1970), pp. 402–03.

[4]Some are described in Quinn, "Divine Conservation, Continuous Creation, and Human Action."

Before doing so, however, we wish to set aside one misgiving to which this doctrine has given rise. Some philosophers have wished to avoid continuous creation theories, on the ground that they imply the doctrine known as occasionalism: that there are no secondary causes in nature, so that no effect in nature is really brought about by natural or secondary causal agents, but rather only by God Himself.[5] We think this objection is misconceived in that it fails to distinguish productive and alterational causation. As Creator, God is directly and primarily responsible for the fact that there is something rather than nothing: that is, it is His creative activity that is causally responsible for the *existence* of the physical universe. To say this is not to say He is directly responsible for the states of things in the universe, or the changes they undergo. By contrast, principles of scientific causation are concerned precisely to explain those states and changes, and they do so by relating them to other states and changes. In all cases, the existence of what occupies a state or undergoes a change is presupposed. Indeed, even where the operation of secondary causes produces what may be held to be a substance (salt, for example), the process by which it is produced is conceived scientifically as a transformation of something that predates it (say, sodium and chlorine, or the particles that make up the atoms of these). That is, even substances are held to be produced through changes undergone by others. In no case is it held that the operation of secondary causes is responsible for the existence of something, where the alternative is the absence of anything whatever. Thus, although there is certainly more to be said on this matter, we see no direct conflict between the doctrine that the creation and sustenance of the universe are one and the same and the claim that secondary causes are operative in nature.

Treatments of divine conservation that call for continuous creation are not, then, to be rejected out of hand. In the next section, we argue in favor of such an approach, based on considerations having to do with the eternity and immutability of God, and with the nature of the creative act itself. But it is important not to leave the case at that for, although we think they can ultimately be answered, there are important objections to the conception of immutability we defend. The most difficult of these has to do with God's omniscience, and is dealt with in

---

[5]By contrast, Malebranche welcomed this consequence, and defended it extensively. See, for example, *Dialogues on Metaphysics*, trans. Willis Doney (New York: Abaris Books, 1980), VII.

section 3. The remainder of the essay is devoted to an argument that is essentially independent of considerations having to do with the nature of God, and that we think shows that created things require God's direct support to continue in existence. In section 4, it is argued that the persistence of the created world cannot be accounted for in terms of any capacity that lies with the very possibilities that are realized when God creates the world, as Leibniz's doctrine of "striving possibles" might be taken to imply. Rather, we hold, created things can be self-conserving only if they themselves have a capacity to continue in existence. Section 5 is aimed at showing that this same result accrues when the relevance of scientific laws to the persistence of the world is considered. In section 6, it is argued that whether created things have a capacity for self-sustenance is a question essentially independent of whether they are ephemeral. In section 7, two versions of the thesis that created things have such a capacity are adumbrated, and in section 8 it is argued that both of these must fail. Our conclusion is that the direct support of God is alone responsible for the continued existence of the things He creates.

2 The Nature of God and *Ex Nihilo* Creation

Since creation is a relation between God and the things He produces, the question whether those things can remain in existence without His support has more than one important dimension. It may be approached not only by considering the nature of created things, but also by considering God's own nature, and what it is for Him to create a world *ex nihilo*. And considerations under these latter headings appear to call for some version of a continuous creation theory. On an orthodox conception of the nature of God, it may be argued that it is wrong to suppose the world can continue in existence after God has finished creating it, simply because it is false that God can cease creating. Perhaps the clearest argument is based on the concept of divine immutability. Traditionally, it is held that God is unchanging, that His being and activity must be conceived in such a way that no predicate can either begin to apply to Him or cease to do so. On the standard conception, indeed, so complete is God's immutability that He is not even subject to the kind of change known as pure becoming. Neither in His experience nor in His activity is God subject to temporal passage. Unlike us, He does not experience different things at different times, or act in different ways at different times. Rather, all predicates that apply to God must do so in a way that precludes His being subject to the limitations of temporal becoming. They may apply to Him tenselessly, or perhaps as signifying a kind of eternal present in which God is somehow directly and simultaneously both knowing and active with respect to all of creation. Now if such a conception of God's relation to time is correct, there is simply no room for the claim that He could cease to create, or cease to create any of the things He does create. Divine immutability is not, on this understanding, a matter of there being some set of predicates, however large, that happen to apply to God throughout the passage of time. Rather, it consists in a relationship of God to time such that, a priori, there can be no question of predicates beginning or ceasing to apply to Him. Thus God simply creates, and creates all that He does create; He does not start and stop. And if this is correct the world cannot persist after God has ceased creating it, for He cannot cease creating it.

Faced with this argument, opponents of the view we uphold would appear to have two options. The first is to accept the formulation of the doctrine of immutability that exempts God from temporal passage, but then seek to introduce some limitation on the object of His creative activity. The second is to argue that this version of the immutability doctrine is false, and that God must be held subject to temporal becoming. We shall consider the first option here, and the second in the next section.

One way of pursuing the first strategy is to grant that God ceaselessly creates all that He does create, yet insist that the object of His creation is the *coming to be* of the universe or the things in it, rather than the *being* of things or their *continuing to be* once they appear. If this is right, then even though God is not subject to becoming, it is only the first appearance of the universe, not its persistence, for which He is directly responsible. There is, however, an argument implicit in the traditional treatment of creation that we think is sound, and according to which this effort must fail.[6] Recall that, where divine creativity is concerned, the relevant contrast in our own experience is that between there being something and there being nothing. We are not, that is, concerned with changes undergone by substances that already exist, or even those changes in which a substance may be held to cease existing while another is made from the same material. Indeed, that the fact of there

[6] *ST* I, Q. 45, A. 2.

being something rather than nothing is the focus of God's creative activity is part of the import of the traditional claim that God creates *ex nihilo*. But where this difference is at issue, there is no room for a distinction between making things come to be and making them be. For if creation is *ex nihilo* it cannot consist in God performing some operation on some material provided prior to creation, and it cannot involve any *process* of things coming to be. That is, where creation *ex nihilo* is concerned nothing short of the *being* of things can be the object of God's will and creative activity. This holds, moreover, even if we conceive of the world as having had, from our point of view, a beginning in time.[7] For even if this were so, the change from there being nothing to there being something took no time, nor was it a change in which any *thing* changed. Thus, short of the first instant at which the world had being, there was nothing God was causing or creating. It is, then, the *being* of things that is the primary object of God's creation, even if there was a time when things came to be.

It is not, then, possible to limit the object of creation to the coming to be of the world, where this is supposed to be distinct from its being, for there is no such distinction. There is, however, another version of this strategy that our opponent might find tempting. For even if the distinction between being and coming to be fails where creation *ex nihilo* is concerned, surely there is a distinction between something's existing at one time and its existing at another. Suppose, then, that the created world had a temporal beginning, and let *t* be the first instant of its existence. Even if there is no becoming in God, and even if creation *ex nihilo* is not a process, one might still hold that the primary object of God's creative action is not the *existence* of the world, but rather *the world's existing at t*. This would again limit the primary object of creation to the first appearance of the world, and its existence thereafter could then be claimed to be a matter of self-sustenance.

We find this view unacceptable for several reasons. First, it is saddled with a presupposition we see no reason to accept—namely, that the world had a beginning in time. Second, the picture of creation this view presents is stilted. Expressions of the form "*x*'s existing at *t*" designate not substances but complex relational states consisting in something's having being at a particular moment. Moreover, because these states include a temporal index they may have to be construed

---

[7]It is worth noting that Aquinas treats this as an entirely separate issue, concerning which no philosophical demonstration is available. Ibid., Q. 46, A. 3.

as eternal. It is not clear that they themselves exist at *any* time (did *Reagan's existing in 1974* exist in 1974?), and it certainly seems clear that they do not endure through time. A fortiori, they could not in themselves be the locus of any self-sustenance on the part of the world, for they are not sustained at all. We can think of no independent reason for requiring that God create the universe in the roundabout way implicit in making these states the primary objects of creation. Nor is it clear by what route this model makes a self-sustaining universe possible. If these eternal states count as the *primary* objects of creation, how is it possible for the things that do exist at a given instant to have the kind of ontological independence that endurance through time requires? It is not obvious that they should count as substances at all, in the sense of enduring entities, rather than as a class of dependent entities with no capacity to continue. In short, it would appear that unless God also created the states consisting in the world's existing at all times after *t*, its endurance would be impossible anyway.

There are, moreover, a number of other difficulties with this way of seeking to limit the object of creation. It is faced, first of all, with the same type of problem that afflicted the previous attempt. That is, it is not clear that where creation is concerned, the supposed distinction between making things be and making them be at a particular time *t* is viable. Simply by causing the world to exist, after all, God would cause it to exist at the first moment of its existence. But the present model of creation reverses this order, and it is not clear that this can meaningfully be done. For if the reversal is to mark a meaningful distinction, we have to be able to suppose that God selects an instant of time *independent* of its being the first moment of the world's existence, and then acts in such a way as to secure its being the case that the world first exists at that instant and no other. But it is in no way obvious that time has the kind of absolute character that would make the selection of such an instant possible, for the instant would have to be individuated independent of any change that occurs at it. If there is such a principle of individuation for instants of time, we have no idea what it would be. If, on the other hand, times cannot be individuated independent of the changes that occur at them, then the supposed distinction between God's causing the world to exist and His causing it to exist at *t* collapses.

But suppose for the sake of argument that instants of time are individuated absolutely, so that there is nothing about time itself that would prevent the selection of *t*. Does the present view then count as a viable model of creation? We think not, for two reasons. First, if it is correct, then God's providence has to include not only seeing to it that the world is fittingly ordered as to relations of before and after among its constituents, but also watching out for its *absolute* timing. The world must appear, that is, when what we may think of as time's pointer is at the proper location. But there could not possibly be a reason for God to create the world at one time rather than another, where time is taken in this absolute sense.[8] All that is reasonable is for God to be concerned with the temporal ordering of what He creates, and this has nothing to do with absolute time. This picture of creation precludes God's being a completely rational being, for while it does not have God doing anything that is positively *ir*rational, it introduces a respect in which His activity as Creator is *non*rational: He must select an absolute moment for the world to appear, when there could be no reason to guide the selection. A God perfect in every respect cannot act in this way.

Second, even if God could select a particular instant for the world to appear, the strong concept of immutability we have been defending would seem to preclude His ever acting in such a way as to secure this result. We who are subject to temporal becoming control the timing of the results of our actions by controlling the time at which we act: for example, we control the time at which a limb moves by controlling the time at which we move it. But this possibility is not available to a God not subject to becoming. God creates the world, but He does not create at *t* as opposed to other times; hence He cannot time the world's appearance by this means. Nor, of course, could He control the time of the world's appearance by making sure some preexisting material changes at *t*, for since creation is *ex nihilo* there is nothing to change. Is there a third option? If so, it would have to consist in God somehow *doing something to t*; that is, He would have to operate *directly* on an independently selected instant so as to be sure the world occupies it. We have no idea what such a supposed possibility would come to, and we suggest that it is unintelligible.

If the traditional understanding of divine immutability is correct,

---

[8] If Leibniz is right, this consideration shows that time has no existence apart from change. *The Leibniz-Clarke Correspondence*, ed. H. G. Alexander (New York: Barnes & Noble, 1956), pp. 26–27. Parmenides employs it in a quite different way, assuming time is absolute and arguing that being could not have come to be. See *The Presocratic Philosophers*, ed. G. S. Kirk and J. E. Raven (Cambridge: Cambridge University Press, 1957), pp. 270–271.

then, there is no room for the claim that God can cease to create, or cease to create anything He does create. Furthermore, the nature of creation is itself such that its object cannot be limited to the coming to be of things, as opposed to their being or continuing to be, or to any supposed first instant of the world's existence. Of necessity, then, it must be through the very same activity that God is responsible for the entire existence of what He creates, for there is nothing short of this that can be the product of His creation. But then there is no way to introduce the possibility of the world somehow sustaining itself in existence after God creates it, and the question whether it does so must surely receive a negative answer.

3 Objections to Immutability

Perhaps, however, the conception of immutability at the foundation of the traditional view is wrong. It may be argued that God cannot be held to be exempt from pure becoming, but rather must be conceived as such that predications of all tenses apply to Him. If this view of God's nature with respect to time is adopted, then the position set forth above is threatened. For to say that God is subject to pure becoming is to hold that His experience and activity have duration. And this at least raises the possibilities that His creative activity might have had a beginning in time, that it might at some time cease, and that it might be intermittent. Thus, even if what is accomplished through creation *ex nihilo* cannot be differentiated with respect to things coming to be and their continuing to be, it might be thought that God could somehow cease to engage in creative activity with respect to the universe at some time after it has already appeared. The issue of whether things could thereafter continue to exist would then be raised anew. We need, therefore, to examine the grounds on which God might be held subject to change, and to discuss their implications for our position.

One argument has it that it must be possible for God to change, for otherwise He could not intervene in the affairs of men. The God of the Judeo-Christian tradition is not the hands-off God of the deist; rather, His love for mankind prompts Him to intervene in our own history. But, the argument runs, this would not be possible for a God all of whose actions are eternal. How can it be true of such a God that by 300 B.C. He had not yet sent His Son, but that by 300 A.D. He had?

It would seem that in order for these things to be true of God, He must Himself behave in different ways at different times.[9] This would entail that He changes, and so is subject to becoming.

The solution to this problem is to be found by drawing out a distinction implicit in the traditional position, between the temporal framework in which God acts and that in which we experience the results of His activity. The temporal framework of God is such that He has direct and immediate access to every instant of the universe's duration. Because this is so, it is possible for Him to perform an eternal action which has effects, in our framework, at one time and not another. That God ceaselessly creates all that He does create does not prevent the *products* of His creativity being ordered by before and after relations, nor is it incompatible with the fact that *we* experience those products seriatim, in a way that is characterized by becoming. The point is just that God does not experience them that way. He is, however, still perfectly able to see to it that the coming of His Son occupies a particular temporal location vis-à-vis other events. The distinction between the eternal activity of creation and its perennial effect in the being of things preserves, then, the possibility of a loving God acting in human history.[10] Indeed, from our own temporal perspective on the results of God's activity in creating the world, *all* of His acts as Creator are acts in history.

It is, then, possible to hold that all of God's actions are simultaneous and unending from the standpoint of His eternity, while still holding that the results of those actions need not be simultaneously present within our own temporal framework. A second type of argument against the traditional concept of immutability may also be dispensed with. It has been claimed that God cannot be immutable simply given the fact that we sometimes refer to Him and sometimes do not. For if we refer to Him at some times but not at others, it follows that there are things that are true of Him at some times but not at others. And from this it would appear that God changes.[11] The traditional doctrine should not, however, be abandoned in the face of this argument. Being referred to by another is a so-called Cambridge or relational property;

---

[9]Nicholas Wolterstorff, "God Everlasting," in *Contemporary Philosophy of Religion*, ed. Steven M. Cahn and David Shatz (New York: Oxford University Press, 1982), p. 78.

[10]For more on this view of God's perspective with respect to time, see Eleonore Stump and Norman Kretzmann, "Eternity," *Journal of Philosophy* 78 (1981), 429–458.

[11]Wolterstorff, "God Everlasting," 95–96. It is worth noting that a similar argument would quickly prove there are no eternal entities whatever, even abstract ones.

its coming to obtain or ceasing to do so signals no intrinsic change in the thing referred to. The real change is in the person who refers. Now the correct construal of the traditional doctrine of immutability requires only that no *intrinsic* property of God's be such that He has it at one time but not at another. He may be allowed to change with respect to Cambridge properties, for this requires intrinsic change only at the "other end" of the relation, and only intrinsic change requires becoming. It is possible, therefore, to allow that God undergoes Cambridge change, while at the same time holding that He undergoes no becoming, and hence remains immutable in the important sense.

There is, however, a more telling argument against divine immutability, based on considerations having to do with God's omniscience. It has been argued that in order to be omniscient God must be subject to temporal passage, for this is necessary in order to know what time it is.[12] The problem can be seen by considering the sentences "It is now 4/26/86," and "It is now 4/27/86." On 4/26/86, the first of these sentences expressed a truth and the second a falsehood; on 4/27/86, the situation was reversed. One way to explain how this can be so is to hold that the propositions expressed by these sentences change their truth value as time passes. But then, the argument runs, God must be subject to temporal passage in order to be omniscient. For He cannot be omniscient unless He knows what time it is, and He cannot know what time it is unless His beliefs change. He must come to believe each proposition about what time it is as it becomes true, and cease to believe it as it becomes false. Indeed, the objection can go further, for it may be wondered how an eternal being can even have *access* to propositions expressed by sentences employing the temporal indexical "now." When such sentences are used, the indexical picks out just the time that is actually occurring. But, it may be argued, only beings subject to temporal passage can be aware of times as occurring and ceasing to occur, and hence only they can be aware of the proposition expressed by any given use of a sentence employing "now." If this is right, then God must be subject to temporal becoming even to have access to these propositions.

This objection raises a number of interesting issues, about both the nature of time and how time enters into God's awareness. A full ex-

---

[12]Norman Kretzmann, "Omniscience and Immutability," *Journal of Philosophy* 63 (1966), 409–421. The claim can be extended to all tensed propositions. See, for example, Wolterstorff, "God Everlasting," 93.

ploration of these matters would take us too far afield, but we do think it is possible to forestall the objection. We shall consider first the problem of God's access to propositions expressed using temporal indexicals, and then return to the issue of whether these propositions change in truth value.

The access problem consists in its seeming to be the case that certain propositions are perspectivally limited, in that only beings subject to becoming can be aware of them. As such, this problem is analogous to problems concerning self-awareness. It has been thought that when someone has a *de se* belief—that is, when he believes something about himself, where the belief is expressed using the indexical "I"—that person accesses a proposition that only he can access.[13] These first-person propositions are quite different from those involved in ordinary *de dicto* belief (belief in a proposition expressed with a sentence using no demonstratives or indexicals), and from those involved in *de re* belief (belief *of an object* that it has a certain property, where the sentence expressing the proposition believed employs a demonstrative such as "this" to pick out the object). If this is right, first-person propositions too are perspectivally limited: they are available only to the person whom the proposition is about. But then they too would raise problems for the traditional construal of omniscience. For if first-person problems can be accessed only by the person they are about, then most of them are unavailable to God—just as, on the objection we are considering, propositions expressed using temporal indexicals would be unavailable to Him. He could therefore not believe these propositions, and so could not be omniscient.

There are, however, theories of indexicals like "I" that do not posit perspectivally limited propositions, yet explain the data that appear to call for them. One such theory calls for a triadic account of belief. On a triadic account, when Hume believes of himself what is expressed by the sentence "I'm Hume," he believes exactly the proposition believed by Heimsohn when Heimsohn believes what is expressed by "He's Hume." Their beliefs are not the same, however, for two reasons.

---

[13]See Roderick M. Chisholm, *Person and Object: A Metaphysical Study* (London: Allen and Unwin, 1976), chap. 1; also the following papers by Hector-Neri Castañeda: "He*: On the Logic of Self-consciousness," *Ratio* 8 (1966), 130–157; "Indicators and Quasi-indicators," *American Philosophical Quarterly* 4 (1967), 85–100; "On the Logic of Attributions of Self-knowledge to Others," *Journal of Philosophy* 65 (1968), 439–459; and "On the Phenomeno-Logic of the 'I,' " *Proceedings of the XIV International Congress of Philosophy* 3 (1968), 260–266.

First, and most obviously, one of them is held by Hume and the other by Heimsohn. Second, and more important, the *belief state* that Hume is in is not the same belief state Heimsohn is in, for the two states play different causal roles: Hume's belief state would lead Hume to respond, "Here I am" to the question, "Where's Hume?" and Heimsohn's would not.[14] Thus the triadic theory of belief eliminates the need for perspectively limited propositions in accounts of personal indexicals, by positing a third *relatum* in believing, namely a belief state. The role of this third *relatum* is to allow first- and third-person speakers to have different means of access to one and the same proposition, thereby explaining the differences between *de se* belief and *de re* or *de dicto* belief.[15]

A triadic theory can also be employed to explain how a being not in our temporal framework can access propositions that we express using temporally indexed sentences. There need not be perspectively limited propositions, available only to us, for the data that appear to call for such propositions can equally be explained by allowing more than one means of access to propositions not perspectively limited. For example, God may have direct and simultaneous access to all propositions that we would express using temporal indexicals, in that the entire sequence of change constitutive of the created order is immediately present to Him. We, by contrast, have direct access to such propositions only sequentially, with the occurrence of particular instants during what for us is a process of temporal passage. If so, then we access these propositions in a way in which God cannot; but that is compatible with both God and us believing one and the same proposition. It does not, then, follow that God cannot access the propositions we express using temporal indexicals merely because He does not share our temporal framework.

The difficulty about the seeming variability in truth value of these propositions can be handled in similar fashion. As far as we are able to tell, the only reasons for thinking that propositions expressed by sentences using "now" change in truth value rest on confusions. One reason is this: what Sam says on Tuesday is true when he says, "It is now Tuesday"; but when he says the same thing on Wednesday, it is

---

[14]John Perry, "The Problem of the Essential Indexical," *Nous* 13 (1979), 3–21. A similar theory is defended by David Kaplan in *Demonstratives*, unpublished manuscript.

[15]For a more complete account of this approach to temporal indexicals, see Jonathan L. Kvanvig, *The Possibility of an All-Knowing God* (London: Macmillan, 1986), chap. 5.

false. But this confuses the sentence used to express a proposition with the proposition expressed. The same sentence is used by Sam on both Tuesday and Wednesday; but the propositions it expresses are different, for they involve different times. Hence nothing need be held to change its truth value. Another reason that could be offered is that in cases like Sam's, the same sentence has the same meaning on two different occasions of use, and so must express the same proposition, which accordingly changes in truth value. But this too is a mistake, for identity of meaning simply does not guarantee identity of propositions. In short, there is no good reason for thinking that propositions expressed by using temporal indexicals change in truth value, hence no good reason for thinking they offer any insuperable obstacle to the traditional doctrine of immutability.

We think, then, that the traditional construal of immutability can be defended against the usual objections, and need not be modified in response to them. Nevertheless, the difficulties raised by the last of these objections are profound, and laying them to rest may well be thought to require a more complete account than we have provided of the nature of time and its relation to God. In order to make our case that the world must be conserved in existence by God conclusive, therefore, we must examine the issue from the point of view of the created order. Thus we turn to the other term in the creation relation: the created world itself.

4 Striving Possibles

From the point of view of the created world, our question is whether there is anything to the character of the things God creates, or at least of some of them, such that simply by bringing them into existence God could somehow secure the continuance of the world. The traditional doctrine of creation has it that this cannot be the case, but the idea that the things God creates could continue to exist without His conserving them implies otherwise. There are at least two ways that this latter conception could be defended. It might, first of all, be argued that it lies in the very character of the possibilities that are realized when God creates things that once they exist, certain things will be self-sustaining. Alternatively, it could be held that the character of at least certain of the products of God's creation includes a self-sustaining feature. The first of these lines of argument can be given as one interpretation of Leibniz's doctrine of "striving possibles," which we will examine first. We will then turn to the question whether the products of creation might include anything with a capacity for self-sustenance.

According to Leibniz, possibilities themselves strive toward, or involve some sort of drive toward, actuality. As he puts it at one point: "Everything possible demands that it should exist, and hence will exist unless something prevents it, which also demands that it should exist and is incompatible with the former."[16] As Leibniz sees it, this competitive striving results in the most perfect possible world, for the degree to which possibles strive to exist is proportional "to their quantity of essence or reality, or according to the degree of perfection which they contain."[17] There is considerable discussion over how this doctrine should be taken. Some hold that it should be taken only figuratively, and that the so-called striving amounts to no more than the degree of attractiveness each possible has for God as Creator.[18] Thus taken, the doctrine offers no obstacle to the account of creation we defend. Others, however, hold that the doctrine should be viewed literally.[19] On this type of account, the striving counts as a real power accorded to each possible, which in the absence of competition from more perfect ones issues inexorably in the possible being realized in existence. If this interpretation of the doctrine is adopted our position is threatened, for it could further be claimed that once existence is attained, the striving for existence manifests itself in a capacity on the part of what exists to be self-sustaining, or to persist in existence without need of support from any external agency.

There are a number of difficulties with the literal interpretation of Leibniz's doctrine, not the least of which is whether it accords to God any direct role whatever in the actual appearance of the world, or even any choice as to whether it will appear once there are possibles. A related question is how the possibles themselves acquire the literal striving imputed to them on this reading of Leibniz. It would seem that unless God is to be completely supernumerary in the creation of

[16]C. J. Gerhardt, *Die philosophischen Schriften von Gottfried Wilhelm Leibniz*, vol. 7 (Berlin: Wiedmann, 1875–90), p. 194.

[17]Ibid., p. 303.

[18]Nicholas Rescher, *The Philosophy of Leibniz* (Englewood Cliffs, N.J.: Prentice-Hall, 1967), pp. 29–30.; David Blumenfeld, "Leibniz's Theory of the Striving Possibles," in *Leibniz: Metaphysics and Philosophy of Science*, ed. R. S. Woolhouse (New York: Oxford University Press, 1981), pp. 77–88.

[19]Christopher Shields, "Leibniz's Doctrine of the Striving Possibles," *Journal of the History of Philosophy* 24 (1986), 343–357.

the world, He must Himself impart to each possible its striving for existence. And indeed Leibniz speaks at one point as though God does impart the striving, and that His doing so is more or less the same thing as His making things exist: "But whatever cause makes [it the case] that something exists, or that a possibility demands existence, also makes [it the case] that all possibles have a striving for existence, since a reason for restricting it only to certain of them cannot be found."[20] But it is hard to see *why* we should understand creation to proceed in this way, and on this point we get little help from Leibniz. The appeal to the Principle of Sufficient Reason in the above passage serves only to support the claim that God does not impart a striving for existence only to *some* possibles. But this argument has force only if it is granted that at least some possibles receive this capacity. If that assumption is denied, the same sort of appeal to sufficient reason will do no good. That is, it would be incorrect to argue that since there is no reason not to impart to possibles a striving for existence, God imparts this characteristic.[21] The Principle of Sufficient Reason requires a *positive* reason for whatever occurs, and thus a positive reason for God to impart the striving. But this argument offers no positive reason; it contents itself with the negative consideration that there is no reason for God not to see to it that possibles strive to exist. This is insufficient, for we can set against this argument the opposite one: Since there is no reason to impart a striving for existence, God does not impart this characteristic. The question, then, is whether to prefer the second or the first argument, and in the absence of some decisive reason for God to impart or not impart the striving the issue remains unsettled.

There are, moreover, reasons for thinking that the literal interpretation of this doctrine cannot be put in a form cogent enough to withstand close examination. Possibles, it is fair to assume, count as some sort of abstract entity—essences, perhaps, or something propositionlike in nature. Now abstract entities exist eternally, and while their existence may depend in some way upon God,[22] they do not require an act of

---

[20]Gerhardt, vol. 7, p. 289. The Latin is: "*Sed quae causa facit ut aliquid existat, seu ut possibilitas exigat existentiam, facit etiam ut omne possibile habeat conatum ad Existentiam, cum ratio restrictionis ad certa possibilia in universali reperiri non possit.*"

[21]Shields interprets Leibniz as giving just such an argument in the passage cited. "Leibniz's Doctrine of the Striving Possibles," 352.

[22]We have in mind here versions of conceptualism according to which such things as universals, propositions, etc. are nothing but *entia rationis*, and never exist independently of minds. Theist versions of conceptualism are able to hold that all such entities exist in the mind of God, thereby allowing for the existence of abstract entities that have never

creation by Him in order to exist. What does require activity on God's part is for possibles to be realized, and that is a matter of their coming to have *instantiations* in the concrete world. On the literal account of striving possibles, this occurs not through direct creation by God, but rather through an indirect operation in which He imparts to abstract entities the capacity to strive toward their own instantiation. But it is not obvious how God could do this, or what good would be achieved if He did. On the first score, note that the capacity to strive toward instantiation could not be a *defining* feature of whatever possibles have it, for if it were they would have it of their own nature, obviating the need for it to be imparted. Nor could the striving be a mere Cambridge property of possibles, for then it would depend on what occurs else-where, and it is the striving of possibles that is supposed, on this account, to *explain* what occurs elsewhere. The striving for instantiation must, then, be either a merely accidental feature of those possibles that have it, or a synthetically necessary, non-Cambridge feature imparted by God. But it is not clear, first of all, that abstract entities can even have features of these kinds. Ordinarily, at least, they are conceived to be such that all of their characteristics are either defining ones, or owing to relations between the abstract entity and other entities such as concrete instantiations, thinkers, and the like. It is not at all obvious that the capacity to strive toward existence should, or even could, count as an exception to this rule. Furthermore, how is it possible for anyone, even God, to operate on an abstract entity in such a way as to impart to it directly a property it would not otherwise have? Certainly mortals can do no such thing, and it is not at all clear how God is able to do it. Even in its formulation, then, this is a baffling doctrine.

Finally, even if God could act on abstract entities in the way this doctrine envisions, it is hard to see how His doing so would further the enterprise of creation. As has been said, creation involves the pro-duction of instantiations of what is possible. But instantiations, at least as usually conceived, are concrete entities, not modified abstract ones, and they are numerically distinct from the abstract entities they in-stantiate. The concept of striving possibles runs counter to this idea. It appears to assert that concrete entities come into existence through

---

been thought of by humans, without having to say that those entities exist entirely on their own. For more on this type of fully theistic metaphysics see Thomas V. Morris and Christopher Menzel, "Absolute Creation," *American Philosophical Quarterly* 23 (1986), 353–362.

a change in some preexisting abstract entity, and constitute a modified version of the abstract entity itself. But this amounts to giving up abstract entities entirely, for it requires that such entities be able to change, in that they themselves can both strive toward existence and come to have it. This alone is incompatible with any conception according to which abstract entities exist eternally, for no eternal entity is metaphysically capable of undergoing intrinsic change. On the other hand, if we retain the principle that instantiations of abstact entities are numerically distinct from the abstract entities themselves, it is at best unreasonable to think that any property imparted to the abstract entity could account for the appearance of its concrete instantiation. It is not, after all, as if the abstract possible could *do* anything with its capacity to strive, or carry out any activity that could result in the production of a concrete entity modeled after the possible.

On a literal reading, then, the doctrine of striving possibles lacks any convincing argument in its favor, and raises far more problems than it solves. To date, at least, it has not been formulated in such a way as to give it any intrinsic credibility, or to pose a serious threat to the traditional account of creation. The existence of a concrete world is not owing to God having put into place something short of such a world that was somehow able to transform itself into one. Nor could any capacity on the part of the world to continue in existence be owing only to a striving on the part of abstract entities to exist. In short, if God's creative activity is not directly responsible for the continued existence of the world, then its continued existence could be owing to nothing short of a self-sustaining feature of the world itself, or the entities in it.

5 Conservation and Scientific Laws

Another argument that the world is self-sustaining can be founded on a certain interpretation of scientific laws. It might be claimed that even the simple chemical principle governing the formation of table salt tells us that if we start by combining sodium and chlorine we are going to wind up with sodium chloride. That is, this principle is diachronic in its import: it tells us something about how the world will be later on if a certain occurrence takes place now. It is hard to see how this principle could be reliable—could even, as is frequently supposed, have some sort of necessity attached to it—if one of the things that could happen when sodium and chlorine are combined is that they both just pass out of existence. At a more general level, one of the guiding principles of physics is that in all physical interactions, the total amount of mass/energy is conserved. The scope of this law includes all physical change, and surely, it might be argued, its purport is in part that once mass/energy exists, it will not simply disappear. This in turn might be taken to indicate that self-sustenance is in fact a characteristic of the physical world, that things are able to persist without the aid of sustaining activity on God's part once they exist at all. In short, this argument concludes, the truth of scientific laws, especially conservation principles, indicates that even if the existence of the physical world requires a theological explanation, its *persistence* does not. Given that it exists at all, the empirical world is perfectly able to sustain itself without help from God.

We believe that this understanding of conservation principles, and of scientific laws generally, is mistaken. As usually formulated, conservation principles do not state without qualification that *anything* is conserved. Rather, they are given as applying only to what are called "closed" or "isolated" systems; only within an isolated system is it held that mass/energy is conserved. And an isolated system turns out to be *defined* as one into which no mass/energy is introduced and from which none is lost. Indeed, the law for the conservation of mass/energy borders, at least, on being a conceptual truth: it holds that within spatiotemporal locations that undergo no net gain or loss of mass/energy, the amount of mass/energy remains the same. How could such a seemingly vacuous principle be of value to science? It is of great value if, as turns out to be the case, it is possible to encounter or devise systems that approximate closely to being isolated, and if, as we urge above, science is concerned not with the question of there being something instead of nothing, but rather only with the changes that occur in things once they exist. In such a setting, requiring that mass/energy be "conserved" amounts to insisting that when we seek to explain a phenomenon scientifically, the principles we articulate and the measurements we take must provide a full accounting at the termination of the phenomenon of the mass/energy that entered into it. So construed, conservation principles turn out to be invaluable aids both to theory formation and discovery, the classic example being that of the neutrino. They are not, however, theological in import, nor do they call for the physical world to persist. Rather, they presuppose that the world is sustained, and they succeed because this presupposition turns out to be correct.

Similar considerations apply to less general scientific laws. The law for the formation of salt offers no guarantee of the persistence of anything. It says only that to the extent that sodium and chlorine do interact within a given spatiotemporal interval, sodium chloride is the result. If there is any diachronic import here at all, it arises from the *prior* fact that, as it turns out, the mass/energy of which sodium and chlorine are composed does in fact persist. But the law for the formation of salt is not a law of such persistence, nor does it entail any such law. In short, scientific laws cannot be invoked to ground the persistence of things. To hold otherwise is to verge on the superstition condemned by Hume in his treatment of causality: that there is some sort of cosmic glue that holds the world together across time, and whose operations are recorded in the findings of science. There is no such thing, nor could any empirical investigation disclose it if it existed. Scientific laws speak only to the transformations of persisting things. Properly understood, they offer no grounding or explanation for the fact that anything in the world is sustained. They do not, for that matter, even state that sustenance is a fact.

Or so we say. But perhaps we are wrong, or scientists have been too timid. It is, after all, a plain fact that many of the things in our experience do persist in existence, at least for a time. The same tree that was in the quad a few minutes ago is there now, and the stars and planets, as well as our own possessions, pets, and friends, do survive, if only for a little while. Perhaps some principle of conservation, whether known to us or not, is at work here after all—a principle that invokes nothing supernatural, and whose truth somehow accounts for the fact that the world or the things that compose it persist through time. The question whether divine activity is needed to sustain the products of creation is equivalent to the question whether there can be a "natural law" of this kind. If traditional belief is correct, there cannot.

What would such a supposed law have to state? It would not be enough for it to say simply that the world or the things in it *are* sustained. That this is true is not in dispute; indeed, taken in this sense even familiar conservation laws are compatible with the belief that it is God who sustains the universe.[23] Rather, the supposed law would

---

[23]Conservation principles become inimical to our thesis only if two conditions are met. First, a "closed system" must be understood simply as a region of space into which no mass/energy enters from another region, and from which none exits. Second, the fact (if it is one) that the quantity of mass/energy in such regions remains the same over time has to be presented either as not requiring explanation, or as owing to a natural capacity

have to treat either the world or the things in it as *self*-sustaining, and it could be true only if a capacity for self-sustenance is an actual *characteristic* of something in the world. Laws, after all, are descriptive in import. They do not *operate* at all, despite our figures of speech, and they do not do anything in or to the world. If they are true, it is because things themselves have features the laws describe. What we must investigate, therefore, is the possibility that some thing or things found *in* the concrete world might have the characteristic of being self-sustaining.

6 An Insufficient Strategy

The project of finding self-sustaining entities in the physical world appears unpromising from the outset. If there are such entities, it is reasonable to suppose that they will count as substances of one kind or another. For the other things we find in our experience—the particular characteristics of things, the states they are in, and the changes they undergo—cannot plausibly be held to exist on their own. Rather, they depend for their existence on there being substances to have characteristics, occupy states, and undergo changes. We may assume, therefore, that the alleged capacity for self-sustenance is associated with substances. If this is right, a natural place to begin looking for it is in the medium-sized ontology of ordinary experience: persons, cats, hills, trees, fields, etc. In thinking about these objects, however, one immediately recognizes their ephemerality. They do persist for some span of time, but inevitably they cease to be, which presents an obvious problem. How could things that have the capacity to sustain their own existence ever cease to be? Is it that the capacity is somehow overridden or destroyed by external forces, perhaps by an exercise of the same capacity in other objects? This answer does not seem adequate, for destruction from without is not always the explanation for a physical object's demise; internal breakdown or decay can serve as well. Might it be, then, that the self-sustaining capacity of a thing goes dry, much

---

of things which, science discloses, renders them stable with respect to existence. But since mass/energy does not exist by logical necessity, its continuing to exist after it first appears is as much in need of explanation as its first appearance. And as for this continuation being due to some natural capacity of mass/energy itself, we are at a loss to understand how scientific investigation could disclose such a capacity even if it were there.

as an engine runs out of fuel after operating for a certain amount of time? But powers or capacities are not well understood in this way. A fuel is a substance; a power or capacity is not, and hence cannot in any literal sense be used up.

Implicitly, then, there appears to be a conflict between ephemerality and the alleged capacity for self-sustenance. The objects of ordinary experience seem not to be self-preserving, but rather to have an intrinsic *potentia ad non esse* that assures that, far from being sustained, they will eventually pass out of existence. It was, no doubt, partly in response to this problem that some philosophers of earlier ages were led to postulate the existence of certain privileged substances—entities that, though not observed in ordinary experience, were held nevertheless to exist, and to be exempt from ephemerality. In Newton's era, for example, atoms were thought to be of such a nature that they would never pass out of existence, either through internal decay or through destruction by external forces. The more familiar, macroscopic entities these atoms composed might pass away, but atoms themselves were deemed imperishable, and to constitute the sole building blocks for all other physical entities. The advantage of this strategy is that by abandoning the realm of ordinary experience, it makes a gain in plausibility. By associating self-sustenance with incorruptibility, it avoids the embarrassment of having to explain how ephemeral substances could have this capacity.

The atomist view is beset, however, with enormous disadvantages. The most obvious is that as far as we know, there are no such privileged entities. To date, physics has disclosed no substances, macroscopic or microscopic, that are not subject to internal breakdown. Even subatomic particles such as neutrons are thought to decay at an extremely slow rate, and they can certainly be destroyed. Nor are any claims of permanence made on behalf of more recently discovered particles. Empirically, then, there appears to be nothing in the physical world that has the character of a Newtonian atom. There are, moreover, theoretical reasons for thinking no such a phenomenon will ever be found. On a very general reading, the second law of thermodynamics would call for any organized state of matter to tend to decline toward disorganization over time. If this is correct then Newtonian atoms, which surely count as organized states of matter, do not exist.

Finally, there is a difficulty arising not from the concerns of physics but from those of philosophical theology. If there were Newtonian atoms, or some other thing that had the property of being created yet indestructible (and hence not even possibly ephemeral), then such a thing would have the capacity for self-sustenance. However, there cannot be any such thing, for such an entity could only exist in violation of God's omnipotence. It has to be within the power of the Omniponent One to destroy that which He has created, and He could not destroy the physical world if the entities of which it is composed were incapable of ceasing to exist.[24] In its classical form at least, then, the atomist view generates severe theological as well as scientific difficulties.

The above problems can be summarized in a dilemma that faces any theory that would seek to locate a capacity for self-sustenance in the physical world. If the supposed capacity is attributed to the substances of ordinary experience, some way must be found to reconcile possession of this capacity with the inevitable demise of the entities alleged to have it. If, on the other hand, self-sustenance is held to be lodged with privileged entities such as those of corpuscularian philosophy, the resulting theory is both scientifically backward and theologically incorrect. An inviting strategy for opposing the view that the products of creation are self-sustaining, then, is to pit it against the fact that everything in our empirical experience is ephemeral.

The defense of the doctrine of divine conservation cannot rest content with this strategy, however. One reason is that it is theologically limited. Traditional belief has it that the products of God's creation include not just physical substances but spiritual ones as well: angels, and perhaps human souls. Spiritual substances do not have the intrinsic *potentia ad non esse* characteristic of the physical objects of ordinary experience, and hence are not ephemeral. Moreover, Christian belief looks forward to the day when our own bodies will be glorified in the Resurrection, and thereafter exempt from forces of decay and destruction. Yet none of these considerations are thought to cast doubt on the

---

[24]It might be objected that it would be no violation of God's omnipotence for Him to create something indestructible, for the resulting limitation on His power would be self-imposed. The situation, it might be argued, is similar to the paradox of the stone, which might be resolved by holding that although God *can* create a stone so big He could not lift it, the resulting limitation on His power is not damaging, since it occurs through His own free action. We hold, however, that this way of dealing with such problems is incorrect. God has to be not merely omnipotent, but also *essentially* omnipotent, where the latter implies that He could not lose His omnipotence, even as a result of exercising His own power. For God to create a stone too big for Him to lift would entail such a loss, and hence even He could not create such a stone. And neither, for the same reason, could He create anything indestructible. For further discussion of these issues, see Thomas P. Flint and Alfred J. Freddoso, "Maximal Power," in *The Existence and Nature of God*, pp. 81–113.

doctrine of divine conservation. Either theologians have been unaware of what is at issue in the doctrine, or the issue is not one connected in any decisive way to considerations regarding ephemerality. Moreover, even where ephemeral substances are at issue it is relevant to our concerns that, although these substances *do* wear down and get destroyed, they do *not* simply disappear. Our concern is not with how long a thing survives, but rather with the fact that it survives at all for more than an instant. Again, there is reason here to think that the issues surrounding self-sustenance are logically distinct from those surrounding ephemerality.

We can put this issue more concisely. The primary focus of our discussion, even where ephemeral substances are concerned, is with the composition between essence and existence they display. Ephemerality, by contrast, has usually been understood to be associated more with the composition between form and matter in physical things. Thus, to attempt to answer the question whether self-sustenance is possible for created things by centering on considerations regarding ephemerality would be to risk missing the heart of the issue. What we hope to show, therefore, is that any claim that a contingently existing being could be self-sustaining is metaphysically misconceived: no created substance, we argue, could have such a characteristic. If we are successful, we will have shown not only that ephemeral substances do not have this capacity, but also that any substance exempt from natural forces of decay and destruction must still be sustained in existence by God.

7 The Nature of Self-Sustenance

For the sake of brevity, we will hereafter refer to the alleged capacity for self-sustenance as *ss*. It may be characterized as follows:

> $ss =_{df.}$ a capacity such that necessarily, if a substance S has ss at t, then, owing to the presence or operation of ss, there will (*ceteris paribus*, at least) be a time t^*, $t<t^*$, such that S will exist at t^*.

Note that by this definition, it has to be due to its possession of ss that S persists. This is meant to distinguish *self*-sustenance from the characteristic of merely *being* sustained, which S would have provided only that it did persist through a temporal interval, regardless of the reason. If ss were defined in such a way that anything that persisted through time had ss for the duration of its persistence, the definition would fail to distinguish between God's sustaining the thing and its sustaining itself.

Suppose, for example, that someone wished to classify the possibilities available to God as Creator as follows. He could, it might be maintained, create things in either of two modes: a perishing mode, or a persisting one. By creating objects in the perishing mode and then sustaining them, God would make the doctrine of divine conservation true; by creating objects in the persisting mode, He would make the doctrine false. If this view is to be maintained, it must be held that the distinction between the two modes is that, in the perishing mode, ss is not given to the objects created, whereas in the persisting mode ss is given. (If one wishes to push harder on the talk of "modes" here, one might wish to claim that ss is an intrinsic characteristic of one way of existing—the persisting mode. Whether ss enters the picture as a characteristic of a mode of existence or as a property of things, though, will make no difference to the outcome.) Our point is that, regardless of how one wishes to formulate the view that contingent things do, or can, exist on their own independent of God's conserving activity, one will have to understand the nature of the things in question in such a way that they include ss. For without ss, there is nothing to distinguish self-sustenance from divine sustenance.

The *ceteris paribus* provision also requires some clarification. It is meant to allow for the fact that where ephemeral substances are concerned, ss must somehow be able to be overridden or frustrated or in some other way cease to be successful, so that S might cease to be. In fact, however, we will not have to be concerned with this possibility, for there are independent reasons for thinking there can be no such capacity as ss in contingently existing beings.

To see this, let us consider what kind of characteristic ss could be. The first important question here is whether ss could count as a physical characteristic of any S that has it. The answer is obviously no where S is a spiritual substance, but the fact is that even if S is a physical entity, ss must be conceived as a strictly metaphysical feature of it. That is, ss cannot be a characteristic like the human power of immunity to disease, or the capacity of sugar to dissolve water. All such powers have a *physical basis*, in that their exercise is due to the operation of physical constituents in the thing having the power. Since they are themselves physical entities, these constituents count as precisely the sort of things the continued existence of which *ss* is supposed to explain. The only way to avoid an infinite regress, therefore, is to make *ss* a strictly metaphysical characteristic, one whose presence and/or operation cannot be reduced to the presence or operations of physical structures within *S*.

A similar argument shows that *ss* cannot be a supervenient characteristic. It cannot have a physical supervenience base, for the reason given above, and we can think of nothing that might count as a metaphysical supervenience base. So *ss* must be a strictly metaphysical characteristic, one whose presence and/or operation cannot depend on the presence or operations of other, more fundamental structures within *S*.

A second important consideration is whether *ss* ought to be conceived as an active power of *S*—i.e., a power that manifests itself in some operation or process by which *S* is sustained in existence. On this point two interpretations are possible, each of which has further implications as to how *ss* must be conceived. On the first interpretation, the *S* that possesses *ss* is understood to be metaphysically in need of constant, active sustenance. That is, it is conceived to be of such a nature that unless it is *actively supported* in existence, it will cease to exist. To avoid the doctrine of divine conservation, this support must come from *ss* rather than God. On such an account, *ss* is construed as an *active power* of *S*, something that operates in or on *S* in such a way as to secure the endurance of *S* through time. The operation of *ss* is here a process that is responsible for the continued existence of *S*.

If *ss* is understood in this way, then the process associated with it must be diachronic rather than synchronic. For if *ss* worked synchronically, its effect would have to be simultaneous with its operation. That is, at each moment *ss* would have to operate in such a way as to sustain *S* at the same moment. But it is obvious that this will not do. For one thing, since the particular powers of things depend for their existence on that of the things that have them, this would mean that *S* and *ss* would be sustaining each other at exactly the same moment. Of course, the type of dependence might be different in each direction; that is, the way in which a substance supports its characteristics may differ from the supposed way in which *ss* sustains *S*. Nevertheless, it is obviously circular to have *S* and *ss* mutually dependent for their existence at *t*. More important, though, no synchronic operation of *ss* could guarantee that an *S* that exists at *t* will *last* until any later moment

t^*. But to provide for this lasting is precisely what it must consist in for ss to sustain S. It simply will not suffice, therefore, to understand ss as an active power that operates synchronically; it must be that the power operates diachronically, if at all.

Assuming ss does operate diachronically, the relationship between the existence of S and that of ss becomes cyclical rather than circular. S at t sustains ss in the way typical of a substance "supporting" its characteristics. But S's own existence at t is owing to the operation of ss before t. In turn, the operation of ss at t secures the existence of S later on, when S in its own turn will support ss. This type of cyclical dependence relation has, of course, a contrived ring to it: one may well suspect it could never exist. Nevertheless, it is necessary to the interpretation of ss as an active power that such a relation be posited. For only in this way can the persistence of S be provided for in such a way that neither S nor ss is supported from without.

Consider now a second approach to the question whether ss is to be viewed as an active power. On this interpretation, S has no metaphysical need for active support, and ss is not an active power. Rather, it simply *consists*, so to speak, in the fact that S requires no active support to continue in existence, that it is not of such a nature that it would cease existing but for some exertion that takes place to support it. This interpretation treats the endurance of S through time as though it were due to a kind of principle of inertia governing temporal existence. Existence, it claims, must be actively supplied to S only when it first comes into being, and may thereafter be retained without effort. It does not claim, however, that nothing could deprive S of existence. S might be destroyed, even by forces of internal decay. All that is excluded is that S require active support simply to continue existing.

The crucial implication of this second interpretation of ss is that on it, ss can only be conceived as an accidental characteristic of S. Indeed, on either of the interpretations given, it is at best problematic whether ss could be essential to S. For suppose ss were part of the essence of S, so that S could not exist without it. Intuitively, this appears to place an undue restriction on God's options in creating the world. It would be one thing for Him to be able to endow created things with an accidental capacity for self-sustenance, for then the persistence of what He creates would remain independently subject to His will. But to make ss essential to what God creates would mean that unless he could somehow contrive actively to destroy them, God would have no say over whether the products of His creation continue to exist once they appear. This type of limitation on God is hardly commensurate with His freedom and power, at least as these are usually understood. Indications are, then, that even if self-sustaining things are possible, it must also be possible for God to sustain those very same things should He choose to do so.

Moreover, where ss is understood according to the temporal inertia model given above, there is an insuperable metaphysical difficulty in taking it to be an essential feature of S. To see this, note first that even if ss is not an active power, it still must consist in a relation of some kind between S (or the essence of S) and S's existence. Whether ss is an active power or not, it still has to *explain* the fact that S persists through time. If this is to be accomplished, then even on the inertial view ss cannot consist simply in the fact that if S exists at t, it will exist at t^*. For that fact alone does nothing to distinguish self-sustenance from divine conservation. If ss is to explain anything, then, it has to consist in some sort of relation between S (or the essence of S) and S's existence.

Yet, if this relation is essential to S, then the necessarily existing abstract entity that is the essence of S has this relation as a proper part. But no relation can obtain apart from the obtaining of those things which are related, and on the inertial interpretation ss is in no way *productive* of continued existence for S. Hence, if the abstract entity that is the essence of S includes ss, conceived as a relation between S (or the essence of S) and S's existence, then S's existence itself is included in the essence of S. It follows that S is a necessarily existing entity, and hence was never created at all. So, at least where ss is not conceived to be an active power, it cannot be essential to S. If it exists at all, it can only be an accidental feature that S possesses.[25]

Analysis of the notion of self-sustenance reveals, then, that if such a capacity exists in created things, it must be a purely metaphysical characteristic of whatever possesses it. Furthermore, ss may be understood in two ways: as an active power that operates diachronically in S, or as a nonactive, relational characteristic that can only be held by

---

[25]A similar argument may also apply to the active power interpretation of ss. There, however, the situation is somewhat different, for if ss is taken to be an active power it must in some way be productive of continued existence for S once S appears, and it might be held that this obviates any need for an independent guarantee that existence will be available as a term in the relation ss embodies. It is, however, not necessary to produce an argument of this kind against the active power interpretation of ss since, as will be seen in the next section, that interpretation must fail in any case.

S accidentally. The burden of the next section will be to show that on either interpretation, there can be no such characteristic.

8 The Impossibility of Self-Sustenance

Consider first the interpretation that takes ss to be an active power. On this account there is supposed to be an operation or process associated with ss, owing to which S is able to endure from some time t to a later time t^*. Could there be such an operation or process? It is hard to see what it would be like, in view of the fact that ss is a completely metaphysical characteristic. Clearly there could be no physical change constitutive of it, or upon which it supervenes. Furthermore, physical or not, the whole notion of such a process is suspect. In it, S is supposed to be able somehow to operate on itself by employing ss, or ss must itself be able to operate in or on S, in such a way as to "propel" S into the future. But this is analogical talk, and if we drop the analogy it is hard to see what we are talking about, if anything. Intuitively, then, the idea that there is such a process has little to recommend it.

The decisive consideration against the active power interpretation of ss is, however, that no such supposed process could achieve the result desired for it. We have seen that on this interpretation, ss must operate diachronically: that is, there is supposed to be a difference between the time at which an increment of the operation of ss occurs, and the time at which that increment sustains S. If, for simplicity, we take this in terms of instants, then the operation of ss at t is supposed to be responsible for the existence of S at a future instant t^*. But this is impossible, for either there is an interval between t and t^* or not, and in each case the position fails. Suppose first that there is no interval between t and t^*. Then since time is a continuum, $t = t^*$, for in a continuum no two points can be adjacent to each other. But if $t = t^*$, then the operation of ss is synchronic, which has already been proven impossible.

Suppose, on the other hand, that there *is* an interval. Then it has to be that an event in the past is able to cause one in the future *without* an intervening sequence of connecting events. This is so because ss is a strictly metaphysical, nonsupervenient power. Since it has this nature, ss cannot operate through any physical sequence of events, and we can think of no metaphysical sequence of events that could fill in here. For *ss* to operate diachronically requires, then, that events be able to have effects at future times without there being any sequence of events connecting the supposed cause and effect. This sort of temporal *actio in distans* is, however, impossible, for it calls for what no longer exists to be causally operative. If t and t^* are taken as instants, then, *ss* cannot operate diachronically.

An equally damaging result can be gotten if we let t and/or t^* be intervals, for then the intervals must either overlap or not. To the extent that they overlap, the operation of *ss* exhibits the circularity characteristic of synchronic operation. If they do not overlap, we are again calling for an event that does not exist to be causally efficacious. Moreover, even where intervals are concerned the argument can proceed in terms of the contribution of *ss* at instants within the intervals, with the same result. It follows that *ss* cannot operate diachronically at all.

It might be thought that this argument is too strong, and that a similar argument would show that there can be no causal relations at all. This is, however, not the case. It is true that the implications of time being a continuum are often overlooked in discussions of causation. If a cause and its effects had to be temporally contiguous there could be no causation, for the nature of time precludes there being contiguous events. Nor, certainly, can a past event cause a future one without an intervening sequence of change to connect the two. There are, however, sequences of events that involve causation. The key to understanding them is to realize that the crucial elements in the sequence are pairs of events that are related as cause and effect, and are simultaneous. To use the classic example, when the cue ball strikes the object ball in a billiard game, there is no reason to suppose momentum is transferred to the object ball before the latter begins to move; indeed, that would be a theoretical impossibility, for the object ball could have no momentum if it had no velocity. Nor is there any way in which the cue ball acts upon the object ball before the object ball begins to react. Action and reaction are simultaneous. Moreover, this is exactly what is to be expected if, as we have argued above, scientific laws are without diachronic import. For since causal relations can always be described using scientific laws, what is true of causation should be commensurate with what is true of those laws. Finally, there is nothing in simultaneous causation of the kind of circularity that would accrue if *ss* were to operate synchronically, for causes are in no way dependent for their existence on their effects. There is, then, nothing in our argument against the active power interpretation of ss that tells against there being causal relations of the ordinary, empirical variety.

Since ss cannot be an active power, we are left with the interpretation according to which it is a nonactive, relational characteristic of S. This understanding of ss suffers from an intuitive implausibility similar to that which attends the active power view. Remember that even on this interpretation, ss has a certain diachronic import. It must still embody the idea that S retains its existence over time. Now when a substance retains a characteristic over time, the explanation usually boils down to one of three things. It may be, first of all, that the characteristic is sustained in the substance by some operation or process. But we have already seen that where the characteristic in question is the existence of S, ss cannot be taken as constituted by any process. A second type of explanation for a substance retaining a characteristic is that the characteristic in question be essential to the substance. Self-evidently, however, this possibility is also foreclosed here: *ex hypothesi*, S is a created substance, and hence one to which existence is not essential. Finally, it may be that the characteristic a substance retains is, though not essential to the substance itself, essential to some material that goes into the composition of the substance. For example, the color of a book, which is not essential to the book, is nevertheless essential to the material that composes the book's surface. But this possibility too is ruled out in the present case. S might, in the first place, be a spiritual substance, and hence not composed of any material. Even in the case of material substances, moreover, there is no reason to suppose existence is essential to anything of which they are made. To hold otherwise is to call into question the entire thesis that there is a God who created the universe, and that thesis is not here in dispute.

It turns out, then, that all of the usual explanations for a substance retaining a characteristic over time are ruled out when the characteristic in question is the existence of a created substance. What the present interpretation of ss does is to call for another type of explanation, one in which the continued existence of S is owing to a relationship between S and its existence, one that appears to be unanalysable, and to consist in no more than the supposed fact that S is, for some reason internal to it, stable with respect to existence. There is little if anything to distinguish this treatment of ss from mere blind insistence that, the traditional doctrine of conservation notwithstanding, the things God creates are self-sustaining. The temporal inertia view is accordingly of dubious plausibility. It is, however, possible to go further. We wish to argue that this understanding of *ss* cannot be made plausible unless it is given an interpretation on which it reduces to the view that it is after all God who sustains the products of His creation.

Recall that where *ss* is viewed as a nonactive, relational characteristic, it can at best be an accidental feature of *S*. But if *ss* is only an accidental feature of *S*, it cannot provide a satisfactory explanation of *S*'s persistence unless we have a further account of how it is that *ss* endures in *S*. That is, instead of worrying about why *S* continues to exist, we have now to worry about why it continues to have *ss*. And the only viable explanation is that God sustains *ss* in *S*.

How do the accidental properties of substances accrue to them? We have already seen one possibility: that they be essential to the material of which the substance is made. There is, however, no possibility that *ss* could accrue to *S* in this way, for we have seen that *ss* must be completely metaphysical, having no supervenience base, physical or otherwise. And again, *S* need not even be a physical substance. Neither would it be feasible to argue that the persistence of *ss* in *S* is guaranteed by the operation of some scientific law, such as a conservation principle. We have already argued that scientific laws do not in themselves do anything. Their truth depends on the characteristics and operations of substances. Indeed, one way to think about *ss* is to view it as exactly the sort of thing that would be needed to account for the usefulness of conservation principles if divine sustenance of creation is denied. Introducing a further conservation principle to ground the persistence of *ss* would be viciously regressive. Finally, to consider a similar strategy, it would be useless to hold that some contingent necessity holds *ss* in place. For then we would have to know what this concept comes to and, since the alleged necessity is supposed to be contingent, what holds it in place.

At this point, a theological response will have occurred to some at least: What sustains *ss* and/or the contingent necessity that accounts for its sustenance is the initial creative act of God. That is, although the endurance of *ss*, and hence of *S*, is indeed to be accounted for by action on God's part, the action in question is not one that takes place or continues after His initial creation. Rather, *ss* and hence *S* perdure only as an effect of God's initial creative act.

This response is not adequate, however; for in this case, there is nothing that can serve as a medium to carry the force of the initial act to a later time at which the effect is to be manifested. In this respect,

God's actions differ from our own. We are able to perform acts that have effects at later times because the universe is so structured, causally and temporally, that intervening events enable our actions to have consequences after they cease. In God's case, no such structure is available to carry the force of His original decision to a realization at some later time. All there could be is the divine resolve to ensure that His original decision be carried out *by carrying it out* at the later time. Nor will it do to protest that, once the causal medium that governs the universe is in place, God can exploit it to make certain that the force of His initial creative act will be carried through to later times, in the sustenance of the things He creates. Perhaps this is possible, though the difficulties discussed earlier concerning conservation laws would indicate otherwise. Even so, however, such a medium is superfluous. For God can exploit it *only if He also sustains the medium itself*. This alternative therefore provides no comfort to those who wish to deny the doctrine of divine conservation, for the fact remains that even here it is God Who sustains things, by continually sustaining a medium that serves as a means to the goal of their preservation.

We do not mean to claim that there can be *no* acts of God that, at least from our own temporal perspective, occur at particular times and have consequences at later times. Such a thing is certainly possible, but the mechanisms involved in such cases are not of a kind that can be adapted to account for the continued existence of the created world. Suppose, for example, that God destroys a physical object at t. If so, that act will have a consequence at a later time: namely, that (unless He somehow later resurrects it) that object does not exist at $t + n$. There is, however, no parity between the continued *non*existence of something that has been destroyed and the continued existence of something that has been created, or of any characteristic of that thing, such as ss is supposed to be. The nonexistence of a thing is a strictly negative state of affairs, and requires no explanation beyond the fact that, once destroyed, things do not just jump back into existence. The persistence of anything is, by contrast, a positive state of affairs, and a contingent one at that, and so requires an accounting. Moreover, as we have argued, the accounting must leave God's omnipotence intact: He must be able to control the means by which something is sustained, lest He be unable to destroy that thing. Short of being able to recreate an object once destroyed, however, God has no control over whether an object exists after it has been destroyed. On the other hand, if God *is* able to recreate objects He has destroyed, then their continued *non*existence requires as much constancy on His part as is demanded of Him by our account of the continued existence of what He creates. He must, that is, continually refrain from recreating the lost object, thus "sustaining" its nonexistence, just as on our view He must constantly sustain the existence of all He creates.

God's activity can also have what for us are later consequences in virtue of the necessity that attaches to the past. In the above case, one consequence at $t+n$ will be that God destroyed an object in the past. Finally, there are consequences realized in virtue of logical, or metaphysical, necessity. One such consequence is that it will be true at $t+n$ that God destroyed an object at t. These consequences are like the continued nonexistence of the object destroyed, in that they too are realized without any required activity on God's part. Again, however, the mechanisms involved are not under God's control, and hence are inappropriate for explaining the continued existence of the created world, or any self-sustaining feature of it. For given that He destroys an object at t, even God cannot bring it about that He will later not have destroyed that object, or not have destroyed it at t. Furthermore, even if these mechanisms were under God's control, they are simply not fit for the task at hand. It does nothing to account for the present existence of any creature to point out simply that God created it in the past, or that He created it at t.

Although it is possible, then, to find certain structures that allow us to speak of consequences of earlier acts on God's part that accrue without His further activity, none of these structures will account for the persistence of the world, or of any alleged self-sustaining feature of it. Hence none of these structures can be used to ground the supposed distinction between God's original creative act of producing ss in S (and/or some alleged contingent necessity held to ground the continuation of ss in S), and the continuing effect of S's retaining ss (or the contingent necessity remaining in place). What is needed, of course, is just the sort of preexisting, causally structured order of things that we as creatures are able to exploit in exerting control over the future. But as we have seen, no such medium is available to God as Creator: indeed, it is precisely the existence of this order of things that God's activity as Creator is needed to explain.[26] And since this medium

---

[26]Nor is the unavailability of causal mechanisms to God to be taken as a limitation upon Him, for the presence of such mechanisms also imposes restraints on agents. It is a distinctive feature of God's freedom that the sorts of constraints the causal structure

is absent, all that can ground the continuation of the world is the divine resolve to continue it in the way begun. And the realization of that resolve is that God continually sustains the world in the way that He began it.

The upshot of these considerations is that it is pointless to try to account for the continued existence of any object S in terms of its possessing ss, where the latter is conceived as a contingently held, nonactive characteristic of S. For on any such view, the persistence of ss in S must in turn be explained, and none of the options considered above will explain it. There remains, we think, only one reasonable explanation. There must be *some* ongoing process that sustains ss in S. To avoid a regress this process must be external to S, and it must be of a kind capable of sustaining a completely metaphysical feature of things. Now we can think of no agency that could be involved in such a process other than God. But if this is right then the fact is, after all, that it is God who continually sustains the existence of the things He creates. The effort to produce a plausible understanding of ss has reduced it to the status of an intervening variable. Indeed, ss cannot even exist as defined earlier, for its definition requires that the continuation of S's existence must result from this purely internal characteristic. If, as we have shown, any role played by an internal capacity for self-sustenance must involve the activity of God as well, then there can be no such capacity. We conclude that ss does not exist, either in ephemeral substances or in any other products of creation. The claim that contingent beings are self-sustaining turns out to be false, for there is no way to give it plausibility without in the end invoking divine sustenance.

9 Conclusion

If the arguments we have given are sound, then it is God alone Who sustains the existence of the things He creates. This can be demonstrated in either of two ways: by considering the nature of God and the creative act, or by considering the nature of the products of creation. An interesting feature of the first strategy is that it leads to the corollary

---

of the world places on us do not, could not, constrain Him. Hence it is not a defect of His power to lack the ability to realize pure effects ("pure" in that they involve no further activity by the individual in question), but rather a mark of His magnificence that He requires no causal means to achieve anything He brings about, and that the limitations that attend such means do not bind Him.

that strictly speaking, it is not even possible to distinguish God's bringing things to be from His sustaining them in existence. This is a satisfying result, for it has been the traditional view, and it is befitting to the divine simplicity that the production and sustenance of the universe should be one and the same.

It is important to note, however, that our main thesis does not depend on the correctness of this strong construal of divine conservation, and the doctrine about God's relation to time that is bound up with it. Our argument that created things can have no capacity for self-sustenance is based on difficulties with the very concept of self-sustenance, not on assumptions about either God's relation to time or the nature of the creative act. Finally, even if, as we believe, the strong construal of divine conservation is correct, it should not be thought that this somehow militates against the scriptural suggestion that in the process of creation there came a kind of point of completion—a point at which, as it is said, "God rested." At its very strongest, our position calls for "continuous creation" only in the sense that it finds no possibility for created things to continue to exist on their own, no possibility for change in God, and no possibility to distinguish, from the perspective of the creative act itself, between God's producing and His sustaining all that He creates. It is perfectly compatible with this that, from the temporal perspective of humans, there occurred a time at which the major elements of creation were all in place. We hold no brief on this issue, but if that is the correct reading of Genesis 2:1–3, nothing we have said gainsays it.[27]

[27]We are grateful to Robert Audi, Robert Burch, Stephen Daniel, Peter Markie, Christopher Menzel, and Philip Quinn for helpful discussions, and comments on earlier drafts of this essay.

2

Divine Conservation, Secondary Causes, and Occasionalism

Philip L. Quinn

The watchmaker God of the deists is said to have fabricated the whole world of contingent things in the beginning, but thereafter it is supposed to behave like a good mechanical device and run on its own without further divine assistance. According to theism, the world of contingent things was not only created by God in the first place but is conserved by God throughout its existence. Many theists even hold that divine conservation of persistent things amounts to continuous creation. On this view, the whole world of contingent things is metaphysically dependent upon God in a very strong sense. There are those who worry about whether this has untoward and unacceptable consequences. It has been urged that one consequence is that there are no secondary causes at all in nature; it has also been suggested that it has the consequence that the only secondary causes in nature are occasional causes. This essay aims to lay such worries to rest.

Whether or not there are secondary causes in nature depends, of course, on what secondary causes are. And as even a superficial acquaintance with contemporary philosophy reveals, there is no consensus among philosophers on this topic. Regularity theories of causation, counterfactual theories of causation, necessitarian theories of causation, and others compete in the marketplace of ideas. I shall argue that taking divine conservation to be continuous creation is consistent with regularity theories, counterfactual theories, and necessitarian theories. So no matter how the controversy among those three approaches to the problem of analyzing causation gets resolved, if it ever does, the view that divine conservation amounts to continuous creation will remain tenable.

In section 1, I rehearse and slightly revise the elements of a theory of creation and conservation I have discussed in more detail elsewhere.[1] In section 2, I formulate a regularity theory of secondary causes based on the celebrated definition of causation Hume proposes in *An Enquiry Concerning Human Understanding* and argue that it and other theories of the same sort, in conjunction with my theory of creation and conservation, have only consequences theists should find quite palatable. In section 3, I lay out the key ideas of the counterfactual theory of secondary causes constructed by David Lewis and try to show that it and more complicated counterfactual theories, in conjunction with my theory, have only consequences theists would approve. And finally, in section 4, I formulate a necessitarian theory of secondary causes and attempt to prove that even it, in conjunction with my theory, has only consequences theists can accept.

1 A Theory of Creation and Conservation

To begin with an enumeration of my ontological assumptions and notational conventions, I assume that time has the structure of a linear continuum and is composed of point instants. I use the letter 't' as a variable of quantification ranging over point instants and the expression 't_1' as a schematic constant designator of point instants. In accord with familiar mathematical practice, I employ the expression 'Δt' to indicate a small temporal increment. I also assume there are concrete individual things such as tables and chairs. I use the letters 'x' and 'y' as variables of quantification ranging over such individuals, and I restrict the domain of quantification to contingent individuals. The expressions 'i_1' and 'i_2' are schematic constant designators of such contingent individuals. I further suppose that there are properties and use the schematic letters 'F' and 'G' to express them. Finally, I suppose there are states of affairs and use the letters 'p', 'q', and 'r' as variables ranging over them. The difference between my use of these letters and their more

---

[1] Philip L. Quinn, "Divine Conservation, Continuous Creation, and Human Action," in *The Existence and Nature of God*, ed. Alfred J. Freddoso (Notre Dame, Ind.: University of Notre Dame Press, 1973), pp. 55–80.

familiar use as propositional variables is that grammatically appropriate substituends for my variables would be nominalized sentences while grammatically appropriate substituends for the ordinary propositional variables would be sentences. Some states of affairs obtain, and others do not.

Following Kim's general strategy, I take events to constitute a species of states of affairs.[2] An event is a state of affairs composed of a contingent individual, a property, and a point instant of time. An event that obtains is said to occur, and it occurs at the instant that is a constituent of it. Because all the individuals that are constituents of events are contingent, all the events that occur do so contingently. I idealize by assuming that an event of finite temporal extension may be replaced for theoretical purposes with an instantaneous event occurring at the midpoint of its duration. As far as I can tell, this idealization does no more harm than replacing an extended body with a point particle at its center of mass for calculational purposes in classical mechanics.

In order to formulate my theory of creation and conservation, I need to assume that there is a two-place relation of bringing about defined on ordered pairs of states of affairs. The primitive schematic locution of the theory is this:

(1) God willing that i_1 exists at t_1 brings about i_1 existing at t_1.

Two things about this locution are worth noting. First, the expression on the lefthand side of the relation-expression picks out states of affairs that are not events. For one thing, God is not a contingent individual, and for another, God's volitions do not occur at times if, as many theists suppose, God is timelessly eternal. Second, the expression on the righthand side of the relation-expression picks out states of affairs that are events just in case existence is a property. I suppose it is not.

I do not claim to have a firm grasp, amounting to a clear and distinct idea, of the relation of bringing about that my theory requires me to postulate. Obviously it must be a rather special relation of metaphysical causation. Beyond that, I think it must be characterized by the following marks in order to answer to the theological purposes it is supposed to serve: totality, exclusivity, activity, immediacy, and necessity. By to-

[2]See Jaegwon Kim, "Causation, Nomic Subsumption, and the Concept of an Event," *Journal of Philosophy* 70 (1973), 217–236.

tality, I mean that what does the bringing about is the total cause of what is brought about; nothing else is required by way of causal contribution in order for the effect to obtain. By exclusivity, I mean that what does the bringing about is the sole cause of what is brought about; causal overdetermination is also ruled out. By activity, I mean that the state of affairs that does the bringing about does so in virtue of the exercise of some active power on the part of an individual involved in it. By immediacy, I mean that what does the bringing about causes what is brought about immediately rather than remotely through some causal chain or by means of instruments. And by necessity, I mean that what does the bringing about in some sense necessitates what is brought about.

Perhaps a bit more light will be shed on the relevant notion of causation if a few words are said about how it functions in inference. The following two schemata seem to me to represent valid patterns of inference:

(S1) p brings about q

p obtains, q obtains

and

(S2) p brings about q

There is no r distinct from p such that r brings about q.

The second of these patterns reflects the fact that bringing about is being understood in such a way that what does the bringing about is the sole and total cause of what is brought about. However, for reasons that will become apparent in section 4, it is important to realize that the following schema does not represent a valid pattern of inference:

(S3) p brings about q
q entails r

p brings about r.

Counterexamples to this schema are not hard to produce. Here is one. Suppose God willing that I exist now brings about my existing now. Since God existing obtains necessarily, my existing now entails God existing. But it is not true and does not follow that God willing that I exist now brings about God existing.

Assuming that enough has been said about the notion of bringing about to generate some understanding of it, I now proceed to state my theory of creation and conservation. It consists of this simple axiom:

(A) Necessarily, for all x and t, if x exists at t, God willing that x exists at t brings about x existing at t.

So the theory says that divine volition brings about the existence of every contingent individual at every instant at which it exists. I claim that there is nothing more to creation or conservation than this. And the theory implies that divine volition brings about the existence of every persisting contingent individual at every instant of, and so throughout, every interval during which it exists. This, I say, amounts to claiming that divine conservation just is continuous creation.

There are those who think there is an important distinction between creation and conservation. They divide the career of a persisting contingent individual into two parts. First there is creation, which takes place at the first instant of existence, if there is one, and then there is conservation, which takes place at every other instant of existence. They seem to suppose that the kind of power required to create something *ex nihilo* is different from the sort of power needed merely to keep it from lapsing back into nonbeing once it has been created. Maybe they imagine God is like an athlete who needs more strength to lift a huge weight than to hold it aloft once it has been lifted.

I consider this view to be mistaken. It seems clear to me that Descartes was correct in saying that "in order to be conserved in each moment in which it endures, a substance has need of the same power and action as would be necessary to produce and create it anew, supposing it did not yet exist."[3] In the case of conservation as well as in the case of creation, that power is whatever mysterious power that God possesses in virtue of which his volitions bring about contingent existence. We speak of creation in the case in which divine volition brings about the existence of a creature at a time and that instant of time is one prior to which there is no other at which that creature existed; and we speak of conservation in the case in which divine volition brings about the existence of a creature at a time and that instant of time is one prior to which there are others at which that creature existed. But the power

---

[3]René Descartes, "Meditation III," *Philosophical Works*, vol. 1, ed. E. S. Haldane and G. R. T. Ross (New York: Dover Books, 1955), p. 168.

and action involved in the bringing about are the same in both cases. I regard it as a merit of my theory of creation and conservation that its axiom expresses this point with tolerable economy.[4]

Now that the elements of a theory of creation and conservation are in place, it is possible to be a bit more precise about what the worry about secondary causes in nature actually is. Ignoring the Special Theory of Relativity in order to make the point vivid, let us imagine that the world of contingent things is partitioned into time-slices by the relation of absolute simultaneity. If the contingent things that exist at a time-slice depend for their existence solely and totally on God's creative activity at that time-slice, then, except for connections among time-slices made from outside nature by divine activity, what exists contingently at one time-slice within created nature is completely independent of what exists contingently at any other. But this appears to leave little or no room for what happens at one time-slice to exercise any influence on what happens at any other by means of a path that remains wholly internal to the created realm. So there seems to be a problem of trans-slice causation, and the possibility of there being secondary causes in nature appears threatened.

Presumably, it is evident to the senses, or something of that sort, that there are, in some sense, secondary causes in nature. So if it were a consequence of my theory of creation and conservation that there are not, it would be appropriate to apply *modus tollens* and to reject the theory. But there are many senses in which there might or might not be secondary causes in nature. The remainder of this essay is devoted to discussing three of them.

2 Humean Regularities and Occasionalism

What sorts of things do philosophers take to be paradigmatic instances of causation in nature? Here is an example that shows up again and again in contemporary discussions. A match, being dry and in the presence of oxygen, is struck at a certain time, and slightly later the match is lit. The event of the match being struck at the one time is a cause of the event of the match being lit at the other. And here is an example adapted from medieval discussions. Our match, being near a

---

[4]See Quinn, "Divine Conservation, Continuous Creation, and Human Action," pp. 67–74, for further discussion of this point.

thimbleful of water, is lit at a certain time, and slightly later the water is heated. The event of the match being lit at the one time is a cause of the event of the water being heated at the other. In the subsequent discussion, I shall use the medieval example to illustrate in concrete terms the general positions under consideration.

A large part of the philosophical problem of causation is to provide a definition, analysis, or theoretical equivalence that will illuminate the causal locution as it occurs in contexts such as those furnished by the two examples. Empiricists have been attracted by a metaphysically minimalist approach to this task that involves analyzing causation in terms of empirical regularities. The idea is often traced back to Hume, though its pedigree might be extended to Gabriel Biel or even to al-Ghazali.[5] In a justly famous passage, Hume says: "Suitably to this experience, therefore, we may define a cause to be *an object, followed by another, and where all objects, similar to the first, are followed by objects similar to the second. Or in other words, where, if the first object had not been, the second never had existed.*"[6] Let us suppose that Hume's "objects" are events, and let us ignore for the time being the second sentence in the quoted passage. From its first sentence, there emerges the fundamental idea of a Humean regularity theory of secondary causes. According to such a theory, the causal locution in our example

(2) The match being lit at a certain time *is a cause of* the water being heated slightly later

is to be parsed as the conjunction of

(3) The match being lit at a certain time occurs
(4) The water being heated slightly later occurs

and

(5) Whenever such a match being lit at a time occurs such water being heated slightly later occurs.

[5]As is pointed out in Alfred J. Freddoso, "The Necessity of Nature," in *Midwest Studies in Philosophy*, vol. 11, ed. P. A. French, T. E. Uehling, Jr., and H. K. Wettstein (Minneapolis: University of Minnesota Press, 1986).
[6]David Hume, "Of the Idea of Necessary Connection," in *An Enquiry Concerning Human Understanding*, ed. Eric Steinberg (Indianapolis: Hackett, 1977), p. 51.

As is usual in such discussions, it is to be understood that (5) is qualified by a *ceteris paribus* clause that incorporates such conditions as there being enough oxygen present for the matches to burn, the matches being in spatial proximity to the water, the water not being in an insulated container, and so forth.

Abstraction from this particular case is straightforward. The schematic causal locution

(6) i_1 being F at t_1 *is a cause of* i_2 being G at $t_1 + \Delta t$

is to be parsed as the conjunction of

(7) i_1 being F at t_1 occurs
(8) i_2 being G at $t_1 + \Delta t$ occurs

and

(9) For all t, if, for some x, x is similar to i_1 and x being F at t occurs, then, for some y, y is similar to i_2 and y being G at $t + \Delta t$ occurs.

The question that requires discussion is whether it is a consequence of my theory of creation and conservation that there are no secondary causes in nature, on this understanding of what secondary causes in nature are.

If it were a consequence of my theory of creation and conservation that there are no secondary causes in nature, then a contradiction would be a consequence of the conjunction of my theory and the hypothesis that an instance of the conjunction of schemata (7), (8), and (9) is true. But what are the consequences of my theory and that hypothesis? I shall now argue that the straightforwardly derivable consequences are ones that theists should find quite palatable and that there is no reason to believe a contradiction is among the consequences of my theory and that hypothesis.

I begin by noting that, except in case of peculiar substituends for 'F' such as "impossible" or "nonexistent," we are entitled to assume instances of the commonplace schema:

(C) Necessarily, for all x and t, if x being F at t occurs, then x exists at t.

Now suppose an instance of (7) is true. From (7) and (C), we get

(10) i_1 exists at t_1.

Then, from (10) and (A), we get

(11) God willing that i_1 exists at t_1 brings about i_1 existing at t_1.

Applying (S1) to (11), we get

(12) God willing that i_1 exists at t_1 obtains.

Applying (S2) to (11), we also learn that no state of affairs other than God willing that i_1 exists at t_1 brings about i_1 existing at t_1. A similar line of argumentation starting from (8) yields

(13) i_2 exists at $t_1 + \Delta t$

(14) God willing that i_2 exists at $t_1 + \Delta t$ brings about i_2 existing at $t_1 + \Delta t$

(15) God willing that i_2 exists at $t_1 + \Delta t$ obtains

and the conclusion that no state of affairs other than God willing that i_2 exists at $t_1 + \Delta t$ brings about i_2 existing at $t_1 + \Delta t$. And, when we start from (9), these results lead us to the conclusion that

(16) For all t, if, for some x, God willing that x exists at t obtains and x is similar to i_1 and x being F at t occurs, then, for some y, God willing that y exists at $t + \Delta t$ obtains and y is similar to i_2 and y being G at $t + \Delta t$ occurs.

Such are the more or less direct consequences of coupling my theory of creation and conservation with the assumption that there are instances of Humean causation in nature.

It seems obvious to me that theists should find these consequences tolerable and perhaps even welcome. All (10)–(15) tell us is that divine volition does indeed take place and brings about the existence of a contingent individual or two in temporal succession. And all (16) says is that there are temporal regularities in at least some of the effects of divine volition, which theists may consider providential in a broad sense. Of course those regularities are constrained by the conditions of the tacit *ceteris paribus* clause, but nothing in my theory precludes divine control over these conditions.

Nor can I see any reason to suppose that a contradiction is to be found among the more remote consequences of conjoining my theory with the hypothesis that there are Humean regularities among events in nature. After all, the assumption that there are Humean regularities among events does not entail that anyone other than God brings about the existence of even a single contingent individual, for that assumption entails nothing at all about metaphysical causation of the sort postulated by my account of creation and conservation. And that account entails only that divine volition brings about the existence of the contingent individuals that are constituents of the events in nature; by itself it entails nothing about the natural relations among those events. Hence it does not rule out there being Humean regularities of succession among them.

There are theists who wish to attribute to divine volition more influence on what happens in nature in situations of the sort I have been discussing than my theory of creation and conservation does. One way to do this would be to add to (11) and (14)

> (17) God willing that i_1 is F at t_1 brings about i_1 being F at t_1

and

> (18) God willing that i_2 is G at $t_1 + \Delta t$ brings about i_2 being G at $t_1 + \Delta t$

and to replace (16) with

> (19) For all t, if, for some x, God willing that x exists at t obtains and God willing that x is similar to i_1 obtains and God willing that x is F at t obtains, then, for some y, God willing that y exists at $t + \Delta t$ obtains and God willing that y is similar to i_2 obtains and God willing that y is G at $t + \Delta t$ obtains.

Such assumptions would give to God a kind of total control and power over what goes on in natural regularities of succession among events. They are not consequences of my theory of creation and conservation, but they can, I think, consistently be added to it.

It is worth emphasizing that the Humean analysis of secondary causation by itself includes no reference to divine activity. Natural events causally related just are such events constantly conjoined. But once this conception gets incorporated into a theistic metaphysics of creation and conservation, it is tempting to suppose that natural causes so understood are not true causes at all. Thus one might come to think with Malebranche that natural causes, so called, are really only occasions of divine activity. He says: "But *natural* causes are not true causes: they are only *occasional* causes that act only through the force and efficacy of the will of God."[7] The strong assumptions discussed but not endorsed in the previous paragraph embody one way in which this thought could be developed. On those assumptions, it is divine volition that brings about both i_1 existing at t_1 and i_1 being F at t_1 and divine volition that brings about both i_2 existing at $t_1 + \Delta t$ and i_2 being G at $t_1 + \Delta t$. Since the true cause of i_2 being G at $t_1 + \Delta t$ is God willing that i_2 is G at $t_1 + \Delta t$, i_1 being F at t_1 is an occasion but not really a cause of i_2 being G at $t_1 + \Delta t$. So, on this view, Humean event-causes are only occasional causes. It might be imagined that anyone who adopts my theory of creation and conservation is implicitly committed to some such occasionalistic view. Louis Loeb, for example, holds that occasionalism is a trivial consequence of the principle that divine conservation is continual re-creation by God.[8] But it is not. The assumptions needed to get to occasionalism are not consequences of my theory at all, and yet my theory is one according to which divine conservation of persisting things just is continuous creation.[9] The reason those assumptions are not consequences of my theory is that, by itself, it entails nothing about whether or how events such as i_2 being G at $t_1 + \Delta t$ are brought about. For all it says, such events have only Humean causes and do not have true causes in Malebranche's sense. I believe this is a result theists could manage to live with, and the empiricist in me inclines me toward it.

There are, of course, familiar difficulties with the Humean approach to the analysis of causation. Not all de facto regularities of temporal succession are causal connections. To adapt an example from Mill, it could be that whenever a certain whistle blows at an automobile works in Detroit, the workers pour out of a certain steel mill in Pittsburgh shortly thereafter. But it is clear that events of these two types would not be causally connected; the regularity joining them would be merely accidental. There are also familiar ways to complicate the analysis in order to escape from counterexamples. The Millian example, for in-

---

[7]Nicolas Malebranche, *The Search after Truth and Elucidations of the Search after Truth,* ed. Thomas M. Lennon and Paul J. Olscamp (Columbus: Ohio State University Press, 1980), p. 449.

[8]Louis E. Loeb, *From Descartes to Hume* (Ithaca: Cornell University Press, 1981), p. 220.

[9]See Quinn, "Divine Conservation, Continuous Creation, and Human Action," p. 73.

stance, can be dealt with by adding a condition of spatial contiguity. I do not know whether the Humean approach can ultimately be made to yield an analysis of secondary causation in nature that is immune from counterexample. However, I am fairly confident that, if this can be made to happen, the resulting analysis, no matter how complicated and sophisticated it may be, will still comport well with my theory of creation and conservation, provided the Humean pattern is followed to the extent of using only de facto regularities in the analysans. If this is done, then coupling my theory with the assumption that there are instances of event causation in nature will only lead to the result that there are de facto regularities of certain sorts among those effects of divine volition that consist of bringing about the existence of contingent individuals in nature. And this is a result no theist I know of would quarrel with.

Nevertheless, there are many philosophers who believe that no pure de facto regularity theory could be the whole truth about secondary causes in nature. As they see it, the very concept of causation requires that there be a modal tie between events causally connected. Constructing a counterfactual analysis of causation is a way of implementing this idea that has enjoyed a good deal of popularity in recent years. This approach focuses on the suggestion made by the second sentence in the passage from Hume quoted above. The next item on my agenda is to discuss the best-known example of this approach.

3 Counterfactual Dependence and Causal Dependence

A simple and ingenious counterfactual theory of causation has been constructed by David Lewis.[10] It has two parts. The first defines truth conditions for counterfactual conditionals; the second defines various causal locutions in terms of counterfactual conditionals.

The definition of truth-conditions for counterfactual conditionals rests on the assumptions that there are possible worlds and that they

---

[10]David Lewis, "Causation," *Journal of Philosophy* 70 (1973), 556–567. My presentation of this theory is adapted from the one given by Marshall Swain in chap. 2 of his *Reasons and Knowledge* (Ithaca: Cornell University Press, 1981).

are ordered in terms of comparative overall similarity to the actual world.[11] It goes as follows:

> (D1) The proposition that if p were to obtain then q would obtain is true = df either (i) there are no possible worlds in which p obtains, or (ii) some possible world in which p obtains and q obtains is more similar to the actual world than any possible world in which p obtains and q does not obtain.

The construction of a definition of a relation of causal dependence between events proceeds in three easy steps. First a relation of counterfactual dependence is defined on pairs of states of affairs:

> (D2) q depends counterfactually on p = df (i) if p were to obtain then q would obtain, and (ii) if p were not to obtain then q would not obtain.

Next the special case of (D2) in which the states of affairs in question are occurrent events is defined as follows:

> (D3) The event of q depends counterfactually on the event of p = df (i) p occurs, (ii) q occurs, and (iii) if p were not to occur then q would not occur.

And then the special case of (D3) in which counterfactual dependence amounts to causal dependence is defined as follows:

> (D4) The event of q depends causally on the event of p = df (i) p occurs, (ii) q occurs, (iii) p and q are distinct events, and (iv) if p were not to occur then q would not occur

More complex causal ideas such as the notion of a causal chain of events and the notion of one event being a cause of another may also be explicated in terms of the relation of causal dependence defined by (D4).

Fearing that additional complexity would be distracting, I shall confine myself to discussing the supposition that there is causal depen-

---

[11]These assumptions deserve extensive discussion, which they get from Lewis in his *Counterfactuals* (Cambridge, Mass.: Harvard University Press, 1973) and, more recently, in his *On the Plurality of Worlds* (Oxford: Basil Blackwell, 1986).

dence among events in nature in the sense specified by (D4). In our simple example of the match and the water, the causal locution

  (20) The event of the water being heated at a certain time *depends causally on* the event of the match being lit slightly earlier

is to be parsed as the conjunction of

  (21) The match being lit at a certain time occurs
  (22) The water being heated slightly later occurs
  (23) The match being lit at a certain time and the water being heated slightly later are distinct events

and

  (24) If the match being lit at a certain time were not to occur then the water being heated slightly later would not occur.

Again abstraction from this particular example is straightforward. The schematic causal locution

  (25) The event of i_2 being G at $t_1 + \Delta t$ *depends causally on* the event of i_1 being F at t_1

is to be parsed as the conjunction of

  (26) i_1 being F at t_1 occurs
  (27) i_2 being G at $t_1 + \Delta t$ occurs
  (28) i_1 being F at t_1 and i_2 being G at $t_1 + \Delta t$ are distinct events

and

  (29) if i_1 being F at t_1 were not to occur then i_2 being G at $t_1 + \Delta t$ would not occur.

As before, the crucial question is whether it is a consequence of my theory of creation and conservation that there is no causal dependence among natural events, given this analysis of what causal dependence is.

So suppose an instance of the conjunction of (26)–(29) is true. Since (26) and (27) are the same as (7) and (8), respectively, the arguments of section 2 show that, when they are conjoined with my theory, they yield only theistically unproblematic consequences such as

(30) God willing that i_1 exists at t_1 brings about i_1 existing at t_1
(31) God willing that i_1 exists at t_1 obtains
(32) God willing that i_2 exists at $t_1 + \Delta t$ brings about i_2 existing at $t_1 + \Delta t$

and

(33) God willing that i_2 exists at $t_1 + \Delta t$ obtains.

Because it is the fact that t_1 is distinct from $t_1 + \Delta t$ that guarantees that i_1 being F at t_1 is distinct from i_2 being G at $t_1 + \Delta t$, (28) is trivial and has no distinctive consequences when conjoined with my theory.

However, assuming that an instance of (29) is true, where its truth-conditions are specified by (D1), and conjoining that assumption to my theory does introduce some novel consequences onto the scene. But, as I shall now argue, none of them should make theists balk.

Since i_1 being F at t_1 is a contingent event, there are possible worlds in which i_1 being F at t_1 does not occur. Hence (29) will be true in virtue of the second rather than the first clause of (D1). The second clause of (D1) tells us that some possible world in which i_1 being F at t_1 does not occur and i_2 being G at $t_1 + \Delta t$ does not occur is more similar to the actual world than any possible world in which i_1 being F at t_1 does not occur and i_2 being G at $t_1 + \Delta t$ does occur. But a possible world in which i_1 being F at t_1 does not occur and i_2 being G at $t_1 + \Delta t$ does not occur might be of any one of the following four types:

(T1) i_1 exists but is not F at t_1 and i_2 exists but is not G at $t_1 + \Delta t$
(T2) i_1 exists but is not F at t_1 and i_2 does not exist at $t_1 + \Delta t$
(T3) i_1 does not exist at t_1 and i_2 exists but is not G at $t_1 + \Delta t$

or

(T4) i_1 does not exist at t_1 and i_2 does not exist at $t_1 + \Delta t$.

And possible worlds in which i_1 being F at t_1 does not occur and i_2 being G at $t_1 + \Delta t$ does occur might be of either of the following two types:

(T5) i_1 exists but is not F at t_1 and i_2 exists and is G at $t_1 + \Delta t$

or

(T6) i_1 does not exist at t_1 and i_2 exists and is G at $t_1 + \Delta t$.

So the second clause of (D1) tells us that some possible world of one of types (T1)–(T4) is more similar to the actual world than any possible world of either type (T5) or type (T6).

My theory of creation and conservation does have consequences for what obtains in possible worlds other than the actual world. Because its axiom (A) begins with a necessity operator, what follows the necessity operator in (A) is asserted by the theory to hold in every possible world. Since the commonplace schema (C) is also necessary, arguments akin to those of section 2 will go through in every possible world. So my theory has the following consequences: (i) in any possible world in which i_1 exists at t_1, God willing that i_1 exists at t_1 brings about i_1 existing at t_1, no other state of affairs brings this about, and God willing that i_1 exists at t_1 obtains; and (ii) in any possible world in which i_2 exists at $t_1 + \Delta t$, God willing that i_2 exists at $t_1 + \Delta t$ brings about i_2 existing at $t_1 + \Delta t$, no other state of affairs brings this about, and God willing that i_2 exists at $t_1 + \Delta t$ obtains. But these are all consequences theists should find acceptable. Moreover, by themselves, they are not provably inconsistent with the claim about similarity at the end of the previous paragraph.

As far as I can tell, there would only be an inconsistency here if, according to the correct account of comparative overall similarity, divine creative volition were to contribute to the determination of similarity in such a way that the consequences of my theory just enumerated and the previously stated consequences of (D1) for the present case could not jointly hold. But I can discover no reason to believe that the correct account of comparative overall similarity will lead to this conclusion. To be sure, similarity of possible worlds is a delicate matter about which there is much disagreement among philosophers.[12] I do not claim to know what the correct substantive account of it is, and so I am in no position to establish that it will not lead to the conclusion in question. But I do think intuitions about concrete examples can be mobilized against that conclusion.

[12]See John L. Pollock, "The 'Possible Worlds' Analysis of Counterfactuals," *Philosophical Studies* 29 (1976), 469–476.

To see how this appeal to intuition works, let us return again to our example of the match and the water. We are supposing that, in the actual world, divine volition brings about both the existence of the match at a certain time and the existence of the water slightly later, the match is lit at the former time, and the water is heated at the latter. Given this supposition, it seems intuitively plausible that some possible world of type (T1) is more like the actual world than any possible world of either type (T5) or type (T6). Why? Well, in worlds of type (T1), divine creative volition continues to bring about the existence of the match at the former time and the water at the latter, and, though they differ from the actual world in that the match is not lit at the former time and the water is not heated at the latter, they need not differ much in other respects. So in some of them the unlit match will still be in the presence of oxygen and in spatial proximity to the water, and the water will still be in an uninsulated container with no other heat sources in its vicinity. By contrast, in worlds of type (T5), though the divine creative volition continues to bring about the existence of the match at the former time and the water at the latter, either a statistically improbable spontaneous or miraculous event of heating occurs to the water at the latter time or some other heat source is brought into its vicinity at the former, because the match is unlit then. Such deviations from actuality seem intuitively large in comparison to those required by worlds of type (T1). And in worlds of type (T6), matters are even worse. Not only is a difference from actuality with respect to divine creative volition required by the nonexistence of the match at the former time; the being heated of the water at the latter time in the absence of the lit match at the former also involves improbable spontaneity, miracle, or the presence of an alternative heat source. Such departures from actuality seem intuitively very large in comparison to those required by worlds of type (T1). So intuition supports the view that the water being heated at a certain time depends causally on the match being lit slightly earlier in circumstances in which the conditions imposed by my theory, according to which the existence of the match and the water at the respective times is brought about by divine volition, are satisfied. From this I conclude that there is some reason to believe that my theory of creation and conservation is consistent with there being natural causal dependence among events as this is construed in the counterfactual theory of causation Lewis has proposed.

So, as I see it, there is, on this view of what causal dependence is, some reason to believe that my theory is consistent with causal dependence in nature and no reason to believe my theory is inconsistent with such causal dependence. Moreover, the way in which Lewis's theory proceeds from the notion of causal dependence to the notion of one event being a cause of another, the second notion being defined in terms of the first, seems to introduce no complications that might give rise to such an inconsistency. I therefore consider myself to have a reasonable basis for the claim that my theory of creation and conservation is consistent with there being instances of secondary causation in nature on this particular counterfactual understanding of what such secondary causes are.

It almost goes without saying that philosophers have subjected Lewis's theory of causation to intense critical scrutiny. Counterexamples to his explication of what it is for one event to be a cause of another have been proposed.[13] More complicated formulations designed to avoid such counterexamples have been worked out.[14] Here I do not have space to delve into the rich but highly technical literature that has accumulated in recent years on the topic of the counterfactual approach to the analysis of causation. Instead I must confine myself to the observation that, to the extent that such theories take off from starting points similar to those embodied in (D1)–(D4), I see no reason to suppose that the further complications they end up by incorporating will generate inconsistencies with my theory of creation and conservation.

It should be obvious, however, that some philosophers are not going to be content with a counterfactual explication of secondary causation in nature, no matter how successful the analysis turns out to be at avoiding counterexamples. Many such philosophers will insist that even secondary causes in nature have to necessitate their effects in some sense stronger than any that counterfactuals by themselves could suffice to explicate. They might say that counterfactual dependence is little better than de facto dependence for getting at true causes. Just as de facto definitions of secondary causation can do no more than tell us what effects a true cause will bring about on certain actual occasions, so also counterfactual definitions of secondary causation can only add to that information about what effects a true cause would bring about on certain counterfactual occasions. In neither case has the notion of

[13]Among the first are those suggested by Jaegwon Kim, "Causes and Counterfactuals," *Journal of Philosophy* 70 (1973), 570–572.
[14]See Swain, *Reasons and Knowledge*, p. 64.

a true cause been adequately analyzed; only a necessitarian theory of causation is capable of providing such an analysis, even for the case of secondary causation in nature.

The necessitarian position certainly deserves a hearing. So the final item on my agenda must be to consider some version of it, if I am to claim fair coverage of the whole spectrum of approaches to the task of constructing an adequate account of secondary causation in nature.

4 Causal Necessity, Concurrence, and Occasionalism Revisited

There are quite a few necessitarian theories of secondary causation in nature in the marketplace of philosophical ideas.[15] However, there is no need in the present context to give a lengthy exposition of any one of them; conceptual machinery already at our disposal allows us to formulate a simple general account of this type. This economy of means is achieved by taking the natural causal relation of primary interest to be closely akin to the one employed in my theory of divine creation and conservation. They function the same way in inference: inferences in accord with patterns (S1) and (S2) are acceptable, and inferences in accord with (S3) are not. And they are characterized by the same marks, except perhaps for immediacy. We may even assume that both involve the same kind of necessity, whatever it turns out to be.

Let 'C' stand for conditions that, together with our match being lit at a certain time, suffice to ensure the presence of the marks of totality and exclusivity. Then in our simple example, the causal locution

(34) The match being lit and being such that C at a certain time *is the cause of* the water being heated slightly later

is to be parsed as

(35) The match being lit and being such that C at a certain time brings about the water being heated slightly later.

And the abstract schematic locution

(36) i_1 being F at t_1 *is the cause of* i_2 being G at $t_1 + \Delta t$

[15]See Freddoso, "The Necessity of Nature."

is to be parsed as

(37) i_1 being F at t_1 brings about i_2 being G at $t_1 + \Delta t$.

As before, the question of concern to us is whether it is a consequence of my theory of creation and conservation that there are no instances of event causation in nature, on this construal of what such causation comes to.

So suppose, as usual, that an instance of the schema (37) is true. Applying (S1) and bearing in mind that i_1 being F at t_1 and i_2 being G at $t_1 + \Delta t$ are events, we obtain

(38) i_1 being F at t_1 occurs

and

(39) i_2 being G at $t_1 + \Delta t$ occurs.

The application of (S2) to (37) yields the conclusion that no state of affairs other than i_1 being F at t_1 brings about i_2 being G at $t_1 + \Delta t$. And, from our commonplace schema (C), (38) and (39), we get

(40) i_1 exists at t_1

and

(41) i_2 exists at $t_1 + \Delta t$.

Next we couple (A), the axiom of my theory of creation and conservation, with (40) and (41). The results are

(42) God willing that i_1 exists at t_1 brings about i_1 existing at t_1

and

(43) God willing that i_2 exists at $t_1 + \Delta t$ brings about i_2 existing at $t_1 + \Delta t$.

And an application of (S1) to (42) and (43) yields

(44) God willing that i_1 exists at t_1 obtains

and

(45) God willing that i_2 exists at $t_1 + \Delta t$ obtains.

So far, so good. These consequences are all theistically benign.

Indeed, it may be thought that they do even better than merely being benign. Implicit in them is a strong version of the doctrine of divine concurrence, according to which the action of divine volition has to collaborate with the activity of every event-cause in nature. Together (37) and (43) tell us both that i_1 being F at t_1 brings about i_2 being G at $t_1 + \Delta t$ and that God willing that i_2 exists at $t_1 + \Delta t$ brings about i_2 existing at $t_1 + \Delta t$. But it is impossible for the event of i_2 being G at $t_1 + \Delta t$ to occur and the state of affairs of i_2 existing at $t_1 + \Delta t$ not to obtain, since the former entails the latter. So the event of i_1 being F at t_1 cannot act to bring about its effect at $t_1 + \Delta t$ unless divine volition actively concurs by bringing about its effect at that time. In terms of our simple example, God and the lit match collaborate to produce the heated water: God provides the water, and the lit match provides the heat.

Is there any way to derive a contradiction from (37) in conjunction with my theory of creation and conservation? I think not. We could get a contradiction if we could derive either

(46) God willing that i_2 is G at $t_1 + \Delta t$ brings about i_2 being G at $t_1 + \Delta t$

or

(47) i_1 being F at t_1 brings about i_2 existing at $t_1 + \Delta t$,

since (S2) applied to (37) yields the negation of (46) and applied to (43) yields the negation of (47). But (46) is plainly not a consequence of the axiom of my theory. As inspection of the form of the consequent of (A) shows, it has consequences of the form of (42) and (43) but not of the form of (46), provided being G is other than existing, because it speaks only of divine volition bringing about the existence of individuals at times. And, though we may assume that

(48) i_2 being G at $t_1 + \Delta t$ entails i_2 existing at $t_1 + \Delta t$,

the derivation of (47) from (37) and (48) has the form of the unacceptable inference pattern (S3). Furthermore, I can see no other ways in which it might be reasonable to think one could construct a derivation of either (46) or (47).

More positively, I think it is clear that no contradiction can be generated as long as event-causes in nature are subject to two restrictions. Because divine volition is said by my theory to bring about all contingent existence and is the total and exclusive cause of such existence, only divine volition brings about contingent existence, and so no event-causes in nature can be causes of existence. So God is the unique cause of contingent existence. In commenting on my earlier discussion of creation and conservation, William E. Mann suggested that I had committed myself to the view that all creation is creation *ex nihilo*.[16] Perhaps the rationale for that commitment is now apparent. If God's bringing about of contingent existence is all the creation there is, as my theory commits me to holding, and divine creation just is creation *ex nihilo*, as I believe, then all creation is creation *ex nihilo*. And, of course, if divine volition does more than bringing about contingent existence and also brings about events in nature, something that is not a consequence of my theory but is not precluded by it either, then no event-causes in nature can be causes of such events.

It is worth nothing that a position inconsistent with there being in nature necessitarian causes of the kind I have been considering can be worked out along lines suggested by my remarks about occasionalism in section 2. On such a view, God's volition brings about not only the existence of every contingent individual whenever it exists but also the occurrence of every contingent natural event. If, for every contingent natural event, God willing that it occurs brings about its occurrence, then, since God so willing is no natural event, according to (S2), no event in nature brings about its occurrence. Needless to say, my theory of creation and conservation does not commit me to this very strong view, and I do not subscribe to it. I consider it no part of the doctrine of divine conservation or the theory that the conservation of persisting things is a kind of continuous creation.

This is not to deny that there are reasons a Malebranchean occasionalist could cite in support of such a view. Malebranche thought that a true cause "is one such that the mind perceives a necessary

---

[16]William E. Mann, "Review of *The Existence and Nature of God*," *Faith and Philosophy* 2 (1985), 195–204.

connection between it and its effect."[17] Apparently the sort of necessary connection in question is to be understood as some sort conceptual necessity that is knowable a priori, for "the mind perceives a necessary connection only between the will of an infinitely perfect being and its effects."[18] The mind perceives no such connections between finite minds and their bodies or between one body and another. Therefore, there are no true causes in nature, and God's will is the only true cause. But there is no need, it seems to me, to accept Malebranche's rather severe constraint on what the mind perceives. It seems plausible to suppose in the light of the history of science that necessary connections in nature can be known by us a posteriori and, perhaps, can be known by us only in that way, if there are any there to be known. So I do not find these reasons compelling. It seems to me one who wishes to hold that there are necessitarian causes in nature can easily resist the rather slight pressure in the direction of occasionalism they generate. And I know of no other reasons for occasionalism that turn out, upon careful examination, to be more convincing than these are.

By way of a conclusion, then, let me briefly summarize my argument. I have examined in detail a specimen of each of three important approaches to providing an adequate account of what secondary causes in nature are. In each case, I have exhibited some of the consequences of the conjunction of my own theory of creation and conservation with the hypothesis that there are instances of secondary causation in nature of the sort specified by the specimen account, and I have argued that these consequences should be welcome or at least palatable to theists. In each case, I have also argued that there are good reasons to believe that my theory of creation and conservation does not have among its consequences the repugnant conclusion that there are no instances of secondary causation in nature of the sort specified by the specimen account and, in the case of the first two approaches, by the more complicated specimens of the same approach to be found in the philosophical literature. I have thereby defended the otherwise attractive view that divine conservation of persisting things is really just continuous creation of them against the charge that it has the consequence that there are no secondary causes in nature, and I have done this in a robust way that covers several rather than just one of the possible

[17]Malebranche, *The Search after Truth*, p. 450.
[18]Ibid., p. 450.

outcomes of the contemporary philosophical debate about the proper analysis of causation. I have also shown that one who holds this view of divine conservation can avoid being tarred with the ugly brush of occasionalism.[19]

[19] I am grateful to John Martin Fischer, Hugh McCann, and David Widerker and to audiences at the 1987 Eastern Division Meeting of the American Philosophical Association, Purdue University, and Western Washington University for stimulating discussion of this essay.

3

Medieval Aristotelianism and the Case against Secondary Causation in Nature

Alfred J. Freddoso

1 Introduction

Central to the western theistic understanding of divine providence is the conviction that God is the sovereign Lord of nature. He created the physical universe and continually conserves it in existence. What's more, He is always and everywhere active in it by His power. The operations of nature, be they minute or catastrophic, commonplace or unprecedented, are the work of His hands, and without His constant causal influence none of them would or could occur.

The Judaic Scriptures speak frequently and eloquently of the pervasiveness of God's causal activity. In a memorable rebuke to Job, Yahweh asks bitingly:

> Who has laid out a channel for the downpour
> and for the thunderstorm a path
> To bring rain to no man's land,
> the unpeopled wilderness;
> To enrich the waste and desolate ground
> till the desert blooms with verdure?
>
> Has the rain a father;
> or who has begotten the drops of dew?
> Out of whose womb comes the ice,
> and who gives the hoarfrost its birth in
> the skies? (Job 38:25–29)

Nor is it only inanimate nature that Yahweh incessantly guides by His invisible hand:

> Do you hunt the prey for the lioness
>   or appease the hunger of her cubs,
> While they crouch in their dens
>   or lie in wait in the thicket?
> Who puts wisdom in the heart,
>   and gives the cock its understanding?
> Who provides the nourishment for the ravens
>   when their young ones cry out to God,
>   and they rove abroad without food? (Job 38:39–41)

And in a cosmic hymn of praise near the end of the Book of Psalms the entire created universe is enjoined to pay homage to the almighty Creator whose decrees it obeys:

> Praise Him, sun and moon;
>   praise Him, all you shining stars.
> Praise Him, you highest heavens,
>   and you waters above the heavens.
> Let them praise the name of the Lord,
>   for He commanded and they were created;
> He established them forever and ever;
>   He gave them a duty which shall not pass away.
>
> Praise the Lord from the earth,
>   you sea monsters and all depths;
> Fire and hail, snow and mist,
>   storm winds that fulfill His word.
> You mountains and all you hills,
>   you fruit trees and all you cedars;
> You wild beasts and all tame animals,
>   you creeping things and you winged fowl. (Psalm 148:3–10)

The Koran is no less insistent upon the ubiquitousness of God's causal activity:

> Allah is He Who raised up the heavens without any pillars that you can see. Then He settled Himself on the Throne, and constrained the sun and the moon to serve you; each planet pursues its course during an appointed term. He regulates it all and expounds the Signs, that you may have firm belief in the meeting with your Lord. He it is Who spread out the earth and made therein firmly fixed mountains and rivers, and of fruits of every kind He has made pairs. He causes the night to cover the day. In all this, verily, are Signs for a people who

reflect. In the earth are diverse tracts adjoining one another, and vine-yards, and corn-fields and date-palms, some growing from one root and others from separate roots, which are irrigated by the same water, and yet We make some of them excel others in the quality of their fruits. Therein also are Signs for a people who understand. (13:2–5)

Even though this essay is concerned only with the role God plays in the production of effects in nature, it is also worth noting that the sacred writers do not shy away from counting even the free actions of rational creatures as products of God's ever-present causal influence: "O Lord, You mete out peace to us, for it is You who have accomplished all we have done" (Isaiah 26:12). In two passages destined to be cited often in the medieval Christian debates over divine causation, St. Paul emphatically reiterates this attribution of good deeds to God: "There are different works but the same God who accomplishes all of them in everyone" (1 Corinthians 12:6); and again, "It is not that we are entitled of ourselves to credit for anything. Our sole credit is from God" (2 Corinthians 3:5). As Paul puts it in summation, "He is not far from any of us, since it is in Him that we live, and move, and have our being" (Acts 17:27–28).

Given such powerful foundational sentiments, it is little wonder that theistic philosophers have through the centuries felt impelled to ad-dress the metaphysical questions quite inevitably prompted by the belief that God is actively involved in the production of effects in na-ture.[1] All have agreed that God is the *primary* or *first* cause of every natural phenomenon. But some have gone on, rather astonishingly, to make the additional claim that God is the *only* cause of such phe-nomena. In other words, they have denied that there is any such thing as genuine *secondary* (i.e., creaturely) causation in nature. In keeping with common usage I will call this position *occasionalism*, and, leaving aside for now various subtle and necessary qualifications, I will take as representative occasionalists al-Ghazali and Gabriel Biel from the Middle Ages and Nicolas Malebranche and George Berkeley from the modern era.[2]

---

[1]On the inevitability of such metaphysical questions being raised about revealed doc-trines and in defense (contrary to much modern theology) of the legitimacy of raising them, the best popular piece I know of is John Courtney Murray, S.J., *The Problem of God* (New Haven: Yale University Press, 1964), pp. 31–76.

[2]I shall be citing the following editions of the works of these four philosophers: al-Ghazali, *al-Ghazali's Tahafut al-falasifah: The Incoherence of the Philosophers*, trans. Sabih Ahmad Kamali (Lahore: Pakistan Philosophical Congress, 1963), problem 17, "Refutation

Occasionalism is a remarkably devout theory of divine causation that (perhaps surprisingly; but then again, perhaps not) managed to attract far wider and deeper support within the increasingly secularized atmosphere of pre-Kantian modern philosophy than it ever did within the unabashedly religious milieu of late medieval scholasticism. Nonetheless, we cannot fully appreciate thinkers like Malebranche and Berkeley unless we understand the fact that their views about the extent of God's causal role in nature, far from popping into existence *ex nihilo* in the seventeenth and eighteenth centuries, emerged instead from a long, even if never dominant, tradition in theistic philosophy—a tradition whose Christian spokesmen have always been eager to trace back to St. Augustine, a hero whom they regard as untainted by the corrupting influence of Aristotelian naturalism.

My aim here is to take a small first step toward determining whether occasionalism can provide theists with a plausible and satisfying philosophy of nature, one that passes both philosophical and theological muster. Specifically, I explore the nature of and motivations for occasionalism, contrast it with the Aristotelianism its advocates have perennially rebelled against, and then confront it with what I take to be the strongest objections hurled at it by three prominent medieval Aristotelians—St. Thomas Aquinas and the sixteenth-century Jesuits Luis de Molina and Francisco Suarez. The Aristotelians do, to be sure, join with the occasionalists in (i) asserting that God is an immediate cause of every natural effect and (ii) rejecting the claim that God's nonmiraculous causal activity in nature is exhausted by His creating and conserving material substances and their causal powers.[3] But in stark

---

of Their Belief in the Impossibility of a Departure from the Natural Course of Events," pp. 185–196; Gabriel Biel, *Collectorium circa quattuor libros sententiarum* 4, pt. 1, ed. Wilfridus Urbeck and Udo Hoffman (Tuebingen: J. C. B. Mohr, 1975), q. 1, "Utrum sacramenta legis novae sint causae effectivae gratiae," pp. 1–36, esp. 14–18 and 27–36; Nicolas Malebranche, *Nicolas Malebranche: The Search after Truth and Elucidations of the Search after Truth*, trans. Thomas M. Lennon and Paul J. Olscamp (Columbus: Ohio State University Press, 1980), esp. *The Search after Truth*, b. 6, p. 2, chaps. 2 and 3, pp. 440–452, and *Elucidations*, Elucidation 15, pp. 657–683 (page references for both *The Search after Truth* and the *Elucidations* will be to this one volume); George Berkeley, *Three Dialogues between Hylas and Philonous*, ed. Robert M. Adams (Indianapolis: Hackett Publishing Co., 1979), and *A Treatise Concerning the Principles of Human Knowledge*, ed. Kenneth Winkler (Indianapolis: Hackett Publishing Co., 1982).

[3]It cannot be emphasized enough that the position being rejected here (viz., that God's action in the ordinary course of nature is exhausted by creation and conservation) is regarded as too weak by almost all medieval Aristotelians as well as by the occasionalists. (Its main medieval spokesman was William Durandus, an early fourteenth-century Dominican bishop who, as far as I know, is the only theologian whose name is explicitly

opposition to the occasionalists, they hold that each material or corporeal substance possesses and exercises its own proper causal powers. Such powers are not, they insist, supplanted or rendered otiose by God's causal activity in nature. Instead, God contributes to the ordinary course of nature only as a *universal* or *general* cause who *cooperates with* or *concurs with* secondary causes.[4] True, as Malebranche was almost maliciously fond of pointing out in retrospect, the medieval scholastics were never able to reach an enduring consensus about the metaphysics of God's "general concurrence" with secondary causes.[5] But here I shall simply ignore their internal disputes and focus instead on their shared antipathy to occasionalism.

In section 2 I formulate what I believe to be the essential thesis of occasionalism. I expound this thesis further in section 3, clarifying along the way the difference between genuine efficient or active causation and so-called occasional causation. Next, in section 4, I identify three conceivable versions of occasionalism (the no-action, no-essence, and no-nature theories) and show how each stems from a distinctive theological motive. I go on to argue in section 5 that while some of the Aristotelian objections to occasionalism are dialectically impotent against all three versions, there are other objections that succeed in pushing the occasionalist toward the no-nature theory, a theory characterized by a "radical" Berkeleyan metaphysics that does away utterly and completely with the Aristotelian conception of the natures of ma-

---

associated with this doctrine by sixteenth-century writers.) In stressing the importance of this historical point in another context, I injudiciously claimed that the scholastics regarded the position in question "as in effect a form of deism." Peter van Inwagen has persuaded me that this use of the term 'deism' is not only historically and philosophically inaccurate but unfortunately inflammatory. So I hereby recant. I would still insist, however, that the near unanimity of the tradition on this point constrains any contemporary theistic philosopher from simply assuming without argument that Durandus's position is theologically orthodox.

[4]Discussions of God's general or universal causation can be found in Thomas Aquinas, *Summa contra Gentiles* III, chaps. 66–70, and *De potentia Dei*, Q. 3, A. 7; Luis de Molina, *Liberi arbitrii cum gratiae donis, divina praescientia, providentia, praedestinatione et reprobatione concordia*, [hereafter *Concordia*], ed. Johann Rabeneck, S.J. (Oña and Madrid: Soc. Edit. Sapientia, 1953) p. 2, "De concursu Dei generali," Q. 14, A. 13, disp. 25–35, pp. 159–222; and Francisco Suarez, *Disputationes metaphysicae*, ed. C. Berton (Paris: 1866; reprinted in two volumes at Hildesheim: Georg Olms Verlagsbuchhandlung, 1965), vol. 1, disp. 22, "De Prima Causa et alia eius actione, quae est cooperatio, seu concursus, cum causis secundis," pp. 802–843. Since those works of Aquinas to be cited here are generally known and widely available, I shall follow the ordinary custom of citing the relevant texts without alluding to any modern editions.

[5]Malebranche, *Elucidations*, pp. 676–680.

terial substances. My main conclusion is, in fact, that anyone espousing occasionalism should accept the no-nature theory, since this is the one form of occasionalism that seems capable of withstanding the Aristotelian onslaught. Finally, in section 6 I briefly indicate for future discussion what I take to be the main strengths of the no-nature theory, as well as its most serious problems.

2 The Essence of Occasionalism

All the thinkers discussed in this essay take causation in the most basic and proper sense to be a relation between substances on the one hand and states of affairs on the other.[6] Typically, substances (agents) act upon other substances (patients) to bring about or actualize or produce states of affairs (effects).[7] So both agents and patients may properly be said to contribute causally to the effects produced, and both acting and being acted upon may properly be thought of as modes of causal contribution. Moreover, since causal contributions involve the exercise of causal powers or, more generally, the actualization of causal tendencies and dispositions, we can also distinguish active from passive causal powers. The active causal powers of a substance delimit the range of effects that might be produced when that substance acts on suitably disposed patients; the passive causal powers of a substance delimit the range of effects that might be produced when that substance is acted upon by suitably positioned agents. (In what follows I presuppose a basic understanding of this distinction between active and passive causal contribution, though I acknowledge that the distinction stands in need of further elaboration.)

In keeping with the above remarks, I take as undefined the causal locution *Substance S causally contributes to state of affairs p's obtaining at time t*. As I am using this primitive locution, it implies that *p* in fact obtains at *t*. However, taken by itself, it has nothing to say about what kinds of substances can be causal contributors. It does not, for example, require that causal contributors be capable of acting freely, or that they

---

[6]The states of affairs in question typically involve states of the substances that are acted upon. Whether all such states must be thought of as involving accidents inhering in these substances is a moot ontological question that would receive different answers from different medieval scholastics.

[7]An *atypical* case would be that of creation *ex nihilo*, wherein there is no patient acted upon.

be endowed with sentient powers, or even that they be living. So the conceptual possibility is left open that some causal contributors, both active and passive, are nonfree, nonintelligent, nonsentient, or non-living substances.

Similarly, this undefined locution says nothing either about the time (if any) at which S makes its causal contribution or about the specific nature of that contribution. So, for instance, S might make its causal contribution to p long before t and not even exist at any time proximate to t. Again, S's causal contribution to p may be more or less direct, more or less closely connected with S's causal tendencies or (in the case of rational beings) intentions, and more or less determinative of the specific character of the effect in question.[8] Finally, S's causal contribution might be either wholly active, wholly passive, or active in one respect and passive in another. (This last alternative occurs, for instance, when a substance brings about changes in itself, or when a substance is employed as an instrument or tool by some "principal" agent.)

I am interested mainly in active or efficient causation, and accordingly I shall now define two further notions:

> (D1) S is an *active* [or: *efficient*] cause of p at t $=df$
>   (i) S causally contributes to p's obtaining at t, and
>   (ii) S's causal contribution to p's obtaining at t is at least in part active.
> (D2) S is a *strong* active cause of p at t $=df$
>   (i) S is an active cause of p at t, and
>   (ii) no substance distinct from S is an active cause of p at t.

The philosophers discussed all hold, first, that no substance other than God can be a strong active cause of any state of affairs, and second, that God is in fact a strong active cause of at least some states of affairs. Each of these tenets is a nonnegotiable element of orthodox western theism. The first is based on sacred writings like those adduced above,

---

[8]Below I will have occasion to allude to the distinction between general (universal) causes and particular causes. Roughly, a substance is a *general* cause with respect to an effect E when its causal influence has had to be channeled (or, better, specified) toward E by some further cause. For instance, the sun is a general cause of this calf's being born. For the heat of the sun is a causal factor in the generation of the calf, but one that is channeled toward the production of a calf (as opposed to, say, a duckling) by further causes (in this case, a cow and bull). As can be seen, the same cause might be more general or less general with respect to different effects.

writings that underscore the radical dependence creatures have on God for their being and causal efficacy (if any). The second is entailed by the doctrine of creation *ex nihilo* as well as by the doctrine, properly understood, that no created thing can remain in existence for any interval of time without being directly conserved by God throughout that interval.[9]

Given the rhetorical excesses of certain occasionalists (Malebranche comes immediately to mind), one might at first be tempted to characterize occasionalism as the thesis that for any state of affairs p and time t, if there is any substance at all that causally contributes to p's obtaining at t, then God is a strong active cause of p at t. This would make God the *sole* efficient cause of *every* effect produced in the created world, including all those involving rational creatures.

In the history of the debate over secondary causation, Aristotelians have sometimes tried to saddle occasionalists with this alarmingly strong thesis and then to discredit them in the eyes of religious believers by pointing out that what follows is a manifestly unorthodox denial of human free choice. For instance, after attributing to Gabriel Biel and Peter D'Ailly the claim that secondary 'causes' bring about nothing at all, Molina continues: "Now if this view is understood to apply to *all* causes *in general*, even to the will and to free choice, as its authors seem to intend, then . . . clearly it must be judged as an error from the point of view of the faith; for it completely destroys our freedom of choice and thus robs our works of every vestige of virtue and vice, of merit and demerit, of praise and blame, of reward and punishment."[10] Suarez inveighs in like manner against those who reject the principle that creatures have and exercise active causal power: "What's more, there are other truths of the faith that cannot stand without this principle. The first and most important of these is the truth of free choice, which cannot consist in anything but a power and manner of acting. . . . Thus the Council of Trent (session 6, canon 4) condemns those who claim that created free choice 'does not act at all, and is purely passive'."[11]

However, as far as I have been able to tell, no important occasionalist has ever in fact intended to deny that there is such a thing as creaturely

---

[9]Conservation must be taken as involving the conferral of existence on the thing in question *and on every proper part of it*. Only then, I believe, can one argue persuasively that conservation is God's prerogative.

[10]Molina, *Concordia*, p. 160.

[11]Suarez, *Disputationes metaphysicae*, disp. 18, "De causa proxima efficiente eiusque causalitate, et omnibus quae ad causandum requirit," p. 597.

free choice or that such free choice involves a genuine active causal power to produce effects. (Just *which* effects is a matter I will take up in a moment.) al-Ghazali and Berkeley, for instance, clearly believe that there are created spiritual substances with the active power of free choice. Even Malebranche, who questions whether free choice can properly be called a 'power', nonetheless recoils from the thought that our sinful deeds might be ascribable solely to God as an active cause.[12] What's more, in the text cited by Molina, Biel is comparing the causal genesis of natural effects with the causal genesis of grace through the sacraments, and in such a context one would not antecedently expect to find any explicit discussion at all of *free*, as opposed to *natural*, causation.[13] So in all fairness we should, it seems, define occasionalism in a way that prescinds from questions concerning God's causal influence on creaturely free choice.

All the philosophers we are dealing with here are libertarians: that is, they hold that a substance S is a *free* cause of p at t only if (i) S has a rational nature, i.e., is endowed with higher intellective and volitional capacities; (ii) S is an active cause of p at t; and (iii) S's causally contributing to p's obtaining at t does not itself obtain by a necessity of nature. This third condition must, of course, be spelled out in more detail, and I have attempted to do this elsewhere.[14] But the intuition underlying it is clear enough for our present purposes: If an act is free, then it does not issue forth in a deterministic manner from the causal history of the world.

Notice, by the way, that despite the tendency of many sixteenth-century Thomists (the Bañezians) to characterize God's causal influence on human action in very strong terms, these thinkers would nonetheless accept all three of the conditions on free causation just laid out. Their dispute with 'strong' libertarians (the Molinists) has to do with the intrinsic nature of God's *contemporaneous* causal contribution to free action rather than with the causal history of the world at the relevant moment. This issue, too, I have dealt with in more detail elsewhere.[15]

We are now ready to state the essential thesis of occasionalism:

[12]Malebranche, *Elucidations*, p. 669.

[13]See Biel, *Collectorium*, pp. 15–18, 31–34.

[14]See my "The Necessity of Nature," *Midwest Studies in Philosophy* 11 (1986), 215–242.

[15]See sec. 2.9 of the introduction to Luis de Molina, *On Divine Foreknowledge (Part IV of the "Concordia")*, Translated, with an Introduction and Notes, by Alfred J. Freddoso (Ithaca: Cornell University Press, 1988).

(OCC) For any state of affairs p and time t, if (i) there is any substance that causally contributes to p's obtaining at t and (ii) no created substance is a free cause of p at t, then God is a strong active cause of p at t.

So, according to occasionalism, God is the sole efficient cause of every state of affairs that is brought about in "pure" nature, i.e., in that segment of the universe not subject to the causal influence of creatures who are acting freely. Interestingly, however, even this seemingly minor limitation on the extent of God's causal influence turns out to be less restrictive than one might at first expect. To see this clearly, and also to get a deeper understanding of the spirit behind occasionalism, we will have to take a brief but, I hope, illuminating excursion into the metaphysics of efficient causation.

3 Real and Occasional Causes

Occasionalists have been wont to draw a sharp distinction between *genuine* or *real* or *proper* causation on the one hand and so-called *occasional* or *sine qua non* causation on the other.[16] Molina gives this concise summary of Biel's discussion of causation:

> He is of the opinion that secondary causes bring about nothing at all, but that God by Himself alone produces all the effects in them and in their presence, so that fire does not produce heat and the sun does not give light, but instead it is God who produces these effects in them and in their presence. Hence . . . he claims that secondary causes are not *properly* causes in the sense of having an influence on the effect; for it is only the First Cause which he affirms to be a cause in this sense, whereas secondary causes, he claims, should be called causes *sine qua non*, insofar as God has decided not to produce the effect except when they are present. . . . He also asserts with Peter D'Ailly that when God produces an effect in conjunction with a secondary cause, e.g., heat in conjunction with fire, He contributes no less than He would contribute were He to produce the same effect by Himself—in fact, He brings about more, since not only does He produce the heat with a concurrence just as great as if the fire were not present, but He also brings it about that the fire too is in its own way a cause of the heat.[17]

[16]On this distinction, see al-Ghazali, *Incoherence of the Philosophers*, pp. 185–187; Biel, *Collectorium*, pp. 15–18; Malebranche, *Search after Truth*, pp. 448–450; and Berkeley, *Principles*, pp. 51–53.

[17]Molina, *Concordia*, pp. 159–160.

On Biel's account, occasional or sine qua non causation turns out to be little more than the mere counterfactual dependence of the 'effect' on the 'cause'. (In fact, to be perfectly accurate, Biel defines *causation itself* wholly in terms of counterfactual dependence, and then treats *proper* causation and *sine qua non* causation as two species of causation so defined—where it is only 'proper' causation that involves the actual *derivation* of the effect from the cause. I will pass over in silence this rather puzzling use of the term 'proper'.) More precisely, x is an occasional cause of y just in case (i) x is posited; (ii) if x is posited, then y is posited; (iii) if x were not posited, then y would not be posited in the same way, and (iv) it is not the case that y's being posited results from the exercise of any causal power on the part of x.[18]

So, for instance, if this fire is an *occasional* cause of the searing of this flesh, then it is not the case that the fire acts in such a way as to sear the flesh. Rather, the fire is an occasional cause of the searing of the flesh simply by virtue of the fact that the *real* or *proper* cause of the searing of the flesh, viz., God, would not have seared the flesh in the same way had the fire not been present. In general, then, an occasional cause is not such that the effect is *derived from* it or *made to occur by* it; nor does it *exercise power* or *exert influence* of any sort. Such conditions are satisfied only by those causes that are *proper* or *real* or *genuine* causes. (Notice, by the way, that classical occasionalists explicitly acknowledge God to be a *real* cause of natural effects; and so, unlike Hume and his progeny, occasionalists are not interested in reducing *all* causation to some sort of mere counterfactual dependence.)

It is clear, I trust, that the primitive causal locution I introduced above was meant to express real or proper causation rather than mere counterfactual dependence. That is to say, S causally contributes to p's obtaining only if p's obtaining derives (at least in part) from S's exercising or actualizing some causal power. Thus, S's presence in a set of circumstances in which p is made to obtain never by itself suffices for it to be the case that S causally contributes to p's obtaining—even if p's obtaining is counterfactually dependent on S's presence.

Now an *occasional* cause is not an *instrumental* cause, at least not if the notion of instrumental causality is explicated plausibly. An instrumental cause is a genuine causal contributor—more specifically, a genuine *efficient* or *active* cause.[19] To be sure, the pen I am using to write

---

[18]Biel, *Collectorium*, pp. 14–15.
[19]For an account of the different types of efficient causes, see Aquinas's *Expositio in VIII libros physicorum Aristotelis*, b. 2, lec. 5 (194b16–195a27).

this paper cannot *on its own* be an active cause of the paper's being written. Nonetheless, it does have active causal powers that are exercised under the right sort of conditions to produce an effect whose specific characteristics derive in part from the nature of those powers. When this particular pen is moved in the right way by the right sort of principal agent, it is an instrumental cause that actively contributes to the paper's being written, and to its being written in black (say) rather than blue or red ink, and to its being written in ink of one consistency rather than of another, etc. By contrast, a merely occasional cause is such that there just is no direct natural connection between its causal properties (if any) and the specific character of the effect.[20] If God alone properly causes the flesh to be seared in the presence of the fire, then there is no exercise of an active causal power on the part of the fire. Thus God is in no sense *using* the fire as an *instrument* to produce the searing of the flesh. Indeed, He could just as easily decide to refrigerate the flesh when it is brought close to the fire—and in that case, according to the occasionalists, the fire would be a "cause" of the flesh's being cooled *in exactly the same sense* as that in which it is now a "cause" of the flesh's being seared. There is thus no natural or intrinsic connection between the character of the effect (searing) and the nature of the fire or its powers. Molina is not slow to seize upon this point in order to demonstrate just how weak the notion of an occasional cause is: "Since God is just as able to make a given thing cold in the presence of fire and to make it hot in the presence of water as vice versa, fire could just as easily be a cause of cooling and water of heating as vice versa. Indeed, since God could create an angel or some other thing in the presence of a rock, a rock could be a cause of creation—which, even though Gabriel concedes it, is obviously as absurd as can be."[21]

Nor can occasional causes be either *advising* causes or *disposing* causes, as these notions are normally understood in Aristotelian theories of efficient causation. An advising cause of an effect *E* is, roughly, a rational agent who—by means of counsel, inducement, provocation,

---

[20]The notion of a 'direct' connection strong enough to ground causal derivation needs further honing here. Suarez, for example, has an objector propose the following sort of connection between fire and heating: Heat inheres in the fire and this is why, even though the fire does not act, God heats (rather than cools) things in the presence of fire. Obviously, any Aristotelian will find this connection still too 'indirect' for true causal derivation. But the example suggests that articulating necessary and sufficient conditions for such derivation might not be very easy. See Suarez, *Disputationes metaphysicae*, disp. 18, p. 595.

[21]Molina, *Concordia*, p. 161. For a reply, see pp. 102–103 below.

request, persuasion, threat, command, prohibition, etc.—influences another agent to contribute freely to E. This, of course, is just the familiar sort of causal influence we ordinarily have on one another's free actions. As should be obvious, an advising cause is a genuine *efficient* or *active* cause. For instance, when I threaten to withhold my daughter Katie's allowance, I bring about in her a change of belief regarding whether her announced course of action is, all things considered, the most desirable. When she then chooses to act in an alternate way, I am said to be an advising cause of this piece of free behavior on her part. In Aristotelian jargon, I am a *perfecting* cause of Katie's new belief and an *advising* cause of the free behavior that issues from that belief.[22]

So no occasional cause is an advising cause, nor is any advising cause as such a mere occasional cause. In some cases this is perfectly obvious: a fire is not a rational agent and hence cannot, as it were, "persuade" God to sear human flesh brought close to it. As we shall see in a moment, however, an occasionalist might be tempted to regard the free choices of rational creatures as, in effect, pieces of advice to God about how He ought to act in the realm of nature.

A substance is a *disposing* cause with respect to an effect E when it produces in some patient a condition required in order for E to be brought about in the way that it is in fact brought about. For instance, the farmer is typically a disposing cause of the corn's growing in the soil: by plowing, planting, fertilizing, etc., the farmer produces (i.e., brings to perfection or completion) in the relevant patients many of the conditions required for healthy cornstalks to be generated in the ordinary way. So, once again, as with the advising cause, the disposing cause of an effect E causally contributes to E by virtue of being a perfecting cause of certain other effects that are preliminary to E. Hence, it cannot be a mere occasional cause of its effects.

Now let us return to (OCC) and to the question of just which states of affairs created substances might, on the occasionalist view, be free causes of. Suppose that Stephen freely puts a kettle of water over a gas flame and that a few minutes later the water begins to boil. To many it will seem evident that Stephen is an active cause of the water's boiling at the time in question. They will reason as follows: True,

---

[22]Suppose that Katie persists in her original intention and acts against my advice. In that case I am not a disposing cause of her behavior—indeed, she acted as she did *despite* my threats. Still, I am a perfecting cause of various psychological states in her, e.g., her belief that I disapprove of the behavior in question.

Stephen could not by himself alone, without relying in some way on the active powers of other substances, have caused the water to boil. Nonetheless, he freely initiated a genuine causal sequence by putting the kettle over the flame. More specifically, by exercising *his* active causal powers he brought it about that other substances (e.g., the gas flame, the metal constituting the bottom of the kettle) were in a position to exercise *their* active causal powers in the relevant way. It follows that Stephen was an active cause of the water's boiling. The only remaining question has to do with *what sort* of active cause he was. Some might argue that he was merely a *disposing* cause who put other substances (e.g., the gas flame) into a position to be perfecting causes of the water's boiling. Others might retort, less plausibly at first glance, that he himself was a *perfecting* principal cause who was using the other substances as his instruments. Yet whatever might be said about that issue, it is beyond dispute that Stephen caused the water to boil.[23]

An occasionalist, however, cannot endorse this line of reasoning. According to occasionalism, the boiling of the water does not in any way derive from the action of the fire or of any other material substance. To the contrary, God alone is a direct active cause of the water's boiling. An immediate consequence is that Stephen cannot be either a principal cause or a disposing cause of the boiling of the water in the ways just suggested. He cannot be a principal cause who uses the fire as his instrument, because the fire is an instrumental cause of the effect only if it is an active cause of the effect. But this is ruled out by occasionalism. Likewise, Stephen is a disposing cause in the manner described above only if the fire is a perfecting cause of the water's boiling. But this, once again, is ruled out by occasionalism.

But perhaps we are being too hasty here. Perhaps we should rethink the whole issue before us in the way that the occasionalist theory ostensibly invites us to, viz., by substituting God for the relevant natural substances such as the fire and the metal pot. Can Stephen in that case be reasonably regarded as an active cause of the water's boiling?

Presumably, to begin with, everyone will agree that Stephen cannot be a principal cause who is using God as his instrument, and so he cannot in that sense be a perfecting cause of the water's boiling.

What's more, occasionalists still cannot grant that Stephen is even a

---

[23]I raise this second possibility, viz., that Stephen is a principal cause who uses the fire, pot, etc., as his instruments, because this is very much the image after which Aquinas models God's relationship to secondary causes. Berkeley, by the way, has some sharp criticisms of the idea that God might use instruments. See *Three Dialogues*, pp. 53–54.

disposing cause of the boiling of the water. Recall that a disposing cause of an effect E produces in some patient a condition *required* in order for E to be brought about in the way that it is in fact brought about. That is, there must be some *intrinsic* or *natural* connection between the disposing cause's preparatory activity and E's being brought about in the way it is. But if occasionalism is true, then there is no such connection between any human action and any effect brought about in nature. Whenever God brings about E, His action in bringing about E, i.e., His causal contribution to E, is exactly the same whether or not there has been any antecedent activity on the part of finite free agents, and regardless of the nature of any such activity.[24] Even if God has decided to act in such a way that He ordinarily brings about E only when finite free agents have first acted in certain ways, this implies only that the finite agents are serving as an *occasion* for God's producing E, not that they are disposing causes of E.

Someone might suggest at this point that Stephen's freely putting the water over the flame renders him an advising cause who by his free action influences God (in a nondeterministic manner) to cause the water to boil.

However, this line of reasoning is also flawed, and in at least two distinct ways. First, all the occasionalists I know of would eschew even the faintest hint that *any* creature has *any* sort of causal power over God's actions. Nor is this attitude peculiar to occasionalists; philosophical theologians have traditionally held that the divine perfection absolutely excludes God's being acted upon as a causal patient by any creature. Second, it seems at least mildly outrageous to claim that *all* of our free actions might be signs to God of what we would like Him to do. Our freely offered petitionary prayers undoubtedly count as such. But can the same be said of, say, Stephen's putting a kettle of water on a stove under ordinary circumstances? Clearly not.

Notice that these arguments are perfectly general. So even though in setting up the example I seemed to be conceding that a finite free agent might cause a change in some other substance (e.g., that Stephen

---

[24]This follows from the fact that according to occasionalism God is a total *particular* cause of every effect in nature. The concurrentists, by way of contrast, hold that there are *two* ways for God to contribute causally to a natural effect: (i) by Himself as a *particular* cause, in which case the nature of the effect is derived from God's causal contribution *alone*; or (ii), more commonly, as a *general* cause (indeed, the *most* general cause) cooperating with secondary causes, in which case the nature of the effect is derived from the secondary causes.

might move the kettle from one place to another), the same considerations will apply to this alleged effect of Stephen's as well. In that case, however, the occasionalist still has not found a way to accommodate the common view that free creatures often make genuine causal contributions to states of affairs that go beyond their own free acts of will and simply bodily movements.

In fact, the occasionalist may not even be entitled to claim that we are proper or real causes of our own bodily movements. For in eliciting (to use the scholastic term) acts of will we might turn out to be nothing more than occasional causes of simple bodily movements. Malebranche enthusiastically embraces this conclusion, since he sees in occasionalism a theoretically satisfying account of how mind and body are interrelated. Mind and body do not causally interact with one another, but this, he avers, is merely a special instance of the more general truth that *no* creature, be it corporeal or spiritual, causally acts upon any other creature. Instead, it is God alone who coordinates created effects in general and who guarantees the customary concatenation of mental and bodily events in particular.[25]

Berkeley, by contrast, has deep misgivings about the claim that free creatures are active causes only of their own acts of will. In the *Philosophical Commentaries* he asserts that "we move our legs ourselves," and that, contrary to what Malebranche thinks, it is not just God who moves our legs on the occasion of our willing that our legs move.[26] And in the *Three Dialogues*, when Hylas charges in effect that (OCC) makes God Himself responsible for the most heinous sins, Philonous replies in part: "I have nowhere said that God is the only agent who produces all the motions in bodies. It is true, I have denied there are any other agents besides spirits: but this is very consistent with allowing to thinking rational beings, in the production of motions, the use of limited powers, ultimately indeed derived from God, but immediately under the direction of their own wills, which is sufficient to entitle them to all the guilt of their actions."[27]

But this reply immediately suggests a difficulty. Suppose that I move my leg and that at the same time the shoe on my foot moves along with it. Can Berkeley consistently grant that I have moved my shoe as

[25]Malebranche, *Search after Truth*, pp. 448–450, and *Elucidations*, pp. 669–671.

[26]Berkeley, *Philosophical Commentaries*, entry 548, in *The Works of George Berkeley Bishop of Cloyne*, ed. A. A. Luce and T. E. Jessop, vol. 1 (Edinburgh: Thomas Nelson, 1948).

[27]Berkeley, *Three Dialogues*, 70.

well as my leg? We have already seen enough to know that on the occasionalist view my leg cannot count as an instrument by means of which I move the shoe. The leg, after all, is a corporeal substance and hence cannot be put into action by a principal agent. The close correlation between the leg's movement and the shoe's is entirely God's doing. Nor, as we have seen, can I plausibly be regarded as a disposing or advising cause of the shoe's moving, and this by virtue of the fact that I *will* to move my leg. It seems to follow from what Berkeley says that I can move my leg and even my foot, but not my shoe!

Though this is by no means the last word, I believe that Malebranche has the better of the argument here. Be that as it may, my purpose so far has merely been to define occasionalism with a modicum of rigor and to show that it must place severe limitations on the causal influence of free creatures in order to remain faithful to its root conviction that God is a strong active cause of effects in nature. In short, according to occasionalism free creatures causally contribute at most to their own basic actions, and it may even be that those basic actions include only their own acts of will.

Another question raised by (OCC) is this: Do occasionalists mean to exclude the exercise of *passive* as well as *active* causal power on the part of creatures? There seems to be no unanimity on this point. Malebranche, for instance, attributes to matter the three essential properties of impenetrability, infinite divisibility, and figure, each of which seems to delimit in some (perhaps fairly minimal) way the sorts of effects that can be produced when a material body is acted upon.[28] So, for instance, if bodies A and B are essentially impenetrable, then God cannot cause B to pass through A (though He could, of course, bring it about that when B comes into contact with A, instead of being deflected it immediately comes to occupy the very same place it would have occupied had it passed through A). By contrast, Berkeley and (in at least one place) al-Ghazali seem to look upon passive powers with as much suspicion as active ones, since both kinds of power would impose restrictions on the manner in which God acts in nature.[29] What's more,

[28]Malebranche, *Search after Truth*, b. 3, p. 2, chap. 8, pp. 243–247.
[29]Thus Berkeley in the person of Philonous: "I only ask whether the order and regularity observable in the series of our ideas, or the course of nature, be not sufficiently accounted for by the wisdom and power of God; and whether it does not derogate from those attributes, to suppose He is influenced, directed, or put in mind, when and what He is to act, by any unthinking substance" (*Three Dialogues*, p. 55). See also al-Ghazali, *Incoherence of the Philosophers*, pp. 187–188.

it is arguable that a corporeal substance's having passive causal powers entails its also having *some* active causal powers, at least to the extent that its passive powers render it apt to be used as an instrumental efficient cause. For instance, even as minimal a property as impenetrability is such that a body that has it can be used by a suitably situated agent (God, at least) as an instrument to deflect other bodies. I will not press this point any further here, but will return to it below.

4 Three Brands of Occasionalism

Given that (OCC) captures the essence of occasionalism, there are at least three interestingly different theories about God and nature that share (OCC). I do not claim that any philosopher has ever actually held either of the first two theories. Rather, I am employing them as "useful fictions" designed to help us (i) isolate three distinct motives for occasionalism and (ii) reconstruct in an informative way the dialectic by which the Aristotelian arguments push all occasionalists in the direction of a Berkeleyan philosophy of nature.

4.1 The No-action Theory

The first, which I will call *the no-action theory*, combines (OCC) with a robust essentialist account of material substance. The essentialist element of the theory (at least as I will be using the term 'essentialist' here) is encapsulated by the following two theses:[30]

(E1) It is metaphysically necessary that for any material substance x, there is a (lowest-level) natural kind K such that x essentially instantiates K.

(E2) For every (lowest-level) natural kind K, there is a nonempty set P of active and passive causal powers such that it is metaphysically necessary that a substance instantiates K if and only if it instantiates every member of P.

So on the no-action theory, nonfree creatures never *exercise* any active causal power, even though each one *has* such power essentially. As we shall see in section 5, something like the no-action theory serves

[30]For an explanation of the notion of a lowest-level species or natural kind, see Michael J. Loux, "The Concept of a Kind," *Philosophical Studies* 30 (1976), 53–61.

as the apparent target of many of the Aristotelian antioccasionalist arguments, despite the fact that in all likelihood no occasionalist has ever actually held this theory. Still, I want to ask what sort of argument a theistic philosopher might be able to give for the no-action theory.

There is an alternative and perhaps more revealing way of stating my objective here. As will become clear in a moment, the best-known arguments for occasionalism involve a denial of essentialism with re-spect to material substances, as defined by (E1) and (E2). But it seems perfectly possible to assert (OCC) or something very much like it with-out even addressing the issue of whether essentialism is true. So even if the no-action theory seems extremely implausible, the following question is still worth considering: Is there any philosophically inter-esting argument for (OCC) that does not involve a denial of either (E1) or (E2)?

Ironically, it is Suarez, rather than any occasionalist, who gives the most penetrating answer to this question. After introducing the thesis that "created things do nothing, but God brings about everything in their presence," he goes on to comment:

> I do not see a foundation for this position that carries any weight. Yet its principal foundation seems to have been that to whatever extent efficient causality is attributed to the creature, to that extent the divine power of the creator is diminished; for either God does everything, or He does not do everything; the latter detracts from the divine efficacy, and for this reason we will show below that it is false and erroneous, since it implies that something exists without depending on God. But if God does everything, then I ask again whether He does it immediately and by a power that is sufficient, or only mediately and by a power that is not sufficient. The latter detracts from the divine perfection. But if the former is true, then any other efficient causation is superfluous, since one sufficient and efficacious cause is enough to produce the effect.[31]

What we have here is a challenge to those who, like the medieval Christian Aristotelians, claim that there is a *via media* between occa-sionalism and the theory on which God contributes to natural effects only *mediately*, i.e., by creating and conserving material substances and their powers. For if God is an *immediate* active cause of every effect brought about in the realm of pure nature, then nonfree creatures are immediate active causes of natural effects only if some such effects

---

[31]Suarez, *Disputationes metaphysicae*, disp. 18, p. 593.

come immediately from *both* God and creatures. But, the argument goes, it is impossible to give a coherent and theologically orthodox account of how an effect might be brought about directly or immediately by both God and a creature—i.e., an account that does not render one of those alleged causal contributions wholly redundant. But God's contribution is on all accounts nonredundant. Therefore, God is the sole active cause of every effect in nature.

This argument is certainly much stronger than Suarez's introductory remark would lead one to believe. How, after all, can God be thought to cooperate or concur with creatures without compromising His perfection in general or His omnipotence in particular? Despite Suarez's evident confidence in the truth of his own position, the scholastics could reach no agreement on this matter—a point that, as I mentioned above, Malebranche was especially delighted to emphasize. So one reason for embracing (OCC) is the conviction that the only philosophically respectable alternative to it is a view according to which God is not an immediate cause of natural effects.[32]

4.2 The No-essence Theory

The second brand of occasionalism is what I shall call *the no-essence theory*. According to this theory, even if material substances have active and passive causal powers, they do not have such powers essentially or by nature. More precisely, the no-essence theory accepts (OCC) but rejects both (E1) and (E2) in favor of the antiessentialist thesis that no material substance has any of its causal powers essentially.[33]

The chief motivation for the no-essence theory is the conviction that if material substances had their causal powers essentially, then there would be constraints on God's power that are both philosophically repugnant and, given the authenticity of certain miracle stories from the sacred texts, theologically untenable. Suppose, for instance, that this human flesh (say, the flesh of Shadrach) is essentially or by nature

[32]As I pointed out in n. 3, the claim that God's nonmiraculous activity in nature is limited to creation and conservation is almost universally found wanting in the theistic metaphysical tradition. For a concise and engaging account of just why this is so, see Molina, *Concordia*, pp. 161–163. I hope to develop Molina's arguments in more detail elsewhere.

[33]Strictly speaking, an antiessentialist could deny just one of (E1) and (E2) or even just their conjunction. However, to simplify the argument, I shall assume that both (E1) and (E2) are being denied. As far as I can see, the differences involved have no bearing on my discussion of occasionalism.

such that if it is exposed to extreme heat in the absence of impediments (e.g., asbestos clothing), it is incinerated; and suppose further that this fire (say, the fire of Nebuchadnezzar's furnace) is essentially or by nature such that in the absence of impediments it automatically, as it were, incinerates unprotected human flesh brought into suitable proximity to it. What follows, the occasionalists claim, is that according to essentialism it is *metaphysically necessary* for this flesh to be incinerated when brought into contact with this fire in the absence of natural impediments—a claim confirmed and, indeed, insisted upon by such *contemporary* essentialists as Rom Harre and Edward Madden.[34] Any alleged human flesh not incinerated under such conditions would not be *real* human flesh; by the same token, any supposedly raging fire that did not incinerate unprotected human flesh brought near it would not be *real* fire. Or so, at least, essentialists seem bound to hold. And yet, the occasionalists retort, the sacred writings tell of God's miraculously sparing (real) human beings thrown unprotected into (real) raging infernos.[35] That is, according to the sacred writings it is metaphysically possible for real human flesh to be exposed to real raging fire and yet not be incinerated. The Bible and the Koran line up on one side, Aristotle and his heathen friends on the other; one must choose between the faith and the philosophers.

This antiessentialist argument should sound familiar, since it is epitomized by the famous philosophical bromide that there is no necessary connection between cause and effect. That is, roughly, there are no nontrivial conceptual limits on what sorts of causal transformations are possible. Thus al-Ghazali:

> In our view the connection between what are believed to be the cause
> and the effect is not necessary. Take any two things. This is not That;
> nor can That be This. The affirmation of the one does not imply the

[34]See Rom Harre and Edward H. Madden, *Causal Powers* (Totowa, N.J.: Rowman and Littlefield, 1975), pp. 44–49.

[35]Specifically, the references are to chap. 3 of the Book of Daniel and to Koran 21:69–70 and 37:98. The miracle of the fiery furnace is not the only such miracle cited in this connection. Aquinas, for instance, alludes to God's keeping the waters of the Jordan from flowing downstream (Joshua 3:15–16). The important factor is that the created substances involved in this sort of miracle at least appear to have a natural inclination toward an effect *contrary to* the miraculous effect. Occasionalists will claim that this appearance is mere appearance, while concurrentists will aver that God accomplishes *this* sort of miracle *by omission*, i.e., by withholding His general concurrence from the ordinary course of nature—even while contrary tendencies remain in the created causes.

affirmation of the other; nor does its denial imply the denial of the other. The existence of the one is not necessitated by the existence of the other; nor its non-existence by the non-existence of the other. Take for instance any two things, such as the quenching of thirst and drinking; satisfaction of hunger and eating; burning and contact with fire; light and the rise of the Sun; death and the severance of the head from the trunk; healing and the use of medicine; the loosening of the bowels and the use of a purgative. . . . They are connected as the result of the Decree of God (holy be His name), which preceded their existence. If one follows the other, it is because He has created them in that fashion, not because the connection in itself is necessary and indissoluble. . . .

Let us consider only one example—viz., the burning of a piece of cotton at the time of its contact with fire. We admit the possibility of a contact between the two which will not result in burning. . . . [The philosophers] reject this possibility.[36]

This, of course, is similar to the billiard-ball argument that Hume found in Malebranche and whose nontheological counterpart he proceeded to make famous in the English-speaking philosophical world. Notice, there is no little irony involved in the fact that al-Ghazali's argument should have been taken over by such a skeptic about miracles as Hume, given that the argument was originally prompted by the belief that God had miraculously saved His faithful servants from being incinerated!

But what exactly is wrong with essentialism? After all, even an essentialist can allow that God is able, say, to change the flesh of Shadrach into stone for the duration of his sojourn in the furnace, or to put an invisible heat-resistant shield between him and the fire.

Occasionalists are wholly unwilling to settle for this concession. God, they will insist, does not have to act *in opposition to* His creatures *from without*, as it were; He does not have to vie with them in order to exercise control over them. Rather, He controls them *from within* as their sovereign Creator and Governor. They are beholden to His word: He can command the fire not to burn the flesh even while it remains fire; He can suspend the flesh's susceptibility to being incinerated without changing it into a different substance or altering its natural kind. Only those whose piety has been corrupted by the philosophers will disagree. al-Ghazali puts it this way:

[The philosophers say:] Whenever we suppose fire with all its qualities, and suppose two similar pieces of cotton which are exposed to fire in

---

[36]al-Ghazali, *Incoherence of the Philosophers*, p. 185.

the same way, how can we conceive that one of them should burn, and the other should not? There is no alternative for the other piece.

(From this idea, they come to disbelieve the story that when Abraham was thrown into fire, burning did not happen, although fire continued to be fire. They assert that this cannot happen, unless fire should be devoid of heat (which would put an end to its being fire), or unless Abraham's person or body should turn into a stone or something else which might resist the influence of fire.)[37]

On al-Ghazali's view, then, material substances may have active (and passive) causal powers as long as God has full control over these powers "from the inside," i.e., as long as no creature has any such power essentially or with metaphysical necessity. So I will take the no-essence theory to consist of (i) (OCC); (ii) the antiessentialist thesis that no material substance has any causal power essentially; and (iii) the claim that every material substance has active causal powers. According to this theory, when God keeps the fire from burning Shadrach, He does not have to act against the fire's natural inclination or tendency to consume Shadrach. Instead, He can merely ensure that the fire lacks this tendency, yet without destroying it or changing it into another kind of thing.

Interestingly, there is some debate about whether al-Ghazali himself is an occasionalist, i.e., whether he accepts (OCC). As a matter of fact, in problem 17 of *The Incoherence of the Philosophers* he sets forth *two* distinct theories. His clear intent, it seems to me, is to find a religiously acceptable alternative to essentialism, since he is convinced that essentialism rules out certain of the miracles recorded by the sacred writers.[38] He finds two such alternatives. The first consists of (OCC) and the antiessentialist thesis; the second includes the antiessentialist thesis along with the dual claim that (i) every material substance *has* active and passive causal powers and (ii) every material substance *exercises* active and passive causal powers. So it is only the first of al-Ghazali's theories that counts as a version of occasionalism, and the argument against calling him an occasionalist must ultimately be based

---

[37]Ibid., p. 188.

[38]The theistic Aristotelians will, of course, demur, insisting instead that one of the prerequistes for the action of a created cause is God's general causal influence. If God withholds this concurrence, there will (miraculously) be no action, even though the substances themselves retain their natures and their essential causal powers. Occasionalists respond by asking for a detailed metaphysical account of God's general concurrence. See my "The Necessity of Nature," 234–236.

on the fact that he seems to retreat from the first theory to the second in the face of objections.

Now whatever position al-Ghazali himself may finally have settled upon, the no-essence theory, as I have formulated it, is a hybrid constructed from the two theories he actually propounded. While the no-essence theory is once again not especially plausible, its very conceivability shows that one can accommodate the antiessentialist motivations for occasionalism without thereby giving up the claim that created substances have causal powers. As such, the no-essence theory provides a possible refuge from the 'prevention or preemption' objection that will be directed at the no-action theory in section 5.

4.3 The No-nature Theory

The third brand of occasionalism is what I dub *the no-nature theory*, and although Malebranche fudges a bit on whether material substances have passive causal powers, he and Berkeley are the champions here, with Biel playing the role of an extremely sympathetic fellow-traveler. In short, this theory consists of (i) (OCC); (ii) the antiessentialist thesis; and (iii) the claim that no material substance has any active or passive causal power at all.[39] The motivation for this theory is not any abstract metaphysical qualm about how one and the same effect might be immediately produced by both God and a creature; nor is it any relatively narrow worry about essentialism's ruling out a certain fairly small class of miracles. It is, instead, the sweeping and startling conviction that the attribution of *any* power at all (especially any *active* power) to *any* corporeal substance is not only unnecessary but blasphemous, not only philosophically confused but downright idolatrous. Malebranche puts the point as follows:

> If we consider attentively our idea of cause or of power to act, we cannot doubt that this idea represents something divine. . . . We therefore admit something divine in all the bodies around us when we posit forms, faculties, qualities, virtues, or real beings capable of producing certain effects through the force of their nature; and thus we insensibly adopt the opinion of the pagans because of our respect for their philosophy. It is true that faith corrects; but perhaps it can be said in this connection that if the heart is Christian, the mind is basically pagan.[40]

[39]This is what I later call the full-fledged no-nature theory. What I dub the modified no-nature theory allows creatures to have passive causal powers.
[40]Malebranche, *Search after Truth*, p. 446.

> To render God all the respect due Him, it is not enough to adore Him as the sovereign power and to fear Him more than His creatures; we must also fear and adore Him in all His creatures. All our reverence must be directed toward Him, for honor and glory are due only Him. . . . Thus, the philosophy that teaches us that the efficacy of secondary causes is a fiction of the mind, that Aristotle's, and certain other philosophers', *nature* is a chimera, that only God is strong and powerful enough not only to act in our soul but also to give the least motion to matter, this philosophy, I say, agrees perfectly with religion, the end of which is to join us to God in the closest way.
>
> We ordinarily love only things capable of doing us some good: this philosophy therefore authorizes only the love of God, and absolutely condemns the love of everything else. We should fear only what can do us some evil: this philosophy therefore sanctions only the fear of God and absolutely condemns all others.[41]

And in the concluding sections of the *Principles*, Berkeley continues the attack on Aristotelian natures:

> If by *nature* is meant some being distinct from God, as well as from the laws of nature and things perceived by sense, I must confess that word is to me an empty sound, without any intelligible meaning annexed to it. Nature in this acceptation is a vain *chimera* introduced by those heathens, who had no just notions of the omnipresence and infinite perfection of God. But it is more unaccountable, that it should be received among *Christians* professing belief in the Holy Scriptures, which constantly ascribe those effects to the immediate hand of God, that heathen philosophers are wont to impute to *nature*. . . . Fain would we suppose Him at a great distance off, and substitute some blind unthinking deputy in His stead, though (if we may believe Saint Paul) *He be not far from every one of us.*[42]

Such memorable passages confirm Charles McCracken's perceptive observation: "The chief goal of the philosophical labours of both Malebranche and Berkeley was the same: to recall Christian philosophy to a recognition of the total and immediate dependence of all things on God. To both, belief in *nature*, if by that term be meant a realm of entities that produce effects by their own power, is the hallmark of the pagan, and the antithesis of the Christian, view of the world."[43]

As our discussion of the no-essence theory revealed, the Aristotelian

---

[41]Malebranche, *Elucidations*, p. 681.

[42]Berkeley, *Principles*, p. 89.

[43]Charles J. McCracken, *Malebranche and British Philosophy* (Oxford: Oxford University Press, 1983), p. 211.

account of substance or individual nature has two distinguishable elements: the bare attribution of causal powers to material substances and the further thesis that each material substance has its basic causal powers essentially. The no-essence theory rejects one-half of this conception of nature, its essentialism. But for a no-nature theorist the mere rejection of essentialism is not an adequate response to the danger posed by "heathen" naturalism, a naturalism that in effect attempts to replace the action of a provident God with that of natures conceived of as intrinsic causal principles. One must instead eradicate *every* vestige of the natures championed by Aristotle and the other pagan philosophers, and this entails nothing less than the complete repudiation of causal power for corporeal substances. What we have here, then, is the most extreme form of occasionalism and, as I will now argue, the only form of occasionalism worth defending.

5 The Aristotelian Objections

The medieval Aristotelians exhibit little patience with those who espouse occasionalism or theories closely resembling it. (Occasionalism is often treated along with theories that limit the active causal contribution of material substances to the production of merely accidental, as opposed to substantial, changes.)[44] In one place St. Thomas goes so far as to call occasionalism stupid, a breach of decorum for which he is roundly applauded by Molina: "Everyone rejects this position, and St. Thomas justifiably calls it stupid. For what could be more stupid than to deny what is obvious from experience and sense perception? But it is evident to the senses that secondary causes elicit and exercise their own operations."[45]

Yet, for all their bravado, the Aristotelians were only partly successful in constructing a reasoned case against occasionalism. Many of their philosophical and theological objections, whatever their "objective" merits, seem in retrospect to be at least dialectically ineffective, especially to those of us who have had the opportunity to read Malebranche and Berkeley.

Take, for instance, the battery of objections that appeal to sensory evidence. Molina points out that such propositions as *The sun gives*

---

[44]See, e.g., Aquinas, *Summa contra Gentiles* III, chap. 69.
[45]Molina, *Concordia*, p. 160.

light and *Fire gives heat*, which he claims our sensory experience shows to be evidently true, would be false if material substances were not active causes of anything.[46] We might add other, perhaps more complex, examples such as *The wind is blowing the leaves around* or *The acid is making the litmus paper turn red* or *The oak tree is sprouting leaves*, but the point is basically the same: If material substances are not active causes, then much of what we ordinarily say in making perceptual reports is literally false.

Along similar but not entirely identical lines, St. Thomas argues that, given the truth of occasionalism, evidently true propositions about sensings themselves, e.g., *I sense the heat of this fire*, would be false. For even if in the presence of fire God produces in me a sensation of heat, He cannot, according to occasionalists, bring it about that it is *the fire's* heat (read: the heat produced by this fire) that I sense.[47]

In yet another vein, St. Thomas argues that if occasionalism were true, then the diversity of effects in nature would not result from a diversity of causes. Rather, the (real) cause in every instance would be the same, viz., God Himself, though the effects would be diverse. But, St. Thomas retorts, "this appears false to the senses. For it is only heating, and not cooling, that results from putting something near a hot object; nor does the generation of anything but a human being result from the semen of a human being."[48]

So in at least three different ways occasionalism runs afoul of common opinions that emanate from and are grounded in ordinary sense experience. But, contends Molina, "what experience attests to should not be denied in the absence of a compelling reason; but not only is there no *compelling* reason, there is not even a *plausible* reason that might recommend the claim that created things do not truly exercise the actions which experience teaches originate from these same causes."[49]

The first-stage occasionalist response to such arguments is to claim that while we perceive the various and diverse effects that occur in nature, we do not perceive that these effects *derive from* or *are brought about by* created causes. At most what is obvious is that these effects are produced *in the presence of* such-and-such corporeal substances. Yet,

---

[46]Ibid., p. 161.
[47]Aquinas, *De potentia Dei*, Q. 3, A. 7, resp.
[48]Aquinas, *Summa contra Gentiles* III, chap. 69.
[49]Molina, *Concordia*, p. 161.

as we saw in our discussion of occasional causation, this sort of presence is in itself a strong enough relation to ground the counterfactual
dependencies that Aquinas's diversity argument points to. We need
make no appeal to the alleged action of material substances.

Furthermore, it is unlikely that any amount of psychological evidence
will be sufficient to settle the question of whether, as common usage
suggests, we actually perceive the wind *blowing* the leaves or the fire
heating the kettle of water.[50] But, the occasionalists urge, even if it
should turn out that almost all our perceptual reports are indeed literally false, we must acknowledge that our linguistic practices have a
myriad of different functions, the overwhelming majority of which do
not require the literal truth of our perceptual statements. Of all the
occasionalists, it is Berkeley who emphasizes this point most forcefully:
"The communicating of ideas marked by words is not the chief and
only end of language, as is commonly supposed. There are other ends,
as the raising of some passion, the exciting to, or deterring from an
action, the putting the mind in some particular disposition; to which
the former is in many cases barely subservient, and sometimes entirely
omitted, when these can be obtained without it, as I think does not
infrequently happen in the familiar use of language."[51]

In fact, to insist on literal truth outside of strict scientific or philosophical contexts will often impede ordinary communication. In reply-
ing to the objection that a philosopher who denied that fire heats or
that water cools would be deservedly laughed at, Berkeley concedes
the point in these celebrated lines: "I answer, he would so; in such
things we ought to *think with the learned, and speak with the vulgar*. They
who to demonstration are convinced of the truth of the *Copernican*
system, do nevertheless say the sun rises, the sun sets, or comes to
the meridian: and if they affected a contrary style in common talk, it
would without doubt appear ridiculous. A little reflection on what is
here said will make it manifest, that the common use of language would
receive no manner of alteration or disturbance from the admission of
our tenets."[52]

As an outspoken rationalist, Malebranche is considerably less reluctant than Berkeley to scorn common opinion and practice. He openly

---

[50]See Harre and Madden, *Causal Powers*, pp. 49–67, for an interesting discussion of
the perception of causation.
[51]Berkeley, *Principles*, p. 19.
[52]Ibid., pp. 44–45.

acknowledges (and laments) that, largely as an effect of original sin, naturalism has become deeply embedded in ordinary thought and language: "We are led by an almost natural prejudice not to think of God with respect to natural effects, and to attribute power and efficacy to natural causes; ordinarily only miracles make us think of God, and sensible impression initiates our view of secondary causes. Philosophers hold this view because, they say, their senses convince them of it; this is their strongest argument. In the end this view is held by all those who follow the judgment of their senses. Now, language is formed on this prejudice, and we say as commonly that fire has the power to burn as we call gold and silver our good."[53]

Occasionalists, then, are not without systematic resources when countering Aristotelian objections that appeal to the evidence of the senses. For even if those who deny that fire heats and water cools are indeed epistemically flawed in some objective sense, they are nonetheless able to articulate a prima facie coherent metaphysical framework from within which arguments of the sort in question will fail to appear compelling.

Even less convincing is the Aristotelian argument charging that occasionalism engenders a sort of causal anarchism. Occasionalism would of course be wholly implausible if it entailed that in any given circumstances C, no one causal transformation is more likely or less likely to occur in C than any other. In that case, to cite al-Ghazali's unforgettable example, you might have good reason to wonder whether the man standing before you now was one of the fruits sold at the market a few hours ago. But in fact occasionalism entails only that such bizarre causal transformations are *metaphysically possible*, not that they are likely or probable:

> If you could prove that in regard to things which 'can exist' there cannot be created for man a knowledge that they 'do not exist', then these absurdities would be inescapable. . . . God has created for us the knowledge that He would not do these things, although they are possible. We never asserted that they are necessary. They are only possible— i.e., they may, or may not, happen. It is only when something possible is repeated over and over again (so as to form the Norm), that its pursuance of a uniform course in accordance with the Norm in the past is indelibly impressed upon our minds.[54]

[53]Malebranche, *Elucidations*, pp. 673–674.
[54]al-Ghazali, *Incoherence of the Philosophers*, p. 189.

Indeed, it is just God's steadfast adherence to certain arbitrarily chosen "norms" that serves as the occasionalist surrogate for Aristotelian natures. That is to say, constant divine intentions provide the stability and regularity in the universe that Aristotelians attribute to the natures of corporeal substances. So instead of invoking causal dispositions, tendencies, and inclinations rooted in the natures of corporeal substances, the occasionalist appeals to God's abiding intention to act in certain fixed ways. Where the Aristotelian will claim that, say, fire has an active causal disposition to heat bodies brought near it, the occasionalist will claim instead that in bringing about natural effects God resolutely follows the (defeasible) rule according to which He heats bodies brought near fire. And where the Aristotelian appeals to the regularity guaranteed by the natures of corporeal substances in order to justify the scientific practice of making inductive inferences about what would occur in counterfactual situations, the occasionalist instead grounds these same inductive practices in the firmness of God's causal intentions. (Notice in passing that this gives occasionalists a great theoretical advantage over their positivist cousins, who generate "the problem of induction" by their agnosticism about the existence and/or nature of the "real" causes of natural phenomena.) In short, every important naturalist concept (nature, law, disposition, power, etc.) has an occasionalist analogue. There need be no substantive disagreement between occasionalists and Aristotelians about what *will* or *would* occur under such-and-such circumstances; there will be disagreement at most about what *might possibly* occur. And even here *theistic* Aristotelians can claim no advantage. They, too, must (or at least *do*) admit that God can prevent the (real) fire from incinerating the (real) human flesh of Shadrach; they, too, must concede that God has the power to transform (or better: transubstantiate) a fruit into a man.[55]

Two types of theological argument used by the Aristotelians are also ineffective. First, the scriptural and patristic testimony cited by the Christian Aristotelians in favor of secondary causation in nature is scanty and, more to the point, counterbalanced by other texts that

---

[55]The theistic Aristotelians differ from the occasionalists in claiming that the admittedly possible bizarre transformations mentioned here have a wholly different sort of causal ancestry from normal causal transformations and are accomplished by God despite natural tendencies to the contrary on the part of creatures. The occasionalists rule out any such tendencies in the creatures themselves and in effect "relocate" them in the divine intellect and will.

seem to support occasionalism.[56] Nor does any Aristotelian I know of make a serious effort to explain the meaning of the latter texts or to argue on hermeneutical grounds that they should be given less weight than texts that militate against occasionalism. Perhaps the Aristotelians simply take it for granted that what is evident to the senses or deeply entrenched in common opinion constitutes a nearly indefeasible constraint on how Sacred Scripture and the Fathers are to be interpreted. At any rate, the most imaginative and ingenious attempt to formulate a decisive argument on this front comes not from an Aristotelian but from Malebranche, who makes an admirable effort to transform the counterintuitive character of the texts supporting occasionalism into a reliable sign of their literal truth.[57]

Second, both Aquinas and Molina argue that God's almightiness is honored more by the view that natural substances possess and exercise their own causal powers than by occasionalism. Thus Molina: "One extols God's power more by claiming that He can effect the operations of all things *both* by Himself *and* through the powers He confers on secondary causes than by claiming that He alone can effect them."[58] Aquinas makes the same point negatively: It detracts from God's power and perfection to deny that He communicates (or is even able to communicate) to creatures the perfection of exercising their own causal power.[59]

But this objection is clearly inconclusive. Occasionalism, after all, assigns to God a much more intensive, if not extensive, causal role in nature than does the concurrentist view held by the Aristotelians. For according to concurrentism, God's active causal contribution to ordinary natural effects is "general" and thus is not by itself sufficient to determine the specific nature of those effects; this is instead a function of the "particular" secondary causes involved.[60] So occasionalists, too, can lay claim to a legitimate sense in which their position celebrates God's power to a higher degree than does that of their opponents.

In summary, then, many of the standard Aristotelian objections seem

---

[56]The longest and most illuminating discussion of this matter is found in Malebranche's *Elucidations*, pp. 672–685.

[57]See ibid., pp. 672–685, esp. 672. I hope to discuss this section of Elucidation 15 at some length elsewhere.

[58]Molina, *Concordia*, p. 161.

[59]Aquinas, *Summa contra Gentiles* III, chap. 69.

[60]Remember that the nature of the effect is derived from its *particular* causes. See n. 8 above.

impotent against a philosophically sophisticated occasionalist. Indeed, it may appear at this point that the most an Aristotelian can hope for against *any* version of occasionalism is a mere standoff. It may appear that there just are no potent objections whose premises have any purchase on convinced occasionalists. This appearance, however, is misleading.

Let's look at the situation a little more closely. The occasionalist must hold either (i) that corporeal substances have no causal powers at all or (ii) that, having such powers, they never *in fact* contribute causally to any effects. That is, an occasionalist must espouse either the no-nature theory or else a weaker no-action or no-essence theory. Let's begin by exploring this second option. How might an Aristotelian respond to it? Consider the following chain of reasoning, which I shall dub the *prevention or preemption* objection:

Suppose for the sake of argument that the no-action theory is true. Now imagine that an ordinary piece of wood falls into a raging fire at a particular time T and that it is completely consumed shortly thereafter. Assume that no creature is a free cause of this effect. (As we saw in section 3, occasionalists seem forced to grant this assumption in any case.) God, then, is the sole active cause of the wood's being consumed. Nonetheless, both the fire and the wood have active and passive causal powers, and these by nature. Now assume that the fire's active causal powers are by and large what we usually take them to be. (If they are not, then alter the example so that the effect *is* one that the fire has the active power to produce.) In that case the fire has at T a natural inclination to consume any piece of ordinary wood thrown into it. Of course, since the no-action theory is true, we know that this inclination is never realized. But why not? There are just two possible answers. The first is that God acts on the fire in such a way as to prevent it from exercising its power to consume the wood; the second is that, without doing anything to the fire, God preempts its action by causing the wood to be consumed before the fire can act on it. In either case, in order to be a strong active cause of the wood's being consumed, God has to ensure that the fire will not exercise its proper causal power.

To put it more generally, the no-action theory entails that in order to produce all natural effects by Himself, God must continually prevent or preempt the causal activity of created material substances. He must, as it were, constantly ward off His own creatures and the powers He has given them in order to play His rightful causal role in the ordinary course of nature—an awkward state of affairs, to be sure, and, embarrassingly, one that flouts the occasionalist's own deepest convictions. For, as we saw in our discussion of the fiery furnace, occasionalists deem it blasphemous even to suggest that God must struggle with His creatures or in any way oppose them from without in order to govern them and exercise control over them. Yet the no-action theory carries with it just this suggestion that Creator and creature tend to work at cross-purposes.

At this juncture the occasionalist might fleetingly contemplate a retreat to the no-essence theory. For if the root problem with the no-action theory is that it attributes to corporeal substances certain essential causal powers, tendencies, and dispositions that God must actively oppose "from without," then perhaps this problem can be solved simply by denying that such causal properties are *essential* to the substances in question. We can see this more clearly as follows:

To prevent or preempt the action of a corporeal substance is to oppose it or frustrate it in some way; otherwise its natural tendencies will be actualized. But if no powers or tendencies are had essentially by any corporeal substance, then God does not have to act against His creatures "from without"; He can instead simply regulate their causal tendencies "from within" to suit His purposes. For example, if He brings it about that the fire simply lacks a causal tendency to consume pieces of wood thrown into it, then He need not prevent or preempt the fire's action. Accordingly, He can be a strong active cause of the wood's being consumed in the presence of the fire without at the same time having to act against or thwart the fire. So, in general, if the no-essence theory is true, then God is able to arrange things in such a way that He never has to frustrate in any way the causal tendencies of any corporeal substance. And there will be just the sort of harmony between Creator and creature that one would antecedently expect.

Perhaps this line of reasoning provides the no-essence theorist with an escape from the 'prevention or preemption' objection. (I am not certain that it does, but shall not dwell on the point here.) Nevertheless, two further arguments are no less damaging to the no-essence theory than to the no-action theory. In fact, the sheer obviousness and power of these arguments may explain why the "prevention or preemption" objection, despite its considerable strength, does not appear in the Aristotelian sources I have cited.

First of all, the no-essence theory, like the no-action theory, entails that each corporeal substance has causal powers and tendencies, and yet that no such causal power or tendency is ever actualized. But this consequence is objectionable in itself, regardless of whether God has to oppose or resist His creatures from without. For what possible reason could a perfectly wise and provident God have for endowing creatures with causal powers, *none of which* they will ever have the opportunity to exercise? Such powers, hidden from view, would be wholly super-fluous, utterly lacking in point, serving no conceivable purpose in the divine providential scheme. St. Thomas expresses this point in two slightly different ways:

> Reason shows that there is nothing in natural things which does not serve some purpose. But if natural things did not do anything, then the forms and causal powers they are endowed with would have no purpose—just as, if a knife did not cut anything, then it would have its sharpness to no avail.[61]

> It is contrary to the notion of wisdom that there should be anything without a purpose in the works of one who is wise. But if created things in no way acted to produce effects, but instead God alone did everything directly, then these other things would be employed by Him to no purpose in the production of effects. Therefore, the position in question is incompatible with the divine wisdom.[62]

This objection seems to be very powerful, especially—but not only—if we make the fairly modest assumption that God could have created a world that appears very much like ours without endowing any cor-poreal creature with active causal powers. After all, if He could have done so, why would He choose instead to create a counterpart universe containing wholly unactualized causal powers? It would be as if He had created many tools (recall the knife) which He then proceeded to ignore in bringing about by Himself alone the very effects that the tools were intended to be instrumental in producing. One need not subscribe to a strong Principle of Sufficient Reason in order to appreciate the point of this argument.

The second objection is a rather subtle one that has both strategic and tactical significance. If corporeal substances cause nothing, then we can have no scientific knowledge. For the chief aim of natural science is to lay bare the natures of the material substances that are real causes of spatiotemporal effects, and the method of science is to

---

[61]Aquinas, *De potentia Dei*, Q. 3, A. 7, resp.
[62]Aquinas, *Summa contra Gentiles* III, chap. 69.

reason from effects to powers and from powers to natures. So if corporeal substances do not act, then scientific reasoning will not help us come to a knowledge of the natures of material things. In short, if occasionalism in any of its forms is true, then natural science is impossible. Thus St. Thomas:

> If effects are not produced by the action of created things, but only by the action of God, it is impossible for the power of any created cause to be manifested through its effects. For an effect does not manifest the power of the cause except by virtue of the action which, proceeding from the power, terminates in the effect. But the nature of a cause is not known through the effect except insofar as its power, which flows from the nature, is known through the effect. Therefore, if created things did not act to produce effects, it would follow that no nature of any created thing could ever be known through an effect. And we would be deprived of all the knowledge of natural science, since in natural science demonstrations are derived mainly from the effect.[63]

This argument is strategically important because it demonstrates how the debate between Aristotelians and occasionalists is readily transformed into a debate over the character and aims of natural science. I shall come back to this in section 6. But here the argument can be used tactically to show that those who accept (OCC) can have no justification for embracing either the no-action theory or the no-essence theory. For if corporeal substances never produce any effects, then, barring divine revelation, none of us will ever know just which powers any given corporeal substance has.[64] Worse yet, scientific reasoning will not even help us establish the general claim that corporeal substances have causal power. So those who believe that material substances never act will, given their own theory, have no justification for attributing to those substances any active causal power at all. Even from within the occasionalist perspective, then, both the no-action theory and the no-essence theory suffer from grave deficiencies. The Aristotelian arguments seem to have rendered a move toward the no-nature theory not only appropriate but mandatory.

But at this point in our dialogue there is likely to be a breakdown in communications—one that helps explain why the most impressive of

---

[63]Ibid.

[64]In fact, if the no-essence theory were true, we would be in a better position to know which powers particular substances *lack*, viz., powers sufficient to bring about the effect that God has in fact brought about. For recall that the no-essence theory is meant to rule out prevention and preemption.

the Aristotelian objections to occasionalism seem question-begging when directed at the no-nature theory. The problem, simply stated, is that the no-nature theory would never occur to a medieval Aristotelian as a coherent possibility worthy of being refuted. To Aquinas, Molina, Suarez, or any other robust Aristotelian, denying active causal power to an entity amounts to nothing less than denying that entity the status of being a substance. As St. Thomas says in the opening chapter of *De ente et essentia* (and here he is simply echoing the Aristotle of *Physics* II), things that exist in the most privileged sense, i.e., the primary beings or substances, are just those things that have natures.[65] And from these natures, in turn, flow the intrinsic causal powers, tendencies, and dispositions that are definitive of the various natural kinds and that are thus possessed by the individual instances of those natural kinds. So it is metaphysically necessary that, say, tomato plants tend to produce tomatoes and that fire tends to incinerate human flesh brought into close proximity to it. What's more, it is just these natures and natural kinds, revealed to some extent and in an imprecise way through ordinary sense experience, that are the objects of systematic scientific inquiry. What, after all, could be more obvious than the contention that in order to have scientific knowledge about a tomato plant, one must acquire a systematic understanding of its causal tendencies and dispositions—more specifically, its principles of generation, development, and degeneration, the conditions under which it flourishes and the conditions under which its development is impeded, etc.? We now know that such inquiry will steer us in directions undreamt of by the medievals—toward postulational biochemistry and evolutionary biology, for instance. But the fundamental guiding idea is the same: The scientific enterprise is aimed at discovering the natures of material substances and providing genuine causal explanations of spatiotemporal phenomena in terms of those natures. To repudiate such natures and the causal powers that flow from them is tantamount to denying that there are any material entities at all and a fortiori to denying that scientific knowledge is possible. To the medieval Aristotelians (and perhaps to others among us as well) such denials seem utterly preposterous. And so they are, as long we take it for granted that corporeal entities must be substances, i.e., beings with natures.

And thus of course we come to Berkeley, whose antinaturalism

---

[65] Aquinas, *De ente et essentia*, chap. 1: "Nature seems to mean the thing's essence as ordered to its proper activity, for nothing is without its proper activity."

knows no bounds. Since corporeal things have no active or passive causal powers, there just are no material substances of the sort that Aristotelian (or, for that matter, Lockean) naturalists have conceived there to be.[66] Only spirits have natures that serve as intrinsic sources of causal power, and hence only spirits are primary beings or substances. There are, to be sure, bodies—those very bodies whose sensible characteristics we continually perceive. But if a mark of substance is the possession of causal power, then there simply are no material or corporeal substances.[67]

Notice, by the way, that Berkeley and the theistic Aristotelians do not disagree about whether corporeal things can exist without being cognized or "perceived." The Aristotelians, after all, do not claim that the ontological independence (or per se existence) of a corporeal substance consists in its ability to exist without being known by any mind. For, according to their theological beliefs, there can be no substance that is not known by the divine intellect. Rather, the disagreement is precisely about whether corporeal things have natures, i.e., about whether they are substances or first beings endowed with causal power.

But perhaps we have moved too quickly here. Perhaps we have overlooked a possible alternative. Berkeley's position is what I shall call the full-fledged no-nature theory. On this view corporeal things *in no way* delimit or determine the effects they are involved in. They have neither active nor passive causal power and hence are not independent beings or substances. Instead, they are "ideas," i.e., mere modes or modifications of spiritual substances. But might an occasionalist not hold, as Malebranche seems to, that even though material substances lack all *active* causal powers, they nonetheless have *passive* causal powers? In this way the occasionalist would be able to affirm both (OCC) and the metaphysical independence of corporeal things. I shall call this the modified no-nature theory.

Such a theory would in effect be putting asunder what Aristotle had joined together, viz., structured or formed matter on the one hand and

---

[66]It is the lack of causal power that, in Berkeley's metaphysics, is prior to and grounds the status, had by each corporeal thing, of being an idea.

[67]The connection between being and power was noticed at least as early as Plato. Thus the Athenian stranger: "I suggest that anything has real being that is so constituted as to possess any sort of power either to affect anything else or to be affected, in however small a degree, by the most insignificant agent, though it be only once. I am proposing as a mark to distinguish real things that they are nothing but power" (*Sophist*, 247d–e).

active causal power on the other. God would supply all the active causal power in nature, while material substances would receive and channel God's causal influence as patients. To be sure, these substances would be wholly inert, but they would at least be "thicker" than on the Berkeleyan view.

Notice, by the way, that the same arguments that led us from the no-action theory to the no-essence theory will dictate that the passive powers in question be nonessential. al-Ghazali, for instance, insists that God could bring it about that of two exactly similar pieces of cotton exposed to equally intense heat in exactly similar circumstances, one is consumed by the heat and the other is not. But if the second piece's susceptibility to being consumed in those circumstances were essential to it, then God would have to thwart that susceptibility in order to keep the cotton from being consumed.[68] So the friend of the modified no-nature theory should presumably hold that any passive causal powers a corporeal thing has are not essential to it.

How plausible is the modified no-nature theory from within the occasionalist perspective? My suspicion is that the very notion of a substance endowed with passive but not active causal powers is incoherent. At the very least, as I noted above, the fundamental passive powers associated with *material* substances in particular (e.g., impenetrability) seem clearly to render the things that have them apt to be used (at least by God) as instrumental efficient causes. But if this is so, then no occasionalist can consistently accept the modified no-nature theory. Since this theory seems to have been Malebranche's, it follows that the arguments presented here support Berkeley against Malebranche, and the full-fledged no-nature theory against the modified no-nature theory.

Any tenacious and epistemically conscientious friend of occasionalism will, I believe, be ultimately led by the Aristotelian objections to embrace the no-nature theory—and the full-fledged version at that. This is what I set out to prove, and I believe that my cumulative argument is a strong one. Yet since the Aristotelian objections examined so far do not appear to undermine the no-nature theory itself, the next step is to evaluate the no-nature theory on independent philosophical and theological grounds. I cannot do this in any depth here, but in the concluding section I will briefly indicate what I take the strengths and weaknesses of the no-nature theory to be.

[68]al-Ghazali, *Incoherence of the Philosophers*, p. 190.

6 Prospects for the No-nature Theory

One of the no-nature theory's chief strengths is, I believe, its ability to provide a very clear and intellectually satisfying account of how the natural sciences are to be integrated into a theistic vision of the universe. Theistic metaphysics seems bound to resist the quintessentially modern dogma that the natural sciences are autonomous in the sense that (i) no alleged source of revelation (e.g., Scripture or Tradition) can rightfully serve in any way to correct or modify their claims, and that (ii) they in no way point beyond themselves to a more ultimate sort of explanation (whether in terms of efficient or final causes) for natural effects. The no-nature theory has the resources to curb these pretensions in a much more direct and simple (some would say simplistic) way than any 'theistic naturalism' can.

Both Berkeley and Malebranche understand (OCC) to be a mortal enemy of the brand of scientific realism that engenders these claims to autonomy. This may not be apparent at first, since Malebranche clearly accepts the existence of unobservable entities with reference to which the fundamental laws of motion are to be formulated—and this makes him a scientific realist in at least one standard sense. However, we must distinguish here between what I shall call *entity realism* and what might appropriately be termed *explanatory realism*. For while Malebranche accepts on scientific grounds the existence of unobservable theoretical entities, the postulation of these entities does not on his view enable us to grasp the causal powers or natures of material substances or to provide *genuine* causal explanations of observable effects—as opposed to "explanations" in terms of *occasional* or what he sometimes calls *natural* causes. Malebranche and Berkeley are both explanatory antirealists. That is, they hold that the purpose of natural science is not to discover the real causes of natural phenomena or the natures of those causes, but to discover and systematize regularities and correlations among the Real Cause's observable effects in nature, and on this basis to make accurate predictions. First Malebranche and then Berkeley:

> The study of nature is false and vain in every way when true causes are sought in it other than the volitions of the Almighty, or the general laws according to which He constantly acts.[69]

[69]Malebranche, *Elucidations*, p. 662.

> If therefore we consider the difference there is betwixt natural philos-
> ophers and other men, with regard to their knowledge of the *phenomena*,
> we shall find it consists, not in an exacter knowledge of the efficient
> cause that produces them, for that can be no other than the *will of a*
> *spirit*, but only in a greater largeness of comprehension, whereby anal-
> ogies, harmonies, and agreements are discovered in the works of na-
> ture, and the particular effects explained, that is, reduced to general
> rules, which rules grounded on the analogy, and uniformness observed
> in the production of natural effects, are most agreeable, and sought
> after by the mind.[70]

So the aim of the natural sciences is merely to give us theories that
are, to use Bas Van Fraassen's apt expression, empirically adequate.
Their aim is emphatically not to find the real (as opposed to natural
or occasional) causes of natural phenomena or to provide a true picture
of the causal mechanisms at work in the created universe. Indeed,
according to the no-nature theory, there are no such causal mechanisms
waiting to be discovered—though this is not to deny that there are
extremely complicated "analogies, harmonies and agreements" that
might suggest such mechanisms to the "pagan mind." When we reach
the inevitable and perfectly legitimate questions about *real* causes, natural science exhibits its inherent explanatory limitations and points
toward metaphysics and theology, to which it is subordinated in the
hierarchy of disciplines. (This is one major point at which occasionalism
breaks with Humean empiricism.) In Malebranche's words:

> I grant that recourse to God or the universal cause should not be had
> when the explanation of particular effects is sought. . . . In a word, we
> must give, if we can, the natural and particular cause of the effects in
> question. But since the action of these causes consists only in the motor
> force activating them, and since this motor force is but the will of God,
> they must not be said to have in themselves any force or power to
> produce any effects. And when in our reasoning we have come at last
> to a general effect whose cause is sought, we also philosophize badly
> if we imagine any other cause of it than the general cause. We must
> not feign a certain *nature*, a *primum mobile*, a *universal soul*, or any such
> chimera of which we have no clear and distinct idea; this would be to
> reason like a pagan philosopher. For example, when we ask how it is
> that there are bodies in motion, or that agitated air communicates its
> motion to water, or rather how it is that bodies push one another, then,
> since motion and its communication is a general effect on which all

[70]Berkeley, *Principles*, p. 68.

others depend, it is necessary, I do not say in order to be a Christian but to be a philosopher, to have recourse to God, who is the universal cause, because His will is the motor force of bodies and also produces the communication of their motion.[71]

The no-nature theory, then, deflates the pretensions of the natural sciences to be autonomous and self-sufficient disciplines that can provide a complete understanding of natural phenomena. If the no-nature theory is true, then the study of nature must inevitably point beyond itself to a more inclusive "wisdom" that investigates the Real Cause of natural phenomena—a wisdom that willingly assigns a prominent place to the study of nature and yet at the same time directs it from without. It is against this background that we must understand the conclusions Berkeley draws from his discussion of the natural sciences in the *Principles*:

> After what has been premised, I think we may lay down the following conclusions. First, it is plain philosophers amuse themselves in vain, when they inquire for any natural efficient cause, distinct from a *mind* or *spirit*. Secondly, considering the whole creation is the workmanship of a *wise and good agent*, it should seem to become philosophers, to employ their thoughts (contrary to what some hold) about the final causes of things. . . . Thirdly, from what has been premised no reason can be drawn, why the history of nature should not still be studied, and observations and experiments made, which, that they are of use to mankind, and enable us to draw any general conclusions, is not the result of any immutable habitudes, or relations between things themselves, but only of God's goodness and kindness to men in the administration of the world. . . . Fourthly, by a diligent observation of the *phenomena* within our view, we may discover the general laws of nature, and from them deduce the other *phenomena*, I do not say *demonstrate*; for all deductions of that kind depend on a supposition that the Author of Nature always operates uniformly, and in a constant observance of those rules we take for principles: which we cannot evidently know.[72]

This mix of theism with explanatory scientific antirealism is very powerful and in many ways very attractive, combining as it does a fitting modesty (even humility) regarding the aims and claims of reason with an optimism about the ability of reason guided by faith to attain wisdom. Thus are avoided the prideful presumption of autonomy for reason on the one hand and an equally destructive pessimism about

[71]Malebranche, *Elucidations*, p. 662.
[72]Berkeley, *Principles*, p. 69.

reason's ability to attain ultimate truth on the other—all of which is extremely desirable from a theistic perspective. What's more, as anyone familiar with the current philosophical scene will realize, no-nature theorists can ride piggyback, as it were, on recent penetrating defenses of scientific antirealism.[73] This adds considerable philosophical weight to the already impressive theological case for the no-nature theory.

Although I myself do not subscribe to the no-nature theory, I am forced to admit that the sort of 'theistic naturalism' I favor has much to learn from and emulate (if it can) in the way occasionalism deals with and situates the natural sciences. The ever-present danger for attempts, like that of the medieval scholastics, to incorporate naturalism into a theistic vision of the world is just that, as Malebranche and Berkeley never tire of reminding us, secondary causes tend to usurp rather than to complement the role of the First Cause. In short, it is ever to be feared that the tail will end up wagging the dog.

Yet while, from a theistic perspective, the no-nature theory provides a much more impressive and satisfying philosophy of nature than most contemporary theistic intellectuals have cared to admit, this theory is not without apparent weaknesses, and these will have to be explored in detail before we can make a final assessment. Three particular problem areas present themselves:

The first is ontological. Just what is the ontology of corporeal things on the no-nature theory? Is Berkeleyan idealism mandatory for the no-nature theorist? If so, can it be made plausible? If it is not mandatory, what are the alternatives? Can bodies have the sort of metaphysical independence characteristic of substances without having any active causal power at all? How so? Might they simply be "bundles" of independently existing sensible qualities? And just what sort of ontology would that entail? (We might also wonder in passing whether such a theory could give a plausible account of the difference between living and nonliving things, or of the difference between finite spirits closely associated with bodies, e.g., human beings, and finite spirits not so attached to bodies, e.g., angels.)[74]

The second problem comes from natural theology. The no-nature theory seems to implicate God too deeply in the causation of physical

---

[73]The best-known, and justly so, of these defenses is Bas Van Fraassen's *The Scientific Image* (Oxford: Oxford University Press, 1980).

[74]The first of these questions is pressed by Suarez in *Disputationes metaphysicae*, disp. 18, p. 595. Malebranche tries to respond at *Elucidations*, pp. 661–662.

evil. Of course, every theistic metaphysics must address questions about why God permits evil. But the no-nature theory has a special problem. Aristotelian theists use individual natures as a causal buffer between God and evil. For they claim that God is only a general cause of the effects of secondary causes, and so they can argue with some plausibility that the defectiveness of evil states of affairs (whether they be moral evils or physical evils) is traceable solely to the causal contribution of the secondary or creaturely causes. The no-nature theory, by contrast, does away with natures, and holds that God is the sole active cause of every state of affairs in nature. So if any such states of affairs are evil or defective, this defectiveness can be traced only to God's causal contribution. But this seems to make God the doer—and not just the permitter—of evil.

In response to this problem Berkeley develops two different lines of argument. The first is to treat the laws of nature (i.e., the rules that God follows) as surrogate buffers between God and evil. The argument is that God's following these general rules is an intrinsic good that outweighs whatever particular evils result from the process. But this clearly will not do, since even when He is following rules, God is still the sole cause of the resultant states of affairs. A more promising reply, though one that stands in need of careful articulation and development, is simply to deny that there is any such thing as natural or physical evil for corporeal things:

> Our prospects are too narrow: we take, for instance, the idea of some one particular pain into our thoughts, and account it *evil*; whereas if we enlarge our view, so as to comprehend the various ends, connections, and dependencies of things, on what occasions and in what proportions we are affected with pain and pleasure, the nature of human freedom, and the design with which we are put into the world; we shall be forced to acknowledge that those particular things, which considered in themselves appear to be *evil*, have the nature of *good*, when considered as linked with the whole system of beings.[75]

This argument may be stronger than it first appears. Since an Aristotelian nature defines normal and/or paradigmatic existence for members of a given natural kind, it follows that doing away with corporeal natures is tantamount to doing away with the objective

---

[75]Berkeley, *Principles*, p. 91.

grounding for the notion of evil (i.e., defectiveness with respect to the norm or paradigm) as applied to bodies. So whereas on the Aristotelian view God merely permits, say, the intrinsic evil of a tree's becoming diseased but does not Himself produce the disease as a particular cause, on the no-nature theory the tree's being diseased is no more an intrinsic evil and no less an intrinsic good than its being healthy. So God can in good conscience, as it were, directly cause the tree to be diseased. In short, given the no-nature theory, there is no independent standard that measures physical or natural good and evil. (Whether this line of reasoning can convincingly be extended to human pain is a moot question, of course.) In any case, the ultimate fate of the no-nature theory depends in large measure on whether or not this argument can be adequately elaborated and defended.

Finally, the acceptability of the no-nature theory must be assessed in the light of revealed doctrines, and the results of this assessment will vary according to denominational allegiance. The "higher" the church, or so it seems, the less acceptable the no-nature theory. For instance, it is fairly clear (though not beyond debate) that no account of substance consistent with the no-nature theory can provide a satisfactory metaphysics for the Catholic doctrine of the Real Presence of Christ in the Eucharist. The no-nature theory may also be incompatible with an orthodox understanding of the doctrine that the sacraments are causes of grace. There are undoubtedly other such examples lurking in the wings.

I hope to discuss all these issues at length in another place. For now I will be satisfied to have shown that occasionalism in general and the no-nature theory in particular are eminently worthy of serious study by today's theistic philosophers. Many contemporary religious thinkers, unduly beholden to Kant and his successors, evidently refuse to take doctrines concerning divine causation as metaphysical truths and seem almost embarrassed by the thought that God might be intimately involved in the production of natural effects—it is as if Berkeley's worst nightmare had come true. Indeed, some even make the astonishing (and astonishingly naive) claim that the natural sciences have themselves established the impossibility of any causal contribution to natural effects on the part of a transcendent agent. (One cannot help but wonder where this sort of information about the deliverances of modern science comes from.) In stark contrast, traditional philosophical theologians almost unanimously regarded as too *weak* even the strong-sounding (to modern ears) claim that God's causal contribution to non-miraculous natural effects consists precisely in His creating and conserving material substances and their causal powers. In this essay I have tried to show by example how we can learn much from an examination of this tradition and its various elements.[76]

[76]A very distant ancestor of this essay was delivered in 1983 to a gathering of the Society for Medieval and Renaissance Philosophy, while a version much more like the present one was given in April 1987 to the annual Notre Dame–Calvin College Philosophy Colloquium. I am especially grateful to Calvin Normore and Philip Quinn for the penetrating questions they posed on those occasions.

4

Individual Essence and the Creation

Linda Zagzebski

1 An Argument for Individual Essences

In this essay I argue that there are individual essences in an interesting sense and show how they can be used to solve a persistent puzzle in philosophical theology. I present two arguments, each of which uses a form of the Principle of the Identity of Indiscernibles and a Principle of Plenitude. The strategy in each case is to show that from these two principles and the hypothesis that there can be two individuals that differ only in one accidental property and what is entailed by that difference, we can derive a contradiction. Each pair of individuals, then, must differ in at least one essential property. Corresponding to each pair of possible objects there is a property that is possessed essentially by the one and lacked essentially by the other. It follows that each individual object possesses a set of properties that is essential to it and that is possessed by no distinct object in any possible world. That is to say, there are individual essences.

The first argument uses a weaker and less controversial form of the indiscernibility principle and concludes that there are individual essences in a sense that may include nonqualitative properties. The second argument uses a stronger form of the indiscernibility principle and has a more interesting conclusion. In that argument I hope to show that each individual in each possible world has a nontrivial individual essence composed of purely qualitative properties.

The final section is devoted to the application of individual essences to solving an important puzzle about the creation. Is God related to possible objects prior to the creation? If so, do they have an explanatory role in it? Many Christian philosophers have thought that God creates from exemplars or models of possible objects that are ideas in his mind. Though this theory has a very powerful explanatory force, it has been criticized as incoherent. This is because it is difficult to make sense of the idea of a possible but nonactual object. In addition, exemplarism seems to require a satisfactory solution to the problem of identifying objects across possible worlds, as well as the problem of analyzing propositions that deny existence to an object. I attempt to show that if there are individual qualitative essences, they go a long way toward making exemplarism coherent.

The two arguments for individual essences require that we distinguish between essential and accidental properties as follows:

> A property E is an essential property of an object O ≡ at every time in every world in which O exists, O has E. It is not possible for O to exist at any time and fail to have E at that time.

I assume without argument that each object has essential properties.

> A property A is an accidental property of O ≡ there is a time in some world in which O exists and has A, and there is a time in some world in which O exists and lacks A. An accidental property of an object, then, is that which it is possible for it to have, but which it need not have in order to exist.[1]

Since the expression "O lacks P" is sometimes ambiguous between the claim that O exists and fails to have P and the claim that O lacks P because it does not exist, I will use the locution "O has $\bar{P}$" to indicate the state of affairs of O's existing and failing to have the property P. So for every object O and property P, if O exists, either O has P or O has $\bar{P}$.

In the following arguments there are two Principles of Plenitude. Both are expressions of the same simple intuition that any state of

---

[1]Since it is useful to have a way of talking about properties of an object without relativizing them to a world, I have chosen a definition of accidental property that has the consequence that some properties that I never have in the actual world are among my accidental properties. It must be remembered, then, that *O has accidental property A* does not entail *O has accidental property A in the actual world*.

affairs that is not prevented from being a possible state of affairs by some necessary truth *de dicto* or *de re* is a possible state of affairs. The essential properties of an object set the limits of the possible properties of the object. Those properties which are compatible with an object's essential properties are possible properties for it, while those which are not compatible with its essential properties are those which it is impossible for it to have. Of course, the possibilities for an object are also limited by the necessary truths, though I assume that these truths are contained in the essence of each object. For example, each object is essentially such that 2 + 2 = 4, God is omnipotent, and so on for all the other necessary truths. Of course, some of the properties possible for an object O will be such that O's having one of them is not compossible with physical laws or the existence of certain other objects or with those objects' possessing certain of their possible properties. This just means that some of the properties that it is possible for an object to have are more compatible with the world as it is than are others. The possession of some of these properties would require very little change in the rest of the world, whereas others would require very dramatic changes. It is still reasonable, though, to think that any combination of states of affairs that is compatible with the existence of all objects figuring in those states of affairs is possible.

1.1 First Argument

PRINCIPLE OF THE IDENTITY OF INDISCERNIBLES (II_1)

In every possible world let ϕ be a variable ranging over complete sets H of the properties of an object in that world. For any property P, H contains either P or $\bar{P}$. Assume the minimum restrictions on the properties in H to prevent triviality.[2]

$$\Box\,(x)\,(\phi)\,[\,\Diamond\ \phi x \rightarrow\ \sim\ \Diamond\ (Ey)\,(\phi y\ \&\ y \neq x)]$$

---

[2]The restrictions needed to prevent triviality require the exclusion of the properties of being identical with one of the individuals in the domain of the individual variables picked out by a *de re* reference. So a property like *being identical with Socrates* would be excluded. In addition, any world-indexed property that is uniquely satisfied by an individual would be excluded. Examples include *being the first president of the U.S. in alpha* and *being the inventor of bifocals in alpha*, where "alpha" is a proper name for the world which is in fact the actual world.

This principle says that if some object x has a certain complete set of properties in one world, there is no distinct object in any world with just that set of properties. Not only does no actual distinct object have exactly the same set of properties as this object, it is not even *possible* that some distinct object have this same set of properties. The properties uniquely belong to that particular object.

II1 is a highly plausible principle. To see this, consider that for any distinct individuals x and y, it is necessary that there be relations R such that it is possible that x bears R to y, and it is not possible that x bears R to itself. So even in worlds in which y does not exist, x will contain within its complete set of properties H properties of the form *possibly bears R to y*, whereas y will contain no such property in any world. It follows that if any x and y are distinct, the complete set of properties one has in any world will never be identical with the complete set of properties the other has in any world.

This argument assumes that any two distinct individuals coexist in some possible worlds and in those worlds there are relations that they bear to each other but not to themselves. Suppose, though, that there are two distinct individuals that never exist in the same worlds. Do they bear any relation to each other that they do not bear to themselves? Presumably they would because they would bear the relation *is not possibly coactual*. But, of course, every object is coactual with itself. Hence, there are no two distinct individuals that have all their relational properties in common. It follows that II1 is true.

FIRST PRINCIPLE OF PLENITUDE (PP1)

If some property A is compatible with the set of essential properties E of an object O, and if O has $\overline{A}$ in some world W, there is another possible world W' in which O has A and that is as similar to W as is compatible with O's having A in W'.[3]

The intuition behind this Principle of Plenitude is that every property and combination of properties that an object is not prevented from having by its essence is something it does have in some possible world. An accidental property of an object just is a property it might have had

---

[3]There will be many such worlds, perhaps an infinite number of them. It could turn out that O's having A is incompatible with the existence of some other object in W. It might even turn out that O's having A is incompatible with the existence of all other objects in W. In that case the world that is just like W except that O has A will not be very close to W at all.

and might have lacked. It is compatible with the essential properties of an object, but is not entailed by them. Given any world in which it lacks the property, it might have had it even though everything else about that object and the world remained the same except for any changes required to maintain necessary truths. But to say it might have been is just to say it is the case in some possible world of that description.

A similar intuition leads us to form a parallel principle for pairs of objects as follows:

SECOND PRINCIPLE OF PLENITUDE (PP2)

If properties A_1 and A_2 are respectively compatible with the set of essential properties E_1 and E_2 of objects O_1 and O_2 respectively, and if in some possible world W O_1 has A_1 and O_2 has A_2, and O_1's having A_1 is compossible with O_2's having A_2, then there is another possible world W' in which O_1 has A_1 and O_2 has A_2, and that is as similar to W as is compatible with O_1's having A_1 and O_2's having A_2.

From the Identity of Indiscernibles, the Second Principle of Plenitude, and the hypothesis that there can be two individual objects that differ only in an accidental property and what that entails, we can derive a contradiction. The argument is as follows:

(1) Assume II1, PP2, and that in W_1 there are two objects, O_1 and O_2, that have all their properties in common with the exception of a single accidental property A_1 which O_1 has and O_2 lacks and whatever that entails.

(2) By hypothesis, O_1 and O_2 have the same set of essential properties E. There is, therefore, nothing in E that precludes O_2 from having A_1 and there is nothing in E that precludes O_1 from having $\overline{A_1}$. Furthermore, O_2's having A_1 is compossible with O_1's having $\overline{A_1}$.

(3) By PP2 there is another world W_3 where O_2 has A_1 and O_1 has $\overline{A_1}$ and all other features of W_3 are identical with those of W_1 except for those entailed by the transposition of properties A_1 and $\overline{A_1}$ between O_1 and O_2.

(4) This violates II1 twice over. The complete set of properties H_1 that O_1 has in W_1 is possessed by O_2 in W_3, and the complete set of properties H_2 that O_2 has in W_1 is possessed by O_1 in W_3. There is nothing that makes O_1, O_1 and O_2, O_2 if what is unique about each is something the other could have had instead. This contradicts (1).

(5) The hypothesis that two objects can differ only in an accidental property and what is entailed by it is therefore false. Each possible individual object has a set of essential properties such that it is not possible that there be a distinct object that has exactly that set of properties. There are, then, individual essences (IEs).

1.2 Objection to First Argument

This argument might be blocked by the following move. Worlds W_1 and W_3 are not both possible worlds because together they violate II1. PP2 must require that the worlds that result from its application be possible. But W_1 and W_3 are not both possible because their description as distinct worlds violates II1, a necessary truth. Hence (3) is false and it is not possible to derive a contradiction from II1, PP2, and the hypothesis that there are two individuals that differ only in an accidental property.[4]

1.3 Answer to Objection

This move on the part of an opponent of the argument commits him to an inconsistency. The reason is as follows:

BEST CASE ARGUMENT

Consider first the best case from the point of view of the objector to my argument. Suppose that there is only a single case in which two distinct objects differ in an accidental property and what is entailed by that difference. Let O_1 and O_2 be this pair of objects and W_1 be the world in which this difference obtains. By hypothesis O_1 and O_2 have exactly the same set of essential properties E. In addition, O_1 and O_2 have the same set of accidental properties in W_1 with the exception of an accidental property A_1 and what is entailed by that difference. Let us say that in W_1 O_1 has A_1 and O_2 has $\overline{A_1}$. The critic of my argument maintains that PP2 must be applied in such a way that it never results in a violation of II1. This means that O_2 is precluded from having A_1 in any possible world while maintaining the rest of the properties it has in W_1, since if it did it would end up indiscernible from O_1 in W_1. So O_2 is prevented by II1 from having A_1 in any world unless in that

---

[4]An analogous objection to a weaker form of the argument was suggested to me independently by both Philip Quinn and Alvin Plantinga.

world one of its other accidental properties differs from the accidental properties of O_1 in W_1. This means that the conjunction of the accidental properties $A_1, A_2, \ldots A_m$ which O_1 has in W_1 is impossible for O_2 in any world. So it is essential to O_2 to have the complement of that conjunction of properties. But it is not essential to O_1 to have the complement of that conjunction of properties $A_1, A_2, \ldots A_m$ since O_1 has that conjunction of properties in W_1. Hence the set of essential properties of $O_1 \neq O_2$ contrary to hypothesis.

WORST CASE ARGUMENT

Furthermore, if two distinct objects can differ only in an accidental property and what is entailed by such a property in one case, there is no reason why there could not be an infinite number of distinct objects corresponding to the set of essential properties of each object, each differing from one of the others by a single accidental property and what is entailed by it. But by the above reasoning, this leads to the conclusion that all of an object's properties are essential to it. It would not be able to change any property at any time, nor could it have different properties at any time in any other possible world, for if it did it would become indiscernible from some other possible object. What's more, if each object has properties that relate it to every other possible object, it would follow from this reasoning that there is only one possible world. But this result is absurd.

What the objection that we are considering fails to appreciate, therefore, is that W_1 and W_3 *are* both possible worlds after all. II1 does not prevent there being a world described as W_1 and a world described as W_3. What follows from II1, though, is that W_1 and W_3 are the same world. My argument shows that $O_1 = O_2$, and hence, $W_1 = W_3$.

1.4 Conclusion

I conclude that no two distinct individual objects can differ only in an accidental property and what is entailed by that difference. It follows that each pair of individual objects differs in some essential property. That is, the minimum difference between two objects is that there be some property E that is possessed essentially by the one and lacked essentially by the other. This is to say that each individual object possesses a set of properties that is essential to it and that no other individual in any possible world possesses. There are, therefore, individual essences in a strong sense.

2 Argument for Individual Qualitative Essences

A qualitative property, or what I call a Q-property, is one that is expressible without direct reference to an individual or a possible world. Examples include *blue, square, humorous, human,* and *funnier-than-the-president*. To put it more vaguely, such properties are purely conceptual entities. They contain no constituents that are not fully accessible within the realm of ideas. A property of this sort has the feature that there is nothing about the formal aspects of the property itself that makes it necessary that it be exemplified by a single object. This is not to say that it is possible for such properties to be exemplified by more than one object. To say so would be to beg the question against the form of the Identity of Indiscernibles I am about to give. All that may be assumed is that there is nothing about being qualitative per se that prevents it from pertaining to more than one individual.

Since the distinction between Q-properties and non-Q-properties has been made in terms of features of the linguistic terms used to express them, a natural question to ask is whether one and the same property can be expressed both by a qualitative and by a nonqualitative linguistic term. I would expect that the answer is no, but if it turns out that some property can be expressed both ways, I will consider it to be qualitative. A Q-property, then, is one that *can be* expressed without direct reference. I assume that each individual has essential Q-properties.

2.1 *The Principle of the Identity of Indiscernibles (II)*

The argument for the existence of individual qualitative essences is parallel to the first argument. II_1 must be strengthened in such a way that it is limited to Q-properties. In place of II_1 we substitute the following principle:

STRONG PRINCIPLE OF THE IDENTITY OF INDISCERNIBLES (II_2)

In every possible world let ψ be a variable ranging over complete sets J of the Q-properties of an object in that world. For any Q-property P, J contains either P or $\bar{P}$:

$$\Box\,(x)\,(\psi)\,[\,\Diamond\,\psi x \to\, \sim \Diamond\,(Ey)\,(\psi y\ \&\ y \neq x)]$$

This is the controversial form of Leibniz's Law. Arguments against it from the possibility of symmetrical universes are well known. I shall not try to defend it against any alleged counterexample, though I shall have something to say later about the impropriety with which such examples are set up. But first I wish to look at another objection to II2 that if valid would be devastating.

The problem is this. A qualitative property, or Q-property, seems to be defined in such a way that it could in principle be exemplified by more than one object. But if this is the case, why couldn't the complete set of an object's Q-properties in principle be exemplified by more than one object? But if so, then it must be possible that some distinct object possess the same complete set of an object's Q-properties, contrary to II2.

This objection turns on an ambiguity in the expression "in principle." If "in principle" means that it is possible in the sense that it is consistent with all logically and metaphysically necessary truths, then it is false that a Q-property is one that in principle can be exemplified by more than one object. The reason is simply that this is inconsistent with II2, a necessary truth. On the other hand, if "in principle" means "is not precluded by the formal features of the linguistic item used to express the property," then it is true that every Q-property (as well as some non-Q-properties) could in principle be exemplified by more than one object. But this can be so even though it remains open whether an analysis of the property would reveal that for reasons having to do with deep logical or metaphysical truths, such a property could not possibly be exemplified by more than one object. So it turns out, for example, that "even prime number" expresses a Q-property, though it is necessarily exemplified by only one object. Many of God's attributes are probably also properties of this sort. Arguably, essential goodness, omnipotence, and absolute independence are properties that could not be exemplified by more than one object. But if this is the case, it requires quite a bit of argument in each case to demonstrate that it is. Such a property is quite different than that expressed by "the most beloved friend of Gorgias," which is tied directly to an individual by the formal features of the term used to express the property.

This brings us to the objection against II2 from symmetrical universes. One alleged counterexample of this type postulates the possibility of a cyclical universe in which all events periodically repeat themselves. Another type of case is the spatially symmetrical universe in which distinct objects with exactly the same relational and nonrelational properties are paired at the ends of axes of symmetry.[5] In an interesting discussion of II, Ian Hacking argues that our laws of nature are so entwined with theories of space and time that such putative examples against II can always be redescribed in ways that save the principle.[6] For example, Kant's two-drop universe could be redescribed as a one-drop universe in a Reimannian space so highly curved that a journey in some direction takes one back to the single drop. Hacking does not claim to have proved that II is necessarily true. All he claims is that the alleged counterexamples are inconclusive, since there is no possible world that must be described in a manner incompatible with II. Once we recognize that such descriptions underdetermine the number of objects in the universe, he says, we are free to choose to adhere to II, and it is largely a matter of aesthetic preference if we do so.

It is up to the objector to II to describe a possible world in which II does not hold. But if Hacking is right, it is not clear that the objector has succeeded, since the attempt to describe such a world can just as well be a description of a world in which II holds. It seems, then, that we must be cautious about the significance of the human power to produce such descriptions. A description that *seems* to contain no inconsistency may not be a description of a possible world, and even if it is, it may still not be clear exactly what world is so described.

A different objection to II is given by Robert M. Adams.[7] Ronald Hoy paraphrases the argument as follows:

(1) Surely it is logically possible to have a universe containing only two objects x and y such that they differ only in that x has some property that y lacks (they are almost indiscernible).

(2) If such a universe as described in (1) is possible, then surely it is logically possible to have a universe like that described in (1) except that x does not have the property that y lacks. (The removal of a property from x does not make it numerically identical to y or decrease the number of distinct objects in the universe).

---

[5]Arguments of this type can be found in Immanuel Kant, *Critique of Pure Reason*, A263 f.–B319 f. Kant speaks of two indiscernible drops of water. In Max Black's well-known version of this argument we are to imagine two solid globes of iron. His discussion is found in "The Identity of Indiscernible," *Mind* 61, 242 (April 1952), 153–164.

[6]Ian Hacking, "The Identity of Indiscernible," *Journal of Philosophy*, 72 (May 8, 1975), 249–256.

[7]Robert Merrihew Adams, "Primitive Thisness and Primitive Identity," *Journal of Philosophy* 86 (January 1979), 16.

(3) Therefore, numerically distinct but indiscernible objects are logically possible.[8]

If the argument I gave in section 1 is right, however, the minimum difference between x and y is an essential property. But then it is not possible that such a property be removed, as Adams asks us to imagine in (2). Of course, the argument I gave for the claim that the minimum difference between x and y is an essential property uses II, and so Adams would, of course, reject that argument. But this shows that the Adams argument does not demonstrate (3). This is because (1) cannot be known unless it is known that II is false.

It seems unlikely, then, that there are any objections to the Identity of Indiscernibles that do not beg the question, or at least rely on the intuition that II is less likely to be true than some putative possibility such as Adams's (1). Of course, my rejoinders to these objections have not demonstrated the necessary truth of II either. What ought we to say, then, about II? It has already been remarked that Ian Hacking suggests that one may simply adopt II as a matter of aesthetic preference. In the paper cited above, Ronald Hoy takes the stronger position that we ought to adopt the methodological principle that one should prefer theories that do not posit distinct entities that are in principle indiscernible. I will not attempt a defense of II in this essay, though I believe it is true. I suspect that ultimately it is not possible to convince a person of the truth of II who is not already inclined to believe it. In this respect basic metaphysical principles may be like basic moral principles. In any case, it is not demonstrably false.

2.2 The Argument for Individual Qualitative Essences

From II2, PP2, and the hypothesis that there are two individual objects that share all their Q-properties with the exception of one accidental Q-property and what that entails, we can derive a contradiction. The argument is parallel to the first argument above:

(1) Assume II2, PP2, and that in W_1 there are two objects, O_1 and O_2, that have all their Q-properties in common with the exception of a single accidental Q-property A_1 that O_1 has and O_2 lacks and whatever that entails.

[8]Ronald C. Hoy, "Identity of Indiscernible," *Synthese* 61 (December 1984), 280.

(2) By hypothesis, O_1 and O_2 have the same set of essential Q-properties E. There is, therefore, nothing in E that precludes O_2 having A_1 and there is nothing in E that precludes O_1 having $\overline{A}_1$. Furthermore, O_2's having A_1 is compossible with O_1's having $\overline{A}_1$.

(3) By PP2 there is another world W_3 where O_2 has A_1 and O_1 has $\overline{A}_1$ and all other features of W_3 are identical with those of W_1 except for those entailed by the transposition of properties A_1 and $\overline{A}_1$ between O_1 and O_2.

(4) This violates II2 twice over. The complete set of Q-properties H_1 that O_1 has in W_1 is possessed by O_2 in W_3, and the complete set of Q-properties H_2 that O_2 has in W_1 is possessed by O_1 in W_3. There is nothing that makes O_1, O_1 and O_2, O_2 if what is unique about each is something the other could have had instead. This contradicts (1).

(5) The hypothesis that two objects can differ only in an accidental Q-property and what is entailed by it is therefore false. Each possible individual object is such that it has a set of essential Q-properties such that it is not possible that there be a distinct object that has exactly that set of properties. There are, then, individual qualitative essences (IQEs).

3 Trivial and Nontrivial Individual Essences

It can be shown that a trivial individual essence for each object follows immediately from any form of II. To see this, enumerate all the worlds in which some object S exists. For each such world, form the infinitely long conjunction of all S's properties (alternatively, Q-properties) in that world. Let C_1 be the conjunction of S's properties in W_1; let C_2 be the conjunction of its properties in W_2, etc. Then form the infinitely long disjunction of these complete sets of properties C_1 v C_2 v ... C_n. Since II states that no object distinct from S shares the complete set of properties S has in any world, it follows that no distinct object possesses C_1 v C_2 v ... C_n. Yet, of course, S has C_1 v C_2 v ... C_n in every world in which it exists, so this disjunctive property is an individual essence of S, but it is trivial because every qualitative property S has in any world appears in one of the disjuncts.[9] This is a quick way to derive IEs from II, but they are obviously uninteresting.

---

[9]This possibility is mentioned by Robert Adams, "Primitive Thisness and Primitive Identity," 10, and by Kit Fine, "Plantinga on the Reduction of Possibilist Discourse," in

How do we know that the individual essences whose existence I have demonstrated are anything more than the trivial individual essence just described? Let us say that an Interesting Individual Essence (IIE) would be a set of Q-properties that appears in every one of the disjuncts $C_1, C_2, C_3 \ldots C_n$ and that no other distinct object has in any world. Can it be shown that there are IIEs? I believe the answer is yes. Suppose that there is no IIE. That is to say, there is no set of Q-properties that appears in every one of the disjuncts $C_1, C_2, \ldots C_n$ of the trivial individual essence of some object O_1 and that no distinct object has in any possible world. Since I am assuming O_1 has essential Q-properties, there is a nonempty set of Q-properties that appears in every disjunct. So if there is no IIE this means that a distinct object shares such a set. Call this object O_2. O_1 and O_2, then, have the same set of nondisjunctive essential Q-properties E. Consider a world W_1 in which O_1 has a set of accidental Q-properties A_1. There is nothing in the essence of O_2 that prevents it from having any of the properties in A_1. But by iterated applications of PP1 it follows that there is a possible world in which O_2 has A_1. Call this world W_2. Since O_2 also has E in W_2 since it has E in every world in which it exists, the complete set of O_2's nondisjunctive Q-properties, essential and accidental, in W_2 is identical with the complete set of the nondisjunctive Q-properties of O_1 in W_1. But since disjunctive properties supervene on nondisjunctive properties, identity of the latter entail identity of the former. It follows that the complete set of O_2's Q-properties, disjunctive and nondisjunctive, in W_2 is identical with the complete set of Q-properties of O_1 in W_1. But this violates II2. Hence, it is impossible that there be an object that lacks an IIE.

So there is an Interesting Individual Essence for each object as well as many trivial ones. In fact, each object possesses infinitely many individual essences. We can, for example, form sets consisting of the disjunction of an individual essence and any impossible property. Furthermore, there will be individual essences composed of sets formed in the following way: Enumerate the worlds in which the object exists. Let the first disjunct be any subset of properties it possesses accidentally in world w_1, the second disjunct any subset of properties it possesses accidentally in world $W_2, \ldots$ the nth disjunct any subset of properties it possesses accidentally in world W_n. As long as each individual pos-

Alvin Plantinga, ed. James E. Tomberlin and Peter van Inwagen (Dordrecht: D. Reidel, 1985), pp. 145–186.

sesses an infinite number of accidental properties in each world in which it exists, there will be an infinite number of disjunctions of this kind that are true of it in all worlds in which it exists. The conjunction of an individual essence of the object and such a disjunction will be an individual essence and there will be an infinite number of individual essences formed in this way as well.

An interesting question to consider is whether all the qualitative properties essential to an object are included in its Interesting Individual Essence (IIE). Suppose an object O has just four nondisjunctive qualitative essential properties, A, B, C, and D. The set composed of these four properties is an IIE. In addition, suppose the set composed of properties A, B, and C is an individual essence as well. No distinct object in any world exemplifies A, B, and C. If such a situation obtained, O would have more than one IIE. But notice that in this case D would not be logically independent of A, B, and C. The reason is just that it is not possible for the set A, B, C to be exemplified without D. If it were possible, there would be a possible world in which something exists that has A, B, and C, but D. By hypothesis there is no such world, since there is only one possible object that exemplifies A, B, C and that object also exemplifies D in every world in which it exists.[10] It follows that by my definition, an IIE may not contain all the non-disjunctive essential Q-properties of the object possessing it, but those it does not contain are necessitated by the possession of the others it does contain. The account I have given of Interesting Individual Essences, then, does not guarantee that there is a unique one for each individual. However, a unique one could be specified (a *very* Interesting Individual Essence?) as the set consisting of all of an object's nondisjunctive, essential Q-properties.

4 Haecceities and Direct Reference

It might be thought that the argument I have given in this essay has the consequence that there are no haecceities. Some philosophers have thought that there are properties that could be characterized as being *this object*—for example, *being-Socrates*. It has also been thought that these properties are not reducible to purely qualitative properties; that is, they are not fully expressible in purely qualitative terms. These

---

[10] I thank Bob Adams for this point.

properties have been called *haecceities*. More broadly, some philosophers think that there are nonqualitative properties, or properties that make an essential reference to an individual in their linguistic expression. Examples might include the properties expressed by "being the first son of Socrates," or "being the person most loved by that man," and again it might be thought that there is something irreducible about the mode in which these properties are expressed. The very same properties could not be expressed in purely qualitative terms.

As far as I can see, there could very well be properties of this kind; at least, nothing I have said precludes their existence. If haecceities are just properties of this sort, then as far as I can see, there may be, and probably are, haecceities. However, my second argument above has the consequence that no pair of individuals can differ in a nonqualitative property without also differing in a qualitative property. That is to say, any set of nonqualitative essential properties supervenes on the qualitative ones. If haecceitism is the doctrine that two individuals may differ only haecceitistically, then I have given an argument for antihaecceitism.

Furthermore, the view I have been defending is not incompatible with the theory of direct reference, a form of which I uphold. On that theory we can and often do refer to a particular individual without referring through any set of qualitative properties that is uniquely satisfied by that individual. But this theory is neutral with respect to the question of whether nonqualitative or haecceitistic properties supervene on the qualitative ones. Robert Adams has pointed out that it follows from the theory of direct reference only that haecceities, or what he calls "thisnesses," are semantically primitive. It does not follow that they are metaphysically primitive.[11] Kripke, for example, claims that it is proper to stipulate possible worlds nonqualitatively, yet he is neutral with respect to haecceitism.[12] Recently, David Lewis has said that though he accepts antihaecceitism, he has no quarrel with direct references:

[11]Adams, "Primitive Thisness and Primitive Identity," p. 10.
[12]Saul Kripke says in the preface to *Naming and Necessity* (Cambridge, Mass.: Harvard University Press, 1980), p. 18: "With respect to possible states of the entire world, I do not mean to assert categorically that, just as in the case of the dice, there are qualitatively identical but distinct (counterfactual) states. What I do assert is that if there is a philosophical argument excluding qualitatively identical but distinct worlds, it cannot be based simply on the supposition that worlds must be stipulated purely qualitatively. What I defend is the propriety of giving possible worlds in terms of certain particulars as well as qualitatively, whether or not there are in fact qualitatively identical worlds."

Anti-haecceitism does indeed imply that any Kripkean specification of worlds could in principle be replaced by a qualitative specification— but not that this replacement is something that the Kripkean specifier had in mind, or something it is feasible to discover, or even something that could be expressed in finitely many words. Even if anti-haecceitism is true, there are two different reasons why we should expect Kripkean specifications to remain indispensable in practice. One reason is just that supervenience falls short of finite definability, to say nothing of manageably concise definability. The other reason is that Kripkean spec- ification, understood as an anti-haecceitist would understand it, makes implicit reference to the not-fully-known qualitative character of this- worldly things. An analogy: consider the class of men wealthier than the Shah of Iran ever was. I have succeeded in specifying a class of men; that same class could have been specified in terms of net worth in dollars; but since the exact wealth of the Shah was a well-kept secret, I cannot substitute the second specification for the first.[13]

It could turn out on my view that each individual has an haecceity or a property that makes the individual that individual, and it could turn out that the haecceity is not reducible to a set of qualitative prop- erties. This may be so even though no distinct individuals differ only haecceitistically. To see why this is so it is helpful to distinguish be- tween the problem of individuation and the problem of differentiation. The former may be thought of as the problem of what makes an entity an individual rather than a nonindividual, as well as what makes an individual the very individual that it is.[14] The latter is the problem of what distinguishes one entity from another. This is a problem even for entities that are not individuals (e.g. abstract objects, natural kinds). On the other hand, even when there is no problem of distinguishing one individual from every other, there may still be the problem of individuation, or what it is about some particular individual that makes it the thing that it is. It was pointed out earlier that it could turn out that the complete set of an object's essential properties is not necessary to distinguish it from all other possible objects (though, of course, I have argued that it must always be sufficient). If all of an object's essential qualitative properties are part of what it is to be that thing, then all of them are necessary to answer what I have called the problem of individuation, though they would not all be necessary to answer what I have called the problem of differentiation. Furthermore, the

[13]David Lewis, *On the Plurality of Worlds* (London: Basil Blackwell, 1986), p. 222.
[14]A related distinction is discussed by Hector-Neri Castañeda in "Individuation and Non-Identity," *American Philosophical Quarterly* 12 (1975), 131–140.

complete set of an object's qualitative essential properties may not be sufficient to explain what it is to be that thing if there are other non-qualitative essential properties that are not reducible to the qualitative ones. If my argument is right, there can be no differences between individuals in their nonqualitative essential properties without differences in their qualitative essential properties, but this does not at all imply that even a complete listing of the qualitative essential properties of a thing gives a complete explanation of what it is to be that very thing. Haecceities may exist and may be theoretically required in answering questions about individuation. Haecceitism and antihaecceitism, though, are theories that arise with respect to the problem of differentiation. On this question I have argued for antihaecceitism.

5 The Creation

5.1 Exemplarism

The traditional theory of exemplarism is a brilliant attempt to explain both how the creation comes to be and how God knows created things. Christian philosophers as far back as the Christian neo-Platonists have held versions of this theory, including Augustine, Bonaventure, Aquinas, Ockham, and Leibniz. Recently, however, the theory has come under attack and it creates a curious puzzle.[15]

Exemplarism is the theory that the ideas of all possible created beings exist eternally in God's mind and act as models or exemplars for those among them that God chooses to create. The explanation of how it comes to be that these ideas are in God's mind is very interesting. The Father knows himself and this act of knowledge is the perfect image of himself. It is the Word, the second Person of the Trinity. As proceeding from the Father, the Son is divine, and as representing the Father, all that the Father can effect is expressed in the Son. If anyone could know the Word he would know all knowable objects, says Bonaventure. All that the Father could create, then, is represented in the Son; that is, all possible beings represent ideas contained in the Son. These ideas are not only of all possible individuals, but also of uni-

---

[15]James Ross, "God, Creator of Kinds and Possibilities," in *Rationality, Religious Belief, and Moral Commitment*, ed. Robert Audi and William J. Wainwright (Ithaca: Cornell University Press, 1986), pp. 315–334.

versals. They are infinite in number since they are the infinitely many ways the Father can be imperfectly imitated. But on some versions of the theory, since God is simple, there can be no real distinction in God save the distinction among the three Persons. So the exemplars are not really distinct from each other, nor are they distinct from the divine essence.

The explanatory force of this theory comes from the fact that, intuitively, creation, if it is significantly free, requires choice, and choice requires not only will but intellect. As Aquinas puts it, since the world was not made by chance, it must have been made by God acting on his intellect. But what is there for God to know but himself? The view that exemplars are ideas of the ways in which God's essence can be mirrored externally links God's knowledge of himself to finite beings in a way that shows how the creation is both nonarbitrary and nonnecessitated. Exemplarism, then, has great explanatory force in understanding the creation.

Exemplarism also gives a plausible understanding of God's present knowledge of his possibilities and hence is supported by the traditional strong views of God's omniscience. God could have created both other individuals and other natures. Had he done so, he obviously would have known that he had. He would have known those individuals and kinds just as well as he knows us and our kind. But surely God knows what he could have done and knows it clearly and distinctly enough to know what he would have known if he had chosen to create such individuals. But those philosophers who support the view called actualism say there aren't any possible but nonactual objects. If there aren't any, there can't be any in God's mind. Furthermore, James Ross objects that there cannot be fully individuating ideas of possible beings prior to their actualization.[16] So whatever God does when he creates, he is not choosing to make a particular possible individual actual. I will argue that if there are individual qualitative essences, there is nothing in the traditional theory of exemplarism that should worry actualists.

5.2 Transworld Identity

Exemplarism has no hope for acceptance unless certain other problems that have been widely discussed in the literature are resolved.

[16]Ibid.

Consider first the problem of identifying individuals across possible worlds. This question has distressed a number of philosophers skeptical about modern modal semantics. The difficulty itself is often posed in a confused way, though there is a genuine problem not far away. Individual essences are not helpful in solving all the problems associated with transworld identity, and I believe some of them are not genuine problems anyway. But individual essences are helpful in solving one of these problems, an important one, and should therefore assuage some of the force of modal skepticism as well as remove one of the obstacles to exemplarism.

What is the problem of transworld identity? Plantinga, Kripke, and others have argued to my satisfaction that one thing the problem is not is that of understanding what assertions of identity across possible worlds *mean*.[17] That is no more a problem than understanding what assertions of identity over time mean. We all know what it means to say that an object at one moment of time is identical with an object at another moment of time. We mean the same thing when we say that an object in one world is identical with an object in another world. That is, the expression "is identical with" means the same thing in both cases. In both statements we intend to pick out the very same individual in different circumstances. Of course, in the case of transtemporal identity we may have a different way of determining the truth of such claims, since we may use spatiotemporal continuity, among other things, and we cannot do that in the case of transworld identity. But this in no way prevents us from understanding what identity claims of either sort *mean*.

The modal skeptic, then, must be looking for something more than the meaning of these statements. One thing he might be looking for is an analysis of the identity relation in terms of other, more primitive relations. He may think he can give such an analysis in the case of transtemporal identity, but not in the case of transworld identity. Now I am not sure there is good reason to look for a way to reduce the identity relation to some more basic relation. But it does seem reasonable to ask what it takes for an object in one set of circumstances to be identical with an object in another set of circumstances. That is, it is reasonable to ask for the truth conditions for identity statements. This may, after all, be more of a problem in the case of transworld

---

[17]This point is convincingly argued by Peter van Inwagen in "Plantinga on Transworld Identity," in *Alvin Plantinga*, pp. 101–120.

identity statements than in the case of transtemporal identity statements, since for the former we cannot bring in spatiotemporal continuity or other causal connections to help us out.

If there are individual essences, the solution to this problem is straightforward. In fact, the solution allows us to express simply the truth conditions for *any* claim of identity, not just transworld identities. Any objects x and y are identical just in case they have the same individual essence. It does not matter whether x and y are specified in their occurrences in distinct possible worlds, or whether they are specified in their occurrences at distinct moments of time in the same world, nor does it matter whether x and y exist in the actual world. This is not to say that the relation *having the same individual essence as* is more primitive than the relation *being identical with*. It is helpful to know that these relations are necessarily coextensive, however, since it gives us the theoretical constraints on the attributions of identity. I suspect that questions about identity conditions are at bottom questions about what it is to be a particular object, and individual essences go a long way toward answering that.

There are other ways in which the problem of transworld identity has been understood. Sometimes the question seems to be an epistemological one, namely, What are the criteria we can use to identify an individual in one world with an individual in another world? Here what is wanted seems to be something that can actually be used in an act of identification. Given what I have said in this essay, there is no reason to think that individual essences will be useful in answering this question, since I have given no reason for thinking that they are grasped in typical situations of a person attempting to make an identification. This in no way affects the metaphysical point, though. If each individual object has an individual essence, the possession of it is both necessary and sufficient for the identity relation to hold and it gives at least a partial explanation of what it is for an object to be the object that it is.

One of the primary theoretical functions of an haecceity is to be the property the possession of which allows an individual in one world to be identified with an individual in another.[18] This, however, is no advance in giving the truth conditions of identity claims since the haecceity just *is* the property of being identical with such

---

[18]This is claimed by David Kaplan in "How to Russell a Frege-Church," *Journal of Philosophy* 72 (1975), 716–729.

and such. To say that an individual in one possible world is identical with an individual in another world just in case they have the same haecceity is to say they are identical just in case they are identical, and that is not very helpful. As I have said, I do not intend to deny the existence of haecceities or the primitiveness of the identity relation. But I do think something needs to be said about the conditions under which identity statements are true, and this haecceities cannot provide.

If there are no nontrivial individual essences, the problem of transworld identity becomes exceedingly difficult because spatiotemporal continuity or other causal relations cannot be appealed to, and since haecceities are unhelpful, there does not seem to be anything left but qualitative similarity. However, qualitative similarity in the absence of the identity of individual essence creates a paradox. This is because two distinct individuals, say a molecule of H_2O and a molecule of NaCl, could be connected by a chain of possible worlds as long as you please, each qualitatively very similar to its neighbor. If the H_2O molecule in the first world is identified with the slightly differing molecule in a neighboring world, and if the chain of neighboring worlds is long enough, small differences add up to very great differences and we might conclude that the H_2O molecule is identical with an NaCl molecule, or some other obviously distinct object. But this is absurd.

An attempt might be made to block the conclusion to this objection by recognizing some set of essential properties for each object, but not an individual essence. This could reasonably be used to block the conclusion above that an H_2O molecule can be identified with an NaCl molecule. But this move cannot prevent the appearance of another paradox, for it would not preclude two distinct H_2O molecules from each being connected by a chain of possible worlds to the same H_2O molecule in another world. In short, the existence of individual essences gives the problem of transworld identity an easy solution, but the lack of IEs creates new paradoxes of identity.

The problem discussed in this section is not a problem limited to possible-worlds semantics. It arises any time a statement is made concerning *de re* possibility for actual or nonactual individuals. Any proposition of *de re* possibility implies that the object that could have had some property P is identical with one that does not, or alternatively, that some object that does not exist but could have, and that might have had some property R, is identical with one that does have property R. The problem cannot be escaped, then, simply by refusing to use possible-worlds discourse.

5.3 Propositions about Nonexistent Entities

Another puzzle connected with exemplarism is a metaphysical one with a long history, going back at least as far as Plato. In contemporary philosophy it is usually discussed within the context of philosophical semantics. This is the problem of giving an analysis of propositions that deny existence to an object; for example, *Pegasus does not exist* or *Socrates does not exist*. When such a proposition is true in some world, it appears to have a designating expression that fails to designate. But how can a sentence successfully express a proposition, much less one that is true, if it contains a nondesignating expression? If in some possible world W the proposition expressed by "Socrates does not exist" is true, who or what is it that has the property of not existing?

To see how the problem arises, consider first a singular existential proposition such as *Socrates exists*. The proper analysis of such a proposition is, of course, problematic, and some philosophers think the proper name can be eliminated in favor of a predicate in a Russellian manner. If the name is treated as a name, though, the truth of such a proposition in a world W seems to require that the individual denoted by "Socrates" in W exists in W. But though this account is reasonable, it makes it difficult to give an analogous account of the proposition, *Socrates does not exist*. If it were analogous, the truth of such a proposition in W would seem to require that the individual denoted by "Socrates" in W does not exist in W, and this does not seem to make sense. Some philosophers think that the paradoxical character of this analysis is an illusion and that this is the right way to analyze such a proposition.[19] The word "Socrates," they say, denotes Socrates with respect to every world, whether or not Socrates exists in the world in question.

Plantinga, however, says such a view is a confusion, and suggests another way to understand singular propositions.[20] The proposition

---

[19]This view is strongly defended by David Kaplan in "Bob and Carol and Ted and Alice" in *Approaches to Natural Language*, ed. Jaakko Hintikka, Julius Moravcsik, and Patrick Suppes (Dordrecht: D. Reidel, 1973), pp. 503–505, and by Nathan Salmon in *Reference and Essence* (Princeton: Princeton University Press, 1981), pp. 36–38.

[20]Alvin Plantinga, "Actualism and Possible Worlds," *Theoria* 42 (1976), 139–160.

(1) Socrates is bald

is not analyzed in terms of its parts, but as a whole. (1) asserts that an individual essence of Socrates is coexemplified with baldness. Of course, since any individual essence is coexemplified with every other, if one of them is coexemplified with baldness, they all are. (1) is true in all worlds in which that is the case and is false otherwise. Since he thinks the individual essences of Socrates exist in all worlds, every other case means just those cases in which an individual essence of Socrates exists but is not coexemplified with baldness. The proposition

(2) Socrates exists

is true just in case an individual essence of Socrates is exemplified. That is to say, it is true in exactly those worlds in which Socrates exists and is false otherwise. When

(3) Socrates does not exist

is understood as the negation of (2), it is true in those worlds in which no individual essence of Socrates is exemplified. So (2) is true in those worlds in which (3) is false, and (3) is true in those worlds in which (2) is false.

This view is reasonable provided that it is reasonable to think of individual essences as existing in all possible worlds. But the only examples Plantinga gives of individual essences are either haecceities, e.g. Socrateity, or certain world-indexed properties. In each case these properties are expressed using proper names, either of individuals or of worlds. But this leaves Plantinga's view vulnerable to an important objection. The existence of an haecceity seems to presuppose the existence of the object exemplifying it. Likewise, the existence of a world-indexed property seems to presuppose the existence of the objects included in the world named in the expression of the property. So the actualist intuition supported by Plantinga, namely, that there are no objects that do not exist, would lead us to say that there are no nonqualitative individual essences of objects that do not exist either. If no nonqualitative individual essence of Socrates exists in any world in which Socrates does not exist, and if Socrates has no qualitative individual essence, there still does not seem to be anything for "Socrates" to denote in (3). On the other hand, if, like Plantinga, it is allowed that

Socrateity does exist in worlds in which Socrates does not exist, there does not seem to be any advance on the Meinongian possibilist ontology Plantinga's actualism was supposed to replace.[21]

If each object in each possible world has an individual qualitative essence, Plantinga's account of the analysis of negative existential propositions can be maintained without vulnerability to the objection just given. Those philosophers unwilling to say that nonqualitative properties exist in all possible worlds are quite willing to say that the qualitative ones do (e.g., Quine and R. Adams). (3), then is true in just those worlds in which an individual qualitative essence of Socrates is not exemplified, and is false if it is exemplified.

The conclusion is that all the singular existential propositions there could have been exist, in fact, in all possible worlds, and have a truth value in all possible worlds. Since there are individual qualitative essences that are unexemplified in the actual world, the corresponding negative existential propositions will be true in the actual world. If those whom Plantinga calls "existentialists" are right, then an haecceity that supervenes on an IQE does not exist in those worlds in which the IQE is unexemplified.[22] Though my view is not committed to their position, the existentialists should find nothing disagreeable about my analysis of negative singular existentials.

5.4 Exemplarism and Individual Essences

If we equate exemplars in the traditional theory with IQEs, exemplarism is considerably strengthened. Since these essences include only purely conceptual properties, they are knowable prior to their exemplification in an actual being. And, as we have seen, they are sufficient to differentiate one possible object from another. So there is no problem about God having the idea of an object prior to its becoming actual. Nor is there any problem about God having from all eternity in the actual world knowledge of what he would have known had he chosen to create a different world or no world at all. In addition, this view has the advantage of being compatible with actualism, but without its limitations. The theory of individual essences allows there to be all the

---

[21]This objection is made by Fine, "Plantinga on the Reduction of Possibilist Discourse," See also Plantinga's response to Fine in the same volume, 329–349.

[22]Alvin Plantinga, "On Existentialism," *Philosophical Studies* 44 (1983), 1–20.

possibilities *de re* there could have been without forcing us to say that there *are* possible but nonactual individuals, nor need we postulate unexemplified haecceities. There are no possible but nonactual individuals, but there are unexemplified IQEs.

So far, I have argued that if my defense of the existence of individual qualitative essences works and if the traditional exemplars are identified with them, exemplarism can answer the most common contemporary charges against its coherence. There is no reason why an exemplar cannot be a necessary object, knowable even if unexemplified, nor is there any reason to think that it is insufficient to determine a unique object if exemplified. That is, each individual essence is such that if any objects x and y result from its exemplification, then $x = y$. It is therefore coherent to say that God chooses from among these IQEs those he wishes to exemplify. This picture, then, explains how it is that God creates both intelligently and freely, as well as how it is that creatures are images of God.

One of the most interesting features of exemplars is the way in which they connect God's essence with that of creatures. Each created thing imitates the divine essence, but no created thing does so fully. If it did, there would be only one such imitation. There is, in fact, one image of the Father that does perfectly imitate him, and that is the Son. There are infinitely many ways, though, of imperfectly imitating him, and this is what we and all other possible creatures do. According to Aquinas, God's essence is the intelligible character of each and every possible being. It is the proper intelligible character of every creature in that each thing imitates the divine essence in a different way, and it is the common intelligible character of every creature in that each imitates the same divine essence.[23] The exemplar of a thing is just what makes it intelligible. It is each object's way of imitating the divine essence. The conceptual or intelligible character of the exemplar is crucial for the theory, then, and it should be apparent that an individual qualitative essence does have such a character. On the other hand, a nonqualitative or haecceitistic essence, such as *being identical with Socrates*, is more problematic for the role of exemplar. This is because it does not seem to be what is intelligible or graspable about the essence of the individual.

[23]Thomas Aquinas, *De veritate*, Q. 2, A. 4, ad 6.

6 Conclusion

I have given an argument for individual qualitative essences in the strong sense that each object in each possible world has a set of qualitative properties that is essential to it and that is possessed by no other object in any world. I argued that each object has, in fact, an infinite number of such individual essences, many of which are trivial, but at least one of which is nontrivial. I have also suggested that if IQEs are identified with exemplars in the traditional account of the creation, some of the most important and persistent objections to exemplarism can be answered. The usefulness of individual essences no doubt goes far beyond the scope of the problems I have discussed here, but I hope I have at least provided a motivation for taking an interest in them and for taking seriously one traditional account of the creation.[24]

[24]I am grateful to Loyola Marymount University for a research award to write this essay under the T. Marie Chilton Chair of the Humanities. I am also indebted to Philip L. Quinn and Alvin Plantinga for their very helpful comments on the argument for individual essences and to Robert M. Adams and Stephen T. Davis, who read and made valuable suggestions on the whole essay.

Part Two

PROVIDENCE AND
CREATURELY ACTION

5

Two Accounts of Providence

Thomas P. Flint

A few years ago, an adjunct Spanish teacher at a major midwestern university was facing significant financial difficulties. Hoping for some assistance, she attended a mass on the feast day of Our Lady of Guadalupe and prayed for help. Shortly thereafter, she was informed that she was the recipient of a financial award for which she had never applied; of which, indeed, she was unaware. The prize was an annual award given in honor of Our Lady of Guadalupe.

Stories such as this strike all of us as intriguing. But while many will view it as merely a happy coincidence that things turned out as they did, those of us who are Christians are inclined to see it as something more—or, at least, are tempted so to see it. We are inclined to think that God's hand was in evidence here. We are likely to speak of such events as not merely fortunate, but providential.

Of course, in saying that this event *was* providential, we do not mean to imply that other events are *not*. We tend to *call* providential those occurrences in which we find the presence of God especially evident, but as Christians we hold that all events are in God's hands. Providence extends over each of God's creatures, whether they or we recognize it or not. Generally, indeed, we *don't* recognize it. For most of us, few events serve to remind us of God's plan for his world, and we spend very few of our conscious moments thinking about divine providence. And this may very well be all for the good.

Still, if and when we *do* pause to think about it, providence provides

147

a rich subject for philosophical reflection. In the history of Catholic thought, such reflection has led to two substantially different explications of the concept of providence. In this essay, I examine these two accounts. Section 1 sets forth the orthodox notion of providence, while section 2 clears the way for presentation of the two divergent explications. The two views are then described in sections 3 and 4. In section 5, I suggest that these opposed theological accounts may well be but the theological reflection of a familiar metaphysical dispute; the ramifications this appears to have regarding the resolution of the theological debate are then discussed. Section 6 provides a brief historical conclusion.

The reader should be aware of three points from the start. First, I am presupposing that it is the traditional, strong notion of providence— a notion the major characteristics of which will be described shortly— that the Christian is concerned to explicate. Many recent writers in the philosophy of religion have been led to abandon one or more of the elements of this classical Christian tenet. I do not here discuss arguments for or against the various dilutions of the concept that have been proposed, but merely assume that it is the robust orthodox notion of providence with which we are concerned. Even those who reject this notion would presumably retain some interest as to how it might be explicated.

Second, the two accounts of providence to be examined here will be those which have been best developed within the Catholic tradition— Molinism and Thomism. To a very large extent, the differences between these two schools map onto differences between Protestants—e.g., between Arminians and mainline Calvinists. Indeed, this essay suggests that *any* orthodox Christian will have only two genuine choices when it comes to providence: a view that is more or less Molinist, or a view that is more or less Thomist. Still, there are advantages to limiting our focus to the dispute among Catholics; for example, the discussion regarding the efficacy of grace is particularly fine grained and revealing in the writings of Thomists and Molinists. Hence, while much of what will be said here has obvious implications for the Protestant dispute, the spotlight will be on the two Catholic positions.

Finally, a note of warning to historians. The view of providence held by the Molinists can clearly be traced to Luis de Molina, the sixteenth-century Spanish Jesuit whose *Concordia* sparked the Catholic controversy over grace.[1] But whether what I shall call the Thomist account

---

[1]Luis de Molina, *Liberi arbitrii cum gratiae donis, divina praescientia, providentia, praedes-*

of providence is a view that Thomas himself would have endorsed is not nearly so clear. I suspect that he would have, but feel far from confident, and realize that the resolution of this thorny question lies well beyond my competence. Hence, the view labeled Thomist here can be confidently ascribed only to a large segment of Aquinas's intellectual heirs, not necessarily to their eponymous philosophical progenitor.

1 The Traditional Notion of Providence

There are at least three components to the strong notion of providence traditionally upheld by Christians. First, as the etymology of the term suggests, providence involves foresight. A God who is provident does not in any significant sense grow in knowledge as time passes;[2] everything that occurs was always foreseen—and foreseen with certainty— by him. Nothing does or can take a provident God by surprise.[3]

But foreknowledge alone hardly suffices to qualify one as provident, for such knowledge could conceivably be had by an utterly powerless or uncaring deity. For providence, then, two more elements are required. A provident God is one who not only knows what will happen, but in some sense or other actively controls what will happen; in Calvin's memorable phrase, providence "belongs no less to his hands than to his eyes."[4] Christians see God as sovereign over his world, as "holding the helm of the universe, and regulating all events."[5] To call God provident yet deny him such control would be, from the orthodox perspective, to contradict oneself.

Finally, providence presupposes that God employs his sovereignty

---

tinatione et reprobatione concordia (hereafter *Concordia*). The first edition was published in 1588; a revised second edition appeared in 1595 and is the one that will be cited in this essay. A modern critical edition of the *Concordia* edited by J. Rabeneck was published in Madrid in 1953.

[2]Obviously, room must be made for the fact that Jesus *did* grow in knowledge; see Luke 2:52.

[3]That God has complete and perfect foreknowledge is not a matter over which orthodox Catholic theologians can disagree, since the First Vatican Council declared the thesis to be *de fide*. See Heinrich Denzinger and Adolf Schonmetzer, eds., *Enchiridion symbolorum*, 23d ed. (Freiburg: Herder, 1963), nos. 3001 and 3003, new numbering (1782 and 1784, old numbering). Many of the scriptural passages supporting this doctrine are cited by Molina in Disputation 52, sec. 8 of the *Concordia*.

[4]John Calvin, *Institutes of the Christian Religion*, bk. I, trans. John Allen (Philadelphia: Presbyterian Board of Christian Education, 1936), p. 222.

[5]Ibid.

wisely and morally. That is, it requires that God exercise his control with some end or purpose in mind, a good end attained in a morally exemplary way. In short, God has a plan in creation, and the execution of this plan gives evidence of his unsurpassable beneficence.

Much more is undoubtedly involved in providence, but I feel we can confidently view the three components thus far noted as those which are most central. For the most remarkable or telling attributes of God are, it would seem, his infinite knowledge, power, and goodness, and the three elements we have highlighted here merely indicate the way in which these three attributes are manifested by a God who is also a Creator.[6]

2 Common Ground in Explicating Providence

Virtually from the start of Christianity, the strong notion of providence that it affirms has been alleged to be at odds with certain evident facts about our world. Divine foreknowledge, we have been told, is incompatible with genuine human freedom. If God knew from the first moment of creation that Cuthbert would, say, buy an iguana in 1998, then (given God's doxastic perfection) it follows with certainty that Cuthbert will buy an iguana in 1998; but if it's thus determined by God's past beliefs that Cuthbert will do so, his doing so could hardly be free. Similarly, we have heard, the suggestion that this world has resulted from the providential activity of a loving God is incompatible with, or at least most improbable given, the evil we see in the world. Each of these charges is, I trust, familiar to contemporary philosophers; equally familiar, I hope, are the various recent discussions that show just how weak such charges really are.[7] Arguments of this kind give the reflective Christian no significant reason to doubt the genuineness of providence.

---

[6]The threefold nature of providence suggested here has obvious similarities to that enunciated by Aquinas. See *Quaestiones disputatae de veritate*, Q. 5, A. 1.

[7]For discussions of the foreknowledge/freedom question, see Alfred J. Freddoso's introduction to Luis de Molina, *On Divine Foreknowledge: Part IV of the Concordia* (Ithaca: Cornell University Press, 1988); George I. Mavrodes, "Is the Past Unpreventable?" *Faith and Philosophy* 1 (1984), 131–146; Thomas Talbott, "On Divine Foreknowledge and Bringing about the Past," *Philosophy and Phenomenological Research* 46 (1986), pp. 455–469; and Alvin Plantinga, "On Ockham's Way Out," *Faith and Philosophy* 3 (1986), pp. 235–269, reprinted in *The Concept of God*, ed. Thomas V. Morris (Oxford: Oxford University Press, 1987). Numerous responses to the problem of evil have been offered; the most impressive and influential, I think, has been that of Alvin Plantinga. See his *God, Freedom and Evil*

Still, questions of another sort *can* be asked—requests not for a defense of the concept of providence, but rather for an articulation or clarification of the notion. Such questions arise more naturally, I think, with regard to God's sovereignty and its connection with human freedom than with regard to his foreknowledge or beneficence, but the discussion of God's foreordination of free actions becomes so intimately connected with the discussion of his foreknowledge that it is somewhat artificial to view any particular element of providence as the one that necessitates clarification. In any case, our attempt to explicate the two major ways of answering such questions will be aided by our approaching them via the framework of possible worlds.

A possible world can be thought of as a maximal possible state of affairs—a state of affairs that specifies a complete history (from beginning to end) of how things might have been. Infinitely many such worlds *exist*, but only one *obtains* or is *actual*, for only one of these complete histories is true. Things *could* have been infinitely many different ways, but they *are* only *one* way.[8]

Now, according to the doctrine of providence, things are the way they are—this world, as opposed to each of the other possible worlds, is *actual*—because of God's creative activity. God knowingly and lovingly willed to create this very world. He didn't merely give a sort of initial impetus to things and then let them proceed on their merry (or miserable) way, not knowing, directing, or caring how things would turn out. On the contrary, his providence, his sovereignty, his control extend to each and every event that takes place. His is a particular, not merely a general, providence.

There are two opposite and extreme interpretations of this thesis of particular providence that orthodox Christians have generally shunned. On the one extreme, one could hold that his world is indeed the result of God's loving activity, yet deny that that activity could possibly have been at all other than it actually was; rather, God's will was necessarily constrained (by his perfect knowledge and goodness, perhaps) to perform a certain creative action. Hence, while the actual world is the result of a divine act of will, that will should not be seen as free to will other than it did. At the other extreme, one might insist

---

(New York: Harper & Row, 1974), pt. 1, and *The Nature of Necessity* (Oxford: Clarendon Press, 1974), chap. 9.

[8]For a fuller discussion of the notion of a possible world being employed here, see Plantinga, *The Nature of Necessity*, pp. 44ff.

upon God's freedom in an utterly unlimited sense. That is, one might see every particular state of affairs that obtains, even a state of affairs such as four's being equal to three plus one, as being such that it was genuinely up to God whether or not it obtained.

On the first of these views, a view often ascribed (somewhat unfairly) to Spinoza and Leibniz, there is really only one possible world, and hence *no* divine freedom; on the latter view, which is often (and perhaps just as unfairly) labeled Cartesian, there is no such thing as an *impossible* world, and thus *unlimited* divine freedom. The first insists that whatever *can* be, *is*; the latter maintains that whatever *can* be, can *not* be. Each position has its attractive features, but each is clearly inconsistent with both orthodox Christian belief and widespread philosophical intuitions regarding modality, and hence the two are best seen as marking the boundaries beyond which the clearheaded orthodox Christian dare not stray.

A traditional and helpful way of marking the middle ground between the two extremes is in terms of God's knowledge. If God's will is free but limited, then presumably he is aware of this fact, and his creative act of will takes place in full cognizance of it. (By his creative act of will I mean his eternal decision to create a certain order of creatures in a certain set of circumstances, an unchanging decision that leads to a multitude of successive temporal acts—e.g., the creation of Adam at this time and place, the bestowal of this grace at this time to this person, and so on—which together can be thought of as constituting God's complete creative action.)[9] Hence, his knowledge of which worlds are possible—what the medievals called his knowledge of simple intelligence, or *natural knowledge*—provides the basis from which his act of will proceeds.[10] That free act of will in turn leads to the world that is actual, and to God's eternal and complete knowledge of that world—his knowledge of vision, or *free knowledge*.[11] Thus, God's natural knowledge is (in a sense) prior to his act of will, which is in turn (in a sense) prior to his free knowledge. The parenthetical qualifiers are needed lest we think of this priority as being a temporal one, for clearly there can

[9] I intend for God's complete creative action to be understood as equivalent to what Plantinga thinks of as God's actualizing the largest state of affairs that he *strongly actualizes*. See *The Nature of Necessity*, pp. 173, 180–181.

[10] The term "natural knowledge" is the one used by Molina; see the *Concordia*, disputation 49 and following.

[11] Again, "free knowledge" is the Molinist term of choice.

never be a time when a provident God is ignorant of what he will do, or of what world is actual. Still, there seems to be a clear analogy from the process of practical reasoning on the human level (where *action* temporally follows *choice*, which in turn follows *deliberation*) to that on the divine level, and thus talk of priority seems apropos.

So, prior to any act of will on his part, God knows which worlds are *possible*. Subsequent to his act of will, he knows which world is *actual*. On these points, all who subscribe to the strong notion of providence will agree. But this state of consensus begins to dissolve as soon as we ask our proponents of providence just how this transition or growth in God's knowledge is supposed to occur. More specifically, how does natural knowledge lead to free knowledge if God's creative act of will includes his willing to create *free* beings?

Freedom leads to a problem because it presupposes the ability to do otherwise. Suppose that Cuthbert will buy that iguana in 1998, and buy it freely. If so, then it must also be true that Cuthbert will have the power to refrain from buying it freely, for without such a power, the act would not be free.[12] So the situation or circumstances in which Cuthbert will find himself in 1998 will be compatible both with Cuthbert's freely buying an iguana and with his refraining from freely buying one.[13] But then it follows that there are two distinct sets of possible worlds that share the same Cuthbertian iguana-buying circumstances (circumstances that we shall call C): the set of B-worlds (B_1, B_2, B_3, and so forth) in which Cuthbert buys the iguana freely, and the set of R-worlds (R_1, R_2, R_3, and so forth) in which he freely refrains. Now it would appear that God, by his natural knowledge, would know that each of these worlds is possible; and let us further suppose that, by a creative act of will, he could directly bring it about that C obtains.[14]

---

[12]Why is the "freely" needed in this sentence? Why not say that, if Cuthbert does something freely, then he must have the power to refrain from doing it—period? The problem is that such conditionals appear to be disconfirmed by certain cases of overdetermination made famous by Harry Frankfurt in his "Alternate Possibilities and Moral Responsibility," *The Journal of Philosophy* 66 (1969), 829–839. While Frankfurt's cases suggest that the ability to refrain from doing x is not a necessary condition of one's doing x freely, they leave intact the principle that, if one does x freely, then one had the power to refrain from doing x freely.

[13]The notion of a situation or circumstance is intentionally left vague throughout this section so as to allow both sides to affirm what is being said here—as, indeed, they would surely wish to do. As we shall see below, such vagueness needs to be eliminated before the distinctions between Thomists and Molinists can be clarified.

[14]This is, of course, most unlikely, since C will almost surely include some activity of

How would this knowledge and this act of will allow him to know whether a *B*-world or an *R*-world will become actual, since either type of world is fully compatible with that knowledge and that act of will? How can God have *free* knowledge, how can he exercise genuine providence, if he creates free beings?

The answer to these questions is evident: providence can be exercised, free knowledge can be present, only if God knows how his free creatures would freely act if placed in various different situations. For example, suppose that God knew that, if he *did* place Cuthbert in *C*, then Cuthbert would freely buy the iguana. Given his knowledge of that counterfactual of freedom, God would know that, should he bring about *C*, a *B*-world would result. To know *which B*-world, he would have to know infinitely many other counterfactuals of freedom, about Cuthbert and about other free beings. And since God's providential activity does not begin in 1998, but has been present since the beginning of time, he must have known from eternity how *any* free creature he might create would freely act in *any* situation in which that being might be placed. Let us call any such counterfactual whose antecedent is complete—i.e., one that, like *C*, specifies the complete set of circumstances in which a creature is placed and left free—a *counterfactual of creaturely freedom*.[15] Provided that God has knowledge of all the true counterfactuals of creaturely freedom, there is no problem with either his exercise of providence or his possession of free knowledge.

Where, then, is the dissension among the advocates of providence? If all agree that the passage from natural to free knowledge requires that God know counterfactuals of creaturely freedom, why speak of there being *two* accounts of providence? Such questions are surely appropriate, and serve to remind us that the two accounts of providence we shall be examining are far more similar

---

agents other than God, and hence will not have been brought about directly and exclusively by him.

[15]For a fuller discussion of such counterfactuals, see my "The Problem of Divine Freedom," *American Philosophical Quarterly* 20 (1983), 255–264. It is worth noting that, in addition to counterfactuals of *creaturely* freedom, there are also true counterfactuals of *divine* freedom—i.e., counterfactuals saying what *God* would freely do were he placed in various different situations. (See below, n. 21.) According to the Molinists, though, these latter counterfactuals need to be strictly separated from the former, for the latter *are* under God's control, while the former are *not*. See Molina, *Concordia*, Disputation 52, secs. 11–13.

than their proponents are likely to remember in the heat of the battle. Still, there is ample room left for combat, and the battlelines are now fairly easy to draw.

Take any true counterfactual of creaturely freedom. Into which category of divine knowledge is this counterfactual supposed to fall? Does it constitute (i) part of God's natural knowledge? Or (ii) part of his free knowledge? Or (iii) does it fall into neither of these categories? While it might appear that there are three possible answers here, only two positions have in fact been defended. This is hardly surprising, for as we shall see, only two positions seem genuinely defensible. Those who answer along the lines of (iii) endorse the *Molinist* view of providence, while those who reject (iii) are led to the *Thomist* position. Whether Thomism is to be characterized more positively as an endorsement of (i) or (ii) is, as we shall see, a question to which no straightforward answer can be given.

Before we compare these two accounts, it would be wise for us to emphasize an oft-overlooked fact. It is sometimes suggested that the debate between Thomists and Molinists hinges on whether or not there are true counterfactuals of creaturely freedom: if there *are*, Molinism is true, while if there *aren't*, Thomism triumphs. But this is surely a misconstrual of the question. Properly understood, Thomism involves no rejection of counterfactuals of creaturely freedom; on the contrary, the Thomist will insist that there are such truths, and that God knows them.[16] For the Thomist no less than the Molinist is a proponent of the strong notion of providence, and as my presentation suggests—and, in truth, as the literature on the issue amply confirms[17]—to deny God knowledge of counterfactuals of creaturely freedom is tantamount to denying him that providence which traditional Christianity requires. For the orthodox, then,

---

[16]Many Thomists, of course, do recognize that their position commits them to an acceptance of counterfactuals of creaturely freedom. For an especially clear example, see Franz Diekamp, *Theologiae dogmaticae manuale*, vol. 1 (Paris: Society of St. John the Evangelist, 1932), p. 204.

[17]Many recent writers have denied that there are true counterfactuals of creaturely freedom. See Robert Adams, "Middle Knowledge and the Problem of Evil," *American Philosophical Quarterly* 14 (1977), 109–117; Bruce Reichenbach, "Must God Create the Best World?" *International Philosophical Quarterly* 19 (1979), 203–212; and William Hasker, "A Refutation of Middle Knowledge," *Noûs* 20 (1986), 545–557. Not surprisingly, none of these writers would appear to endorse the strong notion of providence delineated above in sec. 1.

there can be no question that God knows counterfactuals of creaturely freedom; the question concerns the status of that knowledge.[18] Let us now consider the two answers.

3 The Molinist Account

In order to motivate more clearly the Molinist contention that
God's knowledge of counterfactuals of creaturely freedom is neither
natural nor free, it would be best to highlight a couple of respects
in which the contents of those two types of knowledge are crucially
different.

By his natural knowledge, we have said, God knows which worlds
are possible. This might lead one to think of God's natural knowledge
as a knowledge of all *possible* truths—i.e., to think of the content of his
natural knowledge as an infinite number of propositions of the form,
It is possible that p. While not exactly incorrect, this may not be the most
revealing way to think of God's natural knowledge. For natural knowledge is supposed to be that part of God's knowledge which he by his
very nature believes—that part of his knowledge which could not have
been different from what it is. But to say that God *has to* know a certain
proposition implies that that proposition *has to* be true. Thus, it seems
natural to think of God's natural knowledge as a knowledge of all
metaphysically necessary truths.[19] And since, as we have seen, the orthodox Christian denies that God has any control over such truths,
natural knowledge can be defined as a knowledge of *necessary* truths
whose truth is *independent of* (or *prior to*) any free act of will on God's
part.

Free knowledge exhibits neither of these characteristics. Being that
knowledge which God acquires as a result of his creative act of will,
it includes only *metaphysically contingent* truths, truths that, since God

---

[18]That God knows counterfactuals of creaturely freedom is not quite an article of faith
for Catholics, but it comes close. See Ludwig Ott, *Fundamentals of Catholic Dogma*, ed.
James Bastible, trans. Patrick Lynch (St. Louis: B. Herder, 1964), p. 42. It is also worth
noting that, when discussing his Catholic critics such as Banez (in Disputation 50 of the
Concordia) and Zumel (in Disputation 53), Molina never seriously alleges that his opponents deny that there are true counterfactuals of creaturely freedom.

[19]Given an $S-5$ interpretation of metaphysical necessity, something is possible if and
only if it's necessarily possible. Hence, one who knows all necessary truths will know
all possible truths, and vice versa. So the two ways of conceiving of God's natural
knowledge turn out to be equivalent.

could have prevented their truth by merely creating different situations for his creatures, different creatures, or even no creatures at all, are clearly *dependent upon* (or *posterior to*) God's will.

The double distinction between natural and free knowledge can be graphically displayed as follows:

	Natural knowledge	Free knowledge
Truths known are:	(1) Necessary	(1) Contingent
	(2) Independent of God's free will	(2) Dependent on God's free will

Given such a display, it soon becomes evident why the Molinists hold that God's knowledge of counterfactuals of creaturely freedom constitutes part of neither his natural nor his free knowledge. For truths of this sort—such truths as *If C were to obtain, Cuthbert would freely buy an iguana*—are, as the Molinist sees it, patently not dependent upon or posterior to God's will. If Cuthbert is genuinely free, Molinists insist, then it's not up to *God* what Cuthbert would do in *C*, but up to Cuthbert. Knowledge of such conditionals will surely guide God's providential activity, but their truth or falsity will not be under his control; hence, God's knowledge of them cannot be part of his free knowledge. But neither can it be part of his natural knowledge. For as we have seen, natural knowledge is knowledge of necessary truths. But counterfactuals of creaturely freedom, the Molinist maintains, are *not* necessary truths. Even if it's true that Cuthbert would freely buy an iguana if placed in *C*, it's surely possible that *C* obtain yet Cuthbert *not* freely buy the iguana; if this *weren't* possible, the Molinist will ask, what sense would it make to speak of Cuthbert's action being *free*? Since the relevant counterfactuals are only contingently true, it follows that they are not encompassed by God's natural knowledge.

So God's knowledge of counterfactuals of creaturely freedom stands between his natural and his free knowledge. It is more like natural knowledge in that the propositions known are true independent of God's free will; yet it is more like free knowledge in that the propositions known are only contingently true. Given the in-between status of this knowledge, it is hardly surprising that Molina chose to call it middle knowledge (*scientia media*).[20] Adding middle knowledge to our

---

[20]Throughout the first edition of the *Concordia*, Molina referred to God's knowledge of counterfactuals of creaturely freedom as a special part of his natural knowledge. It

chart, we arrive at a graphic illustration of the Molinists' threefold division of divine knowledge:

	Natural knowledge	*Middle knowledge*	*Free knowledge*
Truths known are:	(1) Necessary	(1) Contingent	(1) Contingent
	(2) Independent of God's free will	(2) Independent of God's free will	(2) Dependent on God's free will

Given middle knowledge, the Molinist is able to offer a clear explication of each of our three components of the strong notion of providence. Prior to creation, God by his natural knowledge knows which worlds are possible. But given middle knowledge, he also knows which worlds are *feasible*—that is, for any creative act of will he might perform, even those acts of will which involve the creation of free beings, God knows which world would as a matter of fact (though not necessarily) result. For instance, since by his middle knowledge God would know whether or not Cuthbert would freely buy that iguana if placed in *C*, he would know prior to creation which type of world was feasible for him, a *B*-world or an *R*-world; knowledge of other counterfactuals would further inform him as to *which B*-worlds or *R*-worlds were feasible.[21] Since every feasible world contains a different divine creative act of will, it follows that, immediately upon deciding which complete creative action to perform, God knows which feasible world will be actual—i.e., he has *free* knowledge. And since the relevant act of will on God's part is presumably one that was always present (that is why it is potentially misleading to speak of God as *deciding* to create), the Molinist can say that middle knowledge allows God always to have had perfect and complete foreknowledge.

Sovereignty is also easily explicable given middle knowledge. Though God has no control over which truths he knows via middle

---

was not until the second edition that he spoke of middle knowledge, and even then, he forgot to make the necessary changes in certain places—e.g., in Disputation 49, secs. 11–15.

[21]For more on feasibility, see my "Problem of Divine Freedom." As noted there, the set of all the worlds that are feasible for God can be thought of as the *galaxy* of worlds with which God is presented, a galaxy that is necessarily a proper subset of the set of all possible worlds. In different possible worlds, God would be presented with different galaxies, and being presented with a galaxy can thus be thought of as what constitutes the situation or circumstances referred to in the antecedents of certain counterfactuals of *divine* freedom. (See above, n. 15.)

knowledge, and thus no control over which possible worlds are feasible worlds, he has complete control over which feasible world will become actual, and he fully exercises this complete control by performing a particular complete creative act. Hence, the Molinist can consistently say that each and every contingent event that occurs is subject to divine sovereignty. If God had, say, wished to prevent Cuthbert's free purchase of that iguana, he could have done so—by seeing to it that Cuthbert was in a situation in which he would freely refrain from buying the iguana; or by directly causing Cuthbert to refrain (unfreely) from entering the pet store; or perhaps even by deciding not to create Cuthbert, or iguanas, at all. Hence, the whole world truly *is* in God's hands: everything that happens was not only foreseen, but either intended or at least permitted by a deity who had full power to prevent it.[22]

Finally, middle knowledge makes it possible for the Molinist to explain just how it is that God's good plan for his world can be achieved with certainty. Given middle knowledge, God would have no doubt as to which worlds were feasible; nor would he have any doubt as to exactly what *he* would have to do—which creatures he would have to create (and when), which laws of nature he would have to institute and sustain,[23] which graces he would have to give which persons, and so on—in order to see to it that any one of these feasible worlds would become actual. We can thus think of God as surveying the feasible worlds prior to creation and choosing one of them—perhaps because of its special fittingness as an illustration of its creator's knowledge, power, goodness, mercy, and the like.[24] God's performance of the various actions that he sees via middle knowledge will lead to this world would thus amount to his executing his plan for creation, and the certainty of that knowledge would thus guarantee the success of that plan.

[22]David Basinger has implicitly denied that the Molinists' God could have specific sovereignty. See his "Christian Theism and the Free Will Defense," *Sophia* 19 (1980), 20–33. I responded to Basinger in "Divine Sovereignty and the Free Will Defense," *Sophia* 23 (1984), 41–52.

[23]I am assuming here that God does have at least some degree of control over which natural laws will apply to the beings he creates. For another opinion, see Alfred J. Freddoso, "The Necessity of Nature," *Midwest Studies in Philosophy* 11 (1986), 215–242.

[24]There is a clear danger of anthropomorphism here; readers should consider themselves warned. Also, talk of fittingness probably cannot be pushed very far. *Any* feasible world would have to be fitting enough for God to create it; otherwise, it wouldn't be feasible in the first place.

Two related points deserve mention here. First, the existence of evil poses no serious objection to this Molinist account of providence. Some of the worlds feasible for God—namely, those which contain no free creatures—surely contain no moral evil, and may well contain no evil at all; but such worlds just as surely exhibit none of the good moral qualities that presuppose genuinely free creatures. If God freely chose to create a world containing moral good—if that was one of the goods he wanted his world to include—he would have to restrict his choice to those feasible worlds containing significantly free creatures.[25] But since *which* worlds are feasible is *not* a matter that is under God's control, it could well turn out that *no* world containing such free creatures included moral good but no moral evil. Indeed, God might well have found that the only feasible worlds containing significant amounts of moral good, or particularly noble instances of it—triumph over especially great temptations, say, or striking cases of repentance and reconciliation—were also worlds that contained significant amounts of evil. If that were so, God might well still decide to create such a world, permitting the evil in order to obtain the good that he know would accompany it.[26]

Second, the manner in which predestination would operate is also explicable given middle knowledge. The orthodox Catholic position on fallen mankind lies squarely between the optimism regarding human nature evidenced by Pelagius and his modern humanist offspring and the corresponding pessimism evidenced by reformers such as Luther. According to the Catholic view, we humans retain after the Fall our ability to perform some good actions without any special divine assistance. But our true happiness is something we cannot attain solely through the use of our own natural powers: the end that we seek— the eternal life of the beatific vision—is not a natural end and cannot be achieved by natural means. The supernatural assistance that each of us requires to attain eternal life is known generically as *grace*, while the particular type of grace we need to perform those salutary acts that God has ordained will allow us to merit eternal life is known as *actual grace*.[27] Actual grace is in turn divided into *prevenient* (or *antecedent*)

---

[25]I follow Plantinga here in speaking of a significantly free creature as one who is free with respect to a morally significant action. See *The Nature of Necessity*, p. 166.

[26]The reply to the problem of evil given here stems from Plantinga; see the work cited in n. 7. I somewhat modified his version of the free will defense in my "Divine Sovereignty and the Free Will Defense."

[27]Salutary acts are those acts of prayer, repentance, faith, and the like that bring one

grace, which precedes and prepares the way for a free act of our will, and *cooperating* (or *consequent*) *grace*, which is concurrent with that free act of will.

Now since God wills that all of us be saved, and since salvation presupposes cooperating grace, it follows that God offers all of us enough cooperating grace for us to merit salvation. So everyone receives *sufficient grace*—i.e., grace that empowers one to perform salutary acts. Of course, this power is not always exercised; some of us do not (or at least *may* not) attain salvation. When cooperating grace does have its intended effect, though—i.e., when it leads to a salutary act—it is called *efficacious grace.*

As the Molinists see it, efficacious grace is not intrinsically different from sufficient grace: it is merely sufficient grace that "works." If a recipient of sufficient grace performs that salutary act which God intended that person to perform, the grace in question is ipso facto efficacious; if not, it is merely sufficient. But whether the person uses the grace for the purpose that God intended is *not* up to God, for it is a doctrine of faith that grace leaves a person free.[28] Efficacious grace, then, is essentially sufficient but only contingently efficacious, and its being efficacious is determined by us, not by God.

How, then, can God will that all be saved, yet predestine only some to glory? How can membership in the elect be up to him if his grace is resistible? Again, Molinists maintain, middle knowledge holds the key. As we have seen, God's universal salvific will requires that he grant everyone sufficient grace. But God can fulfill this requirement in various ways: he can create Cuthbert in numerous different situations, and those situations can include God's bestowing upon him varying degrees of grace (though always sufficient and never irresistible). By virtue of his middle knowledge, God would know prior to creation how Cuthbert would freely react to any such bestowal of sufficient grace. Now suppose that there are feasible worlds in which Cuthbert cooperates with God's sufficient grace, thus rendering it efficacious, and thereby meriting salvation. If so, then God can predestine Cuthbert by choosing to create one of those worlds. God's election of Cuthbert would be free in such a case, for there might well be other feasible

---

into the life of God—that justify and sanctify the person—along with those subsequent good actions generated by the love that accompanies this sanctification.

[28]The Tridentine enunciation of this doctrine was often referred to by Molina in Disputation 53 of the *Concordia*—see pt. 1, sec. 7; pt. 2, sec. 30; pt. 3, sec. 8; and pt. 4, sec. 14. For the actual declaration by the Council of Trent, see Denzinger, n. 1554 (814).

worlds in which the grace given to Cuthbert remains merely sufficient, and there surely are feasible worlds in which Cuthbert doesn't exist at all. Hence, predestination would be genuinely up to God even though the means by which he carries it out (grace) is resistible.[29]

By viewing God's knowledge of counterfactuals of creaturely freedom as genuinely middle knowledge, then, the Molinist is able to explicate his belief in the harmony between human freedom and God's providential activity. Few Christians, I think, can fail to be struck by the power of this ingenious account of providence, nor by the light it might shed on various related topics—prophecy, petitionary prayer, conciliar and/or papal infallibility, and the like.[30] Still, many proponents of the strong notion of providence have rejected, and some have even gone so far as to condemn, the Molinist view of providence. What is the source of their opposition to it? And what alternative picture of God's knowledge of counterfactuals of creaturely freedom have they championed in its place?

4 The Thomist Account

While numerous objections to the Molinist account have been raised, I think it is fair to say that the fundamental criticism that Thomists have leveled against the Molinist explication of providence is that Molinism robs God of the supreme independence and power that he as First Cause is required to possess. If God is genuinely the First Cause, the source of all being, then all contingent beings and all contingent truths must be determined by his will. But if counterfactuals of creaturely freedom were, as the Molinists insist, contingent yet independent of God's will, *they* would limit, *they* would determine, *him*. As Garrigou-Lagrange puts it:

---

[29] A later variation on Molinism known as *congruism* held, in effect, that, even though grace is *not* intrinsically efficacious, God can save whomever he wishes—i.e., that, for any person (indeed, for any "possible person"), God could bestow graces congruent to the situation in which the person is (or might be) placed that would effect that person's salvation. It should be evident that, while the congruist thesis is not incompatible with Molinism, it could at best be contingently true given Molinist presuppositions.

[30] As Alfred Freddoso and I have argued, Molinism also helps provide us with the means to fashion an adequate analysis of the concept of divine omnipotence. See our "Maximal Power," in *The Existence and Nature of God*, ed. Alfred J. Freddoso, (Notre Dame, Ind.: University of Notre Dame Press, 1983), pp. 81–113.

God's knowledge cannot be determined by anything which is extrinsic to Him, and which would not be caused by Him. But such is the *scientia media*, which depends on the determination of the free conditioned future [i.e., the counterfactual or creaturely freedom]; for this determination does not come from God but from the human liberty, granted that it is placed in such particular circumstances; so that "it was not in God's power to know any other thing . . . , but if the created free will were to do the opposite, He would have known this other thing," as Molina says in the passage just quoted. Thus God would be dependent on another, would be passive in His knowledge, and would be no longer pure Act. The dilemma is unsolvable: Either God is the first determining Being, or else He is determined by another; there is no other alternative. In other words, the *scientia media* involves an imperfection, which cannot exist in God. Hence there is a certain tinge of anthropomorphism in this theory.

All the aforesaid arguments bring us to this conclusion: there is no determination without a determining cause, and the supreme determining cause is God, otherwise He would be determined by another. But this is nothing else than the principle of causality.[31]

For the Thomists, then, there are no contingent truths independent of God's will, and hence no middle knowledge; there are only natural knowledge and free knowledge. Where, then, would the Thomists place counterfactuals of creaturely freedom? At first glance, it would seem that they view them as part of God's free knowledge—as contingent truths dependent upon his will. Garrigou-Lagrange writes: "St. Thomas admits only the knowledge of simple intelligence [natural knowledge], which is concerned with possible things, and the knowledge of vision [free knowledge] which, granted a decree, intuits future things. The knowledge of conditioned futures belongs by a reductive process to this latter."[32] The "reductive process" that Garrigou-Lagrange has in mind is undoubtedly something like the following. The Molinists insist that the counterfactuals of creaturely freedom are contingent truths. But no contingent truth can be true independent of or prior to God's will, for as we have seen, such a status would compromise God's divinity. Therefore, the Molinists' counterfactuals of creaturely freedom must be part of God's free knowledge.

---

[31]Reginald Garrigou-Lagrange, *The One God*, trans. Dom. Bede Rose (St. Louis: B. Herder, 1944), pp. 465–466. A similar remark is made by the commentator to the Blackfriars translation of Aquinas's *Summa theologiae* (New York: McGraw-Hill, 1963), Pt. 1, Q. 22, A. 4, pp. 104–105.

[32]Garrigou-Lagrange, *The One God*, p. 464. The same point is made clear by Diekamp; see the work and page cited in n. 16, as well as his *Katholische Dogmatik*, vol. 1 (Munster: Aschendorff, 1949), p. 200.

Yet there is a curious anomaly here. When discussing his position and contrasting it with that of his Thomist opponents, Molina makes it clear that, as he sees it, the Thomists have to situate counterfactuals of creaturely freedom within God's *natural* knowledge.[33] And when we consider the matter carefully, such a conclusion seems quite plausible. Take Cuthbert and his iguana-buying. Suppose it is true that Cuthbert would buy the iguana were he placed in circumstances C—i.e. that $C \rightarrow B$.[34] Now, according to the Thomist, God as First Cause determined that this counterfactual (rather than its negation) be true. Just as his creative activity brought into existence other contingent beings, and made true other contingent truths, so his creative activity guaranteed the truth of $C \rightarrow B$. Indeed, the Thomist would insist that, given all that God himself has done, $C \rightarrow B$ could not fail to be true; God has made it true. If we allow G to stand for God's complete creative activity, then, the Thomists would insist that $G \Rightarrow (C \rightarrow B)$.[35] But from this it follows that $(G \& C) \Rightarrow B$.[36] Now, C is supposed to specify the complete circumstances in which Cuthbert finds himself at the time of his action. Since what God has done would surely constitute a part—yea, a most significant part—of the situation in which Cuthbert finds himself when he acts, it would seem that G must be considered part of C—i.e., $C \Rightarrow G$. But if $C \Rightarrow G$, then $C \Rightarrow (G \& C)$; and since the Thomist is committed to $(G \& C) \Rightarrow B$, it follows by transitivity that the Thomist is committed to $C \Rightarrow B$. That is, the Thomist is committed to saying that it is a metaphysically necessary truth that Cuthbert buy that iguana if placed in circumstances C. And since metaphysically necessary truths are known by God via his natural knowledge, Molina's contention seems eminently defensible.

Something is surely amiss here. Recall that, on the Thomist view, a counterfactual of creaturely freedom such as $C \rightarrow B$ is supposed to be

---

[33]*Concordia*, Disputation 53, pt. 1, sec. 10, and especially Disputation 53, pt. 3, secs. 6 and 10.

[34]I use the single-line arrow to symbolize counterfactual implication, the double-line arrow for entailment (i.e., for metaphysically necessary material implication).

[35]I assume that G does *not* occur in every possible world—i.e., that God's complete creative activity in *this* world does *not* take place in many other worlds. Some Thomists might not like this way of speaking, since they seem to prefer to view God's activity as a constant across different worlds. See, for instance, James Ross, "Creation," *Journal of Philosophy* 77 (1980), 614–629, and "Creation II," in *The Existence and Nature of God*, pp. 115–141.

[36]Suppose $G \Rightarrow (C \rightarrow B)$. From this it follows that $(G \& C) \Rightarrow [C \& (C \rightarrow B)]$. But $[C \& (C \rightarrow B)]$ entails B. Therefore, given that entailment is a transitive relation, it follows that $(G \& C) \Rightarrow B$.

a *contingent* proposition, a proposition whose truth or falsity is *up to God*. Yet Molina says (not implausibly, as we have seen) that the Thomist is committed to viewing the relation between C and B as a necessary one: C → B is true, but only because C *entails* B. How do we account for this discrepancy? Are the Thomists blind to the implication of their position regarding God's all-encompassing causal activity? Or is Molina's description of the view, and our argument in support of that description, misguided in some way?

The problem, I think, hinges on the question of what is to be included in the *circumstances* that the antecedent of a counterfactual of creaturely freedom specify. Thomists have generally been reluctant to allow that the *circumstances* in which a *free* action is performed could be *determinative* of that action. Kondoleon's statement is typical:

> Propositions supposedly the objects of God's "middle knowledge" would not be propositions involving a relationship of strict implication between the antecedent and the consequent, unless, of course, one were to acknowledge a determination of circumstances. In the latter case such a proposition as "If God creates x and places him in circumstances y, then x will do A" would be true if x were determined to do A because of y. While such an explanation would give an adequate account of how such propositions could be true, it would be fatal to free will.[37]

So, according to most Thomists, the circumstances in which an agent is placed do not determine that agent's free actions. And yet, as we have seen, the core Thomist contention is that every contingent event and proposition, including those involving free agents, is completely determined by God; *my* action, even if free, is still determined by *God's* action. The way to reconcile these two positions and to resolve our present perplexity thus seems evident. The Thomist, unlike the Molinist, is not thinking of the circumstances (the condition, the situation) in which an agent acts as including every prior and concurrent divine activity. Exactly what is to be left out of the circumstances is not completely clear. But the Thomist account of predestination offers some definite hints.

On the Molinist view, predestination is executed via grace that is

---

[37]Theodore J. Kondoleon, "The Free Will Defense: New and Old," *The Thomist* 46 (1983), 19. For similar remarks on the determination of circumstances, see Garrigou-Lagrange, pp. 465, 470, and the commentary to Aquinas's *Summa theologiae* cited in n. 31.

intrinsically sufficient but extrinsically efficacious. Thomists reject this scheme, for they see it as placing the ultimate source of one's election in one's own will rather than in God's:

> Let us suppose that Peter and Judas situated in equal circumstances receive equal prevenient grace; then [according to the Molinists] God sees Peter consenting to accept that grace, and hence singling himself out from Judas who does not consent, not on account of the grace, for an equal grace is indifferently offered to each. Therefore it is because the will decides to accept the grace. Thus do all Thomists argue against Molina, and they thus affirm as revealed the principle that can be called "the principle of predilection," namely, that no one would be better than another unless he were loved more and helped more by God.[38]

For Thomists, then, grace that is efficacious is *intrinsically* efficacious; its efficaciousness is not determined by whether or not the human will cooperates with it, for it is not possible that the will *not* cooperate with it. God determines all contingent beings and events, and the way in which he determines us to salvation or damnation is by bestowing or withholding efficacious grace. Molinists, by denying intrinsically efficacious grace, implicitly deny God's determining role and reduce his power: "The theory of the *scientia media* limits the divine omnipotence. For if God, by means of the *scientia media*, foresees that our will under certain conditions will refuse to be moved to perform some good act, then He is already incapable of moving our will so that in these conditions it freely consent to be moved to perform this good act."[39]

Now the general view of predestination that I have just described is pretty much what one would expect of the Thomists, given their emphasis on God's role as First Cause. But the manner in which this view is presented is, I think, revealing of the Thomist notion of a circumstance. For God's bestowal of grace is depicted by Garrigou-Lagrange as something *extra* given to Peter and Judas who are supposed to be "situated in equal circumstances." Similarly, if the conditions in which an agent is placed leave that being free, he implies, then an omnipotent God should be able to act so that the being "in these conditions" does as God wills. What seems clear is that, in each of these cases, God's act of bestowing efficacious grace is viewed as something *external* to the circumstances, something that determines what the agent would

[38]Garrigou-Lagrange, *The One God*, p. 463.
[39]Ibid., p. 466.

do in circumstances that, *taken by themselves*, determine the agent to no particular course of action.

In the case of predestination, then, it seems that what the Thomist wants to exclude from the circumstances of action is any concurrent supernatural activity on God's part. More generally, I think, the Thomist wants to deny that any extraordinary divine action simultaneous with a creature's action should count as part of the circumstances in which that creature acts. All of God's *prior* actions constitute part of the circumstances, as do their ordinary, natural effects up to the time in question. But nothing out of the ordinary (i.e., beyond his constant conserving activity) that God does *at the time* the agent acts is to be thought of as an element in an agent's situation. Since God's bestowal of efficacious grace is *not* included in his ordinary activity, and *is* concurrent with the creature's action, it will not be found among the circumstances in which the action takes place.

If this depiction of the Thomists' view of circumstances is more or less correct, we can quickly resolve our puzzle concerning the Thomists' categorization of counterfactuals of creaturely freedom. Take again $C \rightarrow B$, our counterfactual about Cuthbert. If C is thought of as specifying circumstances *in the limited Thomistic sense*, then most Thomists will insist that the counterfactual is a contingent one that God can make true or false, and that hence is (if true) part of God's free knowledge. On the other hand, if C is thought of as specifying circumstances *in the unlimited Molinist sense* (i.e., as including *all* of God's activity, even that which is simultaneous with the action), then $C \rightarrow B$ will indeed be a necessary truth that God knows via his natural knowledge.

Each of these ways of circumscribing circumstances has something to be said for it, and I doubt that a compelling case could be made for taking either as the more appropriate.[40] So long as we are clear about which notion it is that we are using, we can employ that notion to distinguish Thomism from Molinism. Whichever sense of "circumstance" we employ, God's knowledge of counterfactuals of creaturely freedom will be an instance of middle knowledge according to the

[40]It is interesting to note that a similar disagreement over what is to count as a circumstance seems to lie at the base of the contemporary discussion of compatibilism. (Wilfrid Sellars brings this point to the fore quite clearly; see especially his "Reply to Alan Donagan," *Philosophical Studies* 27 (1975), 150.) One might take this as a sign that the debate over freedom and the Thomist/Molinist dispute are not totally separate. As we shall see, one would be wise so to take it.

Molinist[41]; for the Thomist, there is no room for middle knowledge *however* circumstances are defined.

Since Thomists reject middle knowledge, they will also see no need for us to talk of feasible worlds. For the Molinist, no complete creative action that God might perform will be determinative of any particular possible world; many different worlds *could* result from any such action, and all of these worlds are possible. But, for any such action, God knows which of these worlds *would* result, and hence knows that only that world is *feasible*. For the Thomist, though, the distinction between possibility and feasibility collapses. As First Cause, God completely determines which world is actual. Any complete creative action he might perform is compatible with the actuality of only that possible world which it determines to be actual. Hence, there is a one-to-one correspondence between distinct divine creative actions and distinct possible worlds; and thus, the Thomist concludes, *any* possible world is such that God had the power to actualize it.[42]

It should be evident that the Thomist is able to offer a clear explication of the strong orthodox notion of providence. Since God fully determines which world is actual, the passage from natural to free knowledge is accomplished immediately upon his creative act of will. And since that act of will has eternally been present in God, he has eternally known exactly what was going to happen; that is, he possesses complete and perfect foreknowledge.[43] Since this foreknowledge stems from his all-encompassing causal activity, it is clear that all that happens is truly under his control; the Thomist God is an *active* sovereign who knowingly causes (directly or indirectly) all that occurs. But he is also a *good* sovereign. His creative power is equal to the actualizing of any possible world whatsoever, and he can and does choose a world which is indicative of its maker's wisdom and love.

It is on this last point—the goodness of such a God—that some of the strongest criticisms against the Thomist stance have been leveled.

---

[41]It should be noted, though, that one need not embrace the law of conditional excluded middle in order to be a Molinist. If the sense of "circumstance" employed gives us antecedents that are very thin in terms of content, the Molinist could consistently say that all such conditionals are false. All that is central to Molinism is that there be some conditionals of freedom that are true and known by God prior to his creative act of will.

[42]See Ross, "Creation," p. 614.

[43]It is worth emphasizing that, for the Thomists, it is God's status as First Cause, *not* his presence in eternity, that is primarily to be thought of as responsible for his foreknowledge; see Garrigou-Lagrange, *The One God*, pp. 456–457. Aquinas himself makes the same point in *Quaestiones disputatae de veritate*, Q. 5, A. 1.

For given the Thomist account of providence, the existence of evil in general, and of the especially flagrant kind of evil which results in damnation in particular, would seem to be all but inexplicable. Surely there are possible worlds that contain free beings but no evil, or at least no moral evil, and surely some of these worlds exhibit a large amount and a wide variety of goods. If God is omnibenevolent and can actualize any possible world he wishes, why did he not actualize one of *these* worlds? And even if he *did* have a reason for actualizing a world with moral evil, why did he actualize a world in which some of his creatures become so immersed in evil as to warrant damnation? Given Thomist presuppositions, he could easily have prevented it: by simply offering efficacious grace to all, he could have seen to it that all were saved, and none reprobated. Why did he not do so? Where does God's universal salvific will fit in given the Thomist view?[44]

Troubling as such questions may appear, Thomists are not without replies. Frequently, such replies hinge on the notion that it is fitting or appropriate that God create a world whose inhabitants exhibit a variety of grades of being. Hence, it was fitting that God create not only immaterial, incorruptible beings, but material, corruptible beings as well. Since corruption is natural to such beings, it is not to be expected that God will always prevent the evil of corruption from befalling them, for there would be something almost contradictory in God's creating a being and then systematically frustrating its natural tendencies. Much the same goes for the moral agents God has created. Fallen human nature leaves us naturally inclined toward sin and perdition. For God to save even some of us is a purely gratuitous act on his part; by no means is he required to save *all* of us. In fact, a world in which only some are saved may well be a more fitting illustration of the divine nature, for not only are God's mercy and kindness made manifest through his saving of the elect, but in addition his justice— more specifically, his *vindictive* or *retributive* justice—is evidenced by his permitting some to remain in sin and subsequently punishing them with damnation. Nor, says the Thomist, need we deny that God wills that all of us be saved, for we can consistently say that God in his goodness offers sufficient grace to all. Those who are damned could have done otherwise and have no reason to curse God for their fate.

---

[44]It is not quite *de fide* that God wills all to be saved; see Ott, *Fundamentals of Catholic Dogma*, pp. 188–189. Nevertheless, I am aware of no Thomist who would deny God's universal salvific will.

True, they *would* have done otherwise if and only if God had given them intrinsically efficacious graces to do otherwise, but that fact in no way eliminates the fact that God in his goodness offered sufficient grace to all and thereby manifested his universal salvific will.[45]

Molinists push Thomists on many of these points, and some Thomists (like some Calvinists) end up conceding that there is an apparent harshness, a seeming arbitrariness, in God's salvific action. But Thomists will insist that this appearance is more than outweighed by the hard evidence of Scripture (e.g., the ninth chapter of Paul's letter to the Romans) and the philosophically demonstrable implications of taking seriously the belief that God is the First, complete and universal, Cause. Besides, the Thomist will remind us, Molinists have similar embarrassing questions of their own to deal with, even on the question of predestination. For example, if Cuthbert is damned in the actual world, but saved in some other feasible world, does it not at least appear that God has arbitrarily excluded Cuthbert from heaven? How can the Molinist say that God truly *willed* that Cuthbert be saved if God created him in a situation that God knew—and knew with certainty—would result in Cuthbert's damnation, when he could just as easily have actualized one of those worlds in which Cuthbert is saved? The point of such questions is not to suggest that God would actually be cruel, or even less than perfectly good, on the Molinist scheme. Rather, they simply serve to remind us that no one who ascribes to the orthodox position regarding reprobation will find it easy to reconcile that doctrine with the belief in an all-loving God. For all of us, Thomists and Molinists alike, there is need here for faith.[46]

5 The Metaphysical Foundation of the Dispute

The mention of faith should serve to remind us that the difference between Thomism and Molinism is not, properly speaking, a religious

---

[45]The emphasis on vindictive justice is clearly present in Aquinas—see, for example, *Summa theologiae*, Pt. 1, Q. 23, A. 5—but has been pushed with evident relish by Thomists such as Garrigou-Lagrange; see *The One God*, p. 705. See also Kondoleon, "The Free Will Defense," p. 35.

[46]In an excellent discussion of the Wesleyan/Calvinist dispute, Jerry Walls has suggested that the ground-level difference between the two sides has more to do with the concept of divine goodness than that of human freedom. As this paragraph suggests, I have my doubts about this. See his "The Free Will Defense, Calvinism, Wesley, and the Goodness of God," *Christian Scholar's Review* 13 (1983), 19–33.

difference. Though Thomists have been wont to call Molinists semi-Pelagian innovators, and Molinists have returned the favor by labeling their opponents Calvinists, such colorful language is more a sign of the heat of battle than of genuine doctrinal difference. In truth, there is not one article of faith or biblical passage that either a Thomist or a Molinist will reject. And though the point could be argued, I think it is fair to say that neither party is dissembling: there simply is no way to resolve the dispute by appealing to Scripture or tradition.[47] What we are faced with, then, are two distinct and incompatible theological explications of a common religious faith.

Of course, the fact that there is no religious resolution available does not imply that the debate is hopeless. Might it not be that the theological divergence is traceable to a more fundamental divergence of some sort? If not a credal divergence, what kind of disagreement might account for the dispute?

One answer—an answer that has surely occurred to many readers by now, and that undoubtedly all but leapt at many when reading the Thomist explanation of how one denied efficacious grace nonetheless could have acted otherwise—seems particularly revealing. The dispute between Thomists and Molinists *is* rooted in a more fundamental dispute—a metaphysical dispute. All of their theological differences stem from a core philosophical difference regarding the necessary conditions of free human action.

Consider first the Molinist stance. What notion of freedom would most naturally lead to such a theological system? Clearly, I think, it is that which is commonly called libertarianism. The libertarian insists that the circumstances (even if broadly construed) in which a free agent acts are not determinative of the agent's action. But then, any proposition affirming that a free agent would act a certain way in a certain situation would have to be both contingent and (if the situation were inclusive enough) not under God's control. For if it weren't contingent, the *circumstances* would determine one's free action, while if it were under God's control, then *God* would be the ultimate determiner of one's free action, and neither of these consequences is compatible with the full-blooded libertarian assertion that nothing and no one other

---

[47]Passages from Scripture that the Thomists emphasize include Psalm 135:6, Proverbs 21:1, 1 Corinthians 4:7, Romans 8:28–9:33, Philippians 2:13, and Ephesians 1:11 and 2:8–9. Among the Molinists' favorite passages are Wisdom 4:11, Sirach 31:8–11, 1 Samuel 23:1–13, Deuteronomy 30:15–20, and Matthew 11:21 and 23:37.

than the agent determines the agent's free action. As we have seen, one can uphold the strong concept of providence only if one agrees that there are true counterfactuals of freedom. Therefore, any libertarian who affirms providence will have to say that all such conditionals are contingent propositions known by God but not under his control. That is, the libertarian will have to embrace the concept of middle knowledge. And once middle knowledge is accepted, Molinism is all but inevitable.

So the path from libertarianism to Molinism seems clear. It would be gratifying if a similar trail to Thomism could be discerned. It would be especially gratifying if that trail set off from a view concerning human freedom. And it would most gratifying of all if that starting point were none other than that alternative to libertarianism known commonly as compatibilism. Now it might well seem that proponents of contemporary compatibilism who wished to endorse the strong concept of providence would indeed be led toward the Thomist position, for if physical determinism is true, it will presumably be seen by the theist as merely the means by which God determines all events, including free human actions. One might thus be led to think that the road from compatibilism to Thomism is as clear as that from libertarianism to Molinism. Unfortunately, things are not quite so simple, for at least two reasons.

In the first place, the preceding discussion of compatibilism ignores a crucial distinction. Some compatibilists maintain that it is *possible* that free human actions be physically determined, while some also maintain that it is *necessary* that such actions be physically determined. Those in the first but not the second group, whom we may call *soft compatibilists*, say that the truth or falsity of determinism is irrelevant to the question of human freedom; those in the latter group, the *hard compatibilists*, insist that a human action can be free only if it is determined.[48] While it may be true that hard compatibilists will be led toward a Thomist elucidation of providence, it is at least less clear that the same can be said for soft compatibilists.

Second, and more important, it is fairly clear that relatively few of those who have called themselves Thomists would accept either of the forms of compatibilism delineated above. As we have seen, Thomists

---

[48]Most of the more strident classical compatibilists (such as Hume, Mill, and Schlick) were clearly hard compatibilists. In recent days, many if not most compatibilists (including Sellars, Lehrer, and Kenny, to name but a few) seem to have gone soft.

generally reject the idea that human freedom is compatible with what they call a determinism of circumstances, and as several of them make clear, the upshot of this rejection is that human freedom could not exist in a world where all actions were determined by the laws of nature and the prior history of the world. In denouncing modern-day compatibilism, hard or soft, most Thomists have been as vociferous as the Molinists.

So it would be misleading to represent Thomism as the compatibilist view of providence, as opposed to the Molinists' libertarian view, for as we have seen, Thomism neither entails nor is entailed by what we generally call compatibilism. Still, I think it is fair to characterize Thomism as a compatibilist position, provided we expand the notion of compatibilism in a manner that I shall now try to explicate.

One clear way of characterizing the distinction between libertarian and compatibilist views of freedom is in terms of principles setting forth necessary conditions of human freedom. As a first approximation, one might suggest that the affirmation of

> (A) Necessarily, for any human agent S, action A, and circumstances C, if S performs A freely in C, then it is possible that S refrain from performing A freely in C

is what is definitive of the libertarian position, while compatibilism is characterized by the denial of (A). Unfortunately, such a suggestion is simply false; most compatibilists would have little trouble accepting (A). As they see it, one cannot plausibly consider the entire past history of the world as being part of the circumstances in which an action is performed.[49] And if not, then the circumstances in which a free agent acts are, even according to the staunchest defender of determinism, logically and physically compatible with that agent's having acted otherwise.[50]

The failure of (A) to discriminate between libertarians and compatibilists can easily be rectified by removing any ambiguity regarding the notion of circumstance. For consider:

[49]See the reference to Sellars in n. 40.

[50]I am assuming here that the determinist is one who believes that determinism is operative only if formulated at the level of microphysical entities and laws, not at the level of, say, minds and psychological laws. Those who espouse the latter kind of determinism—those whom Sellars refers to as *vulgar* determinists ("Reply to Alan Donagan," 156)—might well have problems with (A).

(B) Necessarily, for any human agent S, action A, and time t, if S performs A freely at t, then the history of the world prior to t and the laws of nature are jointly compatible with S's refraining from performing A freely.

I think that (B) does allow us to distinguish between libertarians and compatibilists, the former affirming and the latter denying this principle. Indeed, (B) *may* also allow us to set off some Thomists from their Molinist opponents. For while all Molinists would, I take it, affirm (B), some Thomists—namely, those who think God's all-determining activity operates exclusively through natural laws and bestowals of prevenient grace—might reject it.[51] Still, I suspect that most Thomists would have little trouble endorsing (B). For as they see it, the actions by which God determines our free actions are not prior to, but concurrent with, those actions. If Cuthbert performs some salutary action, the Thomist will insist, that action was determined by God's bestowal of intrinsically efficacious grace. But, as we have seen, such grace is generally viewed as cooperating rather than prevenient. It is present *when* one acts, but not *before* one acts; otherwise, one would have the dreaded determinism of circumstances. Analogous points could be made, from the Thomist viewpoint, regarding God's concurrence with Cuthbert's nonsalutary free actions: God's determining activity is not to be thought of as something that occurs temporally prior to Cuthbert's action. So, while (B) allows us to separate libertarians from compatibilists, it does not go far in distinguishing Molinists from Thomists.

Nevertheless, it seems clear that the kind of divine activity that the Thomists see as compatible with human freedom would not be deemed compatible by those with libertarian inclinations. For the heart and soul of libertarianism is the conviction that what an agent does freely is genuinely up to the agent to do freely or refrain from doing freely; no external circumstance, no other agent, does or even can determine what I do freely.[52] Physical determinism, which sees my actions as

---

[51]See, for example, Thomas Loughran, "Theological Compatibilism" (Ph.D. diss.: University of Notre Dame, 1986).

[52]A clear early statement of this libertarian intuition is found in the writings of that grand old man of libertarianism, Thomas Reid: "If, in any action, [a man] had power to will what he did, or not to will it, in that action he is free. But if, in every voluntary action, the determination of his will be the necessary consequence of something involuntary in the state of his mind, or of something in his external circumstances, he is not free; he has not what I call the liberty of a moral agent, but is subject to necessity." As the discussion following makes clear, Reid is using "circumstances" in the broad Molinist

determined by physical laws and *prior* states of the universe, is clearly at odds with this core insight. But súrely the Thomist picture of *simultaneous* divine determinism will strike the true libertarian as equally destructive of human freedom. And, indeed, if external determination *is* incompatible with human freedom, does it really make that much difference just how the determination is accomplished? Are the movements of a hand puppet any more under its own control than those of a windup doll? In sum, if we think of compatibilism in the broader sense as the view that a free action *can* be externally determined, does it not appear that Thomism is indeed ultimately rooted in compatibilism?

If we wish to articulate this broader notion of compatibilism in terms of a principle along the lines of (A) and (B), the following would seem to do the trick:

> (C) Necessarily, for any human agent *S*, action *A*, and time *t*, if *S* performs *A* freely at *t*, then the history of the world prior to *t*, the laws of nature, and the actions of any other agent (including God) prior to and at *t* are jointly compatible with *S*'s refraining from performing *A* freely.

The affirmation of (C) can, I think, be seen as virtually definitive of the libertarian position, and that position does indeed leave the advocate of strong providence little choice but to embrace Molinism. Suppose we call Compatibilism that broad notion of compatibilism which is constituted by the rejection of (C). It would be convenient if Compatibilism stood to Thomism as libertarianism does to Molinism; but, alas, things are not quite so easy. For just as there is a distinction between hard and soft compatibilism, so there is a distinction between hard and soft Compatibilism. Hard Compatibilists feel that free human action is not only *compatible* with divine determinism, but in fact *requires* it; soft Compatibilists refuse to make the latter and stronger claim. That is, while all Compatibilists agree in rejecting (C), they differ over a principle such as

> (D) Necessarily, for any human agent *S*, action *A*, and time *t*, if *S* performs *A* freely at *t*, then the history of the world prior to *t*,

---

sense; for him, a paradigm case of an unfree action would be one that was determined by an external agent. See his *Essays on the Active Powers of the Human Mind* (Cambridge, Mass.: MIT Press, 1969), p. 259.

the laws of nature, and the actions of God prior to and at t jointly entail that S performs A freely at t.

Hard Compatibilists endorse (D), while soft Compatibilists reject it along with (C).

With hard Compatibilism, we have indeed found a notion of freedom that, if endorsed, seems to lead the believer in providence inexorably toward Thomism. Soft Compatibilism, though, is more baffling. On such a view, there are some possible worlds in which God *does* determine our free actions and other possible worlds in which he *doesn't*. There may even be worlds in which some of our free actions are divinely determined, and some are not. What follows—Thomism or Molinism? Or does neither view follow? Should the soft Compatibilist perhaps be thought of as providing us the material to fashion a *third* account of providence?

Though I doubt that sure answers to such questions can be offered— after all, just what are the identity conditions for *accounts?*—I think we do ourselves little good by taking soft Compatibilism too seriously, or by honoring it as the root of a third explication of providence.

Why not take soft Compatibilism seriously? For one thing, because it seems to have so few advocates. Indeed, few Christians seem to have even considered such a stance, let alone endorsed it. And when we consider the position more carefully, it is easy to see why. After all, if God *can* determine Cuthbert's actions while leaving them fully free, why on earth would he fail to do so? For example, if God *can* offer Cuthbert the Thomists' intrinsically efficacious grace yet still leave Cuthbert's actions as free and meritorious as such actions can be, what possible reason could he have for offering Cuthbert only the Molinists' extrinsically efficacious grace? Such considerations are, of course, far from logically conclusive; God could have reasons of which we are unaware. Still, they do lead us to wonder whether, if Compatibilism is true, there are any possible worlds in which God doesn't determine all of our free actions. If a theist is inclined toward Compatibilism at all, it is hard to see why he or she would reject hard Compatibilism.

Even if there were reasons to favor soft over hard Compatibilism, though, I doubt that we would want to view soft Compatibilism as grounding a genuinely distinct explication of providence. For if soft Compatibilism is true, then God can in effect choose which type of world including free human actions to create—one in which those actions are divinely determined, or one in which they are not, or one in which some are and some aren't. If God chooses the first kind of world, his providence will be exercised in precisely the way envisaged by the Thomists. If he chooses the second type of world, the Molinist picture will be exactly correct. And if he chooses the third, the Thomist explication will cover some events, the Molinist account the rest. In a sense, then, soft Compatibilists would not really be offering a third account of providence; they would merely be saying that it's up to God which of our two accounts will apply.

So I think we can safely ignore soft Compatibilism and view libertarianism and hard Compatibilism as the two views of freedom toward which a Christian might be drawn, metaphysical views that, given one and the same religious faith, generate radically different theological accounts of providence. If Scripture or tradition definitively favored one of these views of freedom, then the theological question could be answered; but, again, neither the Bible nor the Church appears clearly to address the metaphysical debate. And if that is so, then the dispute between Thomists and Molinists is resolvable only if the dispute between libertarians and Compatibilists can be settled on philosophical grounds.

What are the prospects of such a resolution? Consider first the debate between libertarians and compatibilists, a millennial contest replete, to be sure, with intricate arguments launched by each camp, but at least as noteworthy for the plethora of exquisite invectives it has inspired.[53] Such vituperative language is not without reason. For the arguments by which each side has attempted to prove its position, and thereby best its combatant, have never been very successful. While their failure could conceivably be the result of the stupidity or intransigence of one

---

[53]Readers will, no doubt, have their own favorite examples of the salty language that has peppered this dispute; here, I shall recount only three especially memorable ones. Kant referred to the typical compatibilist stance as a "wretched subterfuge" and chided such compatibilists for thinking that "with a little quibbling they have found the solution to the difficult problem which centuries have sought in vain and which could hardly be expected to be found so completely on the surface." His opinion was seconded by William James, who labeled compatibilism "a quagmire of evasion." On the other side, Schlick considered it "one of the greatest scandals of philosophy" that one still had to expend time and energy discussing libertarianism, since the truth of compatibilism had long since been established by "certain sensible persons" such as Hume. See Immanuel Kant, *Critique of Practical Reason*, tr. by Lewis White Beck (Indianapolis: Bobbs-Merrill, 1956), p. 96; William James, "The Dilemma of Determinism," *The Will to Believe and Other Essays in Popular Philosophy* (New York: Dover, 1956), p. 149; and Moritz Schlick, "When Is a Man Responsible?", *Free Will and Determinism*, ed. Bernard Berofsky (New York: Harper & Row, 1966), p. 54.

side or the other, I doubt that any honest observer of the dispute could come to such a conclusion. Rather, neither side has been converted because no demonstrative arguments for either position have been devised. The dispute between libertarians and compatibilists is ultimately a dispute over the necessary conditions for human freedom. Libertarians feel that something like (B) states such a necessary condition; compatibilists feel it does not. But neither side has offered anything approaching a proof of the truth or falsity of (B). In the absence of such a proof, the controversy stands little chance of abating.[54]

Are the chances for resolving the dispute between libertarians and Compatibilists any better? I see no reason to think so. Is it likely that either side can produce an argument for or against (C) that is anything more than a slight variation on one of the arguments for or against (B)? As we have already seen, the heart of libertarianism lies in the intuition that external determination of a free human action is impossible; how and when that external determination takes place is of little consequence to the true libertarian. But then, the switch from compatibilism to Compatibilism is unlikely to break the dialectical impasse. Libertarians will still insist, and Compatibilists still deny, that external determination robs agents of control over, and hence responsibility for, their actions. Compatibilists will still insist, and libertarians deny, that human actions that are not ultimately externally determined are random, out-of-the-blue, inexplicable happenings. In short, the debate will continue more or less unchanged, with little likelihood of a definitive conclusion.

If the prospects of proving or disproving either libertarianism or Compatibilism are as bleak as I have suggested, then so are the chances of resolving the dispute between Molinists and Thomists. For the two theological views are simply the images that naturally appear when a common religious faith is observed through divergent metaphysical lenses. If metaphysical consensus is unattainable, theological diversity is all but assured.

This is not to say that the Christian should maintain a tepid neutrality on these two pairs of views. Indeed, it seems to me that one can build a strong case for preferring the Molinist picture of providence to that

---

[54]Despite my conviction that libertarianism is true and that the arguments against it are weak, I doubt that the compatibilist alternative is demonstrably false. For a defense of compatibilism against a common libertarian attack, see my "Compatibilism and the Argument from Unavoidability," *The Journal of Philosophy* 84 (1987), 423–440.

painted by the Thomists. The libertarian assumption upon which Molinism depends seems clearly right to me: a free action simply cannot be determined by anything or anyone other than its agent. Furthermore, the Compatibilist position that undergirds Thomism leads to a disanalogy between divine and human freedom that strikes me as most peculiar. For though the Compatibilist will insist that *our* free actions are determined externally, the *Christian* Compatibilist can hardly contend that *God's* free actions are determined externally. So the Christian Compatibilist must admit that there are some free actions (namely, God's) that are free in the sense in which libertarians say *our* free actions are free. But if there is no incoherence in the notion of libertarian free action, are not most of the considerations favoring Compatibilism rendered otiose, at least for the Christian? How could one contend, say, that a self-determined action would be a random happening, or that the agent would not be responsible for an action not determined by his or her character, when one has no choice but to hold that *God's* free actions *are* self-determined, and are *not* determined by his character?

So it seems clear to me that the Molinist perspective on providence is by far the stronger of the two. Even so, it also seems clear to me that the case is insufficient to justify the hurling of anathemas at the Thomists. The reasons offered above for rejecting Compatibilism hardly amount to a conclusive refutation of that position. No dyed-in-the-wool Compatibilist will share my intuition regarding the core libertarian assumption on the necessary conditions of freedom. Nor, I suspect, would many Christian Compatibilists be moved by my distaste for the disanalogy between divine freedom and human freedom that Christian Compatibilism requires. While I think that Compatibilists would be mistaken in each of these reactions, I don't see how one could truly demonstrate to them the error of their ways. In sum, I doubt that there are compelling reasons for a Christian to endorse either libertarianism or Compatibilism. And if my suspicions are accurate, the dispute between Molinists and Thomists is destined to endure.

6 A Historical Postlude

I end with a brief historical note. While it can be debated whether the concept of middle knowledge and the theological system that flows therefrom originated with Molina,[55] there can be no doubt that the appearance of his *Concordia* in 1588, by publicizing a position so at odds with the dominant (though, at the time, still developing) Thomist view, ignited a fiery and extended debate among Catholic theologians. Charges and countercharges were made to the bishops and the leaders of the Inquisition in Spain. Eventually, Pope Clement VIII appointed a commission to advise him as to whether or not the new Molinist position should be declared heretical. On three separate occasions, this commission recommended that various Molinist theses be condemned. Indeed, we are told that, as Molina lay dying in Madrid in April of 1600, rumors spread through the city that he had indeed been condemned by the pope, and that the works of the newly declared heretic were now warming the hands (though still not the hearts) of his Dominican detractors in Rome.[56]

But the rumors were false. Clement avoided making a final decision, choosing instead to have the issue debated before him and the commission by the theologians from the two sides. The disputations that followed lasted nearly four years (March 20, 1602—March 1, 1606), and in fact outlasted Clement, who died in 1605—grateful, perhaps, that he was not called upon to render judgment. His successor,[57] Paul V, had been present as a cardinal at the earlier disputations, and saw them through to their conclusion. In the end, the commission recommended that forty-two propositions of Molina be condemned.

The long-awaited papal decision finally arrived in August of 1607. Refusing to take the course of action consistently counseled by his commission, the pope declared that the Molinist position had not been shown to be at odds with the faith. Both Molinists and Thomists were to be allowed to promulgate their teachings, but each side was strictly admonished to desist from condemning the other. Any final decision on the matter, Paul declared, would come from Rome; until such a decision was reached, theological tolerance was to be shown by all concerned.

---

[55]Molina himself insisted that only his terminology was novel; the concept of middle knowledge, he maintained, was present in the writings of the Fathers of the Church. See his *Concordia*, Disputation 53, pt. 2, sec. 22.

[56]See the article on the *congregatio de auxiliis* in *The New Catholic Encyclopedia*, vol. 4 (New York: McGraw-Hill, 1967), pp. 168–171.

[57]Actually, Clement's immediate successor was Leo XI. But Leo's pontificate lasted less than a month. He was followed by Paul V.

And so the matter rests to this day. No final decision was ever made, and none appears forthcoming.

If the thesis of this essay regarding the ultimate source of the dispute is correct, Paul's decision seems entirely appropriate. But is appropriateness all that we can discern therein? Might it not be that Molinists, and perhaps even Thomists, can justly discern in this story the workings of that very providence which each side upholds?[58]

[58]This research was supported by a grant from the American Council of Learned Societies under a program sponsored by the National Endowment for the Humanities. I owe thanks to many people for their help with this project, especially to Fred Freddoso.

6

God's Freedom, Human Freedom, and God's Responsibility for Sin

William E. Mann

> God is the cause of every event that takes place in
> the world, just as he is the creator of the whole
> universe as it now exists.
>
> —MOSES MAIMONIDES

The God of Judaism, Christianity, and Islam is a personal being, to whom various kinds of cognitive and volitional activities are correctly ascribed. He is said to be supremely knowledgeable, powerful, and loving, and to work his ways intentionally in the affairs of humans. He is also thought to be supremely free, free of many of the constraints to which humans are subject. He freely created the world, could have chosen to create a different world or not to create at all; he freely responds or refrains from responding to his creatures; he freely offers his divine grace for our salvation. The traditional theological position— more often presupposed than articulated—is that God is maximally free, as free as any being possibly could be.

What is it for God to be free? The conceptions of freedom with which we are most familiar are intended to apply to humans. It might be that any attempt to transfer these conceptions wholesale to the case of God requires modification, if not abandonment. Consider the case of knowledgeability. Tied intimately to the notion of knowledgeability in humans are such operations as learning, memory storage and retrieval, and inference. Yet there is a powerful case to be made that knowledgeability in God involves none of these operations.[1] It is still correct

---

[1]See, for example, William E. Mann, "Epistemology Supernaturalized," *Faith and Philosophy* 2 (1985), 436–456.

to say that God is knowledgeable, but knowledgeability may be realized in God in a way quite different from the way(s) in which it is realized in humans.

I wish to discuss three general theories about human freedom. Each has had its philosophical champions. I shall argue that a certain set of traditional theological assumptions entails that freedom is realized in God in a way significantly different from the way in which it is realized in humans. The difference seems to pose a threat to human freedom and to imply that God is morally culpable for human sin. Rather than abandon the set of theological assumptions, I shall argue that the alleged consequences do not follow from it.

1 What Means This Freedom?

The classic debate about human freedom and its compatibility or incompatibility with determinism has produced two general, competing theories about what it is for a person to be free.[2] Using the traditional terminology, we can distinguish between *liberty of indifference* and *liberty of spontaneity*.

Let us characterize liberty of indifference in this fashion:

> (LI) Agent A is free at time t with respect to situation s if and only if A has it in his power at t to bring it about that s and A has it in his power at t to refrain from bringing it about that s.

The crucial, undefined notion in this characterization is the notion of an agent's having something in his power. The intuitive idea behind the notion is that if A is free with respect to s, then it is up to A whether A brings about s or not. In particular, the causal history of the world up to time t is indecisive with respect to A's bringing about s or not. An exhaustive list of all the causal laws governing the world, conjoined with an exhaustive list of all the situations that obtain or have obtained in the past (relative to t), entails neither that A brings about s nor that

---

[2] A useful discussion of these two theories, or families of theories, is contained in various writings of Anthony Kenny: "Descartes on the Will," in *Cartesian Studies*, ed. R. J. Butler (Oxford: Basil Blackwell, 1972), pp. 1–31, esp. sect. 2; "Freedom, Spontaneity and Indifference," in *Essays on Freedom of Action*, ed. Ted Honderich (London: Routledge & Kegan Paul, 1973), pp. 87–104; and *Will, Freedom and Power* (Oxford: Basil Blackwell, 1975), esp. pp. 122–161.

A brings about not-*s*.[3] We can presume the list to include all the facts about *a*'s psychological states: there is nothing about A's character, beliefs, desires, and the like that, when conjoined with relevant laws of human behavior (if there are any), implies that *A* will choose *s* over not-*s* or vice versa.

It is not accidental that the conception of freedom as liberty of indifference has been championed by libertarians, those philosophers who are incompatibilists and who believe that persons are free. If freedom requires the absence of determination by causal laws, then (LI) gives the libertarian enough leverage to express his case. Of course we may wonder whether anyone really is free according to this conception of freedom. We may even ask whether anyone would want to be free in this way. The debate will have just begun. I shall not pursue it further at this point. We should note, however, one feature of (LI) that seems plausible and that will receive further attention. If *A* is free at *t* with respect to *s*, and if at *t A* refrains from bringing it about that *s*, it still might be that *s* obtains at or after *t* without A's agency. A's refraining at *t* from bringing it about that *s* typically does not preclude B's bringing it about at *t* that *s*. Smith can turn off the water tap or leave it on. At *t* Smith refrains from turning it off. At *t* Jones, under no relevant causal influence of Smith, turns off the water tap. So although Smith refrains at *t* from bringing it about that the water tap is off, nevertheless at *t* the water tap is off. Smith's freedom, construed as liberty of indifference, is in no way compromised by this sort of situation. We may say in a case like this that if *A* is free à la (LI) with respect to *s*, then *A* is *decisive about A's not bringing it about that s*, but that *A* is not *decisive about whether s obtains*.

As an approximation to the notion of freedom as liberty of spontaneity, let us say the following:

> (LS) *A* is free at *t* with respect to *s* if and only if either *A* brings it about at *t* that *s* because *A* wants at *t* to bring it about that *s*

---

[3]There are some problems here involving "future-infected" situations that obtain before *t*. If *t* is 1987 and if in 1986 the situation, *A's bringing about s a year hence*, obtained, then the past history of the world up to *t* is not indecisive with respect to *A's* bringing about *s*. We should understand the notion of freedom as liberty of indifference as having a device to expunge such situations from the causal history of the world up to *t*. See Alfred J. Freddoso, "Accidental Necessity and Logical Determinism," *Journal of Philosophy* 80 (1983), 257–278.

or A refrains from bringing it about at t that s because A wants at t to refrain from bringing it about that s.[4]

Compatibilists, those philosophers who are determinists and who believe that persons are (sometimes) free, are attracted to some variation of (LS), because it allows (i) that a person's wants are themselves causes; (ii) that wants are themselves caused; and (iii) that to be free is simply for there to be some sort of harmony between one's wants and one's actions. In contrast to libertarians, compatibilists can insist that the causal history of the world before t either implies that A brings it about that s or implies that A does not bring it about that s. A freely brings it about that s if and only if A's desire to bring it about that s is the proximate causal vehicle that delivers A's bringing it about that s. A freely refrains from bringing it about that s if and only if A's desire not to bring it about that s is causally sufficient for A's not bringing it about that s. In the latter case it could still be that s obtains. Smith desires at t not to turn off the water tap; his desire brings it about that he refrains at t from turning off the water tap. Smith thus freely refrains at t from turning off the water tap even though Jones turns off the water tap at t. Can we then say in a case like this, as we did when examining (LI), that A is decisive about A's not bringing it about that s, but that A is not decisive about whether s obtains?

A wily compatibilist will say that we can. It is clearly true that A is not decisive about whether s obtains: the water tap is off even though Smith refrained from turning it off. The compatibilist will urge that it is also true that A is decisive about A's not bringing it about that s. Smith's desire was to refrain from turning off the water tap, and that desire was effective in preventing Smith from turning off the water tap. That is all that is needed. In general, for A to be decisive about A's not bringing it about that s just is for A's desires to be effective in bringing it about that A refrains from bringing it about that s. The compatibilist's notion of decisiveness is a different notion from that of the libertarian's, but that is to be expected, since the notions of liberty of indifference and liberty of spontaneity are themselves different.

---

[4](LS) has the consequence of judging an agent to be unfree with respect to any of his actions that he desires neither to do nor to refrain from doing. This result is counterintuitive. It is at least as implausible to say that an agent is free with respect to *all* such actions. The problem would be to figure out a way of making discriminations within this class of cases without abandoning the appeal to desires. Nothing in this essay hinges on our pursuing these issues further.

Foes of compatibilism have argued that (LS) gives us a deceitful account of human freedom, because in telling us that we are free if our actions are in conformity with our desires, it neglects to address the issue whether we are free with respect to the desires we have. Our desires in turn are the products of causal processes that were initiated long before we were born, if determinism is true, and so it is alleged to follow that we cannot help but have the desires we have.[5] More sophisticated versions of (LS) have attempted to rebut this criticism, either by introducing higher-order desires or by distinguishing causal pedigrees of the desires we have, or both.[6] It would take us too far afield to pursue this debate further. Instead, I wish to focus on a third theory of human freedom that straddles liberty of indifference and liberty of spontaneity.

Libertarian defenders of freedom as (LI) seek to locate human freedom in the interstices of the natural network of event causation. To be free, a person's action must issue from an act of that person's will, where it is understood that the act of will either is uncaused or has the agent as its cause. (In the latter case it is alleged that agent causation is different in kind from event causation.) Compatibilist defenders of freedom as (LS) locate human freedom in the harmony between a person's desires and actions, even if more sophisticated versions find need to augment the harmony. The third type of theory connects freedom with reason. A person's actions are free insofar as they are the expression of that person's rational decisions. Elements of this conception of freedom are to be found in the writings of the great Rationalist philosophers, including Spinoza, Kant, and Hegel. There are significant differences among them as to what constitutes the permissible input of considerations if a decision is to be counted as genuinely rational, differences that are reflected in the notions of viewing things *sub specie durationis* as opposed to *sub specie aeternitatis*, heteronomy versus autonomy of the will, *Willkür* informed by *Wille*, *Moralität* as

---

[5]For a sustained discussion and defense of arguments of this type, see Peter van Inwagen, *An Essay on Free Will* (Oxford: Clarendon Press, 1983).

[6]See Gerald Dworkin, "Acting Freely," *Noûs* 4 (1970), 367–383; Harry G. Frankfurt, "Freedom of the Will and the Concept of a Person," *The Journal of Philosophy* 68 (1971), 5–20, (reprinted in *Free Will*, ed. Gary Watson [Oxford: Oxford University Press, 1982], pp. 81–95); Wright Neely, "Freedom and Desire," *The Philosophical Review* 83 (1974), 32–54; Gary Watson, "Free Agency," *The Journal of Philosophy* 72 (1975), 205–220, (reprinted in *Free Will*, ed. Watson, pp. 96–110); and Gerald Dworkin, "Autonomy and Behavior Control," *Hastings Center Report* 6 (1976), 23–28. Watson's anthology contains a useful bibliography.

opposed to *Sittlichkeit*.[7] We can safely ignore those differences and concentrate instead on a generic characterization of what freedom is, according to this loosely affiliated tradition.

Consider the following principle:

> (RO) *A* is free at *t* with respect to situation *s* if and only if either (i) *A* chooses at *t* that *s* because *A* realizes at *t* that *s* is rationally preferable to not-*s*; or (ii) *A* chooses at *t* that not-*s* because *A* realizes at *t* that not-*s* is rationally preferable to *s*; or (iii) *A* chooses arbitrarily at *t* that *s* or *A* chooses arbitrarily at *t* that not-*s* because *A* realizes at *t* that *s* is not rationally preferable to not-*s* and that not-*s* is not rationally preferable to *s*.

No philosopher has enunciated precisely this characterization of freedom. There are several different ways in which it could be modified and amplified, yielding a family of conceptions of freedom as involving rationality. We may call (RO) and its cognates *liberty of rational optimality*. Our understanding of liberty of rational optimality will be deepened by examining several features of (RO) in detail.

A full-fledged theory about agent freedom built around (RO) would incorporate a theory of rational preference and an axiology, that is, a theory about what sorts of things have intrinsic value and hence are worthy of our rational choice. There can be vigorous disagreement in both areas of theorizing. It is fortunate that nothing in this essay depends on fleshing out the notion of rational preferability.

It is a fine question whether (RO) is compatible with determinism. Any attempt to answer that question would have to deal with such

[7]On Spinoza, see the *Ethics*, bks. 4 and 5, esp. bk. 4, propositions 62–66; Stuart Hampshire, "Spinoza and the Idea of Freedom," *Proceedings of the British Academy* 46 (1960), 195–215; and Stuart Hampshire, "Spinoza's Theory of Human Freedom," *The Monist* 55 (1971), 554–566.

On Kant, see the *Critique of Pure Reason*, esp. the Third Antinomy (A444/B472–A451/B479, A532/B560–A558/B586); the *Groundwork of the Metaphysic of Morals*, esp. chap. 3; the *Critique of Practical Reason*, esp. pt. 1, bk. 1, chap. 1; Lewis White Beck, *A Commentary on Kant's Critique of Practical Reason* (Chicago: University of Chicago Press, 1960), esp. chap. 11; Ralf Meerbote, "Kant on the Nondeterminate Character of Human Actions," in *Kant on Causality, Freedom, and Objectivity*, ed. William L. Harper and Ralf Meerbote (Minneapolis: University of Minnesota Press, 1984), pp. 138–163; and the essays by Terence Irwin, Ralf Meerbote, Allen W. Wood, and Jonathan Bennett in *Self and Nature in Kant's Philosophy*, ed. Allen W. Wood (Ithaca: Cornell University Press, 1984), pp. 31–112.

On Hegel, see the *Philosophy of Right*, esp. sects. 4–28, 142–157; and Richard L. Schacht, "Hegel on Freedom," in *Hegel: A Collection of Critical Essays*, ed. Alasdair MacIntyre (Garden City, N.Y.: Doubleday & Company, Inc., 1972), pp. 289–328.

issues as whether reasons are causes. And so it would seem that some versions of (RO) might be compatible with determinism and that other versions might not be. Once again, none of our present concerns depend on our giving a determinate answer to the question.

There are cases in which A rationally chooses that s but is unable to bring it about that s. A defender of (RO) must be prepared to say that so long as A's choice is rationally optimal, A is free, even if A cannot effectuate the choice. There are some important issues here concerning the extent of such cases. A defender of (RO) will want to limit the scope of such cases by invoking the notion of rationality itself. It is natural to suppose, for example, that no one can rationally choose a situation that is logically impossible, and that no one can rationally choose a situation that intrinsically requires that that person do something that he knows he cannot do. Nevertheless, we expect there to be a residuum of cases in which an agent freely chooses a rational outcome and in which the agent cannot bring about the outcome. It is incumbent on a defender of (RO) to spell out the principles that cover those sorts of cases.

The conception of freedom delineated by (RO) makes an agent's freedom *relative* with respect to the agent's reasons while at the same time the agent's freedom is *objective* with respect to the agent's reasons. (RO) is relative to A's reasons in the sense that any choice that A makes, in order to count as a free choice, must take into consideration A's own actual circumstances, obligations, relations to others, and the like. Even so, (RO) is objective in the sense that A's freedom does not hinge on *whatever* A may happen to believe or desire. In order to be free with respect to s, A must consciously realize where the weight of reason rests vis-à-vis s and choose s for that reason. An example may serve to illustrate the two features of relativity and objectivity. Suppose two people are at a party. Neither has scruples about social drinking; both in fact have found that a bit of restrained drinking has helped them in the past to overcome feelings of awkwardness and shyness in social settings. Both have abstemious spouses who can drive them home should they overindulge. But there is one crucial difference between them. He is self-employed and has no formal commitments tonight or tomorrow. She is a surgeon presently on call. Relative to the circumstances, his choosing to drink would be rationally preferable to his choosing not to drink, while her choosing to drink would definitely not be. Yet once the circumstances are fully exposed, it can be seen that his decision to drink and her decision not to drink are both objectively rational. Hence, according to the conception of freedom depicted by (RO), both choices are free.

Clause (iii) of (RO) applies to the case in which A knows that the reasons for alternative s are in equipoise with the reasons for not-s. What (iii) claims is that in such a case, the rational choice is to choose arbitrarily. In the fourth *Meditation*, Descartes frets about this circumstance: "But that indifference which I experience, when no reason urges me to one side more than to the other, is the lowest grade of liberty, and it is evidence of no perfection in it, but only a defect in intellect, or a certain negation. For if I always saw clearly what is good and true, I would never deliberate about what is to be judged or chosen, and thus, although clearly free, I could nevertheless never be indifferent."[8]

Descartes appears to believe that in reality there are no rational ties, and that to be in a state of subjective equipoise between two alternatives is to be in a cognitively deficient state, constituting the "lowest grade of liberty." Consider Buridan's ass, Brunellus. Equidistant from two equally attractive bales of hay, Brunellus has no more reason to head for one rather than the other, and so dies of starvation. What went wrong? I take it that Descartes thinks that there must be some objective features of the situation favoring one of the bales over the other, and that had Brunellus only attended to those features, he would not have starved. Let us call Descartes's view—that there never really are two alternatives that are exactly equally preferable, and that the belief that there are is based on incomplete knowledge of the situation—the "Great Chain of Value."

On Descartes's view, Brunellus starved because of cognitive imperfection; equal distances were his *pons asinorum*.[9] Suppose that I offer

[8]René Descartes, *Meditations* IV. My translation is based on the Latin text in *Oeuvres de Descartes*, ed. Charles Adam and Paul Tannery, vol. 7: *Meditationes de prima philosophia* (Paris: Leopold Cerf, 1904), p. 58. In contrast, Eleonore Stump and Norman Kretzmann assert that "the clearest instances of free choice are cases of choosing between equally good contrary alternatives" ("Absolute Simplicity," *Faith and Philosophy* 2 (1985), 353–382; the passage is on p. 366).

[9]Stump and Kretzmann seem willing to console Brunellus's donkey-shade with the observation that he died while instantiating a paradigm case of free choice. If anything, cases of choosing between equally good contrary alternatives most clearly illustrate not free choice but *random* choice. Suppose that I offer you a choice between a one- and a five-dollar bill. Barring some extraordinary stage-setting, you will gladly choose the five over the one. Your choice is not random. You have a good reason for choosing the five. It seems obvious that this kind of case is the clearest instance of free choice, a case, that is, in which one chooses between *unequally* good contrary alternatives. It may be that a choice between a good and an evil is a less clear instance of a free choice. If someone

you one or the other, not both, of two crisp, new one-dollar bills. You take one, probably not articulating to yourself the reasons why you take it rather than the other. Indeed, you may *have* no reasons to articulate. If the Great Chain of Value is true, then we might say that in the case of choosing one dollar bill over the other, you really are attending to some feature of the situation that makes it objectively preferable to pick that bill, and that your performance is a success, whereas Brunellus's performance was a failure. Alas, your success may not be a cognitive success. According to the Great Chain of Value, there is one and only one right dollar to choose. The corollary is that there is a *wrong* choice in this case, and you may have made it. But if there is a wrong choice to be made, in what could its wrongness be plausibly grounded? Conversely, if there is a right choice, in what could its rightness be grounded? Reflection on the seeming arbitrariness of any answer one tries to give provides motivation for rejecting the Great Chain of Value.

Clause (iii) of (RO) maintains that in cases of rational equipoise, an agent, if acting freely, will choose arbitrarily. Confronted with two equally attractive one-dollar bills, you could flip a coin to determine whether to take the one on the left or the one on the right. What you have done is initiate an unbiased procedure that will determine an outcome in a situation of rational equipoise.

Of course you need not have done anything as formal as flipping a coin in order to pick one of the dollars. Moreover, the coin-flipping strategy merely pushes the phenomenon of arbitrariness back one step: Why is it that heads is assigned to the dollar on the left? In the typical case you simply pick one dollar without undergoing any such procedure. Life is full of such episodes. "Pick a card, any card." You simply pick one; to go through a tedious pairwise comparison of all fifty-two cards would be a sign of psychopathology. Jacob Horner, the protagonist of John Barth's *End of the Road*, is afflicted by the inability to choose in trivial situations. The Doctor who discovers him immobilized in Baltimore's Pennsylvania Railroad Station attempts to remedy the deficiency: "Above all, act impulsively: don't let yourself get stuck between alternatives, or you're lost. You're not that strong. If the al-

---

offers me a choice between $1,000 (no strings attached) and slow torture, I may say that I was made an offer "I could not refuse." For a defender of freedom as liberty of rational optimality, there is no doubt that my choice of the $1,000 is free, and that my saying that I could not refuse it is simply a remark about the overwhelming weight of reason on one side of the choice.

ternatives are side by side, choose the one on the left; if they're con-secutive in time, choose the earlier. If neither of these applies, choose the alternative whose name begins with the earlier letter of the alpha-bet. These are the principles of Sinistrality, Antecedence, and Alpha-betical Priority—there are others, and they're arbitrary, but useful."[10] What distinguishes Horner from the normal case is that Horner must consciously internalize and invoke a set of randomizing strategies. In the normal case of apparent equipoise it is not so clear that we *invoke* a strategy—even unconsciously—as that our behavior simply *instan-tiates* some strategy or other.

Brunellus's failure is not necessarily that he failed to detect which bale was rationally preferable, as the Great Chain of Value would have it, nor even that he had not internalized either of the principles of Sinistrality or Dexterity. It may be that the most we can say about failing to choose in cases of equipose is that the behavior instantiates no strategy at all; that is, that the behavior is rationally inexplicable.

With (LI) and (LS), we noted a distinction between A's being decisive about A's not bringing it about that s and A's being decisive about whether s obtains. Something analogous can occur with (RO). A can be decisive about A's not choosing s yet not be decisive about whether s obtains. Freedom of choice does not always imply successful imple-mentation of choice, although, as I have suggested, the boundaries of tolerable exceptions are far from clear.

The most distinctive consequence of the notion of liberty of rational optimality runs contrary to intuition. Recall the case of the surgeon on call choosing not to drink. Her so choosing is free qua rationally op-timal. But had she chosen to imbibe in those circumstances, *that* choice would not have been free. In general, (RO) implies that we are unfree whenever we choose a rationally suboptimal alternative. There are maneuvers that a defender of (RO) can deploy to make this implication more palatable than it may be initially. For example, one might insist on distinguishing freedom from responsibility, claiming that there are actions for which we are responsible even though we did not perform them freely. It is clear that a burden of explanation lies on someone prepared to make that case.[11]

The distinctive differences among the three theories of freedom can

---

[10]John Barth, *The End of the Road* (New York: Bantam Books, 1969), p. 85.

[11](RO) shares *some* features of a theory put forward by Susan Wolf in "Asymmetrical Freedom," *Journal of Philosophy* 77 (1980), 151–166.

be brought out by asking of each of them what it is *not* to be free. According to (LI), *A* is unfree if, whether he knows it or not, he lacks the power to do otherwise than what he does. Unfreedom is a kind of powerlessness. If *A* decides to remain in a room when in fact he is locked in the room, then *A* may have acted *voluntarily*, but he has not acted *freely*. (Proponents of [LI] typically assume that if *A*'s actions were causally determined, then that kind of determination would render him powerless in the relevant way.) According to (LS), unfreedom is a sort of lack of fit between desire and action. *A* acts unfreely if he is doing what he does not want to do; or, on more sophisticated accounts, if *A* is doing what he does not want to do, all things considered; or if *A* is doing what he wants to do but does not want to have the want(s) that he in fact has; or if *A* is doing what he wants to do but his wants have had the wrong sorts of causal ancestry, or are now impervious to reflective revision . . . and so forth. According to (RO), unfreedom is a kind of ignorance or a kind of irrationality. *A* chooses unfreely if he lacks the relevant knowledge about his choice-situation (including, perhaps, self-knowledge). *A* may choose to do what is in fact the rational thing to do, but if he chooses for the wrong reasons, his choice is unfree. It is interesting to ask whether *A* can choose not-*s* if *A* fully realizes that the weight of reason is on the side of *s* over not-*s*. A defender of (RO) is not committed by that doctrine alone to hold that the rationally optimal course of action, when recognized, will always be chosen. Irrational factors may swamp reason on occasion. What a defender of (RO) is committed to holding is that on those occasions, the agent's choice is unfree.

It would be valuable to discuss the merits and weaknesses of these three theories more fully. A natural and healthy tendency would be to explore hybrid varieties of the theories.[12] Our present concern, however, is to see how the purer strains might apply to the case of God.

2 Of Divine Bondage

It seems straightforward enough to say that whichever theory one favors as a theory about human freedom, that theory can be applied

[12]Michael A. Slote believes that the newer versions of (LS) already incorporate rational constraints of the type embodied in (RO); see his "Understanding Free Will," *Journal of Philosophy* 77 (1980), 136–151.

to God. Moreover, on any of the theories, the way in which freedom is realized in God, it would seem, may be different from the way in which it is realized in humans, but the differences are comprehensible and entailed by the notion that God is not subject to the limitations to which humans are subject. That is, God is free in whatever way humans are claimed to be free, but, in virtue of his possessing certain divine attributes, God, unlike humans, is *maximally* free.

Thus, an agent lacks freedom construed as (LI) if the agent lacks the power to do otherwise. To lack a power, it would seem, is to lack either an ability or an opportunity (or both). But traditional theistic belief maintains that God is omnipotent and omniscient, a being able to do, roughly, anything that can be done, and knowledgeable about every situation. It is hard to see, then, how God could ever lack a genuine power to do otherwise.[13] And so, given God's omnipotence and omniscience, it appears that he is maximally free under the conception of freedom as (LI).

Versions of (LS) ascribe lack of freedom to an agent if the agent acts in frustration of his first-order desires, or first-order all-things-considered desires, or second-order desires, or if the agent's desires were induced by the wrong sorts of causal mechanisms. Once again, given God's omnipotence and omniscience, one cannot envision how one of his desires could be frustrated, or have been inculcated in a coercive or compromising way. Nothing could coerce God. It would seem that the only thing that could frustrate one of God's desires would be another of God's desires of equal or greater strength, and the frustration would have to be at the level of logical incompatibility; otherwise both desires could be satisfied. So if God had logically incompatible desires, he would have a taint of unfreedom. However, since God is omniscient, his having logically incompatible desires is not something that could escape his attention. Since God is omnipotent, he ought to be able to modify his system of desires if he detects inconsistency among them. And, one presumes, God would have an overriding higher-order desire for consistency among his desires. If all this is so, then no frustration of desires could threaten God's maximal freedom, construed as (LS).

Consider, finally, (RO). According to this conception, ignorance and irrationality are the sources of unfreedom. If God is omniscient, then

---

[13]Some philosophers have alleged that God does not have the power to change the past, and that he does not have the power to sin. I believe that properly understood, these claims, if true, do not impose any limitations on God's power.

it cannot be that he is ever unfree on account of lacking knowledge. Many theists believe that God is the *standard* of rationality; thus, that no action of his could be rationally suboptimal.[14] So if freedom is a matter of rational optimality, it follows once again that God is maximally free.

Yet it may be that other theological considerations place constraints on our speculating about God's freedom. I wish to examine the impact that three theological theses have on the attempt to characterize God's freedom along the lines indicated above. Two of the theses are familiar and indeed are implicit in the doctrines of God's omniscience and omnipotence. The third is more controversial.

An entailment of God's omniscience is that for any situation whatsoever, if that situation is the case, then God knows that that situation is the case. Nothing can escape God's ken. God's omniscience comprises more than this entailment, one presumes, but all we need at present is this entailment. Let 'K' denote a two-place relation corresponding to $\{x$ knows that $\sigma\}$,[15] where 'σ' is a variable taking situations as its values, and let 'g' be an individual constant translating 'God.' Then the first thesis, (OM), can be expressed symbolically as

$$(OM) \ (\sigma)(\sigma \to Kg\sigma).$$

An entailment of God's omnipotence, in tandem with the thesis that God has no incompatible desires, is the thesis that God's will is unimpedible. Nothing can thwart God's willing activity. Introducing 'W' to represent a two-place relation corresponding to $\{x$ wills that $\sigma\}$, we can express the thesis of the unimpedibility of God's will as

$$(UW) \ (\sigma)(Wg\sigma \to \sigma).$$

The third, more controversial thesis is an entailment of the doctrine of divine simplicity. That doctrine maintains that God has no complexity of any kind. In particular, it maintains that there is no plurality of activity in God. There is just one divine activity, which from some points of view it is appropriate to call his *knowing*, from other points of view his *willing*, from still others his *loving*, and so on. It should be

---

[14]For a discussion of this thesis, see William E. Mann, "Modality, Morality, and God," *Noûs* (forthcoming).

[15]I use braces to function analogously to Quine's quasi-quotes.

emphasized that the thesis claims that God really does know and really does will: it is just that his knowing and his willing are not two separate operations. For any situation, God's knowing that situation just is identical with God's willing that situation. The third thesis is a necessary equivalence entailed by this identity, namely,

$$(KW)\ (\sigma)(Kg\sigma \equiv Wg\sigma).$$

The identity that licenses (KW) has its attractions. I have argued elsewhere that it is an important component for steering a middle course between Platonism and Cartesian possibilism with respect to God's relation to the necessary truths, and between objectivism and subjectivism with respect to God's relation to absolute moral values.[16] Hence I am loath to give up (KW). I am equally loath to give up (OM) or to place any restrictions on what situations are values of the variable σ: I do not believe that there are any situations that are unknown to God. Moreover, for reasons sketched above, involving God's omnipotence and his complete self-knowledge, I accept (UW) in full force: whatever God wills to be the case is the case. But the conjunction of (OM), (UW), and (KW), with no restrictions placed on the range of values for 'σ', yields some surprising results.[17]

Consider (UW). If 'σ' is unrestricted in its range, then one sort of situation to which (UW) extends is a situation in which God does not will that some situation (call it 's') be the case. That is, a legitimate substituend for 'σ' might be '∼Wgs'. But if '∼Wgs' is an acceptable substituend for 'σ', then (UW) entails

$$(1)\ (Wg{\sim}Wgs \rightarrow {\sim}Wgs).$$

(OM) and (KW) jointly entail

$$(T1)\ (\sigma)(\sigma \rightarrow Wg\sigma),$$

that is, for any situation whatsoever, if that situation is the case, then God wills that it is the case. The contrapositive of (T1) is

[16]See my "Modality, Morality, and God."
[17]Much of the following material has its roots in reflections on chap. 5 of James F. Ross, *Philosophical Theology* (Indianapolis: Bobbs-Merrill, 1969), which deals not with God's freedom but with God's omnipotence. See my "Ross on Omnipotence," *International Journal for Philosophy of Religion* 8 (1977), 142–147.

$$\text{(T2) } (\sigma)(\sim Wg\sigma \rightarrow \sim\sigma),$$

which entails in particular

$$\text{(2) } (\sim Wgs \rightarrow \sim s).$$

Since '$\sim s$' is a value of 'σ', (T1) entails

$$\text{(3) } (\sim s \rightarrow Wg\sim s).$$

(2) and (3) entail

$$\text{(4) } (\sim Wgs \rightarrow Wg\sim s),$$

and (1) and (4) entail

$$\text{(5) } (Wg\sim Wgs \rightarrow Wg\sim s).$$

Since 's' was chosen arbitrarily, (4) and (5) are instances of general theses about God's willing activity, namely

$$\text{(T3) } (\sigma)(\sim Wg\sigma \rightarrow Wg\sim\sigma)$$

and

$$\text{(T4) } (\sigma)(Wg\sim Wg\sigma \rightarrow Wg\sim\sigma).$$

(T3) and T4) are noteworthy: if they are true, they indicate two ways in which God's willing is different from ours. According to (T3), God's not willing a situation to be the case entails that he wills that situation not to be the case. And (T4) says that God's willing not to will a situation to be the case entails that he wills that situation not to be the case. It is clear that such theses do not hold for us. Smith's not willing that s does not entail that Smith wills that not-s: Smith may have no attitude whatsoever toward s. Similarly, Smith's willing not to will that s does not entail that Smith wills that not-*s*: Smith may not care one way or the other.[18]

Since (T3) and (T4) are perfectly general with respect to situations, we can construct from them theses dealing with negations. Replacing 'σ' with '$\sim\sigma$' and deleting double negations, we get

$$(T5) \quad (\sigma)(\sim Wg\sim\sigma \rightarrow Wg\sigma)$$

and

$$(T6) \quad (\sigma)(Wg\sim Wg\sim\sigma \rightarrow Wg\sigma).$$

By (T5), if God does not will that a situation not be the case, then he wills that it be the case, and by (T6), if God wills that he not will that a situation not be the case, then he wills that it be the case. Once again it is clear that theses like (T5) and (T6) do not hold for us.

(T4) and (T6) indicate that certain kinds of second-order willing in the case of God boil down to first-order willing. But in fact, given (OM), (UW), and (KW), it is easy to show that (T4) and (T6) can be strengthened into biconditionals:

$$(T7) \quad (\sigma)(Wg\sim Wg\sigma \equiv Wg\sim\sigma)$$
$$(T8) \quad (\sigma)(Wg\sim Wg\sim\sigma \equiv Wg\sigma)$$

Moreover, given (OM), (UW), and (KW), we can establish the following two results:

$$(T9) \quad (\sigma)(WgWg\sigma \equiv Wg\sigma)$$

[18](KW) allows us to construct epistemic analogues to theses (T3) and (T4):

$$(T3K) \quad (\sigma)(\sim Kg\sigma \rightarrow Kg\sim\sigma),$$

if God does not know that a situation is the case, then he knows that it is not the case, and

$$(T4K) \quad (\sigma)(Kg\sim Kg\sigma \rightarrow Kg\sim\sigma),$$

if God knows that he does not know that a situation is the case, then he knows that it is not the case. Analogues of (T3K) and (T4K) do not hold of us, but it should not be surprising that they hold of a genuinely omniscient being.

$$(T10)\ (\sigma)(\sim WgWg\sigma \equiv Wg\sim\sigma)^{19}$$

In light of these four biconditional theses, we seem to be able to say either that all cases of iterated willing on God's part boil down to cases of first-order willing, or that all cases of first-order willing steam up into cases of higher-order willing. These results are just what a defender of the doctrine of divine simplicity would expect. God's willing to will that s is *equivalent* to God's willing that s, according to the simplicist's interpretation of (T9), because God's activity of willing to will is *identical* with his activity of willing.

Theses (T1)–(T10) are thus the spawn of (OM), (UW), and (KW). Now let us see what effect the theses have on an attempt to extend the three theories of human freedom to God.

When we examined (LI), we noted that it might be that an agent, A, is decisive about A's not bringing it about that s but not decisive about whether s obtains. A may thus freely refrain from bringing it about that s even though s obtains through some independent agency. But if (OM), (UW), and (KW) are true, then this distinction cannot characterize God. It is natural to suppose that for God to refrain from bringing about s is for God not to will that s, that is, for '$\sim Wgs$' to be true. But in that case, (T3), which is itself entailed by (OM) and (KW), entails that '$Wg\sim s$' is true. And (UW) in turn entails that '$\sim s$' is true. So it is logically impossible, given (OM), (UW), and (KW), for '$\sim Wgs$' and 's' to be simultaneously true. Put in English, what we have just seen is that God's refraining from bringing about s formally entails God's bringing about not-s.

Analogous results follow for (LS) and for (RO). A defender of (LS) cannot make room, when A is God, for a consistent distinction between A's being decisive about A's not bringing it about that s and A's not being decisive about s. As we have just seen, the distinction cannot be between God's not willing that s and s's obtaining anyway. It is tempting to apply one of the insights of sophisticated versions of (LS) and

---

[19]Here are the four epistemic versions of (T7)–(T10):

> (T7K) $(\sigma)(Kg\sim Kg\sigma \equiv Kg\sim\sigma)$
> (T8K) $(\sigma)(Kg\sim Kg\sim\sigma \equiv Kg\sigma)$
> (T9K) $(\sigma)(KgKg\sigma \equiv Kg\sigma)$
> (T10K) $(\sigma)(\sim KgKg\sigma \equiv Kg\sim\sigma)$

(T9K) applies the controversial "KK thesis" of epistemic logic—if one knows, then one knows that one knows—to God. If the thesis is true of anyone, it should be true of an omniscient being.

appeal to a higher-order act of willing to represent God's being decisive about his not bringing it about that s. The construction that comes to mind is '$Wg \sim Wgs$', God wills that he not will that s. But given (T4), that construction collapses into '$Wg \sim s$', which, in virtue of (UW), entails '$\sim s$'. Once again the distinction cannot be consistently made in the case of God.

If we make the reasonable assumption that God's choosing is God's willing, then we find that the same result holds for (RO). God's not choosing (not willing) s is tantamount to God's choosing not-s, by (T3).

If we accept (OM), (UW), and (KW), then we cannot on any of our three theories of freedom distinguish in God's case between his being decisive about his not bringing it about that s and his not being decisive about whether s obtains. To put it in other terms, the way in which freedom is realized in an omniscient, unimpedibly omnipotent being, in whom knowing and willing are necessarily identical, entails that that being is decisive with respect to every situation.

Recall that the way in which maximal knowledgeability, omniscience, is realized in God may preclude his undergoing such human phenomena as learning. It is implausible to think that that kind of alleged difference constrains God's knowledge in any way. To say that God knows everything without learning anything amounts to saying that whatever there is to be known is known already by God. The alleged differences in the way in which knowledgeability is realized in God as opposed to humans seem to be benign: they do not appear to conflict with God's being omniscient or with anything else theists typically want to affirm.[20] Can we say that the same is true about the way in which freedom is realized in God? Is God's being decisive about every situation a benign consequence of the way in which maximal freedom is realized in him?

There are three troublesome objections here, all of which devolve from what might be called, to preempt a term of abuse, the Problem of God's Ubiquitous Meddlesomeness. The first is that God's being universally decisive compromises, ironically, his claim to maximal freedom. For there is one sort of thing God is not free to do that I am free to do—forbear from being decisive about a situation. From the theses we have canvased, it follows that '$(\sim Wgs \ \& \ \sim Wg \sim s)$' entails '$(s \ \& \ \sim s)$' and that '$(Wg \sim Wgs \ \& \ Wg \sim Wg \sim s)$' entails '$(s \ \& \ \sim s)$'. God is, so to

---

[20]Although I cannot argue the case here, I do not think that God's not having to learn about any situation poses a threat to human freedom.

speak, condemned to be free. It is not at all clear that this consequence is benign.

The second objection is tied to the first. If God cannot forbear from being decisive about every situation, then there is no room for the exercise of genuine freedom in his creatures. Consider your choosing to read this essay. It is a situation that God unimpedibly willed, and given that he did, you could not have chosen not to read it. Of course he could have unimpedibly willed that you not choose to read this paper, but in that case, you could not have chosen to read it. In either case you cannot be free.[21]

The third objection comes hard on the heels of the second. If every situation is a product of God's unimpedible will, then God is causally responsible for sinful actions. It is not just that God passively allows humans freely to sin. It is rather than he unimpedibly wills those situations which consist in human sin. Suppose that Jones hypnotizes Smith so effectively that Smith, not aware that the suggestion was planted by Jones, murders Johnson. Whatever we want to say about Smith's responsibility for the murder, we certainly want to impute blame to Jones. Smith, we may even think, was merely a helpless instrument of Jones's nefarious activity. Now on the view of the nature and extent of God's willing activity that has emerged above, God is like Jones, only more so. But this result belies the theistic claims that God does no evil and causes no one else to do evil.

One remedy for the Problem of God's Ubiquitous Meddlesomeness is to reject one or more of the theses that generate the problem. Another remedy is to assert that the problem is not as bad as it seems.

3 Free at Last

The first objection that defines the Problem of God's Ubiquitous Meddlesomeness maintains that on a view that accepts (OM), (UW), and

[21]Nelson Pike has made a beguiling case for saying that God's omnipotence is compatible with human freedom if we understand God's omnipotence to involve "over-power." But for God to have over-power with respect to a situation just is for him to be able to forbear from being decisive about its obtaining or not obtaining. Thus the theses that we have uncovered about God's freedom knock the props out from under the structure Pike designed to preserve human freedom from God's omnipotence. See Nelson Pike, "Over-Power and God's Responsibility for Sin," in *The Existence and Nature of God*, ed. Alfred J. Freddoso (Notre Dame: University of Notre Dame Press, 1983), pp. 11–35.

(KW), God cannot forbear from being decisive about s; therefore, God is not maximally free. The proper response to the objection is to grant the premise but to deny that the conclusion follows from it. 'God cannot forbear from being decisive about s' has a *de re* and a *de dicto* reading:

> God's nature is such that he does not have the ability to forbear from being decisive about s.

> The proposition that God forbears from being decisive about s is necessarily false.

Both readings will pass muster for a theist who maintains that God is necessarily sovereign and that the notion of God's necessary sovereignty entails that no situation escapes God's determination. When we noticed that God cannot forbear from being decisive about s, what we noticed, in effect, was that '($\sim Wgs$ & $\sim Wg\sim s$)' cannot possibly be true. It follows then that '(Wgs v $Wg\sim s$)' must be true. In general we have

$$(T11)\ (\sigma)(Wg\sigma\ v\ Wg\sim\sigma).^{22}$$

(T11) adds nothing to what we already had; (T11) is formally equivalent to (T3). But (T11) gives us a vivid depiction of the ubiquity of God's sovereignty.[23] Moreover, (T11) allows a theist to explain that what was alleged to be a lack of an ability on God's part is more accurately described as a lack of a limitation. God's "inability" to forbear from being decisive about s is thus akin to God's "inability" to bring about his own nonexistence. Just as the latter is a consequence of God's necessary existence, so is the former a consequence of his necessary sovereignty.

But if necessary sovereignty entails lack of forbearance on God's part, then necessary sovereignty eliminates human freedom, according to the second objection contained in the Problem of God's Ubiquitous Meddlesomeness. If God is decisive about every situation, then there are no situations about which humans can be genuinely decisive.

---

[22]Compare (T11) with

$$(T11K)\ (\sigma)(Kg\sigma\ v\ Kg\sim\sigma).$$

[23]Although I shall not defend the position here, we should understand (T11) as extending to necessary truths (including necessary truths about God) and absolute moral values. See my "Modality, Morality, and God" for an account of how God is responsible for them all.

At the heart of the second objection is the concern that if God is decisive about all situations, then we are powerless in two ways: God's unimpedible will to bring about *s* supplies all the power *needed* to bring about *s*, and God's decisiveness about *s* precludes us from having the power to bring about any situation contrary to *s*. The first point is that God's will seems to render any power that we might have otiose or epiphenomenal. The second point is especially troubling for a defender of (LI). If *A* brings it about that *s*, then *A*'s having been free with respect to *s* requires that *A* had it in his power to refrain from bringing it about that *s*. But if God unimpedibly willed that *s*, and, for that matter, unimpedibly willed that *A* bring it about that *s*, then *A* did not have it in his power to refrain from bringing it about that *s*; thus, for a defender of (LI), *A* did not bring about *s* freely.

Suppose that Smith is contemplating two different ways of building his house. He is sufficiently skilled in carpentry, masonry, plumbing, and wiring to build it himself; or he can engage the services of a contractor, Jones, to do it for him. If Smith chooses to build the house himself, then we can say, in stilted terminology, that Smith brings it about that Smith's house is built. If Smith decides to have Jones build his house, then we can say that Smith brings it about that Jones brings it about that Smith's house is built. The second case illustrates two general principles. If *B* is a two-place relation corresponding to {*x* brings it about that σ}, then bringing-about is *transitive*,

$$\text{(TB)} \quad (x)(y)(\sigma)(BxBy\sigma \rightarrow Bx\sigma).$$

So, for example, if Smith brings it about that Jones brings it about that Smith's house is built, then Smith brings it about that Smith's house is built. Moreover, cases of iterated bringings-about preserve the *efficacy of the proximate agent*,

$$\text{(EP)} \quad (x)(y)(\sigma)(BxBy\sigma \rightarrow By\sigma),$$

so that if Smith brings it about that Jones brings it about that Smith's house is built, then Jones brings it about that Smith's house is built.[24]

Here is the picture that emerges. When Smith hires Jones to build Smith's house, the bringing-about of Smith's house is, if you will, a

---

[24](TB) and (EP) are standard theorems in the logic of action. See Ingmar Pörn, *The Logic of Power* (Oxford: Basil Blackwell, 1971), p. 14.

joint venture. Both of them bring it about that Smith's house is built. Of course the way in which Smith brings it about differs from the way in which Jones brings it about. Jones "does all the work," but it is the contractual activity of Smith that authorizes Jones's work and makes the work count as building Smith's house. In the circumstances described, Smith could have been the proximate agent of his house's being built, but chose instead that Jones be the proximate agent. Smith thus differs from many of us, for whom the only way we could bring it about that our houses are built is by having someone else build them. There are, in other words, some situations which some of us can only bring about indirectly, through the agency of someone (or something) else.

You may have anticipated the moral of the story. God's willing a situation just is his bringing about that situation, and so we have the following necessary biconditional:

$$(\text{WB}) \ (\sigma)(Wg\sigma \equiv Bg\sigma).$$

By partial substitution of equivalents, (WB) sanctions versions of (TB) and (EP) that pertain to God:

$$(\text{TB}') \ (y)(\sigma)(WgByσ \rightarrow Bg\sigma).$$

$$(\text{EP}') \ (y)(\sigma)(WgByσ \rightarrow By\sigma).$$

On the view we have been investigating, every situation that obtains obtains because it is willed by God, whose unimpedible willing is his unimpedible bringing-about. Yet some situations obtain because they are genuinely brought about by humans. Those situations are joint ventures between God and humans. God's willing them is sufficient to bring them about, but it does not follow that the humans who bring them about are thereby rendered inert by God's will, any more than Jones's activity is rendered ineffectual by Smith's bringing it about that Jones builds Smith's house. If you bring it about that s, then God brings it about that s *and* brings it about that you bring it about that s. Perhaps for any situation that we bring about, God could have brought about that situation directly, without our participating, as Smith could have built his own house without Jones's aid. Perhaps not.[25] Even if he can, the point remains that if God brings it about that you bring it about that s, then God brings it about that *you* bring s about, and not even God can do *that* without your bringing about s.

If the unimpedibility and ubiquity of God's will are compatible with humans' having the power genuinely to act, they might nevertheless be incompatible with humans' having the power genuinely to act otherwise. This is the second point of the second objection. If you freely brought it about that s, à la (LI), then you must have had the power, at the appropriate time, to refrain from bringing it about that s. But if, at that time, God unimpedibly willed that s and that you bring it about that s, as he surely did, then you did not have it in your power to refrain from bringing it about that s.

The second premise is the culprit. You had the power to refrain from bringing it about that s if and only if God willed that you had the power to refrain, according to a view that endorses (OM), (UW), and (KW). There is nothing contradictory in the notion of God's willing both that you bring it about that s and that you have the power to refrain from bringing it about that s. What follows, if he does will both situations, is that you do not exercise your power to refrain. It does *not* follow that you *cannot* exercise your power to refrain. Let us inspect the logic of the situation more closely. Suppose that the following propositions are true.

[25]The sixty-third proposition condemned by bishop Stephen Tempier in the Condemnation of 1277 was "*quod Deus non potest in effectum cause secundarie sine ipsa causa secundaria*," that God cannot bring about an effect of a secondary cause without the secondary cause itself (*Chartularium Universitatis Parisiensis*, ed. Henricus Denifle and Aemilio Chatelain, vol. 1 [Paris: Delalain, 1889], pp. 543–555; proposition 63 is on p. 547). The good bishop seems to have been unaware that the proposition has a compound sense and a divided sense. *In sensu composito* the proposition is

God cannot bring it about that there is an effect of a secondary cause which is not an effect of that secondary cause,

which is not the proposition the bishop set out to condemn: the Condemnation insists on the omnipotence of God, but does not extend omnipotence to include the ability to do the logically impossible. The offender is the original proposition interpreted *in sensu diviso*:

There is an effect of a secondary cause which is such that God cannot bring it about without that secondary cause.

The second interpretation raises some interesting questions about God's omnipotence and the so-called necessity of origins. Can God make a genuine Chippendale chair without bringing it about that Thomas Chippendale makes the chair? Is a chair qualitatively identical to a chair made by Thomas Chippendale itself a Chippendale chair?

(6) God unimpedibly wills that you bring it about that *s*.

(7) God unimpedibly wills that you have the power to refrain from bringing it about that *s*.

(6) and (7) imply, among other things,

(8) You bring it about that *s*

and

(9) You do not exercise the power you have to refrain from bringing it about that *s*.

(6) and (7) do *not* imply

(8') Necessarily, you bring it about that *s*,

or

(9') Necessarily, you do not exercise the power you have to refrain from bringing it about that *s*.

(8') and (9') would be implied by

(6') Necessarily, God unimpedibly wills that you bring it about that *s*

and

(7') Necessarily, God unimpedibly wills that you have the power to refrain from bringing it about that *s*,

eked out with necessary truths to the effect that if God unimpedibly wills a situation, that situation obtains, and that if you bring about a situation when you have the power to refrain, then you do not at that time exercise your power to refrain. But it would take extremely powerful arguments to force us to accept propositions as strong as (6') and (7').

The traditional problem of evil is a problem of understanding how a perfectly good, all-knowing, all-powerful God can allow the existence of evil in his domain. The problem—more accurately, the family of problems—is the most severe test of the enterprise of philosophical theology and of religious belief. As it surfaces from the theses we have been examining, the problem can only appear to be even worse. The most monstrous deeds in the history of humankind will all have been joint ventures between God and human perpetrators, and so we must ask not why God *passively allows* evil to exist but rather why he *actively wills* evil to exist, brings evil about, is a willing conspirer in the evil-doer's activity.

I cannot offer a theodicy on behalf of the view developed in this essay. I can do something considerably more modest, namely, argue that the view fares no worse on the problem of evil than other views that maintain that God only allows evil to exist, and suggest the direction that I think an adequate theodicy must take.

Consider yet another earthly analogy. Smith intentionally supplies Jones with the weapon, the training, and the opportunity to kill a healthy, blameless Johnson. It is clear that if Jones is successful, Smith is at least as morally accountable for Johnson's death as Jones is. Now let us change the case. Smith has not supplied Jones with any assistance. But Smith is in the same room with Jones, watching Jones prepare to kill Johnson. Smith knows that unless, he, Smith, intervenes, Jones will be successful. Smith has it in his power to intervene so subtly and effortlessly that Jones will not even realize that it is Smith who has thwarted his plans. Smith elects not to intervene, allowing Jones to kill Johnson. Is Smith any the less morally accountable in this case than in the first case? Notice that the question is not about causal responsibility but moral accountability. Suppose that Johnson's survivors become informed of the power that Smith had but did not exercise. They are entitled, it seems to me, to regard Smith with the same moral outrage that they may hold for Jones. Philosophers have vigorously disagreed about whether there is a significant moral difference (and not simply a causal difference) between killing and letting die. That difference is not the one exemplified in our two cases, however: What they illustrate is a distinction between killing and allowing to be killed.

In the case of God especially, a being who is perfectly good, all-knowing, all-powerful, and against whom no other being can prevail, there is no plausible moral difference between his actively bringing about a situation that is evil and his passively allowing a situation that is evil to be brought about. We sometimes excuse human agents for not intervening when they might have because we think that the cost of intervention to them would have been inordinately high. We sometimes loathe and sometimes pity those who fail to intervene because of their stupidity, cowardice, venality, callousness, or other sorts of character flaws. But we do not suppose that God has or could have any of those human liabilities. And so God's passively allowing a situation that is evil to be brought about is on a par, morally speaking, with his actively bringing about that situation. The distinction between passivity and activity does no moral work in the case of God.

This conclusion meshes with (although it is not entailed by) the metaphysical result that there is no difference between God's not bringing it about that s and God's bringing it about that not-s. Independent of that, the conclusion has the bracing effect—as one says when one tries to make a virtue of necessity—of forcing theists to face the problem of evil in its starkest form. Saying that God actively brings about evil situations makes matters no worse for the prospect of theodicy than does saying that God passively allows evil situations to be brought about. The question now is just how bad that makes matters for the prospect of theodicy.

I want to argue that the claim that God brings about situations that are evil does not imply that God *does* evil; thus, that the claim is compatible with the doctrines that God is morally perfect and impeccable. It will help to consider what seems to be the hardest kind of case for my contention. Under what circumstances, if any, are all the elements of the following scenario true?

(1) A knowingly and willingly brings it about that B knowingly and willingly brings it about that s.

(2) A knowingly and willingly brings it about that s (From [1] by [TB]).

(3) S is a situation that is evil.

(4) In knowingly and willingly bringing it about that s, B does something that is wrong.

(5) In knowingly and willingly bringing it about that s, A does not do anything that is wrong.

What we are seeking is not an *excuse* for A's action but a *justification* for it. To excuse an agent's action is to acknowledge that although what the agent did was wrong, the agent should not be blamed or punished for it, or should only be blamed or punished to a diminished degree. Some of the sorts of considerations offered as excuses—for example, factual ignorance and duress—do not apply here, since we are supposing that A acts knowingly and willingly. Other sorts, such as physical weakness and mental abnormality, do not apply in the case in which A is God. In any event, what is wanted is not something that presupposes that what A did was wrong, but rather that, appearances to the contrary notwithstanding, what he did was not wrong.

There are at least two ways in which A's action might be insulated from a charge of wrongdoing. It might be that A's intentions, purposes, and goals justify his action. Or it might be that A enjoys a special status or plays a special role that makes his action "privileged." Let us put together a case that combines both features.

If John's parents do not prevent him, he will break his sister Mary's favorite toy, because she heedlessly broke one of his favorite toys. By deciding not to restrain John, John's parents bring it about that he brings it about that Mary's toy is broken; thus, they bring it about that Mary's toy is broken. What John does is wrong. What John's parents do is not wrong, even though they bring about what John brings about, namely, that Mary's toy is broken. How can that be? The wrongness of John's action (in distinction from the badness of the situation that is the action's result) lies in the intention or motive with which John commits the action. John acts in retaliatory rage, with the intention of inflicting suffering on Mary. In contrast, John's parents act out of love for their children, with the intention of using the episode to illustrate vividly to John and Mary the futility of pursuing a policy of tit for tat. They believe that only by allowing John to act out his rage will he come to feel, through seeing Mary suffer, the bitter emptiness of his action. They believe that Mary will learn to be more careful with things that are not hers. They hope that each child's witnessing the suffering so easily inflicted on the other—and so easily inflicted *by* the other—will strengthen, not weaken, the children's empathy and the bonds of sibling affection. Because they are the children's parents, they occupy a special moral status that confers on them a network of rights, duties, liberties, and immunities with respect to the children. Suppose a casual friend had been present instead of the parents, with the same beliefs and hopes that the parents did in fact have. It is not obvious that the friend's decision not to restrain John is above moral reproach. The friend's action smacks of presumption, of arrogating to himself a course of action that may only rightly be followed by the parents.

The example portrays a way in which items (1)–(5) can all be true. Moreover, it suggests two strategies for dealing with the problem of evil that are available to a theist attracted to the doctrines contained in this essay. God's plans for us are not transparent: now we see through a glass darkly. It is not immediately obvious to Mary why her parents endorsed John's breaking her toy. But if Mary's moral growth can only proceed by means of this or similar sorts of experiences, then the point of her parents' action can only be clear to Mary after she has become what they had hoped she would become. So it may be that God can bring about certain kinds of moral and spiritual growth in us only by confronting us with genuine evils. And it may be that the point of his activity can become clear to us only as a result of our facing the travails. Furthermore, God's relation to us as loving Creator invests in him, we may suppose, certain rights and responsibilities, privileges and immunities, that may be reflected with some accuracy in some of the aspects of the human relations of parent to child, lawgiver to subject, judge to judged. Mary would be entitled to complain about the family friend's decision not to restrain John, but perhaps not about her parents' identical decision. We would be guilty of overlooking the unique moral position that God occupies if we thought without further argument that anything God does to us is on a par, morally speaking, with anything a stranger might do to us. This observation cuts two ways. Things impermissible for a stranger to do to us may be permissible for God, but God may also have responsibilities to us that no stranger does.[26]

These remarks scarcely begin the task of theodicy. It would be foolhardy to assume that the two strategies will handle adequately all legitimate questions about God's justice. My purpose has not been to argue that the two strategies are adequate or complete, but only to show how the project of theodicy can get off the ground within the framework of assumptions made in this essay.

To recapitulate, the assumptions are that God is omniscient, that God's will is unimpedible, and that in God there is no real distinction between knowing and willing. The three theories of freedom coalesce in the case of God. Qua omnipotent, God enjoys maximally realized liberty of indifference. Qua sovereign, he enjoys maximally realized liberty of spontaneity. Qua supremely rational, he enjoys maximally realized liberty of rational optimality. One may take a methodological moral from this peaceful coexistence. There is nothing about the three theories themselves that makes them incompatible with each other:

---

[26]This sort of possibility is compatible with ethical absolutism and with the thesis that God has no obligations to his creatures.

one being exemplifies them all. The good news is that that fact might encourage us to try to construct hybrid versions of the theories. The bad news is that their simultaneous realization in God may depend essentially on his being a being in whom knowing and willing are not two things. Human psyches do not enjoy such integration.[27]

[27]An earlier version of this essay benefited from the critical comments of Hilary Kornblith and Derk Pereboom.

7

The Place of Chance in a World Sustained by God

Peter van Inwagen

In this paper, I want to examine a number of interrelated issues in what might be called the metaphysics of divine action: creation, sustenance, law, miracle, providence, and chance. Thus my title is rather narrow for the topics considered. But it is the topic *chance* that I shall be working toward. My discussion of these other topics is a prolegomenon to my discussion of chance. (My discussion of chance, is, in its turn, a prolegomenon to a discussion of the problem of evil; but that is a topic for another time. In the present essay I shall lay out some implications of what I say about chance for the problem of evil, but I shall not directly discuss this problem, much less suggest a solution to it.)

I will begin with a discussion of God's relation to a certain object that might variously be called "the world," "the universe," "Creation," "the cosmos," or "nature." It is necessary for us to have a picture of this thing. I will provide a picture that is scientifically naive and philosophically tendentious: the world consists of a certain number of small, indivisible units of matter I shall call "elementary particles"; there is only one type of particle, and there are always just the same particles, and they are in constant motion in otherwise empty infinite three-dimensional space ("the void").

This picture could be called a Newtonian picture, although I don't insist on the absolute space or the "absolute, true, and mathematical time" of Newton. It is, as I have said, from a scientific point of view, a naive picture. But if it were replaced with the sort of physical world picture provided by quantum field theories like quantum electrodynamics and quantum chromodynamics, I do not think that this replacement would affect in any essential way the philosophical points I want to make. I therefore retain the naive picture—not that I am equipped to carry on the discussion in the terms provided by any other picture.

The picture is philosophically tendentious. It presupposes that the created world is entirely material. But that could easily enough be changed. Anyone who wants to suppose that the created world contains, for example, Cartesian egos, may simply reject my assumption that the elementary particles are all indivisible units of matter, and assume that some of them are nonspatial and are capable of thought.[1] (A similar device could accommodate angels conceived as St. Thomas Aquinas conceives angels.) The generalizations I shall make about "elementary particles" in the sequel do not in any *essential* way presuppose that elementary particles are spatial, nonthinking things. And the generalizations I shall make about created persons do not in any essential way presuppose that no created person is a Cartesian ego.

Having given this naive and tendentious picture of the world or nature, I relate it—in a burst of simplistic picture-thinking—to God in the following way.

God created the world by bringing certain elementary particles into existence at some particular moment—six thousand years ago or twenty billion years ago or some such figure. These particles were at the moment of their creation suspended in the void—which is sheer emptiness, and not a physical object like the modern spacetime or the modern quantum vacuum—and possessed of certain initial velocities. Each, moreover, possessed certain causal powers; that is, each possessed a certain intrinsic capacity to affect the motions of other particles.

Now these particles were (and are) not capable of maintaining themselves in existence or of conserving their own causal powers. For one of them to continue to exist, it is necessary for God contin-

---

[1]Unless this philosopher accepts the Platonic doctrine of the preexistence of the soul (as well as its immortality), he will also want to reject my assumption that there are always the same elementary particles.

uously to hold it in existence. For it to have the same set of causal powers—the same set of capacities to affect the motions of other particles—at a series of instants, it is necessary for God at each instant to supply it with that set of causal powers. For that matter, for a particle to have *different* sets of causal powers at two or more instants is for that particle to be supplied with different sets of powers at those instants. To say that God once created, and now sustains, the *world* is to say no more than this: that God once created and now sustains certain particles—for the world, or nature, or the cosmos, or the universe, is nothing more than the sum of these particles. Moreover, every individual created thing is the sum of certain of these particles, and the point that was made about the created universe as a whole can be made about each individual created thing. If, for example, God sustains a bridge in existence and preserves its causal powers—its capacity to bear a ten-ton load, for example—this action is just the sum of all the actions He performs in sustaining in existence and preserving the causal powers of the elementary particles that are the ultimate constituents of the bridge; the powers, that is, by which they so affect one another as to continue to form a configuration that exhibits a certain degree of stability.

And this is the entire extent of God's causal relations with the created world. He does not, for example, *move* particles—or not in any very straightforward sense. Rather, the particles move one another, albeit their capacity to do so is continuously supplied by God. Here is an analogy. Suppose that two pieces of soft iron are wound round with wires and a current passed through the wires. The two pieces of iron then become electromagnets, and, if they are close to one another and free to move, they begin to move in virtue of the forces they are exerting upon each other. It would be odd to say that the generator that is supplying the current to the wires was moving the two pieces of iron. It is more natural to say that the generator is moving only electrons, and that the pieces of iron are *moving each other*, this movement being a function of their relative dispositions and the causal powers that are (in a sense) being supplied to them by the generator.

This is everything I want to say about the way in which God acts in and sustains the created world—with one omission. We have not yet raised the question whether the causal powers of a given particle are constant over time. Let us suppose that this is at least very nearly true:

Each particle always, or almost always, has the same causal powers.[2] That is, God always, or almost always, supplies it with the same set of causal powers. Now we have assumed, for the sake of convenience, that there is only one type of elementary particle. It seems reasonable to suppose that causal powers are the only relevant factor in classifying elementary particles into "types." It would follow that the causal powers possessed by a given particle at a given time are almost certainly identical with the causal powers possessed by any other particle at any other time. (This picture of God's action in the world has an interesting consequence. Consider again the example of God's sustaining a bridge in existence and preserving its causal powers. The particles that compose the bridge would have existed even if the bridge had not, since there are always the same particles, and—almost certainly—they would have had the same causal powers. It follows that what God does in sustaining the bridge in existence and preserving its causal powers is something He would have done even if the bridge had never existed, although, in that case, this action would not have fallen under the description "sustaining the bridge in existence and preserving its causal powers.")

Now suppose that God occasionally (and only momentarily) supplied a few particles with causal powers different from their normal powers. Such an action would cause a certain part of the natural world to diverge from the course that part of the world would have taken if He had continued to supply the particles in that part of the world with the usual complement of causal powers. Such a divergence would, presumably, spread—with decreasing amplitude—till it encompassed the entire universe. The early stages of such a divergence we shall call a *miracle*. For example, imagine that God momentarily supplies unusual

[2]This note is addressed to those who believe that there are created rational immaterial beings. It was suggested in the text that anyone who believed in such creatures could accept most of what I say if he rejected my assumption that all "particles" were material, and assumed that some "particles" were immaterial and rational. If anyone avails himself of this suggestion, he must take care to except thinking, immaterial "particles" from the generalizations about particles that are made in the following discussion of the metaphysics of miracles, since it would seem obvious that, e.g., a Cartesian ego's causal powers will hardly ever be constant over time. Such a being's causal powers will vary with time (if for no other reason) because its internal representations of its circumstances will vary. If I took Cartesianism seriously, I would try to elaborate the model of the created world presented herein to provide a more comfortable niche for immaterial human minds; but I don't and I won't. As for angels, while I take them seriously, I know nothing of their metaphysical nature and thus have no idea of what sort of elaboration of the model would be needed to provide a more comfortable niche for them.

causal powers to the particles composing the water in a certain pot, in such a way that those particles (in virtue of their momentarily abnormal effects on one another) follow trajectories through the void that they would not normally have followed, and that, as a consequence, they rearrange themselves into the configuration we call "wine"—at which moment God reverts to His usual policy and continues to supply each of the particles with its normal causal powers.[3]

I like this account of miracles better than either of the two alternative accounts I know of. On one account, a miracle is an "intervention" into the course of nature by God. But the word 'intervention' seems to imply that nature has some sort of native power, independent of God's, and that in working a miracle, God has, as it were, to *overpower* some part of nature. No theist can accept such a picture of the relation of God to nature; this account of miracles provides a better description of what the deist says God *doesn't* do than of what the theist says God *does* do.[4]

---

[3]This definition of *miracle* is tailored to fit our account of the created world and its relation to God, an account that is in many respects too simple to be satisfactory. If the account were elaborated, our definition of *miracle* might have to be modified. For example, we have assumed, for the sake of simplicity, that there are always just the same particles. If we were to assume instead that God sometimes—but very rarely—annihilated particles, or created particles *ex nihilo* subsequently to the first, great Creation, then we should want to count as miracles the initial stages of the divergences occasioned by such actions from what would have otherwise been the course of events.

If we were to assume that God sometimes moved particles otherwise than by supplying them and neighboring particles with abnormal causal powers—that He sometimes moved particles "directly"—such episodes, too, should be counted as miracles. (It is not entirely clear to me, however, that the alleged distinction between God's moving particles "directly" and "indirectly" is ultimately intelligible. To adapt a remark of Frege's, sometimes I seem to see a distinction, and then again I *don't* see it.)

[4]When this paper was read to the Society of Christian Philosophers, the commentator charged the author with deism. (Talk about *odium theologicum!*) In this he claimed to be following medieval Latin authority: The position I propound, that alterations in the created world are not directly caused by God, "is stigmatized as (in effect) a form of *deism* by almost every important medieval Christian philosopher." Well, it would have to be "in effect," since the words *deista* and *deismus* occur in no medieval manuscript—or if they do, this is not known to the editors of the Oxford English Dictionary, who derive the French *déiste* directly from *deus*. Since 'deist' (when used in a dyslogistic sense; it has sometimes been used to mean 'theist') has never meant anything but "person who believes in a Creator on the basis of reason alone, and who denies revelation, miracles, Providence, and immanence," "in effect" cashes out to this: Someone who denies that God directly causes alterations in the created world denies God's immanence. But a God who continuously sustains all things in existence and continuously conserves their causal powers is immanent enough for me. In such a God, "we live and move and have our being" (Acts 17:28); "in him all things hold together" (Col. 1:17). (I hold, moreover, that no created thing *could possibly* exist at a given moment unless it were at

According to the second alternative account, a miracle occurs when God causes an event that is a "violation of the laws of nature." I like this alternative better than the other, but I have a rather technical objection to it. Let us call a contingent proposition a *law of nature* if it would be true if God *always* supplied the elementary particles with their normal causal powers, and would, moreover, be true under any conditions whatever that were consistent with this stipulation. For those who are familiar with the philosophical use of the concept of "possible worlds," here is a more precise definition: A proposition is a law of nature in a possible world *w* if it is a con-

---

that moment held in existence by God; and no created thing *could possibly* have causal powers at a given moment unless it were at that moment supplied with those powers by God.)

The alternatives to this position are occasionalism and concurrentism. Occasionalism is one of those high-minded philosophical depreciations of God's works that come disguised as compliments to God's person. As, for example, Docetism devalues the Incarnation, occasionalism devalues the Creation. What God has made and now sustains is substance, not shadow. Concurrentism is the doctrine that God must cooperate with a created thing in order for that thing to act on another thing. I find this doctrine hard to understand. Does it credit created things with the power to produce effects or does it not? In the former case, why is God's cooperation needed to produce the effect? In the latter case, Creation is devalued.

The commentator also endorsed a curious medieval argument that is supposed to show that a certain sort of miracle requires either occasionalism or concurrentism. Consider the three young men in the fiery furnace. If fire and flesh really had intrinsic causal powers, powers that could be exercised without God's cooperation (the argument runs), then God could have preserved the three young men only by altering the powers, and hence the natures, of the fire or the flesh—in which case they would not have *been* fire or flesh. There seems to me to be little to this argument. The causal influence of the fire would have had to pass from one place to another to affect the flesh, and God could miraculously block this influence at some intermediate point in space without in any way altering the fire or the flesh. Interestingly enough, in the apocryphal "Song of Azariah in the Furnace" (which the Jerusalem Bible inserts between Daniel 3:23 and the Song of the Three Children), just this line is taken: "But the angel of the Lord came down into the furnace [and] drove the flames of the fire outward, and fanned in to them, in the heart of the furnace, a coolness such as wind or dew will bring, so that the fire did not even touch them or cause them any pain or distress." The commentator does consider this sort of possibility, but suggests that it represents God as engaging in an unseemly struggle with a creature; "resisting the power of the fire," as he puts it. Similarly, I suppose one might argue that God would not, whatever the Psalmist might say, send His angels to support one, lest one dash one's foot against a stone. That would be "resisting" the power of the stone or of gravity or something. Such mindedness is too wonderful for me; it is high, I cannot attain unto it. But if one must have a high-minded account of the preservation of the three young men, here is one consistent with what is said in the body of the essay (in a slightly modified version, which takes into account a little elementary physics): As the photons are on their way from the fire to the flesh, God ceases to sustain most of the more energetic ones in existence.

tingent proposition that is true in all possible worlds in which elementary particles *always* have the causal powers they *always or almost always* have in *w*. Now if the proposition L is a law of nature, then we can say that an event *violates* the law L if the particles whose joint activity constitutes that event follow, while the event is going on, trajectories that are inconsistent with the truth of L. Roughly: An event violates a law if the law says that no events of that sort happen. A *miracle*, then, is an event that violates one or more laws. (It follows from this account of law and miracle that, if there are any miracles, then some laws of nature are false propositions. Some philosophers insist that, by definition, a law of nature, whatever else it may be, must be a true proposition. I can't think why.) I said that I had a rather technical objection to this account of the concept of miracle. The *objection* is simply that this account is not equivalent to the one I favor: Some events that my account labels 'miracles' this account does not. "Technical" comes in in explaining why. It comes down to this: The two accounts coincide only if the laws of nature are deterministic; that is, only if, given the present state of the world, the laws of nature are so strict that—miracles aside—they tie the world down to exactly one future, a future determined in every detail. For suppose that the laws are *indeterministic*. Suppose that they are sufficiently "loose" that they permit a certain event *A* to have either of two outcomes, *B* or *C*, and they don't determine which will happen. They allow history to fork, as it were, to go down either of two roads. Suppose that *A* has happened and suppose that God wants *A* to be followed by *C* and not by *B*. Suppose that, to achieve this end, God supplies certain particles with abnormal causal powers of such a nature that *B has* to happen. (Speaking very loosely, you might say that He locally and temporarily replaces the indeterministic laws with deterministic ones.) Then *B* will be a miracle by the account I have given, but not by the violation-of-laws-of-nature account. I prefer so to use the word 'miracle' that this event counts as a miracle. If you disagree, you may regard my use of the word as idiosyncratic.

It will be convenient in what follows to have a uniform way in which to describe God's actions with respect to the created world, a mode of description that comprehends both His ordinary sustaining of particles in existence and His miraculous departures from the ordinary. I shall suppose that whenever God brings about some state of affairs involving created beings, His doing this is the same action as His issuing a certain *decree*—a pronouncement of the form "Let such-and-such be" or "Let the following be so: . . . ." For example, "Let there be light" is a decree, and God's issuing or pronouncing this decree is the same action as His creating light. For technical reasons, I shall want to suppose that God's decrees are, as philosophers say, "closed under entailment." This means that if God issues certain decrees—say a decree that p and a decree that q—and if, as a matter of absolute or metaphysical necessity, if p and q are true then r must also be true, then it follows that God, in decreeing that p and q, also decrees that r. For example, suppose that one of God's decrees is "Let the waters be divided from the waters"; suppose that, as many philosophers, myself included, believe, it is a matter of absolute or metaphysical necessity that if there is water, then there are protons. Then it follows that in issuing this decree, God also issues the decree "Let there be protons." (It will, however, be convenient to except necessary truths from the closure requirement: Let us say that if God decrees certain propositions, and these propositions jointly entail p, it follows that God decrees p, provided that p is a contingent proposition.)

In this "decree" language, we may represent the action of God with respect to each elementary particle at a given moment as follows. His action consists in His then issuing a decree of the form "Let *that* now exist and have such-and-such causal powers." If God wished to annihilate a certain particle, therefore, He would not do something *to* the particle, as I might hit a vase with a hammer if I wished to destroy it. He would simply stop issuing such decrees. (But in our rather simple model of the relations of God to the world, we tacitly assume He never ceases to hold any particle in existence, since we assume there are always the same particles. This feature of our model is not essential to any of the points made in this essay, and could be removed at the cost of putting up with a slightly more complex model.) And for God to work a miracle is for Him temporarily to decree different causal powers for certain particles from the ones He normally decrees. God's actions with respect to the entire created world at any moment subsequent to the Creation are simply the sum of His actions at that moment with respect to all the particles composing the world.[5] Thus, God's action

---

[5]We shall presently discuss God's action at the *first* moment, the moment of Creation. In what follows in the text and in subsequent notes, generalizations about what God

in the created world at any given moment consists, on this model, in His issuing a vast number of decrees—as many as there are particles—of the form, "Let *that* now exist and have such-and-such causal powers".[6] His issuing these decrees is identical with His sustaining the world.

---

does at particular instants should be understood as referring to instants subsequent to the first.

This way of talking raises the question: What, exactly, is the relation of God and His actions to *time* in our model of God's relation to the world? Let us say the following. First, we shall assume that the existence of time, of "before" and "after," is a function of the existence of the physical world: If there had been no world, there would have been no such thing as time, and one can make no sense of talk of temporal relations except in reference to the physical world. As both St. Augustine and Stephen Hawking have insisted, it makes no sense to ask what happened *before*—at least in the literal, temporal sense of the word—the world existed. (Hawking employs this analogy: You might as well ask what is happening north of the North Pole.) Secondly, we shall assume that some of God's decrees can be assigned dates (dates provided by the processes of the physical world, the only dates there are): We can ask with respect to a time *t* what decrees God *then* issues. (I shall not attempt to prove that these two assumptions are consistent.) Because of our closure condition, however, it is possible that there be decrees of God that are not issued at any particular time. (An example of such a decree can be found in n. 11.) I do not insist that the two assumptions I have made about God and time represent the ultimate metaphysical truth. Those who hold that God is entirely "outside time" are faced with certain authoritative documents—such as the Bible—which, on the face of it, say that God does one thing at one time and another thing at another time. Such philosophers generally have some way of interpreting assertions of this sort so that these assertions are seen to be compatible with their theory of an extratemporal God. They should feel free to interpret my assertions about God's actions at particular times in the same way.

[6]But, owing to our closure condition, He does not issue *only* those decrees; He also decrees, at any given moment, any contingent proposition entailed by the totality of that vast ensemble of decrees about individual particles. Or, at any rate, this follows if we interpret our closure condition (which, as stated, does not refer to time) as having this consequence: If, at *t*, God decrees certain propositions, and these propositions together entail the contingent proposition *p*, then at *t*, God decrees that *p*. Thus, at an instant *t*, God then decrees every proposition that is true in all possible worlds in which, at *t*, there are the same particles as there are in actuality and in which each of these particles has at *t* the same causal powers it has in actuality.

We should note that the thesis that God decrees at *t* that a certain particle then exist and then have certain causal powers does not entail that He decrees at *t* that it then be at any particular place. "Let *that* now exist and have such-and-such causal powers" is not the same decree as "Let *that* now exist and be *right there* and have such-and-such causal powers." (A similar point applies to velocity and the higher derivatives of displacement.) More generally: From the thesis that God at *t* is sustaining the universe, it does not follow that He then decrees the particular *arrangement* of particles that in fact obtains at that time. Here is an imperfect analogy. From the fact that a gardener is now tending the flowers in a certain garden (and is thus in a sense now sustaining them in existence) it hardly follows that he is now determining the way they are now arranged. I return to this point in n. 11.

Let us now turn to the question, What is the place of chance in a world sustained by God? Can chance exist at all in such a world? Or, if it does exist, must its realm not be restricted to trivial matters—say, to such matters as where a particular sparrow falls—if its existence is to be consistent with God's loving providence?

In order to approach these questions, let us ask what it would be for there to be chance in the world. There are various things that can be meant by the word 'chance.' What I shall mean by saying that an event is a "chance" occurrence, or a state of affairs a "matter of chance" or "due to chance," is this: The event or state of affairs is without purpose or significance; it is not a part of anyone's plan; it serves no one's end; and it might very well not have been. A chance event, in other words, is one such that, if someone asks of it, "Why did that happen?" the only right answer is: "There *is* no reason or explanation; it just happened".[7] But you must treat this statement charitably. I do not mean to imply that a "chance" event in this sense has no explanation of *any* sort. If Alice suddenly remembers that she had promised to buy a box of crayons for her son, and turns into an unfamiliar street in search of an appropriate shop, and is struck and killed by a car whose brakes have failed, her death may well be a "chance" occurrence in the sense I mean—someone who did not believe in divine providence

[7]Some philosophers believe that there are impersonal but intelligible "world-historical" processes, and that these processes somehow confer intelligibility or significance on certain of the events that issue from them. For such an event there would be an answer to the question, Why did that happen? If there are such world-historical processes, one would not want to call their products "chance" events, despite the fact that—assuming that the world-historical processes are not instruments of God's purpose—they are not a part of anyone's plan (unless it were the plan of a personified abstraction like History). The primary purpose of the qualification "It might very well not have been" is to deny the status of a "chance" event to an event—as it may be, the rise of capitalism—that is a necessary product of some impersonal but intelligible world-historical process like the Labor of the Concept or the Dialectic of History. Since the idea of such processes is a vague one, I will not attempt to be precise about the meaning of "It might very well not have been." I will explicitly and formally exclude only metaphysically necessary events (if such there be) and metaphysically necessary states of affairs from the category "might not have been." (Thus, if Spinoza is right, no event or state of affairs can be ascribed to "chance.") Readers for whom Spinozism, and historicism of the Hegel-Marx-Spengler variety, are not live options can safely ignore the qualification "It might very well not have been." In any case, the *theist* will say, first, that Spinozism is false, and secondly, that either there are no "world-historical" processes, or, if there are, their existence is ordained by God and any necessary product of such processes will therefore be a part of someone's plan. The theist, therefore, may ignore the qualification "It might very well not have been." I shall do so in the sequel.

would almost certainly say that it was—even though in one sense her death has an obvious explanation: She was struck by a car. But if her grieving husband were to cry in despair "Why did she die?", it would be a cruel joke to tell him that she died because she was struck by a large, heavy vehicle moving at fifty miles an hour. That is not the sort of explanation he would be asking for. By calling an event a "chance" event, I mean that it has no explanation of the sort Alice's husband might ask for: It has no purpose or significance; it is not a part of anyone's plan.

It does seem that there are many events of this sort; some horrible, some benefic, some of no consequence to anyone. But there are people who believe that this seeming is mere seeming and that either there are no chance events in this sense, or, if there are, they are always events that are of no consequence to anyone. I have in mind those people who believe in divine providence and who take a certain view, which I shall proceed to describe, of divine providence. Such people think that God not only *knows* of the fall of every sparrow, but that the fall of every sparrow is a part of God's plan for His creation. Presumably they think that the exact number of hairs on one's head is also a part of God's plan. Other people may find the attribution of every detail of the world to providence bizarre, but say that at any rate all those events that would be accounted important by human beings—Alice's death, for example—must have a place in God's plan. A person who takes this view will say that when Alice's grieving husband asks, "Why did she die?", there is an answer to this question, an answer that God knows even if no human being knows it. My purpose in the remainder of this essay will be to suggest that this is wrong. I want to suggest that much of what goes on in the world, even much of what seems important and significant to us, is no part of God's plan—and certainly not a part of anyone *else's* plan—and is therefore due simply to chance.

If there is chance in a world sustained by God, what are its sources? Where, as it were, does it "come from"? Let us recall our picture of God's relation to the world: The world consists of elementary particles, and God created the world by creating these particles simultaneously at some moment in the past; God sustains each of them in existence and continuously "supplies" each of them with its causal powers; following the Creation, the world evolved in a manner determined, insofar as it *was* determined, by the causal powers of its constituent particles; the causal powers supplied to a given particle are normally invariant, but God may, of His own good pleasure, momentarily supply certain particles with different sets of causal powers from the ones they normally receive from Him, and, if He does this, then a miracle occurs.

If God has this relation to the created universe, what is meant by His "plan" for the created universe? I believe that we should, as a first approximation, identify God's plan with the sum total of what He has decreed. (I say "as a first approximation" because I will presently qualify this definition). Thus, if God has issued the decree "Let there be light," then the existence of light is a part of His plan. If He has *not* issued the decree "Let there be lies," then lies are no part of His plan. We should remember that a plan—God's plan or anyone's—may take account of a certain possibility without requiring that that possibility be realized. For example, bank robbers planning their getaway may *plan for* the contingency of leaving the city by air—they have bought airline tickets—but not *plan to* leave the city by air. Leaving the city by air is not a part of their plan in the way that arriving at the bank at 3:00 P.M. is. We should also remember that the fact that God knows that something will happen does not mean that that thing is a part of His plan. God may, therefore, have known before there were any rational creatures that some of them would someday tell lies, and His plan for the world may contain measures for dealing with lies should any lies be told; but it does not follow from these things that lies are a part of His plan. Now here is the qualification of our definition of God's plan that I alluded to a moment ago. It may happen that God sometimes issues decrees in response to events that He has not decreed. For example, suppose that a young man is dying following a car wreck and that God had not decreed that that car wreck should occur. Suppose the young man's mother prays that his life be saved, and that God grants this prayer by performing a miracle in virtue of which the man recovers. We shall not count this miraculous recovery as a part of God's plan, since it was contingent on an event—the car wreck—that God had *not* decreed. We might call the decree God issued to bring about the man's recovery a *reactive* decree, since it was issued in reaction to an event that God did not bring about. We may define a reactive decree of God's as a decree He would not have issued had some event not decreed by Him not occurred. Our revised definition of God's plan is:

God's plan consists of the totality ef all His decrees other than re-active decrees.[8]

If this is the correct picture of God's relation to the created world and His plan for it, there would seem to be, within such a world, at least three possible sources of chance, or of events or states of affairs that are not a part of God's plan: the free will of rational creatures, natural indeterminism, and the initial state of the created world. (I call these *three* sources of chance, but I realize that proponents of various philosophical theories may hold that every instance of some one of these sources is also an instance of one of the other two. For example, a philosopher who holds that free will and determinism are incompatible will probably maintain that every instance of human free will is also an instance of natural indeterminism.)

Let us first consider human free will. I take it to be obvious that if God decrees (I do not mean *commands*) that a certain human being on a certain occasion behave in a certain way, then that human being loses his freedom of choice on that particular occasion. When, for example, God "hardened Pharoah's heart," Pharoah—at that particular moment—did not *freely* choose to forbid the Hebrews to leave Egypt. Thus, if there is such a thing as human free will, it cannot be that all of our choices are like Pharoah's. And it is certainly not obviously the biblical picture of God's relation to man that all of our choices *are* of that sort. For example, Ecclesiasti-

---

[8]Or we might call this totality "God's unqualified plan" or "God's eternal plan" or "God's plan *ante omnia saecula*." We could also speak, for any contingent proposition *p*, of "God's plan given that *p*": If the conditional "if *p* then *q*" is a part of God's eternal plan, and if *p* is true, then *q* is a part of "God's plan given that *p*." If *q* is a part of God's plan given that *p*, and if *p* is not a part of God's unqualified plan, then *q* will be a part of God's plan given that *p*, but not a part of God's unqualified plan. If *q* is a part of God's plan given that *p* (but not a part of God's plan *ante omnia saecula*) and if *p* is a proposition that we all know to be true—or which we and all of our coreligion-ists believe to be true—it will be natural for us to speak of *q* as being "a part of God's plan"; in fact it would be inadvisable for anyone to speak otherwise, except (as in the present case) when engaged in highly abstract theological speculation. Thus, Christians may properly speak of the Incarnation as being "a part of God's plan," even if there would have been no Incarnation if there had been no Fall: for, surely, there is some contingent proposition *p* (perhaps "Man falls from his original perfection," or the conjunction of this and various other propositions) such that the Christian will believe that *p* is in fact true and also believe that "If *p*, then God becomes man" is a part of God's eternal plan.

We should note that God's eternal plan is not (at least according to orthodox Christian theology) a necessary product of the Divine Nature. "There is a created universe" is a part of God's eternal plan, but not, orthodoxy has it, a necessary truth.

cus says of God (15:4): "He himself made man in the beginning, and then left him free to make his own decisions." (Admittedly, Christians have to deal with some difficult passages in Romans on this point.) If we have free will, therefore, the manner in which any particular person exercises this free will is no part of God's plan, and likewise the consequences of free acts, even if they occur thousands of years after the act, are no parts of God's plan. I must point out that this is not an attempt to *absolve* God of responsibility for the consequences of the free acts of creatures. After all, that an event is not part of one's plans does not necessarily mean that one is not responsible for it. If the man who fell among thieves had died beside the road from Jerusalem to Jericho, this would not have been a part of any plan of the priest or the Levite, but they would nonetheless have been responsible for his death. Whether God should be held responsible for the evils caused by the abuse of human free will—and He could certainly prevent most of these evils, if not all of them—is not the present question. I am arguing only that they are not part of His plan for the world, which is a relatively weak thesis.

A second source of chance in the world is natural indeterminism. Indeterminism is the thesis that the distribution of all the particles of matter in the universe at a given moment, and their causal powers at that moment, do not determine the subsequent behavior of the particles. In other words, an indeterministic universe is one in which a given state of affairs can have more than one outcome. The Greek atomists held that atoms—what are now called elementary particles—could swerve in the void, and something very much like this is true according to modern physics. If God's causal relations with the world are confined to continuously holding the elementary particles in existence and continuously supplying them with their causal powers, then He does not decree the outcomes of such "swerves in the void," since the "swerves" are not determined by the causal powers of the particles. And the consequences of such undetermined events can show up at the level of ordinary observation, if they are sufficiently amplified. A Geiger counter is an amplifier designed for this purpose. (Another effective amplifier can be found in the collisions of rolling spheres. Imagine a billiard table on which perfectly spherical, perfectly elastic billiard balls are in motion, without loss of kinetic energy to friction or to collisions with the sides of the table. Imagine a second billiard-table-and-balls setup that is as close to be-

ing an absolutely perfect duplicate of the first as the laws of nature allow. If the "laws of nature" are those of nineteenth-century physics,
the second table will be an absolutely perfect duplicate of the first
sans phrase, and the behavior of the balls on the second table will—
presumably—duplicate exactly the behavior of the balls on the first
table forever. Suppose, however, that a rolling billiard ball exhibits
the position-momentum and time-energy uncertainties predicted by
Heisenberg. For an object as big as a billiard ball, these uncertainties
are minuscule indeed. Nevertheless, the capacity of the collisions
of rolling spheres to magnify slight deviations is astounding: Within
a few minutes the arrangements of balls on the two tables will be entirely different.)

Since the actual physical world seems in fact to be indeterministic,
it is plausible to suppose that there are a great many states of affairs
that are not part of God's plan and which, moreover, cannot be
traced to the free decisions of created beings. I very much doubt
that when the universe was (say) 10^{-45} seconds old, it was then
physically inevitable that the earth, or even the Milky Way Galaxy,
should exist. Thus, these objects, so important from the human
point of view, are no part of God's plan—or at least not unless their
creation was due to God's miraculous intervention into the course of
the development of the physical world at a relatively late stage. I
see no reason as a theist, or as a Christian, to believe that the existence of human beings is a part of God's plan. This may seem a
shocking statement. Let me attempt to palliate the shock. First, I do
not claim to *know* that the existence of our species is not a part of
God's plan. Secondly, I am sure that the existence of animals made
in God's image—that is, rational animals having free will and capable of love—*is* a part of God's plan. I am simply not convinced that
He had any *particular* species in mind. Thirdly, I do not deny God's
omniscience. I do not deny that He knew from the beginning that
humanity would exist; but what is foreknown is not necessarily
what is planned. Fourthly, *having* come into existence, we are *now*
in God's care and the objects of His love and the instruments of His
purpose. Here is an analogy: When my wife and I decided to have a
child, we did not decide with respect to some particular child to
have *that* child, as a couple might decide with respect to some particular child to adopt *that* child. But now that our child is in existence, she, that very individual and no other, is in our care and is
the object of our love. I concede that if God knows the future in

every detail, then He knew before humanity existed that that particular species would exist; and my wife and I did not know of Elizabeth van Inwagen, before her conception, that she, that very individual, would exist. But if God knew from the beginning of time, or even "before all worlds," that humanity would exist, it does not follow that He decreed the existence of humanity; He may for all I know have issued no decree more particular than "Let there be a species in My image and likeness."

I now turn to the third source of chance in the world: the initial state of things. (I ignore the problem presented by the fact that, according to most of the current cosmological models, although the world has a finite age, there was no first instant of its existence—or if there was a first instant, the world was then of zero volume and infinite density, an idea that seems to make no sense.)

At the first moment of the existence of the physical universe there were, let us say, $(2.46 \times 10^{80}) + 2319$ particles,[9] each having a certain set of causal powers, a certain position in space, and a certain velocity. No doubt this "initial arrangement" (so to call it) suited God's purposes; if it did not, of course, there would have been some other initial arrangement. But is it conceivable that this was the only one out of all possible initial arrangements that suited God's purposes? Is it conceivable that God chose this arrangement because it was better for His purposes than *any* of the infinitely many alternatives? Well, I find that very hard to believe. I don't mean to deny that God could hold all of the infinitely many possible initial arrangements before His mind at once, and then say, "Let *that* one be." (Of course this is mere picture-thinking, treating God as if He were just like a human being, with the minor difference that He is infinite. But picture-thinking is all we are capable of. When I say I don't mean to deny this, I am saying that I don't mean to deny that it's the best picture.) I do, however, doubt whether any *one* of the alternatives *could* be superior to all the others. To me that sounds as absurd as saying that, if an artist wants to draw a portrait in chalk, then one particular arrangement of calcium, carbon, and oxygen atoms, out of all the possible arrangements, must be the arrangement that would constitute the best possible piece of chalk for the job.

Well, suppose there are various alternative initial arrangements that would suit God's purposes equally well. Doubtless if there is more

[9]Or, better, think of a number of this order of magnitude that isn't mostly zeros.

than one such arrangement there are infinitely many. But let us suppose for the sake of simplicity that there are just two, X and Y. We are supposing, that is, that for God's purposes to be accomplished, either X or Y must come into existence, but it makes no difference which; it is a matter of sheer indifference to Him. Now if God wishes either X or Y to come into existence, what decree shall He issue? There would seem to be three possibilities:

    (1) "Let X be"
    (2) "Let Y be"
    (3) "Let either X or Y be."[10]

Leibniz, though he does not talk of things in exactly these terms, might be interpreted as saying, first, that (3) is impossible because God creates only "complete" states of affairs, fully detailed ones, "possible worlds"; secondly, that God cannot issue either (1) or (2), because that would be for God to act without a sufficient reason for His action; and, thirdly, that there must, therefore, be a *best possible* initial state, since there in fact is a created world.

I would deny the first of these assertions. It does not seem to me to be logically or metaphysically impossible that God should decree that either X or Y should be without decreeing that X should be and without decreeing that Y should be. Suppose God does decree that *either X or Y exist; suppose Y thereupon comes into existence.[11] Then it is no part

[10]We must be careful about what we mean by calling (1), (2), and (3) *three possibilities*, since, by our closure condition, if God issues either (1) or (2) He ipso facto issues (3). The three possibilities I mean to call attention to are: God issues (1); God issues (2); God issues (3) *without* issuing (1) or (2).

[11]The moment Y comes into existence, there will, of course, be a particular number of particles and each will have a determinate position and velocity and complement of causal powers. It is at *that* point that God must, if He is to sustain the world He has created, begin issuing "a vast number of decrees—as many as there are particles—of the form 'Let *that* now exist and have such-and-such causal powers'." Here is another imperfect horticultural analogy. Suppose I plant a tree in my garden. Within certain limits, it may not matter much to me where the tree is. I may, within these limits, choose a spot at random. But once I have planted the tree and it is firmly rooted at a particular spot, I must tend it where it is. It's no good watering a spot ten feet to the left of the tree, even if my purposes would have been as well served by planting the tree at that other spot.

I said in n. 6 that it does not follow from the fact that God at *t* issues decrees that then sustain the universe in existence that He then decrees the current arrangement of particles. I will now go further and say that, if our model of God's relation to the world is anything like right, then at at most *one* instant does He then decree the current arrangement of particles: the first. And if the decree of God that brings the universe

of God's plan that Y—*as opposed to X*—exist, and the result of His decree might just as well have been the existence of X. We may therefore say that Y exists owing simply to chance, and that every result or consequence of Y that would not *also* be a result of X is due to chance. There could, therefore, be chance events even in a wholly deterministic world that was created and is sustained by God. If, moreover, we assume that God cannot, after all, decree that either X or Y exist except by decreeing that X exist or else decreeing that Y exist, this will not remove the element of chance from the world. It will simply locate the ultimate source of that chance within the internal life of God, rather than in the results of an indefinite decree. For if God must issue a decree that X exist or else issue a decree that Y exist, and if He has no reason to prefer one of these states of affairs to the other—if it is really, from God's point of view, six of one and half a dozen of the other—then there seems to be no way to avoid the conclusion that some analogue of a coin toss takes place within the Divine Nature. An analogy is provided by Buridan's Ass; this unfortunate animal, you remember, is forced to choose between two equally attractive and accessible piles of hay. If the poor creature is not to starve, it must make an arbitrary

---

into existence is indefinite (like "Let either X or Y be"), then at *no* instant does He then decree the current arrangement of particles. (Moreover, the existence of a first instant of time is a consequence of the limitations of our model: A more sophisticated model would allow for the possibility that, while the temporal sequence has a greatest lower bound, it has no earliest member.) It would, however, be possible for God to decree the arrangement of particles at t without *then* decreeing it. Suppose, for example, that at t_o (the first moment of time), God then decrees a perfectly definite arrangement of particles; suppose that at every instant in the interval having t_o as its earliest member and t as its earliest nonmember, He then decrees the existence of the same particles that existed at t_o and also decrees a deterministic set of laws; and suppose that at t He then decrees the existence of the same particles that existed at t_o. Only one arrangement of particles at t will be consistent with this set of decrees and it therefore follows that God decrees the arrangement of particles at t. Since, however, He does not issue all of these decrees *at t*, we cannot say that *at t* He *then* decrees the current arrangement of particles. But, of course, if the theory presented in the text is correct, God does not, even in this sense, decree the arrangement of particles at any time: There are, in fact, possible worlds in which God has issued the same decrees He has issued in actuality, and in which no particle is where it is in actuality. Nevertheless, God may have (and if any revealed religion is true, *has*) decreed many of the features the universe has at any given moment: that it then contain living creatures, for example. It should be evident from what has been said in this note and in n. 6 that we cannot validly deduce from the two premises: (i) God has decreed that at t there be living creatures, and (ii) at t, God then issues decrees that sustain in existence all the living creatures there are at that moment, the conclusion that at t God then issues the decree that there be living creatures at that moment.

choice. And, presumably, within each animal—even within rational animals like ourselves—there exists some mechanism, some biological analogue of a coin toss, for making arbitrary choices. Occasional reliance upon such a mechanism is not beneath the dignity of an animal, even a rational animal, but I find it wholly incongruous to suppose that the Divine Nature contains anything remotely resembling a coin-tossing mechanism. To suggest this seems to be almost to suggest that the Lord of all is, as Zeus was said to be, one of the subjects of the goddess Tyche or Chance. I prefer to think that God is capable of decreeing that a certain indefinite condition be satisfied without decreeing any of the indifferent alternative states of affairs that would satisfy it. However this may be, the following result seems secure: If there are alternative initial arrangements of particles, any of which would have served God's purpose for His creation equally well, then certain features of the world must be due to mere chance. How pervasive these features may be, and how important they might seem to us, are, of course, further questions, questions that are not answered by anything that we have so far said. And this same result, the existence of states of affairs due to chance, follows from our consideration of human freedom and natural indeterminism. I do not doubt that all three sources of chance have in fact been in operation, and that many of the features of the actual universe are due to them—perhaps even features as prominent as the human race or the Local Group. I do not think that such a view of the place of chance in the formation of the universe is incompatible with the proposition that God is the Maker of all things, visible and invisible. Even if the planet Mars (say) is not a part of God's plan, it is entirely composed of particles that He made in the beginning and which exist from moment to moment only because He continues to hold them in existence and which continue from moment to moment to form a planet only because He is continuously supplying them with the causal powers by which they mutually cohere. I suppose that *we* exist only by chance, and yet it is in God that we live and move and have our being. And, as I have implied, creatures that, like us, exist by chance, may well be filling a divinely ordained *role*, and in that sense be serving God's purposes—rather as individual soldiers may be serving a general's purposes, even though the battle plan the general has drafted does not include any of their names. (But again, the analogy is imperfect, for the general, we may suppose, neither knows nor cares about individual private soldiers—even if he is concerned about their collective welfare—whereas God knows all about each of us, and loves each of us with a depth and intensity that is without human parallel.)

If what I have said so far is correct, then it seems very likely that among the events that are due simply to chance and not part of God's plan are certain evils; or perhaps even *all* evils. In the remainder of this essay I want to examine this idea and its consequences.

If much of the world is due to chance, and if much of the world is infected with evil, then it would be reasonable to suppose, on purely statistical grounds, that at least some evil is due to chance. Many theists, moreover, ascribe the very existence of evil to an abuse of the divine gift of free will by created beings. If that speculation is correct, then the very existence of evil is a matter of chance; that is, there is simply no answer to the question, Why is there evil? and it is not correct to say that God planned to create a world containing evil. Since people seem to be particularly likely to misunderstand the point of suggestions like this one, I will repeat something I have said before: This suggestion is in no way supposed to be a "solution to the problem of evil," since it is consistent with the proposition that before evil ever was, God knew that there would someday be evil and could have prevented it. I mention the point that (if evil is wholly due to the creaturely abuse of free will) evil is not a part of God's plan for His creation, simply to distinguish this point from the points I wish to discuss. The points I wish to discuss involve particular evils and their relation to God's plan.

What I want to say about particular evils is best made clear by illustration and example. I will consider two evils, one *very* particular—the accidental death of a particular person—and the other more general. I will discuss the more general evil first. I think that the existence of a certain disease will provide a good illustration of the point I want to make. For the sake of a concrete example, I will discuss rabies—an arbitrary choice, except that I have deliberately chosen a rather horrible disease. (A disease like rabies falls in the category that students of the problem of evil call "physical" or "natural" evil. But in what follows, I will make no explicit use of the distinction between natural and "moral" evil.) I see no reason to suppose that God has decreed the existence of rabies. In my view, the rabies virus simply evolved and it might not have. If the initial arrangement of things had been slightly different, or if the indeterministic course of the natural world had taken a slightly different turning in the remote past (on any of uncounted billions of occasions), the particular disease we call rabies would never have come into existence. (But other diseases might have. If the rabies virus had never evolved, the world's catalogue of diseases might have been a bit less horrible—or it might have been a bit more horrible.) Is there any reason a theist should want to deny this? Although *I* think that there is no explanation of the existence of evil—I don't deny that there is an explanation of the fact that God *permits* evil—I can see why a theist would want to say that there must be an explanation of the existence of evil. Although I think that there is no explanation of the fact that many people die in agony—I don't deny that there is an explanation of the fact that God *allows* people to die in agony—I can see why a theist would want to say that there must be an explanation of the fact that many people die in agony. Well, suppose there were explanations of these things. Suppose there were a good explanation of the fact that there is evil. Suppose there were a good explanation of the fact that some people die in agony. Why should the theist want or expect an explanation of the fact that one of the evils is the particular disease rabies, or of the fact that some of the agonizing deaths are due to that disease? By the same token, if there is an explanation of the fact that God *permits* the existence of evil and agonizing death (even if there is no explanation of the existence of these things), why should anyone want or expect an explanation of the fact that rabies is one of the evils or is one of the causes of the agonizing deaths that God permits? I think that this point is an important one, for theists are often challenged to produce an explanation—even a *possible* explanation—of the existence of this or that evil, or of God's permitting that evil to come to be or to continue. And many theists, in their pride, construct fanciful explanations of particular evils as divine punishments. (Christians who explain particular evils—like the Bubonic Plague or the AIDS virus—as divine punishments are neglecting the story of the tower at Siloam and the story of the man born blind.) But there is no reason that the theist should believe that there are any such explanations. This point is even more important in connection with the misfortunes of individual persons, to which I now turn.

Let us consider again the case of Alice who, by sheerest chance, turned into a certain street and was killed by a car whose brakes had failed. Let us borrow a term from the law and call her death an example of *death by misadventure*. Although I think that there is no explanation of the existence of death by misadventure—I don't deny that there is an explanation of the fact that God *permits* the existence of death by misadventure—I can see why a theist would want to say that there must be an explanation of the existence of death by misadventure. Well, suppose that there were an explanation of the fact that there are deaths by misadventure. Why should the theist want or expect an explanation of the fact that *Alice*, then and there, died by misadventure? By the same token, if there is an explanation of the fact that God *permits* the existence of death by misadventure, why should anyone want or expect an explanation of the fact that God permitted *Alice* to die by misadventure? Why should there be an answer to the question, "Why did *Alice* have to die that way"? Suppose that the driver of the car had seriously considered having his brakes checked a few days ago, when he first noticed certain ominous symptoms, that he freely decided to put it off till he was less busy, and that, if his deliberations had gone the other way, Alice would now be alive and well. Suppose that God's relation to Alice and the driver and their circumstances was confined to sustaining certain elementary particles (such as those that composed Alice and the driver and the braking system in the latter's car) in existence and supplying those particles with their normal causal powers. God would, of course, have known that the accident was to occur and could have prevented it by a miracle—one unnoticed by any human being, if He wished. If it really is true that God has a general reason for permitting deaths by misadventure, need He have a particular reason for permitting *this* death by misadventure? Why?

It is clear that many theists think that He *must* have such a reason. Every now and then, in Billy Graham's newspaper column and similar places, one finds explanations—admittedly speculative—of how a particular death by misadventure (or robbery or rape or illness) might serve God's purposes. I am not, as some are, morally offended by these explanations, but I find them singularly unconvincing, even as speculations. I certainly do not want to deny that *sometimes* particular deaths by misadventure, and other misfortunes of individual persons, may be such that God has a special reason for allowing those very misfortunes. I do not want to deny that God sometimes miraculously intervenes in the course of nature—say, in answer to someone's prayer for a loved one's safety—to *prevent* such misfortunes. I do not wish to deny that God sometimes intervenes miraculously in the course of nature to *cause* individual misfortunes. I want to deny only that there is any reason to suppose that, for every individual misfortune, God has a reason for not preventing *that* misfortune. (The English word *misfortune* is rather a milk-and-water word. My use of it *faute de mieux* should not be allowed to obscure the fact that my thesis comprehends events like the sudden death of a young woman who, had she not *happened* to turn down a certain street, might well have lived a long, happy, and useful life. Some would use the word *tragedy* for such events, but, in my usage at least, the word 'tragedy' carries the inescapable implication that the event to which it applies is, above all, a *meaningful* event, the very implication I want to avoid.)

Why should a theist deny any of this? One reason might be a conviction that there could not be a *general* explanation of God's allowing deaths by misadventure unless there were, for each such event, an explanation of His allowing *it*. A conviction, that is, that a general explanation of God's allowing deaths by misadventure could only be the sum of the explanations of his allowing this one and that one and the other one. I see no reason to believe this. After all, most theists believe that there is a general explanation of God's allowing sin—as it may be, a refusal to interfere with the free choices of creatures—that is independent of such reasons as He may have for allowing this, that, or the other sin. If this belief is correct, then, even if God had *no* special reason for allowing Cain to murder Abel, *no* reason peculiar to that act, *no* reason beyond His general policy of not interfering with the free choices of His creatures, it would not follow that He had no general reason for allowing sin. By analogy we may speculate that even if God had *no* special reason for allowing Alice to be struck by a car, *no* reason peculiar to that event, *no* reason beyond His general policy of allowing deaths by misadventure (whatever exactly the reasons underlying that policy might be), it would not follow that He had no general reason for allowing deaths by misadventure.

Or a theist may feel that it is simply not *fair* to Alice that she should die young, and that this unfairness could be acceptable only if God had a special reason for allowing her premature death. (A complication arises here. Most theists believe in an afterlife, and thus may be inclined to say that, in theory at least, an early death is not necessarily a misfortune. But this complication is due to a feature of the example that is not essential to the problem; it would not have arisen if, instead of assuming that Alice died when struck by the car, we had assumed that she lived out her normal span, but crippled and in pain.) One might point out that, if God indeed does allow people to be subject to Fortune and her wheel, then He has given everyone the same chance. Suppose, moreover, that He has a good reason for allowing us to be (to some extent) at the mercy of Fortune. If Fortune's wheel is fair, how, then, can the losers say that they have been treated unfairly? If the twins Tom and Tim both wish to propose marriage to Jane, and they take this problem to their father, and he orders them (this is in the old days) to draw straws, and Tim loses, can he say that he was treated unfairly by his father because his father had no special reason for denying him the opportunity to propose to Jane? No, the situation demanded a lottery, and Tim has no complaint unless the lottery was unfair. It will probably occur to someone to protest that *life's* lottery is *not* fair and that everyone does *not* have the same chance. (For example, someone living in Beirut has a greater chance of sudden violent death than someone living in Zurich.) But whatever problem this fact may raise for the theist, it does not seem to have anything in particular to do with chance. It is simply a special case of whatever problem is raised for the theist by the fact that life's blessings are not distributed equally. People are not equal in wealth, intelligence, native strength of character, or physical constitution. No one supposes that these inequalities are always a matter of desert. (What could one do to deserve greater native strength of character than someone else?) It may be that there are good reasons, known to God, for these inequalities. But such good reasons would not make the inequalities *fair*—not unless the reasons in some way involved desert. The theist may say all sorts of things in response to this difficulty: that the potter may do as he likes with his clay, for example, or that we deserve little from God and that no one gets less than he deserves and that it is not unfair for some to get more than they deserve provided no one gets less. But whatever the theist says about inequalities in the distribution of, say, intelligence and strength of character, I don't see why he shouldn't say the same thing about inequalities in the distribution of (for example) the probability of sudden violent death. In a nutshell: If it is fair that we should all be subject to chance in some degree, then it would seem to be unfair that we should be subject to unequal chances only if unequal distribution of any sort of advantage or disadvantage is unfair. It might be good at this point to remember the words of the Preacher (Eccl. 9:11–12):

"I returned, and saw under the sun, that the race is not to the swift, nor the battle to the strong, neither yet bread to the wise, nor yet riches to men of understanding, nor yet favor to men of skill; but time and chance happeneth to them all."

For man also knoweth not his time: as the fishes that are taken in an evil net, and as the birds that are caught in the snare; so are the sons of men snared in an evil time, when it falleth suddenly upon them."

If what I have said is true, it yields a moral for students of the problem of evil: Do not attempt any solution to this problem that entails that every particular evil has a purpose, or that, with respect to every individual misfortune, or every devastating earthquake, or every disease, God has some special reason for allowing it. Concentrate rather on the problem of what sort of reasons a loving and providential God might have for allowing His creatures to live in a world in which many of the evils that happen to them happen to them for no reason at all.[12]

[12]This essay owes a great deal to chap. 6, "The Ordainer of the Lottery," of P. T. Geach's *Providence and Evil* (Cambridge: Cambridge University Press, 1977). I doubt, however, whether Professor Geach would approve of everything I say. I do give "real assent to the doctrine that all events however trivial fall within the ordering of Providence" (p. 116); I do not, however, take that doctrine to entail that God has chosen the number of hairs on my head, or even that He chose Matthias over Joseph Justus to fill the vacant apostolate of Judas. As to the latter case, we have not been told anything about this; what we may presume is that God was content that Matthias should hold that office. I *think* that Geach believes something stronger than this. Proverbs 16:33, which Geach cites, refers (I believe) only to the rather special case of the sacred lots, and, in any event, "the way it falls out is from the Lord" is open to various interpretations.

This paper was read at a conference on the philosophy of religion at Cornell University in February 1987 and at a meeting of the Society of Christian Philosophers in Chicago in May 1987. On the latter occasion, the commentator was Alfred J. Freddoso, some of whose spirited animadversions I have addressed in nn. 4 and 7. (Freddoso's essay in this volume contains much that is relevant to n. 4 and to other matters discussed herein.) Different, but equally spirited, animadversions have been communicated to me by Eleonore Stump; these have mainly to do with the implications of the paper for the problem of evil. I hope to discuss these elsewhere. I thank Norman Kretzmann, Richard Swinburne, Lawrence H. Davis, and, especially, William P. Alston for helpful criticisms.

An extremely interesting book (not yet published in the United States) has come into my hands too late to influence this essay: *God of Chance*, by D. J. Bartholomew (London: S.P.C.K., 1984). This book brings the expertise and perspective of a statistician to bear on the question of the relation of chance and God's action in the created world.

8

Freedom and Actuality

John Martin Fischer

1 Incompatibilism

I shall begin by setting out a familiar argument for the incompatibility of God's foreknowledge and human freedom to do otherwise.[1] I will not at this point be specifying what I take to be the total set of divine attributes. Rather, I will simply fill in as many divine attributes as are required to develop a version of the argument for incompatibilism. At the outset, I should point out that I am using "God" as a proper name of an individual who has the divine attributes essentially.

I assume that God is essentially eternal in the temporal sense. That is, it is necessarily true that if God exists, then He exists at all times. This conception of God's eternality implies that God is "sempiternal" in all possible worlds in which He exists; in any possible world in which God exists, there is no time at which He does not exist.

Second, God is essentially omniscient. It is necessarily true that, if God exists, then for any time t and proposition p, God knows (and thus believes) at t that p if and only if p is true at t. Now, let us adopt, for the sake of the argument, an admittedly controversial

---

[1]For similar developments of the argument, see Nelson Pike, "Divine Omniscience and Voluntary Action," *Philosophical Review* 74 (January 1965), 27–46; and John Martin Fischer, "Freedom and Foreknowledge," *Philosophical Review* 92 (January 1983), 67–79, and "Ockhamism," *Philosophical Review* 94 (January 1985), 80–100.

(but certainly not entirely implausible) assumption concerning the fixity of the past:

> (FP) For any agent A, time t, action X, and property P, if it is true that if A were to perform X at t, then some individual who actually possessed P at some time prior to t would *not* have possessed P at this prior time, then A cannot do X at t.

(FP) must be interpreted so as to apply only to temporally "genuine" or "nonrelational" properties. There is a distinction between temporally nonrelational (intrinsic) and temporally relational (extrinsic) properties that is parallel to the distinction between spatially nonrelational and spatially relational properties. The distinctions are notoriously hard to explain and characterize, but at least we can point to relatively clear cases of each of the kinds of properties. The property of being east of San Francisco is a spatially relational property of Sam (who is in Connecticut), whereas the property of having blue eyes is a spatially nonrelational property of Sam. The property of eating dinner prior to going to the movies is a temporally relational property of Jill, whereas the property of eating dinner is a temporally nonrelational property of Jill (relative to the time at which she has dinner). I shall assume that God's beliefs at a time t are temporally genuine properties of God at t. In general, believing some proposition at t seems to be a temporally nonrelational property of the individual who holds the belief at t.[2]

A further assumption of the argument is that "future contingents" are determinately true (or false) prior to the times they are "about." So if Robert cooks dinner on Tuesday, then it is true on Monday that Robert will cook dinner on Tuesday, etc. Also, I assume that God's existence is "counterfactually independent of any action that a human has it in his power to perform":

> (CI) If God exists, then if it is true that if a human agent were to perform an act X, God would not exist, then the agent cannot perform X.

Thus, even if God's existence is not metaphysically necessary, it cannot depend on whether a human agent does something that is

[2]For an argument that God's beliefs should be construed as temporally nonrelational properties, see John Martin Fischer, "Hard-Type Soft Facts," *Philosophical Review* 95 (October 1986), 591–601, esp. 595–599.

in his power to do. (Of course, [CI] is entirely compatible with—although weaker than—the assumption of God's necessary existence.) The intuitive idea here is that if God exists, then His existence should not depend on whether I (say) go to a basketball game tonight or clench my fist now.[3]

Now for the argument. Suppose that Jane actually goes to the movies on Tuesday. So it was true on Monday that Jane would go to the movies on Tuesday. It follows that God believed on Monday that Jane would go to the movies on Tuesday. One of the following three conditionals must be true:[4]

(1) If Jane were to refrain from going to the movies on Tuesday, then God would have held a false belief on Monday.

(2) If Jane were to refrain from going to the movies on Tuesday, then God would not have existed on Monday.

(3) If Jane were to refrain from going to the movies on Tuesday, then God would have held a different belief from the one He actually held on Monday.

But (1) must be false, in virtue of God's essential omniscience. And if (2) were true, then Jane couldn't refrain from going to the movies on Tuesday (via [CI]). And if (3) were true, then Jane couldn't refrain from going to the movies on Tuesday (via [FP]). (This is because [3] implies that if Jane were to refrain from going to the movies on Tuesday, God wouldn't have had a genuine property on Monday that He actually had— the property of believing that Jane would go to the movies on Tuesday.) So Jane could not have refrained from going to the movies on Tuesday. And it is obvious that the argument can be generalized to apply to any human action. If God exists and has the properties specified above, then it appears that no human agent is free to do other than what he actually does.

2 Incompatibilism and Immutability

The argument for incompatibilism presented above does appear to be valid, but its soundness can be challenged in various ways. One way

---

[3]For a development and explanation of the independence assumption, see Fischer, "Ockhamism," 88–94.

[4]If a different conditional—one with the common antecedent and a disjunctive consequent—were true, the same kind of argument could be developed; I suppress this possibility for the sake of simplicity.

to deny its soundness is to claim that God's belief on Monday that Jane would go to the movies on Tuesday is not a temporally genuine property of God. This strategy would accept (FP) but deny its applicability to the incompatibilist's argument.

Another possible way to deny the soundness of the argument is simply to deny (FP). That is, one could say that there are some cases in which a human agent can at a time t_2 so act that an individual who possessed some temporally genuine property at some prior time t_1 would not have possessed that property at t_1. On one version of this approach, one claims that "God believes at t_1 that Jane will go to the movies at t_2" is a "soft" or temporally relational *fact* about t_1, and that Jane can at t_2 so act that a soft fact about t_1 would not have been a fact. This is a kind of "Ockhamistic" strategy. It claims that there are some soft facts about the past relative to a time that one can at that time "falsify," and that some of these facts are "composed of" an individual who has a temporally genuine property (say, at t_1). Further, it claims that one can at t_2 falsify the soft fact about t_1 by so acting at t_2 that the individual would not have had the genuine property at t_1. This kind of Ockhamism suggests that one can "bootstrap" to the "alteration" of a genuine *property* relative to a time by falsifying a soft *fact* about the time.

The first approach to denying the soundness of the argument rests on the controversial claim that believing a certain proposition is *not* a genuine property of God at a certain time. In general, it seems to me that believing a proposition should be considered a temporally genuine property relative to a time. And so it seems to me that when God believes a proposition at a time, He has a temporally genuine property (of so believing) at that time. The second approach rests on two crucial and controversial claims: (i) the claim that God's believing at t_1 that Jane will go to the movies at t_2 is a *soft* (relational) fact about t_1; and (ii) the denial of (FP) insofar as the pertinent property is part of a certain sort of *soft* fact.

A third strategy (which is also contentious) *accepts* that believing a proposition at t_1 is a temporally nonrelational property with respect to t_1 *and* that God's believing a proposition at t_1 is a *hard* (i.e., temporally nonrelational) fact about t_1. This strategy (like the second approach) denies (FP), and *also* claims that human agents can sometimes have it in their power so to act that *hard* facts about the past would not have been facts. On this approach, one does not "bootstrap" to a denial of (FP) via claiming that God's beliefs are soft facts about the pertinent times. Rather, one denies both (FP) and the fixity of hard facts about the past. In this essay I consider the position that is common ground between the second and third strategies; that is, I consider the kind of compatibilism that *rejects* (FP)— *multiple-pasts compatibilism.*

The multiple-pasts compatibilist accepts

> (3) If Jane were to refrain from going to the movies on Tuesday, then God would have held a different belief from the one He actually held,

but denies that (3) implies that Jane cannot refrain from going to the movies on Tuesday. It is not claimed that Jane can initiate a causal chain that begins on Tuesday and ends on Monday. Rather, the claim is that Jane can do something on Tuesday (i.e., refrain from going to the movies) that is such that, if she were to do it, God would have known (and thus believed) on Monday that she would do it on Tuesday. It is often alleged that, since the compatibilist is *not* here committed to backward-causation, there is no incoherence in the position.

I wish to point out that multiple-pasts compatibilism, whatever its merits in other respects, is inconsistent with God's having a certain sort of immutability. It is frequently suggested that God's perfection—His supremacy—implies that He is immutable. But of course there are various different conceptions of immutability that depend, in part, on whether God's eternality is conceived of temporally or atemporally. We shall here employ the temporal conception of immutability.

Let me describe a very basic and (I hope) intuitive idea of immutability. Suppose that this chair is brown at t_1, and imagine that it is immutable as regards its color. Then its immutability implies that I (and all other agents) cannot make the chair nonbrown at t_2. Of course, we start with some sort of distinction between "intrinsic" and "extrinsic" properties of an object. And then we say that an object is immutable only if all its intrinsic properties are such that, if they are possessed at some time t_1, then no agent can so act that they are *not* possessed at any later time t_2. Let us call the sort of immutability that satisfies this condition *immutability I.*[5]

---

[5]This condition cannot provide a sufficient condition for the pertinent sort of immut-

Evidently, the multiple-pasts compatibilist's God cannot possess Immutability I. We are assuming, of course, that *believing that Jane will go to the movies on Tuesday* is a temporally intrinsic property of God (relative to the time at which the belief is held). And given the facts on Tuesday, God believes on Sunday that Jane will go to the movies on Tuesday. Thus, if Jane can on Tuesday so act that God would not have had this belief on Sunday (and thus on Monday), God isn't immutable in the first sense: although He actually has a certain temporally genuine property on Sunday, some agent can so act that He would not have had this property on Monday.

Of course, if Jane can refrain from going to the movies on Tuesday, Jane can act in such a way that God wouldn't have had his "actual" belief on Monday, Sunday, Saturday, and so on. That is, if Jane had refrained from going to the movies on Tuesday, God would have known from the beginning of time (if there was one) that Jane would refrain. Thus, on multiple-pasts compatibilism, there is *one* kind of immutability possessed by God. On this picture, an object is immutable only if no agent can bring it about that it has property P at t_1 and then lacks it at t_2.[6] This is a "world-relative" conception of immutability; according to this sort of immutability, in no possible world in which God is immutable does He possess an intrinsic property at t_1 and not at t_2. This kind of immutability is a sort of divine "stability" or "reliability".[7] An object has *immutability II* only if no agent can bring it about that it has P at t_1 and then lacks P at t_2. In contrast, an object is immutable I only if, given that it has P at t_1, no agent can bring it about that it lacks P at t_2. Thus, an object can be immutable II without being immutable I: the necessary condition for immutability I is stronger than that for immutability II. Now the multiple-pasts compatibilist

---

ability, because we can conceive of a possible world in which there are no agents and in which some object has some property at t_1 and can fail to have it at t_2. A more general characterization of immutability I would be as follows: an object is immutable I insofar as all its intrinsic properties are such that, if they are possessed at t_1, then it is not possible that they not be possessed at any later time t_2. Of course, the kind of possibility relevant to this definition cannot be logical possibility, but must be some weaker kind of possibility.

[6]The sort of considerations raised in the previous footnote also apply to immutability II.

[7]For such a conception, see Thomas V. Morris, "Properties, Modalities, and God," *Philosophical Review* 93 (January 1984), 35–55.

can grant immutability II to God, even while denying God immutability I.

Before I discuss the two different conceptions, I shall make a few small points. God is constantly changing His merely extrinsic or relational properties, such as the property of *being worshipped by John*, and so on. (I take it that spatially and temporally extrinsic properties are species of the genus, extrinsic properties). But I simply assume here that such changes in extrinsic properties do not attenuate God's immutability, properly interpreted. Further, God changes from believing (on Monday) that Jane *will go* to the movies on Tuesday to believing (on Tuesday) that Jane *is going* to the movies on Tuesday, etc. But it can be argued that this sort of change does not involve two different beliefs, but rather, two different ways of holding, or perhaps temporal perspectives on, the *same* belief. It is not obvious that *this* sort of change implies that God is mutable in any interesting sense.

Which sort of immutability—I or II—more faithfully reflects our conception of God? I do not know the answer to this question. If one decides that attributing freedom to God's creatures is quite necessary, then one will presumably opt for immutability II (insofar as one is a multiple-pasts compatibilist). But it is interesting at least to note that according to this approach God would not have the stronger kind of immutability—immutability I. This might undermine God's claims to perfection and supremacy.

In light of this sort of worry, one could respond that the kind of property I have discussed—having a certain belief—is not the kind of property pertinent to God's immutability. Rather, the properties relevant to God's immutability are the more "general" properties that comprise the divine attributes. And it is true that with respect to (say) omniscience, God is both immutable I and immutable II. This is certainly a coherent option open to the multiple-pasts compatibilist; but it is unclear exactly *why* temporally genuine properties such as beliefs should not be relevant to God's immutability. Further, it is useful to notice that the multiple-pasts compatibilist is *committed* to such a conception of the properties relevant to immutability, if he wishes to maintain that God has immutability I.

In this section I have pointed out that there are two different notions of immutability. The multiple-pasts compatibilist can agree that God is immutable II, but unless he speaks only of certain "general" divine attributes, he *cannot* say that God is immutable I. Multiple-pasts compatibilism is in tension with a very attractive conception of immutability, one that might seem to follow from God's perfection and supremacy. So even if one grants the multiple-pasts compatibilist's highly controversial assumption that one can "affect" genuine properties possessed in the past, the position may not be coherent, relative to the *total* set of divine attributes. Of course, I have not *established* any incoherence; the multiple-pasts compatibilist might be willing to settle for immutability II, but it is useful to see that this is the *price* of multiple-pasts compatibilism.[8]

3 WI Compatibilism

In Section 2 I claimed that *even if* one denies (FP), there is a problem for compatibilism: God cannot be construed as possessing immutability I. Since I believe that the denial of (FP) is itself implausible, I believe that the multiple-pasts compatibilist is committed to *two* rather damaging and problematic claims. In this section I shall develop an alternative version of compatibilism; this version of compatibilism might seem to allow the compatibilist to *accept* both (FP) and God's immutability I. Thus, this kind of compatibilism is promising insofar as it purports to avoid both problematic commitments of multiple-pasts compatibilism.

[8]After having written this paper, I received extremely valuable comments from Philip Quinn, who raises the following objection to requiring that God possess immutability I. Someone who believes that God has immutability I should also hold that God has immutability I*: an object is immutable only if its intrinsic properties are such that, if they are possessed at some time, then events cannot so happen that they are not possessed at any later time. Now it is obvious that an argument similar to the one presented in the text would show that God's immutability I* is incompatible with indeterminism in nature. On a certain (plausible) conception of atomic physics, radioactive decay takes place indeterministically. So when a certain radium atom decays at time t_n, it is compatible with the laws of nature and the past relative to t_n that it not decay: in this sense of *can*, it could have been the case that the atom did not decay. But then although God actually believed (let us say at t_o) that the atom would decay at t_n, it could have been the case that He believed (at say t_1) that the atom would *not* decay at t_n. Thus God would not possess immutability I*.

Quinn's point is that God's immutability I* is incompatible with indeterminism in nature and thus that it is not reasonable to require that God possess immutability I. If this is correct, then the price of settling for immutability II would not be too high. If one agrees with Quinn about this, the considerations in the following sections should be construed as germane primarily to (FP): that is, even if the denial of immutability I is not unreasonable, the denial of (FP) certainly is controversial, and it is important to investigate the possibility of a compatibilism that can embrace (FP).

The approach that I propose to consider here involves a *world index-ation* of the contents of God's beliefs. So suppose that the actual world is W_1. And imagine again that Jane goes to the movies on Tuesday. Then God believes on Monday that Jane will go to the movies on Tuesday *in* W_1. But God knows not just what actually happens, but what possibly happens as well. So if it is possible that Jane refrains from going to the movies, then God has true beliefs about which worlds are the possible worlds in which Jane refrains from going to the movies on Tuesday. Thus, if W_2 is a world in which Jane refrains, then God believes on Monday that Jane will refrain from going to the movies on Tuesday *in* W_2. On the world-indexed picture of God's omniscience, God has at each time a complete catalogue of true beliefs about all possible worlds. At each time, God knows not only what happens (and will happen) but what is possible.

I shall call the sort of compatibilism that issues from acceptance of the world-indexed picture of God's omniscience *WI compatibilism*. WI compatibilism is attractive insofar as it appears to be consistent with both (FP) and God's immutability I.

Consider first (FP). Suppose (as above) that Jane goes to the movies on Tuesday in W_1. It is true that if Jane were to refrain from going to the movies (let us say in W_2), then God would have believed on Monday that Jane would refrain from going to the movies on Tuesday in W_2. But the truth of this conditional is entirely consistent with Jane's freedom on Tuesday to refrain from going to the movies, even given (FP). This is because God actually held the same belief that He would have held on Monday, if Jane were to refrain: the belief that Jane will refrain from going to the movies *in* W_2. On Monday, God has a complete catalogue of true beliefs about future times in *all* possible worlds—in W_1, W_2, W_3, etc. God believes on Monday that Jane will go to the movies on Tuesday in W_1, that Jane will refrain from going to the movies on Tuesday in W_2, etc.[9] Apparently, in virtue of the world in-

---

[9]As I have described things, it seems that all possible worlds are immersed in time and that God, who is also in time, looks at these worlds from a viewpoint outside of any particular possible world. But I need *not* make this assumption. I could make essentially the same points by placing God *in* the pertinent possible worlds. On this picture, in all the relevant possible worlds, God holds the complete catalogue of true, world-indexed beliefs. So, God believes on Monday *in* W_1 that Jane will go to the movies on Tuesday in W_1, that Jane will refrain from going to the movies on Tuesday in W_2, etc. And God believes on Monday *in* W_2 that Jane will go to the movies on Tuesday in W_1, that Jane will refrain from going to the movies on Tuesday in W_2, etc. The metaphysical

dexation of the contents of God's beliefs, the catalogue of God's beliefs would not change if Jane were to refrain from going to the movies on Tuesday. Thus, it appears that the WI compatibilist can *accept* (FP): Jane's freedom to do otherwise on Tuesday apparently need not be construed as the freedom so to act that God would not have possessed some property on Monday that He actually possessed on Monday. WI compatibilism thus appears to be a "fixed-past" version of compatibilism, even on the assumption of the temporal genuineness of God's belief.

Also, it should be clear how WI compatibilism might be thought to be consistent with God's immutability I. Suppose that Jane actually goes to the movies on Tuesday. Then God believed on Sunday that Jane would go to the movies on Tuesday in W_1. If Jane can refrain on Tuesday, then she has it in her power so to act that God would have believed on Monday that she would refrain from going to the movies on Tuesday in (let us say) W_2. But it is *not* the case that whereas God has some genuine property P at t_1 (the property of believing on Sunday that Jane will go to the movies on Tuesday in W_1), Jane can bring it about that God wouldn't have this property at t_2 (i.e., on Monday). This is because if Jane were to refrain on Tuesday in W_2, it still would be true that on Monday God believed that Jane would go to the movies on Tuesday *in* W_1. Of course, if Jane were to refrain, then God would have believed that Jane would refrain from going to the movies on Tuesday in W_2; but he would have *actually* had this *same* world-indexed belief. So we have (as yet) found no property possessed by God on Sunday that is such that Jane can bring it about that it is not possessed by God (say) on Monday.

WI compatibilism, then, is attractive. World indexation of the content of God's beliefs seems to allow the compatibilist to deny that God's beliefs are of the form: "that Jane will go to the movies on Tuesday." Rather, God's beliefs are explicitly world-indexed: He believes on Monday that Jane will go to the movies on Tuesday *in* W_1, etc. This picture of the content of God's beliefs evidently allows the WI compatibilist to respond to the objections raised by the incompatibilist.

But I believe that WI compatibilism, as thus far developed, is unacceptable. It is vulnerable to objections that are similar to those developed above. The dialectical situation is as follows. The incom-

---

issues developed in this paper are neutral with respect to assumptions about whether or not God is situated within possible worlds.

patibilist claims that the compatibilist must say that there is at least one temporally genuine property P possessed by God at a time t that is such that a human being can at a later time so act that God would *not* have possessed P at t. Above, the incompatibilist suggested that the pertinent property is something like *believing that Jane will go to the movies on Tuesday*. But the WI compatibilist can apparently *deny* that God possessed *this* property, and he can point out that the pertinent world-indexed property that *is* possessed by God is indeed outside of Jane's power to affect. But it clearly does *not* follow that there is *no* property that accords with the incompatibilist's claim. That is, it does not follow from the WI compatibilist's response that there is *no* property P such that it is temporally genuine, possessed by God at a time t, and such that a human being can at a later time so act that God would not have possessed P at t (on the assumption of compatibilism).

Suppose, again, that Jane goes to the movies on Tuesday in the actual world, W_1. It follows from God's omniscience that God believed on Monday that W_1 is the actual world. But if Jane were to refrain from going to the movies on Tuesday, then (let us say) W_2 would have been the actual world. So if Jane were to refrain on Tuesday, then God would have believed on Monday that W_2 is the actual world. So there is a property—believing that W_1 is the actual world—that is (by the supposition of this essay) temporally genuine, possessed by God on Monday, and that is such that Jane can on Tuesday so act that God would not have possessed it on Monday (insofar as Jane can indeed refrain from going to the movies on Tuesday). If this is correct, then even WI compatibilism is committed to the denial of (FP) with respect to *some* property.

Further, it is clear that WI compatibilism cannot accept God's immutability I. The property of believing that W_1 is the actual world is such that God possesses it on Sunday and nevertheless Jane has it in her power on Tuesday (if compatibilism is true) so to act that He would not have possessed it on (say) Monday. Thus, even WI compatibilism is committed to God's mutability I, with regard to *some* property. So WI compatibilism seems to be no more plausible than the compatibilism with which we started—multiple-pasts compatibilism.

I shall now point to a further problem with WI compatibilism. On the supposition that Jane actually goes to the movies on Tuesday, God believes on Monday that Jane will go to the movies on Tuesday in W_1. Also, He believes on Monday that W_1 is actual. But these two beliefs appear to *entail* the index-free belief that Jane will go to the movies on Tuesday. So it seems that even on WI compatibilism, God must have the index-free belief, to the extent that God's beliefs are closed under entailment. Indeed, since God is omniscient, He knows the pertinent entailment, and thus He must have the index-free belief, to the extent that God's beliefs are closed under known entailment.

Now it might be thought that the WI compatibilist could simply insist that the world-indexed belief is the proper *analysis* of the index-free belief. That is, one might claim that *Jane will go to the movies on Tuesday* is properly analyzed as *Jane will go to the movies on Tuesday in W_1*, and thus that God "really" has only the world-indexed belief. But this move is obviously unacceptable. The world-indexed belief cannot be the same belief as the index-free belief, because the world-indexed belief is a *necessary* truth, whereas the index-free belief is contingent. (The world-indexed belief is necessary insofar as "W_1" is the name of a completely determinate world that already "includes" Jane's going to the movies on Tuesday.) So it seems that, despite world-indexation of *some* of God's beliefs, *others* will be index free, and WI compatibilism will have exactly the same sort of problem as multiple-pasts compatibilism.

One way to deny that God must have index-free beliefs would be to deny that God's beliefs are closed under entailment (and known entailment). But this is an entirely unacceptable conception of God's omniscience; it is implausible to suppose that God is an "epistemically irresponsible" or negligent or in any way "nonideal" agent. The argument of this section, then, can be summarized as follows. Even if some of God's beliefs are world-indexed, there will be *some* property of God—a belief about which world is *actual*—in virtue of which WI compatibilism must deny both (FP) and God's immutability I. Further, if God's beliefs are closed under entailment, then even if some of God's beliefs are world- indexed, *other* beliefs (say, about what human agents will do) will be index-free; and in virtue of God's having these index-free beliefs, the WI compatibilist must confront exactly the same problems as the multiple-pasts compatibilist.

4 Freedom and Actuality

In this section, I shall sketch and explore a possible way of defending WI compatibilism against the arguments presented above. I intend to show how questions about the relationship between God's existence and human freedom connect in an interesting way with another set of issues in metaphysics.

The problems for compatibilism arose from God's beliefs about the actual world. Now a compatibilist might respond that God does not have any beliefs about "the actual world," because there is no single, unique actual world. This kind of compatibilism combines world indexation of God's belief-contents with the metaphysical doctrine of "indexical possibilism."

Let us begin by distinguishing *possibilism* from *actualism*.[10] The possibilist about possible worlds claims that all possible worlds are concrete objects. But there are two versions of possibilism: an absolutist version and an indexical version. Absolutist possibilism claims that there is a unique possible world that possesses the property of *actuality*; the other possible worlds, although concrete and in some sense existent, are not actual or "real." Indexical possibilism claims that all possible worlds are equally "actual" and equally "real." On the indexical view, each possible world is actual "relative to itself," but there is no nonrelative truth about which world is "the actual world."[11]

In contrast, actualism claims that possible worlds are abstract entities—propositions, states of affairs, properties, etc. (depending on the particular version of actualism). The actualist might say that possible worlds are abstract particulars (such as sets), or universals; but the point is that they are abstract. The actualist claims that there is one actual world that "corresponds to" this concrete universe: on one version of actualism, the actual world is "the way this concrete universe is," whereas other possible worlds are "ways this universe might have been." The actualist is a reductionist: he wishes to reduce talk of other possible worlds to talk about this one. That is, he does not engage in talk about other possible worlds as unreducible concrete objects.

Actualism and absolutist possibilism share an *absolute* conception of actuality: there is a unique world that is *the* actual world. Indexical

[10]I follow McMichael's characterization of the distinction: Alan McMichael, "A Problem for Actualism about Possible Worlds," *Philosophical Review* 92 (January 1983), 49–66. For a related distinction, see Robert Merrihew Adams, "Theories of Actuality," *Noûs* 8 (1974), 211–230.

[11]David Lewis is an indexical possibilist: "Anselm and Actuality," *Noûs* 4 (1970); *Counterfactuals* (Oxford: Basil Blackwell, 1973); and *On the Plurality of Worlds* (Oxford: Basil Blackwell, 1986).

possibilism denies this claim; it argues for ontological parity. On this view, an inhabitant of W_1 would be speaking truly if he said that W_1 is the actual world, but this statement must be understood as embodying a kind of relativism that springs from indexicality: he must be interpreted as saying that W_1 is actual *relative to* W_1. On indexical possibilism, there are no true, "nonrelative" actuality claims.

There are many interesting metaphysical issues involved in the debates between actualists and possibilists, and between "absolutists" and "indexicalists." I shall not discuss these issues here. Rather, I am concerned to discuss the connection between indexical possibilism and compatibilism about God's existence and human freedom. It should be evident that indexical possibilism implies that God would not have any (nonrelativized) beliefs as to which world is *the* actual world, and thus, that the objections to WI compatibilism based on such beliefs would be unacceptable. It is interesting to see that a WI compatibilist who accepted indexical possibilism could block the traditional objection based on the fixity of the past, as well as the objection based on God's immutability I.

To see how indexical possibilism helps the WI compatibilist, imagine again that Jane goes to the movies on Tuesday. Note that if Jane were to refrain from going to the movies on Tuesday, then God would have believed on Monday that Jane would refrain from going to the movies on Tuesday in W_2. And of course, as was argued above, this world-indexed belief is a belief which God *actually* held (i.e., held in W_1) on Monday. So there would be *as yet* no violation of (FP) or immutability I (as pointed out above). Further, God does not (and would not have) any nonrelativized beliefs about the actual world, so there appear to be no ways of generating violations of (FP) or immutability I in the manner presented above. (Note that God actually believed on Monday that W_1 is the actual world *relative to* W_1, but He would have had exactly the same *relativized* actuality-belief, had Jane refrained from going to the movies on Tuesday—let us say, in W_2.) Thus, indexical possibilism helps the WI compatibilist to block the objections based on (FP) and immutability I. The WI compatibilist who accepts indexical possibilism can embrace (FP), God's immutability I, the temporal genuineness of God's beliefs, and the closure of God's beliefs under entailment (and known entailment).

If indexical possibilism is accepted, then we can say that the closure of God's beliefs under entailment (and known entailment) does not lead to ascribing to God index-free beliefs. But it might be pointed out that, even if one doesn't ascribe index-free beliefs to God as a result of the necessity of His inferring them from other beliefs He has, it nevertheless might be the case that God has index-free beliefs. And insofar as index-free propositions such as *Jane goes to the movies on Tuesday* are indeed *true* in possible worlds (specifically, W_1), and God is omniscient as defined above, then God must believe in W_1 that Jane will refrain from going to the movies on Tuesday.

The WI compatibilist could make two responses. First, the objection seems to assume that God is inside particular possible worlds, and it might be avoided by assuming that God is not situated within possible worlds. But it is not obvious that God is not situated in possible worlds, so this response is unappealing. The WI compatibilist should simply insist that the contents of God's beliefs *must* be world-indexed. Thus, insofar as index-free propositions are indeed true, God does not believe all the truths that there are. In order for WI compatibilism to provide a method of responding to the incompatibilist's argument, it must insist that God's beliefs are all world-indexed. Thus, such a compatibilist must adopt the following conception of God's essential omniscience: It is necessarily true that, if God exists, then for any time t and *world-indexed* proposition P, God knows (and thus believes) at t that P if and only if P is true at t.[12]

Now I do not have a knockdown objection to indexical possibilism, and thus I do not have a decisive argument against the conjunction of WI compatibilism and indexical possibilism. But I shall sketch a basic complaint about employing indexical possibilism to rescue compatibilism, and then I shall present two worries about indexical possibilism. The first worry concerns the theological acceptability of indexical possibilism, and the second worry concerns the relationship between indexical possibilism and practical reasoning. Thus, the two worries are particularly germane to the relationship between indexical possibilism and compatibilism.

The first thing to say about indexical possibilism is that it is, at best, an extremely controversial metaphysical thesis. A defense of compatibilism that employed the assumption of indexical possibilism would thus be very weak; it would be no less controversial than indexical possibilism itself. There are philosophers who wish to be compatibilists

---

[12]Of course, it will now be controversial whether God's omniscience has been attenuated significantly by denying God some true beliefs—the index-free truths. I *do* think that the WI compatibilist is committed to this picture of God's omniscience, but it is not clear that this is an unacceptable picture. After all, given that God believes all the world-indexed truths, exactly what information has been denied God?

but who are not indexical possibilists, and clearly this sort of defense of compatibilism (which embraces indexical possibilism) would be unacceptable to them. This kind of compatibilism is based on too "special" and contentious a presupposition.

Consider a possible world (W_3) in which everyone (and there are many persons) suffers terribly throughout his life. This is certainly a conceivable world, and it would appear to be metaphysically possible. Now it seems to me to be highly implausible to suppose that, simply in virtue of its conceivability and metaphysical possibility, it would follow that W_3 is equally real as our world—that there is no difference in respect of reality and actuality between our world and W_3. (Of course, this is just to remind us of the surface implausibility of indexical possibilism).

But let us imagine that the indexical possibilist is correct that W_3 and our world are equally real. I think that this is certainly in contrast with the standard theological assumption that God created our world W_1 *rather than* (say) W_3, and that He did so *for a reason*. That is, it is a standard theological assumption that God made this world *the* actual world, and that He had a good reason for doing so. Indeed, in presenting a theodicy—a response to the problem of evil—it is standardly supposed that one needs to explain why God created (i.e., "made real") *this* world rather than another world. This kind of response would be irrelevant, if indexical possibilism were true.

To be sure, indexical possibilism would allow one to dispose of the problem of evil. This is because (under indexical possibilism) it is a necessary truth that all possible worlds are equally real, and thus it is no real limitation of God that He created *this* possible world. God never had the choice of making this world rather than another world *the* real world. But whereas indexical possibilism would in principle permit this sort of response to the problem of evil, I think that this implication of indexical possibilism points to its theological inadequacy (or at least its inconsistency with very appealing, natural theological presuppositions). The indexical possibilist's God is one who did *not* make this world rather than W_3 real, and who literally could not prevent the existence of an entire world of intensely suffering (innocent) persons— a world in which the people and their suffering are as real as we are. But this is surely not the traditional (or a very plausible) conception of God.[13]

---

[13]Parallel to indexical possibilism's dissolution of the problem of evil is its dissolution of the problem of skepticism about our own actuality (Lewis, "Anselm and Actuality,"

The first worry about indexical possibilism, then, has to do with the theological acceptability of this doctrine. The second worry has to do with the relationship between indexical possibilism and practical reasoning.[14] To focus on this second worry, let us take for granted a possible-worlds analysis of freedom, according to which an agent A can (in world W_1) do X just in case there exists some world "suitably related" to W_1 in which A does X. The intuitive problem for indexical possibilism is as follows. If it is granted that A can either do or not do something—e.g., give some money to charity—then why should A care about *what* he actually does? Insofar as the worlds in which he does the thing and in which he does not do it are equally real, then why should it matter to the agent what he does in this world? Given a specification of the actions that he *can* perform (and given indexical possibilism), it becomes rather mysterious what the point of practical reasoning would be.

Now an indexical possibilist might respond as follows. Agents must be considered worldbound.[15] If A exists in world W_1, then A cannot exist in any other possible world. Rather, there are "counterparts" of A in some other possible worlds. We can now combine the possible-worlds analysis of freedom with counterpart theory as follows: to claim that A can do X in (say) W is just to claim that a *counterpart* of A, A', does X in some world "suitably related" to W. But since agents care about what *they* (rather than their counterparts) do, there is a point to practical reasoning.

But I find this response unconvincing. The WI compatibilist who adopts indexical possibilism wants to preserve the truth of certain claims about human freedom, even if God exists. But if the claims about freedom simply amount to facts about what an agent's *counterparts* do, and one cares about what one (and *not* one's counterpart) does, then the claims about freedom will be cold comfort. The kind of freedom claims secured by this sort of compatibilism would be uninteresting and irrelevant to agents.

---

186) and the problem of why there is something rather than nothing (see Peter van Inwagen, "Indexicality and Actuality," *Philosophical Review* 89 (July 1980), 403–426.

[14]I owe this point entirely to David Widerker, to whom I am deeply indebted.

[15]Of course, David Lewis develops just such a theory in "Counterpart Theory and Quantified Modal Logic," *Journal of Philosophy* 65 (1968), 113–26. Interestingly, Peter van Inwagen says (concerning a different point from that concerning practical reasoning), "I doubt it is an accident that Lewis is the originator of both Counterpart Theory and the indexical theory" ("Indexicality and Actuality," 417).

The worry that arises from the nature of practical reasoning can now be set out rather more explicitly. The WI compatibilist who adopts indexical possibilism wishes to secure human freedom, even if God exists. But on this approach, either the freedom claims *are* interesting and relevant but the point of practical reasoning is lost, or there is a point to practical reasoning but the freedom claims are attenuated.

5 Conclusion: Freedom, Immutability, and Actuality

One kind of compatibilist (the multiple-pasts compatibilist) admits that beliefs are temporally genuine properties, but denies that certain temporally genuine features of the past are fixed—i.e., denies (FP). This sort of compatibilist must also deny that God has a certain sort of immutability—immutability I; that is, the denial of God's immutability I is part of the price of multiple-pasts compatibilism (unless one restricts the properties pertinent to immutability).

Further, I have sketched an alternative form of compatibilism that embraces the world-indexation of the contents of God's beliefs: WI compatibilism. This sort of compatibilism seems at first to preserve both (FP) and God's immutability I (even while admitting that God's beliefs are temporally genuine). However, in order to secure these results, the WI compatibilist must endorse indexical possibilism.

I am tempted to call WI compatibilism *Leibnizean compatibilism*, for the obvious reason that Leibniz held that God had knowledge of all the different possible worlds. But the problem is that the plausibility of WI compatibilism depends on indexical possibilism, which is profoundly un-Leibnizean. Perhaps the conjunction of WI compatibilism with indexical possibilism should be called *Lewis-style compatibilism*.[16]

It is interesting to note that such a compatibilism is possible. It might have been thought that the only way a compatibilist could maintain (FP) and God's immutability I would be to insist that God's beliefs are not temporally genuine; but the conjunction of world indexation of

[16]To my knowledge David Lewis has not explicitly considered this sort of position, and I have no idea whether he himself would adopt it. Lewis argues for indexical possibilism at length in Lewis, *On the Plurality of Worlds*. I believe that the kind of compatibilism developed in this paper must at least be taken seriously.

God's beliefs with indexical possibilism shows this supposition to be false. I hope that it will have been worthwhile to reveal a connection between two apparently unrelated sets of issues in metaphysics: questions about freedom and questions about the nature of actuality. Ultimately, I believe that WI compatibilism is unsatisfying precisely because its plausibility depends on its conjunction with indexical possibilism. The acceptability of WI compatibilism rests on a highly contentious metaphysical assumption.[17]

[17] I have benefited greatly from extremely useful discussions with David Widerker, and also from his comments on a previous version of this essay. Also, I thank Phil Quinn for his insightful comments.

Part Three

THE NATURE OF
THE DIVINE AGENT

9

Divine and Human Action

William P. Alston

Unlike most others in this volume, this essay is not a direct discussion of divine action. Rather, it raises questions of "second intention" concerning the kind of concepts we are able to form of divine action, and it considers the bearing of this on our situation vis-à-vis God.

What concepts are applicable to God depends, of course, on what God is like.[1] If, for example, God is a personal agent in the same fundamental sense as ourselves, albeit one that is immaterial and unlimited in fundamental respects, many concepts applicable to human beings will be applicable to Him, perhaps with a little doctoring. There is no space here to defend a position on the nature of God. I will be thinking of God as (i) immaterial, (ii) infinitely perfect, and (iii) timeless, in that His own being, His own life, does not involve temporal succession. The third of these assumptions is particularly controversial, but I forgo any defence in this place.[2] I shall be considering what sort of action concepts could be truly applicable to such a Being.

It is a familiar truism that our concepts of God, at least those that go beyond such bare ontological features as self-identity, are derived

---

[1] To establish a conclusion about the kinds of concepts applicable to God, or even to argue for such a conclusion, we have to say something about what God is like, thereby claiming to apply certain concepts to Him. Thus the enterprise is inevitably infected with a certain circularity.

[2] For an impressive exposition and defense of the doctrine see Eleonore Stump and Norman Kretzmann, "Eternity," *Journal of Philosophy* 78 (1981), 429–458.

from our concepts of human beings; and this would seem to be particularly obvious with respect to my topic. Our thought of God as agent is clearly modeled on our understanding of human agency. Thus a natural and frequently taken approach to our problem is to start with human action concepts and determine how much of them is transferrable to the divine case. In traditional terms, can we speak *univocally* of divine and human action? Or, better, to what extent can we speak univocally of divine and human action? As the last formulation indicates, I take seriously—indeed advocate—a position rarely taken on this issue, viz., partial univocity. The field has been dominated by, on the one hand, those who see no difficulty in a wholesale univocity, and on the other hand, those who hold that no term can be univocally applied to God and to us. This latter group is divided into those who suppose that some irreducibly analogical relation holds between divine and human senses of terms, and those who take the terms in question to be applied figuratively or "symbolically" to God. It is odd that the partial-univocity possibility has not received more attention. After all, a partial overlap of meaning is an excessively familiar semantic phenomenon. Just to take the most obvious example, the terms for two species of the same genus share the generic feature and differ, tautologically, with respect to the differentia. I conjecture that partial overlap of meaning has been ignored because of the prominence of those who, like Tillich, construe the otherness of God so radically as to leave room for no commonality of meaning, leading in turn to an overreaction by those who feel that unless univocity receives a compensatory stress our talk about God will founder in a morass of pan-symbolism. In any event, it is the partial-univocity thesis that I wish to explore and defend.

However, the univocity issue has a determinate sense only to the extent that there are determinate boundaries around the meaning of a term. To go at it from the other side, insofar as what belongs to the meaning of a term, as contrasted with what is obviously true of the things to which the term applies, is not fixed, there is no determinate issue as to whether another term, or that term in another application, bears the same meaning. And it has been forcefully pointed out in recent decades by Quine and others that it is very difficult (impossible, according to Quine) to discern such boundaries. Let's take an example directly relevant to the concerns of this essay. It is a basic fact about human action that one cannot perform an action the necessary conditions of which include changes in the world outside the agent, without doing so by moving one's body in certain ways. Does that mean that it is part of the *meaning* of 'S closed a door' that S brought it about by movements of S's body that a door was closed? This obviously has a crucial bearing on whether human action terms can be univocally predicated of God; for if that is part of the meaning, then, since God has no body, no action term with that meaning could be truly predicated of God. In "Can We Speak Literally of God?"[3] I argued that this is not part of the meaning, that it is a (conceptually as well as metaphysically) *contingent* fact about human beings that one can only bring about changes in the external world through movements of one's body, and that it is no part of the meaning of action terms, including those that in fact apply to human beings, that this should be the case. However, I must confess that the matter is not crystal clear. Again, is it part of the meaning of 'S succeeded in achieving his purpose that T' or 'S carried out her intention to do A' that there is some temporal separation between the initiation of the having of the purpose or the forming of the intention, on the one hand, and the achievement of the action on the other? This will have an important bearing on whether notions of purpose and intention can be applied in the human sense to an atemporal deity. Again, I don't find this very clear. I am not for a moment suggesting that *no* line can be drawn between meaning and the facts of the world, between the dictionary and the encyclopedia. It is clearly part of the meaning of 'intention to do A' that the intender have some tendency to do A, and it is clearly not part of that meaning that intenders not infrequently fail to carry out their intentions. Nevertheless, in the most interesting cases it is often unclear where the line is to be drawn. If it is drawn so as to circumscribe meaning most narrowly, there will be much more of a chance for univocal terms across the divine-human gap; if it is drawn more generously less will carry over to the divine case.

Even if we cannot settle all these boundary disputes to everyone's satisfaction in a clearly objective fashion, our problem will remain. It would be misguided to suppose that the question of how we should construe divine action is tied to the details of the ways in which conceptual content is encoded in the meaning of one or another linguistic item. The more fundamental issues concern how much of the *way we*

---

[3]In *Is God GOD?*, ed. A. D. Steuer and J. W. McClendon, Jr. (Nashville, Tenn.: Abingdon, 1981), pp. 146–177.

think of human action can be carried over to our thought of divine action. It is of secondary importance how much of this is carried by the meaning of one or another linguistic expression.

It seems to be agreed on all hands that concepts of human intentional actions (we shall be restricting ourselves to intentional action) are to be understood in terms of the role of psychological, motivational factors like intentions, desires, attitudes, beliefs, and so on. To (intentionally) close a door is not just to make some particular sort of bodily movement. Nor does it just consist in a bodily movement of the agent's leading to a door coming to be closed. That overt pattern does not count as a case of S's intentionally closing a door unless it constitutes the carrying out of an intention to close the door in question, unless it was done because S had an interest in the door's being closed . . . The dots indicate that there is a variety of ways in which psychological antecedents or concomitants of the overt activity are thought to enter into the concept of intentional human action. There are differences both as to what sorts of psychological factors play a crucial role, and how they are related to the more overt aspects of the action, e.g., causally or otherwise. Although these differences are of the first importance for the project of developing an adequate account of human action, they are peripheral to our concerns here, with an exception to be noted. For the sake of concreteness let's adopt Donald Davidson's lingo, though not putting it to the same uses, and say that S intentionally closes a door just in case S performs the overt movements that lead to the door's being closed because S has a "pro-attitude" toward a state of affairs, A, and a belief that the door's coming to be closed either is or is likely to lead to a case of A.[4] In more informal terms, S intentionally brings about a state of affairs B only if there is a state of affairs, A, which might or might not be identical with B, for the sake of which S is doing what leads to the bringing about of B.

If something like this is along the right line, then the question of whether we can carry human action terms over to the divine case can be divided into two main parts: (i) Can psychological motivational concepts be applied to the divine case? (ii) What about the bodily

[4]See Donald Davidson, "Actions, Reasons, and Causes," *Journal of Philosophy* 60 (1963), 685–700, for his version of this. In "An Action-Plan Interpretation of Purposive Explanations of Actions," *Theory and Decision* 20 (1986), 275–299, I present reasons for objecting to the idea that the crucial psychological factors are to be thought of, as Davidson and many other theorists do, as antecedent causes. Again, these differences are not crucial for the present discussion.

movements that get thus motivated and lead to the crucial external result? I shall discuss these in reverse order.

1 Action and Motivation

It is clear that human beings bring about changes in the external world by moving their bodies in various ways, and so, as pointed out above, if this fact is (partly) constitutive of the meanings of human action terms, then that will prevent these terms from being truly applied, in just the same sense, to an incorporeal agent. However, if everything else carries over we can still apply closely analogous terms. Whereas in the human case the appropriate psychological background leads to bodily movements that result in the door's being closed, we can think of the structure of a divine action of closing a door as being just like this except for the shortcircuiting of the bodily movement part. That is, in the divine case the sort of psychological factors that led in the human case to the bodily movements that were designed to get the door closed will, in the divine case, lead directly to the "external" result, in this case the door's being closed. More exactly, this would be the pattern of God's closing the door as a "basic act," one done not by way of doing something else. Of course God could do everything He does as a basic act, but He may well choose to do some things by doing other things. Thus the Old Testament tells us that God got the Israelites out of Egypt not by directly bringing it about that they were instantaneously somewhere else, as He perfectly well could have done, but by altering the configuration of the water in a lake or inland sea in order to make it possible for them to cross. In any event, whatever it is that God does directly in any particular project will follow immediately on the relevant psychological antecedents. Thus the absence of bodily movements in the divine case will not prevent us from applying to Him human action concepts, or concepts that can be simply derived from them.[5]

The second part of the question will occupy us for most of the re-

---

[5]If someone were to ask at this point "How on earth can God bring about external results directly?", I would have to rule the question out of order. I am setting out to explore not the "mechanism" of divine action, if there can be any such thing, but rather its conceptualization, what sort of concept we can form of God's doing something. Whatever that concept may be, it most certainly will not contain any specification of how God manages to bring off what He does.

mainder of this essay. Let's begin the discussion by looking more carefully at what we need to carry over from the human side in order to come as close as possible to univocity. The basic idea of the approach to intentional action with which we are working is that overt changes (to use a term that is neutral as to whether movements of the agent's body are involved) constitute, or constitute the overt aspect of, an intentional action only if they result from a psychological structure that involves at least a "goal-setting" state (our "pro-attitude") and a cognitive guidance state—one that provides "information" as to actual or probable connections in the world, information that is needed to determine how the goal state may be reached. The category of *pro-attitude* stretches over a wide variety of conative factors—wants, desires, aversions, longings, yearnings, attitudes of various sorts, scruples, commitments, and so on. (Actually we are speaking of "con-attitudes" as well as pro-attitudes. In the sequel I shall frequently use the term 'attitude' for the general category, leaving '*pro* or *con*' to be tacitly understood.) Different items on this list work differently, have different antecedents, manifest themselves differently in consciousness, and so on. Now it is doubtful that the divine nature provides any basis for such discriminations. God is subject to no biological cravings, rooted in the need for survival. Since He is perfectly good He wants nothing that runs contrary to what He sees to be best, and so there is no discrepancy between what He wants and what He recognizes to be right and good. He does not pursue goals in sudden gusts of passion or uncontrollable longing. For the divine case we can safely confine ourselves to the generic category. As for the cognitive guidance factor, we could ignore that, as far as the motivation of behavior is concerned (though we would still think of God as possessing perfect knowledge), if God were to do everything He does as a basic act. But since we want at least to leave open the possibility that this is not the case, we will have to make room for God using His knowledge to determine what will lead to what.[6] In the human case it seems that the appropriate

---

[6]These issues deserve much more discussion than is possible here. For one thing, since anything God brings about in the world will have innumerable consequences, it might be thought that God will be indirectly bringing about all those consequences, and so it is impossible that God should not do many things indirectly. But it must be remembered that we are restricting ourselves to *intentional* action, and it cannot be assumed that God intends to bring about all the consequences of everything He brings about, even though He will, of course, know about them. Second, if we were to take God to be "omnidetermining," deciding every detail of His creation, then He would have no need to guide His action by His awareness of relevant features of the world. For He

generic term for this side of the matter is *belief*. For human beings choose means to attain their goals in the light of what they believe to be the case, whether or not these beliefs are correct and whether or not they count as knowledge. But God will not possess any "mere beliefs," beliefs that do not count as knowledge, since He has complete knowledge of everything knowable. Moreover, as I have argued elsewhere[7], the category of belief would seem not to be applicable to God at all, since, among other reasons, there is a point in using the concept only where there is a possibility that the subject may take something to be the case without knowing it to be the case. Thus, it would seem that the cognitive side of the divine motivational structure should be restricted to knowledge.

Thus our question becomes: Can we use the same concepts of "attitudes" and "knowledge" of God and man? Let's begin with the former. In supposing that God has a pro-attitude toward my becoming sanctified, am I attributing the same sort of thing to God that I am attributing to you when I suppose that you have a pro-attitude toward winning the race? Clearly there will be enormous differences between what is involved in God and in you having such an attitude. There is no question of assimilating the details of the divine psychology to human psychology. But is there a significant core that is common to divine and human attitudes? Clearly the answer to this is going to depend not only on what God and we are like but also on what is or can be meant by speaking of attitudes in either case. So let's turn to this latter issue.

This is, of course, just a particular form of the more general issue as to how to construe intentional psychological states, including but perhaps not restricted to "propositional attitudes." What we are calling 'attitudes', at least in their human realisations, would seem to belong to the latter category. To want, or to have an interest in, a chocolate fudge sundae would seem to involve a certain favorable conative attitude toward the proposition *my eating a chocolate fudge sundae*, or some-

---

would have chosen every such feature in the original act of creation, which was carried out on the basis of no knowledge of "the situation," there being none. If, on the other hand, as we are assuming, God has chosen to refrain from deciding some features Himself (e.g., free choices of human beings, together with their contributions to the way things go), leaving them up to the created agents in question, then He will have to "look and see" how those things have been constituted, where that is relevant to his decisions as to how to bring about a certain state of affairs.

[7] "Does God Have Beliefs?" *Religious Studies* 22 (1986), 287–306.

thing of the sort. On the current scene there are two prominent approaches to the understanding of such states. On the one hand, there is the view identified with Bretano, and represented on the current American scene by Chisholm, that intentionality is a basic, unanalysable feature of psychological states. The generic feature of being "directed onto" an object, propositional or otherwise, is a basic feature in the sense that it cannot be explicated in terms of other concepts. This view leaves it open as to whether each of the various forms taken by intentionality, e.g., believing, hoping, fearing, or desiring that p, is itself basic and irreducible to others, or whether some of these forms can be taken as basic and the others explained in terms of them. But at the very least the position will hold that the difference between knowing that p and having a pro-attitude toward p is unanalysable in terms of anything else. In particular, a positive attitude toward a state of affairs—taking it to be desirable, gratifying, attractive, worth while, a good thing, or whatever—is a basic underivative feature of our mental life. No doubt such attitudes, in conjunction with other facts, have various consequences for behavior, thought, and feeling; but it would be a grave mistake to suppose that the intrinsic nature of attitudes can be specified in terms of such consequences.

On this view, there would seem to be no bar to the univocal predication of some intentional concepts to God and to us. If *taking a state of affairs to be a good thing* is a basic, unanalysable relation of an intelligent agent to a (possible) state of affairs, there is nothing in the concept to limit it to an embodied, finite, imperfect, or temporal agent. Why shouldn't God, as we are thinking of Him here, relate Himself in such a manner to possible states of affairs? There would seem to be no basis for a negative answer.

2 Functionalism

However, many contemporary Anglo-American philosophers are unhappy with the idea that concepts of intentional states are unanalysable. We are committed to finding analyses; *c'est notre metier*. Various suggestions have been made as to how to unpack concepts of intentional states; currently the most popular one is *functionalism*. The basic idea of functionalism is that "psychological states are type individuated by their distinctive role within a complex network of states mediating the perceptual conditions and behavior of organisms or systems."[8] The concept of a belief, an attitude, or an intention is the concept of what performs a particular *function* in the psychological economy, a particular "job" done by the psyche, just as the concept of a loudspeaker is the concept of what performs a certain function, viz., converting electronic signals to sound. Of course, the specification of psychological functions is far more difficult and complicated than the specification of audio functions. The above quote indicates the dominant approach to this by contemporary functionalists. The fundamental role of the psyche is to mediate between perceptual or other informational input and behavioral output; and a particular psychological role is a particular piece of that overall mission, a particular way in which one state interacts with other states and with informational input to influence behavior. Thus, e.g., a belief that it is now raining is a state that interacts with an intention to go outside, a desire to remain as dry as possible, and a belief that carrying an umbrella is the best way to stay as dry as possible, to elicit the behavior of carrying an umbrella. Other components of the total functional role of this belief include its interacting with the belief that it has been raining for the past six days to infer that it has been raining for a week, and its interacting with the strong desire for sunny weather to produce a feeling of despondency. Clearly a complete analysis of even a very specific psychological concept would be an enormously complicated affair, perhaps beyond our powers.

In previous publications[9] I have argued that psychological and action concepts of a generally functionalist sort can be applied to God, even viewing the divine nature as I am in this essay. No doubt, the challenge has contributed to the attractiveness of the project. Functionalism is generally associated with a physicalistic view of human beings, and computer analogies have played a large role in its development. It would be quite a coup to show that concepts derived from this milieu could be applied to a being that is incorporeal, timeless, and absolutely infinite. But there was also a positive lead. A major emphasis within functionalism has been the idea that since a certain kind of psycho-

---

[8]Robert van Gulick, "Functionalism, Information, and Content," *Nature and System* 2 (1980), 139.

[9]"How to Speak Literally about God", in *Is God GOD?*, pp. 146–177, and "Functionalism and Theological Language," *American Philosophical Quarterly* 22 (1985), 221–230. In the first-mentioned essay I was only dealing with problems introduced by divine incorporeality. In the second I was thinking of God just as I am here, but I believe that I can now do a better job of bringing functionalism to bear on the problem.

logical state is that which carries out a certain function, whatever its intrinsic character, one and the same psychological state concept might be applied to beings of widely different inherent natures, to biological organisms (of various physical and chemical sorts), to computers, even, perhaps, to angels. Put in another way, the fact that Y is widely different in constitution from X will not in itself prevent a univocal application of psychological state concepts, provided the crucial sort of function is being performed. Analogously, provided X has the capacity to convert electronic signals to sound it is a loudspeaker; its composition, internal mechanism, and external appearance can vary widely, as audio buffs can testify.

To be sure, at best there will be large differences between the human and divine psyche. Going back to van Gulick's summary account of functionalism, God is not an organism, though He may be a "system," depending on just how we use that term. Nor does God receive information through sense perception. And if van Gulick is thinking of "behavior" types as constituted by types of bodily movements, that part of the picture doesn't carry over either. So let's see how we can generalize the account to the divine case. First let's replace "organisms or systems" with "agents."[10] As for "perceptual conditions," the lack of sense organs is no disability for God just because God, being omniscient, has no need for any such means of acquiring information. Since the "input" drops out of the picture, the functionalist model will be simplified to the following: psychological states are type individuated by their distinctive role within a complex of states that gives rise to action.

Note that the functionalist interpretation of psychological concepts is, at least when we neglect input, simply the "motivational background" conception of intentional action stood on its head. An intentional action is one that stems from attitudes, beliefs, and the like in a certain way, and attitudes, beliefs, and the like are to be construed in terms of the way in which intentional action stems from them. At a later stage we shall look at the apparent circularity this introduces.

The following qualification should also be made explicit. Since I am aspiring only to exhibit a partial overlap between concepts of divine and human action, even if the overlap is solely functional in nature it need not exhaust our concepts of psychological states in either context. Thus I need only maintain that our concept of human belief, desire,

---

[10]The full implications of this shift will appear shortly.

or intention, is *at least in part* the concept of a role in the motivation of behavior, in order to have a basis for partial univocity.

I have already suggested that the divine psyche is dramatically simplified as compared with the human. I am loath to agree that it is as bare of distinction as, e.g., the Thomistic doctrine of divine simplicity would have it, but it lacks bases for many of the distinctions between different types of human attitudes, and it equally lacks our distinctions between different degrees of firmness of belief. For present purposes we can think of the divine motivational structure as made up of (i) attitudes toward various (possible) states of affairs,[11] and (ii) complete knowledge. We can then think of divine action as arising from a pro-attitude toward some goal state and the knowledge that the action in question will realize that goal state (or will probably do so, in case free choices of creatures have a role here, and God lacks "middle knowledge" of how each free creature would act in each situation in which that creature might find itself). Of course, in a limiting case, the action in question is just the bringing about of that goal state; this is the case in which God realizes His purpose directly. In terms of this simple model we can think of a divine pro-attitude toward G as, at least in part, the sort of state that, when combined with knowledge that doing A is the best way of achieving G, will lead to God's doing A. And, pari passu, knowledge that doing A is the best way of achieving G is the sort of state that, combined with a pro-attitude toward G, will lead to God's doing A.

3 A More Complex Model

However, this model is much too simple in a number of respects. (The complications to be set out now should also be read back into the oversimplified account given earlier of what sort of motivational background makes an action intentional.) First, and most obviously, God presumably, and humans certainly, will have pro-attitudes toward mutually exclusive states of affairs. For example, God may have both a pro-attitude toward all human beings enjoying eternal felicity and a pro-attitude toward inveterate sinners being suitably punished for their

---

[11]These attitudes will be construed differently depending on whether we think of values as chosen by the divine will or whether we think of God as recognizing values that are independent of His will. But we need not take sides on this controversy for purposes of this essay.

sins. And, assuming that a suitable punishment would involve the lack of eternal felicity, even God can't have it both ways. Or God might have a pro-attitude toward Jacob being the (one and only) bearer of a certain revelation and also a pro-attitude toward Michael's having that status, in which case He will have to sacrifice at least one of these desiderata. Thus in order to allow for at least the possibility of incompatible divine goal states, we will have to introduce a tendency notion and say, instead of the above, that a pro-attitude toward G is the sort of state that, in conjunction with the knowledge that doing A is the best way to attain G, will give rise to a *tendency to* do A. How are we to explain this notion of a *tendency*? The rough idea is that a tendency to do A is a state that, in the absence of sufficient interference or blockage, will issue in doing A. It is, so to say, being prima facie prepared to do A. What interferences or blockages there can be will vary from case to case, and so that specification need not be included in the most general concept of a tendency.[12] Second, and perhaps most important, we must construe the relation of tendencies to action in such a way as to preserve the divine freedom. Here my account in "Functionalism and Theological Language" was defective. Because of divine timelessness I gave up thinking of attitudes as causes of action, but I replaced this with the idea that "a functional concept of S is a concept of lawlike connections in which S stands with other states and with outputs."[13] This has the double disability of rendering God subject to natural laws and of denying God any real freedom of choice, at least if the laws in question are thought of as deterministic. As far as the first problem is concerned one might replace the notion of law governedness with the notion of the nature of God being such that a tendency (formed by an attitude-knowledge interaction of the sort we have described) that is not successfully opposed will issue in action. But that still leaves the second problem. Are we really prepared to think of God's behavior as issuing automatically from the interplay of motivational factors? Wouldn't that make God into a mechanism, a system the output of which is determined by the interplay of its parts, rather than a supremely free agent? Wouldn't that represent God as less free than us?

While these considerations are quite sound, they do not show the

---

[12]If that did have to be included the definition would become circular. For the most important interference with a given tendency is other tendencies to incompatible actions.

[13]"Functionalism and Theological Language," p. 225.

above account to be mistaken, but only incomplete. What we must do is to recognize that among the factors that can prevent a tendency from issuing in action is the divine will. To say that God is supremely free implies that He has the capacity to refrain from doing *A* whatever the strength of a tendency to do *A* that issues from His attitudes and knowledge. This is not, of course, to say that God wills at random, nor is it to deny that He can be depended on to act in accordance with His nature and to act for the good. It is only to say that God's free choice is interposed between any tendencies issuing from His nature and His activity. God's activity is the activity of a free agent in the most unqualified sense. Not only are the things He directly brings about the result of "agent causality" rather than "event causality," even where the events or states are states of His own psyche; it is also the case, if this is indeed a separate point, that no exercise of this agent causality is determined by anything, not even by states of Himself.

These claims about divine freedom have often been taken to conflict with the attribution to God of essential goodness. If God is essentially good then it is metaphysically impossible that He should act in any way other than the best. A proper discussion of this issue must await another occasion. Suffice it to say that God's freedom of choice will have to be construed as a freedom to choose whatever is logically (metaphysically) possible; and if God is essentially good that makes many choices metaphysically impossible that otherwise would be possible. Within those constraints, however, it can still be maintained that God always has a free choice among metaphysically possible alternatives. And however we construe the divine goodness and its relation to action, there will be situations in which there is no unique action to which God's nature constrains Him. Just to take the major putative example of this, Christian theology has traditionally maintained that the divine goodness does not constrain God to create anything other than Himself.

Since a given attitude-knowledge combination does not by itself necessarily issue in action, either in the divine or the human case, we are led to recognize another sort of motivational factor that mediates between the field of tendencies and overt behavior, determining the character of the latter. If everything proceeds in accordance with event causality and the agent itself does not constitute a factor to be reckoned separately, we need not think of this mediating factor as being different in kind from the various tendencies. It is, as Hobbes says of the will, simply the strongest current tendency, the winner in the struggle among competing tendencies. However, if the agent (as a whole, or *as* an agent) always has, or can have, the last word, we must recognize a quite different sort of factor, an internal act of the agent, an act of will, volition, or whatever, that does, or at least always can, control the gates to the external world (for embodied agents, the gates to bodily movement). Again, the human agent is more complex than the divine. Since a temporal agent can form intentions for the future, we must distinguish *intention to do A*, which may not issue immediately in doing *A* and which may dissipate before *A* ever gets done, and a *volition to do A*, ("executive intention") which issues in doing *A* unless the external world (external to the psyche) prevents it. Since there can be no intention for the future in a timeless agent, for God we need only recognize volitions (executive intentions) as leading from the field of tendencies to the actual thing done. As the above discussion indicates, for a given agent, divine or human, sometimes the strongest tendency will issue directly (automatically) in action, and sometimes there will be (may be) a free choice of the agent, made in the light of the current tendency field but not determined thereby (the tendencies "incline without necessitating"), that determines what is done. In the former case we shall speak of the immediate psychological determinant of action as an *executive intention*; in the latter case we shall speak of *volition*.

Although I can only hope to scratch the surface of human motivation in this essay, there is one additional feature I had better make explicit. The bridge between the tendency field and overt action (the volition or executive intention) is not best thought of, as the above remarks would suggest, as confined in its intentional object to the action done (the state of affairs the bringing about of which constitutes the action). For one thing, the agent may, in one volition or intention, launch itself onto a complex activity, involving a number of subordinate stages, each designed to lead to its successor. Thus, if I form the intention to go to my office, this requires me to intend to perform a number of sequentially linked actions of arising from my chair, suitably garbing myself, unlocking my front door, etc. etc. Again, where God decides to restore the kingdom of Israel this involves His doing a number of things to lead up to this. In such a case what is formed, as the immediate psychological determinant of overt activity, is better termed an *action plan*, something that involves a mental representation of the structure of the complex activity intended. And in the case of a temporal agent this action plan will monitor and control the evolving sequence of steps to the final goal.[14] Even where no such sequence of results is intended, the intentional object of the executive intention or volition will typically involve not only the defining result of the action in question but also that for the sake of which the action is entered on. Even if my intention is the simple one of opening the door, my intention will also involve an awareness of why I am doing it, e.g., to let someone in; and so even here we have an action plan, though of limiting simplicity. In fact, the reason or purpose for which I do something, as I argue in "An Action-Plan Interpretation of Purposive Explanations of Actions," is best construed as given by the structure of the action plan involved.

We can now read these additional complexities back into the account of intentional action. One intentionally brings about B iff the bringing about of B is due to (is the carrying out of) an executive intention or a volition to bring about B. That intention or volition, in turn, is to be understood, in part, in terms of the way in which it stems from a field of tendencies, and if what I have just been saying is well taken, it bears marks of this origin in the structure of its own intentional object.

Let's return to the functionalist account of intentional mental states in the light of this enriched model. Attitudes and cognitions are to be understood in terms of the way in which they interact to engender action tendencies. Tendencies, in turn, are to be understood partly in terms of this origin and partly in terms of the way they interact with each other to either determine executive intentions or to influence volitions, as the case may be. Finally, executive intentions and volitions are to be understood in terms both of their background and of the way they determine overt action. This whole functionalist contribution to our concepts of such states can be thought of as deriving from conditionals like the following:

1. If S has a pro-attitude toward G, then S will have a tendency to do whatever S takes to be a way of attaining G.

2. If S has a tendency to do A, then if this tendency is not successfully opposed by a stronger tendency or by an act of will, S will do A, if the external world cooperates in the right way.[15]

We must be clear that we have deviated from the usual functionalist account by introducing free acts of will into the picture. This means that we are countenancing an irreducible concept of agency (currently

---

[14]See my paper "An Action-Plan Interpretation of Purposive Explanations of Actions," for an elaboration of this idea.

[15]This last qualification becomes vacuous in the divine case.

termed 'agent causality'), the concept of an agent's directly bringing something about, where this something is to be explained in terms of the agent's exercise of its powers, rather than by any sort of event or state as a cause, and where this activity on the part of the agent is not causally determined by anything, not even its own states, though it may well be influenced by them. This is not a notion that can be given a functionalist interpretation, so far as I can see, without losing its distinctive contours. What is directly engendered by agency, the volition, can itself be partly construed in functionalist terms. But the concept of an agent's bringing something about, as we understand that here, resists any such explication.

The attentive reader will not have missed a certain circularity in this functionalist treatment of the divine psyche. Divine intentional action is what issues from a certain motivational background, and the elements of that background are in turn construed in terms of the way in which they lead to action. If all divine action issues from divine acts of will, it might be thought that we could ignore the business about pro-attitudes, tendencies, and so on in explaining divine action, thereby avoiding the circularity. But that only makes the circle smaller. It is an essential part of this program to construe volitions functionally too. If we leave out of account the way in which volitions are influenced by attitudes and the like, the only way to say what a volition is, is to say that it is an internal act of the agent that determines overt action (in the case of finite agents, within the limits of bodily capacity and external opportunity).

I'm afraid that I see no alternative to biting the bullet and admitting the circularity. Intentional action and conative psychological factors are to be understood in terms of their interrelations. For the human case, unlike the divine case, one might try to get out of the circle by construing the behavioral output in terms of bodily movements rather than full-blooded action. But this would require us to construe at least some of the attitudes and beliefs as taking bodily movements as intentional objects; and it seems to be the exception rather than the rule that human action is guided by beliefs, etc., that have to do with specific bodily movement types, rather than the results or significance of bodily movements. When we speak, e.g., the relevant purposes, beliefs, and intentions have to do with what we are saying rather than with what we are doing with our vocal organs to get it said. Even in the human case we are saddled with the circle. The way out is to recognize that functionalism cannot be a reduction of intentionalistic concepts (of actions and psychological states) to non-intentionalistic concepts, physicalistic or otherwise. It must be construed as a partial interpretation, exhibiting the conceptual interrelations of actions and intentional psychological states, thereby shedding considerable light on their nature.

The functionalist treatment of divine knowledge has thus far been restricted to the knowledge of means-end connections, hardly even the tip of the iceberg. Of course the cognitive guidance of behavior extends far beyond these narrow bounds. Depending on features of the particular case, bits of information other than means-end connections will be relevant to one or another divine project. Thus, e.g., God will want to know the details of the Israelites' observance or nonobservance of the convenant in deciding how to deal with the threat from Assyria. But unless we want to assume that everything God knows is relevant to some decision He makes or might make, that will still leave much knowledge without a functionalist interpretation. For humans the account can be eked out by reference to sources of informational input. Knowledge (belief) varies in lawful ways with sensory input, as well as interacting with conative factors to guide behavior. We have noted that this maneuver is not available for the divine case. Nevertheless there is a divine analogue of input to which we may appeal. Since God is essentially omniscient, He knows that p for every true p. Therefore, as we might say, the facts of the world constitute "input" for the divine psyche. Knowledge is the aspect of the divine psyche that varies lawfully, indeed with logical necessity, with the facts. It is that divine psychological state that takes all and only facts (true propositions) as its intentional objects. It is thereby distinguished from all other divine psychological states.[16]

Let's take stock. I have indicated how one can give a functionalist construal of psychological and action concepts that enables us to give at least a partial account of such concepts in their divine application and thereby to articulate some commonality between our thought of human and divine action and motivation. In both cases an action can be thought of as a change that is brought about by a volition or intention, where that is formed against the background of action tendencies that are formed by the interaction of attitudes with cognition. I am not claiming that concepts of divine and human actions, conative factors,

---

[16]Note that if we were to take God to be what I called "omnidetermining," we would not be able to distinguish knowledge in this way. For in that case the divine will would also have every fact as its intentional object.

etc., are exactly the same, even in their functionalist component. On the contrary, there are many differences, some of which follow from points already made in this essay. For one thing, the form of the interactions may be different. Perhaps there is a relation of event or state causality between attitudes and cognitions on the one hand and action tendencies on the other in the human case but not in the divine. And, most obviously, attitudes and beliefs are typically related by temporal succession to the action tendencies they determine in the human case; the action is "generated" or "given rise to" by the attitudes and beliefs in a temporally literal sense of these terms. This is especially obvious where there is a process of conscious deliberation as to what to do, but there are also unconscious and non-centrally directed temporal processes of tendency formation. Whereas there can be no such internal *processes* of tendency formation for a timeless agent. Moreover, if a functionalist concept of a psychological state type, P, is spelled out by the way in which states of that type interact with others in the motivation of behavior, then any differences in the total motivational field will be reflected, to some extent, in the concept of each type of state. And we have noted several such differences. Human intentions or volitions lead to the corresponding action only if the external world, including the agent's body, cooperates in certain ways, but no such qualification is needed for divine motivation. Human beings exhibit a great variety of cognitive and conative states that is not matched by the divine psyche; and at least some of these differences make a difference in the way the total motivational structure issues in behavior. For example, biological cravings influence action tendencies differently from the way in which internalized general moral principles do. Again, in the human case different degrees of firmness of belief will make a difference to the strength of tendencies formed, a difference quite inapplicable to the divine case. For another difference on the cognitive side, God, being omniscient, will know everything entailed by a given piece of knowledge, so that, assuming that the inferential interrelations of cognitions enter into a functionalist account of cognitive states, this will work out somewhat differently on the two sides of the divide. But despite all these differences, there is a basic commonality in the way in which attitudes combine with cognitions to determine action tendencies, and the way in which action tendencies are related to the final active volition or executive intention. There will be crucial conditionals in common, of the sort listed earlier. In both cases, e.g., if the agent has a pro-attitude toward G and a cognition that doing A is a way to realize G, then the agent will have a tendency to do A.[17]

Since it may still be doubted that any functionally construed psychological concepts can apply to a timeless being, I should say a word about that. We can assure ourselves of the intelligibility of this conception by taking as our model a physical system—mechanical, electromagnetic, or thermal— in which the values of some variables at a given time are a determinate function of the values of other variables at that same time. This gives us the idea of *simultaneous* "subjunctive" or "counterfactual" dependence, in contrast to the dependence of states on those that precede them in time. To be sure, there are other features of these systems that do not carry over to our timeless divine agent. For one thing, the value of a given variable at a particular time will have resulted from temporal processes of interaction within the system; for another, the relations of contemporaneous dependence reflect the subjection of the system to laws, and we don't want to think of God as subject to laws. Nevertheless, it seems clear that it is not a conceptual or otherwise necessary truth that relations of contemporaneous dependence are dependent on these other features. Hence we are able to form the conception of a being (a "system") in which some factors depend on their relations to others for being what they are, even though there are no temporally successive processes of formation, nor any subjection to laws. More specifically, we are to think of God as realising a complex structure of attitudes, knowledge, tendencies, executive intentions, and volitions in the "eternal now," a structure that involves the kinds of dependence we have been talking about. Thus, let us say, it is true eternally of God that He wills that the Church be inspired by the Holy Spirit to develop the doctrine of the Trinity because He has

---

[17]One might suppose that if it is possible to give a (partial) functionalist account of divine action and motivational concepts along the lines we have been suggesting, it is not so important to show a basic commonality among these concepts and their analogues in our thought about ourselves. For the search for univocity has been fueled largely by the fear that without it we will not be able to apply terms and concepts to God directly, literally, and straightforwardly, that we will at best be able to speak of Him metaphorically or symbolically. But if my suggestions in this essay are on the right track we can forge concepts that apply directly to God, whether or not they overlap with concepts that apply to human beings. I think this reaction is justified as far as it goes; but I think it is also true that unless our understanding of divine purpose, intention, and will had at least as much commonality with human motivational concepts as I have been alleging, we would, justifiably, doubt that the divine states in question deserve to be called 'purpose,' 'intention,' and so on.

a pro-attitude toward the Church's making explicit the most fundamental truths about Himself (at least those suitable for our condition),
and He knows that this development is necessary for that. Note that
although there is no temporal succession within the divine life there
is temporal succession between the things brought about by God in
the world, the external aspects of His activity. Thus although His *will*
to choose Israel and His *will* to become incarnate are embraced without temporal succession in the eternal now, it does not follow that
the results brought about in the world by these volitions are
simultaneous.[18]

4 Beyond Functionalism

That's the good news; now for the bad news. The concepts I have been
adumbrating are very thin, to say the least. All we have are concepts
of positions in a structure of mutual dependence, "counterfactual dependence," to use a currently fashionable phrase. God's being favor-
ably disposed toward G and God's doing A are the sorts of things that
are related to each other, and to other states and activities, in the ways
we have been laying out. God's having a pro-attitude toward the re-
juvenation of Israel is the sort of state that is such that if God knows
that giving a certain commission to Ezekiel is the best way to bring
this about, then God will have a tendency to give that commission to
Ezekiel. And that tendency is the sort of state that is such that an agent
that has it will give that commission to Ezekiel unless sufficient interferences are present. Among such interferences is a divine decision
not to give that commission to Ezekiel. And what is a divine decision
(not) to do A? It is a state such that . . . And so it goes. I have laid out
a certain structure of what depends on what in what way, but as to
what it is that stands in these relations of dependence I have said
virtually nothing. There are only two places at which this system of
mutual dependencies gets anchored in something outside it: (i) For
any proposition p, p entails that God knows that p, as well as vice
versa; (ii) for any p, God's willing that p entails that p, but not vice

---

[18]For more on this point see Stump and Kretzmann, "Eternity," and my "Divine-
Human Dialogue and the Nature of God," *Faith and Philosophy* 2 (1985), 5–20.

versa. But this makes little contribution to our grasp of the nature of the internal states that stand in the specified functional relations.[19]

Of course I have said that the functionalist account only claims to be a partial account. But that's just the rub. How do we fill in what it leaves out? In the human case we have a lot to go on that we are lacking in the divine case. First, and most obviously, we have our own first-person sense of what it is like to want something, to be afraid of something, to believe that something will occur, to hope for something, to feel that one ought to do something, to intend to do something, and so on. But we can hardly pretend to any such insight into what it is like to be God, or even to have purposes, intentions, and the like in the way God does. Thomas Nagel has gained fame (or significantly added to it) by pointing out we don't have much idea of what it is to be a bat. How much less are we in a position to know what it is like to be God. Moreover, we can see how our concepts of human motivational factors are enriched by aspects that must be absent if God is as we have been supposing Him to be. Just consider temporality. Our conception of human purposes and intentions is partly constituted by our understanding of the way in which the purpose or intention holds fast through a variety of changing circumstances, providing a basis for changing our approach to the goal as we encounter unforeseen difficulties and complications. And our conception of the relation between an intention to bring about G and actually bringing about G is partly constituted by our realization that one can have the intention even though G is not yet brought about. Again, our understanding of what it is to make a decision or form an intention is partly constituted by our sense of how a decision is the terminus of a *process* of deliberation. But none of this is applicable to a timeless deity. Again consider God's supreme perfection. This prevents our making use of any analogue of the way in which our understanding of human acts of will is enriched by our awareness of effort of will in struggles against temptation. In the human but not in the divine case, our ability to distinguish between willing, intending, or deciding to do A, on the one hand, and doing A, on the other, is partly dependent on the fact that the former will not issue in the latter unless one receives the right sort of cooperation

---

[19]Indeed there is some question as to whether our account even entails that the system constitutes a distinctively *personal* agent. See Ned Block, "Troubles with Functionalism," in *Minnesota Studies in the Philosophy of Science* 9, ed. C. W. Savage (1978), pp. 261–325, for some doubts along this line. To be sure, since we have opted to construe the "output" of the system in rich, intentionalistic *action* terms, that may suffice to dispel the doubts.

from the external environment. Finally, consider the point that even if God is temporal, He will, being supremely perfect, have at any moment a perfect knowledge of whatever is the case at any time. Hence He will know just what situation He will be reacting to at any point in the future *and what His reaction will be*. And that means, in effect, that His decision as to what to do in that situation has already been made; He will never decide on the spot how to react. Again, even though God be temporal, He cannot go through any genuine process of deliberation as to what to do at t, or any process of genuine *formation* of an intention to do something at t, since at every previous moment He will already know what He will do at t. These contributions to our understanding of our own motivational structure are unavailable in the divine case, not only because of timelessness but also because of omniscience.

Thus, the account we have offered of concepts of the divine psyche and divine activity leaves them quite sparse. Even if we help ourselves to an unanalysed conception of personal agency, we are still left with only a tenuous conception of the knowledge, attitudes, and volitions of the divine agent. Is this enough? Enough for what? I would suppose that we do not need more for theoretical purposes, just because we have no right to expect a satisfactory theoretical grasp of the divine nature and doings. That is, we would need much more to attain a satisfactory theoretical grasp, but such is, by common consent, un-suited to our condition. However, there are more practical needs to be considered as well. There is the need for guidance, direction, inspi-ration, assistance in attaining salvation, in leading the kind of life and becoming the kind of person God intends us to. For these purposes do we need more of a grasp of the divine psyche and activity than we are provided by my austere conditionals?

Whether or not it would be possible for people to receive adequate guidance in the religious life while deploying only the meager concep-tual resources I have allowed, it is clear that this is not the way it goes in actual theistic religions. If you think of the Bible and, more generally, of practically oriented religious literature, it is at once apparent that God is represented as deliberating, forming purposes and intentions in the light of developing events as they occur, acquiring knowledge of events as they transpire, exhibiting features that attach only to tem-poral, imperfect agents. It may be said that those who write, and those who read with approval, such works simply do not share the concep-tion of God with which I have been working. I have been dealing with the "God of the philosophers," while theirs is the "God of the Bible" or the "God of simple believers." But this reaction fails to take account of the point that those who explicitly advocate the conception I was using typically take the Bible as authoritative, and also speak and write in these terms themselves when their purpose is homiletical, pastoral, or edificatory. Thus, there seems to be a deeply felt need to represent God and His doings in a much more concrete way than I have provided. Moreover, I think we can see why this should be the case. For the practice of the religious life, we need to think of ourselves in genuine personal interaction with God: in prayer, in the action of the Holy Spirit within us, in God's providence for our needs, in seeking enlightenment from Him, and so on. But the conception I have offered of a timeless "personal system" of functionally interrelated psychological states simply does not present anything with which we can coherently conceive ourselves to be in dynamic personal relations of dialogue, support, love, or instruction. To this it may be objected that a functionalist account of the human psyche does not represent human beings as incapable of genuine interpersonal relations. But first, in the human case, we can draw on our intimate familiarity with ourselves and each other; the functionalist account is not our sole resource. And second, the functionalist account of the human psyche does not represent it as a timeless, infinitely perfect agent.

Thus, it seems to be a practical necessity of the religious life to represent God as much more like a created, imperfect temporal agent than what I am taking to be a sound theology will allow. We must, for devotional and edificatory purposes, think of God as finding out what happens as it occurs and forming intentions to deal with developing situations as they develop, even though an omniscient being, whether timeless or not, would know everything about the future at any given point in time.

I would like to consider what bearing this has on the central concerns of this essay, even though I cannot enter into a proper discussion. One reaction to the points I have just been making would be to abandon the view that God is timeless and that He eternally possesses complete knowledge of the future. Many religious thinkers have taken this line. But here I want to stay within the previously announced constraints and consider what moves are open. Clearly, given those constraints, this more concrete picture cannot literally apply to God. Thus with respect to whatever in the picture goes beyond my austere functional account, we will be thrown back on the familiar array of alternatives that are open, with respect to the total meaning of theological predicates, to those who deny that any terms (concepts) we can form can be literally applied to God: the alternatives of analogy, metaphor, symbolism, etc. The problem is not quite as urgent for me as for them, just because I recognize that there is an abstract core of predicates that are literally true of God. But given the ineluctability of the more concrete characterizations, it is a genuine problem. The answer would seem to lie somewhere in the general territory of metaphor and symbol.

I hope that I have said enough to indicate both that there is a hard literal core to our talk about divine action and that, for the religious life, we need to go beyond that in ways that launch us into the still not sufficiently charted seas of the figurative and the symbolic.

10

Being and Goodness

Eleonore Stump and Norman Kretzmann

1 Introduction

Parts of Aquinas's moral philosophy, particularly his treatments of the virtues and of natural law, are sometimes taken into account in contemporary discussions, but the unusual ethical naturalism that underlies all of his moral philosophy has been neglected. Consequently, the unity of his ethical theory and its basis in his metaphysics are not so well known as they should be, and even the familiar parts of the theory are sometimes misunderstood.

We think Aquinas's naturalism is a kind of moral realism that deserves serious reconsideration. It supplies for his virtue-centered morality the sort of metaethical foundation that recent virtue-centered morality has been criticized for lacking.[1] Moreover, it complements Aquinas's Aristotelian emphasis on rationality as a moral standard by supplying a method of determining degrees of rationality.[2] And when Aquinas's naturalism is combined with his account of God as absolutely simple, it effects a connection between morality and theology that offers an attractive alternative to divine-command morality, construing morality not merely as a dictate of God's will, but as an expression of his

---

[1] See, e.g., Robert B. Louden, "On Some Vices of Virtue Ethics," *American Philosophical Quarterly* 21 (1984), 227–236; Gregory E. Pence, "Recent Work on Virtues," *American Philosophical Quarterly* 21 (1984), 281–297.

[2] See pp. 291–292 below.

nature.[3] Finally, Aquinas's brand of naturalism illuminates a side of the problem of evil that has been overlooked, raising the question whether recent defenses against the problem are compatible with the doctrine of God's goodness.

Aquinas's ethics is embedded in his metaphysics, only the absolutely indispensable features of which can be summarized here. Consequently, we can't undertake to argue fully for his ethical theory in this essay. For our purposes it will be enough to expound the theory, to consider some of the objections it gives rise to, and to point out some of the advantages it offers for dealing with recognized issues in ethics and philosophy of religion.

2 The Central Thesis of Aquinas's Metaethics

The central thesis of Aquinas's metaethics is that *the terms 'being' and 'goodness' are the same in reference, differing only in sense.*[4] What does Aquinas mean by this claim, and what are his grounds for it?

It will be helpful to begin with an observation about terminology. Contemporary metaphysics uses cognates of some Latin words crucial to Aquinas's presentation of his theory, but the terms 'essence', 'actual', and 'exists', for example, have acquired meanings different from the meanings Aquinas understood the corresponding Latin terms to have. For instance, he does not identify essential characteristics with necessary characteristics; as he uses those terms, all essential characteristics are necessary, but not all necessary characteristics are essential. Furthermore, in Aquinas's usage what is actual is opposed to what is potential rather than to what is merely possible, as in standard contemporary usage. As he understands it, what is actual is, fundamentally, what is in being; and what is in being is, ordinarily, what exists.

---

[3]See our article "Absolute Simplicity," *Faith and Philosophy* 2 (1985), 353–382; esp. 375–376.

[4]Thomas Aquinas, *Summa theologiae* (*ST*) Ia q. 5, esp. a. 1. We are interpreting Aquinas's "*sunt idem secundum rem*" as "are the same in reference" and "*differunt secundum rationem*" as "differ in sense." Aquinas's treatment of this thesis about being and goodness is a particularly important development in a long and complicated tradition, on which see Scott MacDonald, "The Metaphysics of Goodness in Medieval Philosophy before Aquinas" (Ph.D. diss., Cornell University, 1986). See also Michael Hönes, "Ens et Bonum Convertuntur: Eine Deutung des scholastischen Axioms unter besonderer Berücksichtigung der Metaphysik und Ethik des hl. Thomas von Aquin" (inaugural diss., Albert-Ludwigs-Universität, Freiburg 1. Br., 1968).

But, as we'll see, his conception of being is broader than the ordinary conception of actual existence.

Goodness is what all desire, says Aquinas, quoting Aristotle,[5] and what is desired is (or is at least perceived as) desirable. Desirability is an essential aspect of goodness. Now if a thing is desirable as a thing of a certain kind (and anything at all *can* be desirable in that way, as a means, if not as an end), it is desirable to the extent to which it is perfect of that kind—i.e., a whole, complete specimen, free from relevant defect.[6] But, then, a thing is perfect of its kind to the extent to which it is fully realized or developed, to the extent to which the potentialities definitive of its kind—its specifying potentialities—have been actualized. And so, Aquinas says, a thing is perfect and hence desirable (good of its kind) to the extent to which it is in being.[7] That's one way of seeing how it is true to say that a thing's goodness is its being.

Offering the same line of explanation from the standpoint of the thing rather than a desirer of the thing, Aquinas says that everything resists its own corruption in accordance with its nature, a tendency he interprets as its aiming (naturally) at being fully actual, not merely partially or defectively in being. Thus, since goodness is what all things aim at or desire, each thing's goodness is its full actuality.[8]

In another gloss on Aristotle's dictum Aquinas takes the sense of 'goodness' to be brought out in the notion of that in which desire culminates.[9] Now what is desired is desired either for the sake of something else, for the sake of something else and for its own sake, or solely for its own sake. What is desired solely for its own sake is what the desirer perceives as the desirer's final good, that for the sake of which it desires all the other things it desires, that in which the hierarchy of its desires culminates. But what each desirer desires in

[5]See, e.g., Thomas Aquinas, *Summa contra Gentiles* (SCG), I 37.4 (n. 306); III 3.3 (n. 1880); Aristotle, *Nicomachean Ethics* I 1,1094a1–3.

[6]Kinds must be broadly conceived of in this connection. For an exhibit at a plant pathology conference a stunted, diseased specimen of wheat may be perfect of its kind, just what's wanted. But the kind at issue in that case is not wheat, but wheat-afflicted-by-wheat-mildew. Alternatively, it might be said that the goodness of an exhibit, like that of other artifacts, is related to the rational purposes of its users, in which case the kind at issue is not wheat, but exhibit-specimen-of-mildewed-wheat.

[7]*ST* Ia q. 5, a. 1.

[8]See, e.g., SCG I 37.4 (n. 306); ST IaIIae q. 94, a. 2. Rational agents have goals over and above their natural aims, and so the objects of their conscious desires are sometimes only perceived by them as good and not also actually good for them.

[9]*SCG* III 3, passim.

that way is the fulfillment of its own nature, or at least that which the desirer perceives as the very best for the desirer to have or be.[10] Each thing aims above all at being as complete, whole, and free from defect as it can be.[11] But the state of its being complete and whole just is that thing's being fully actual, whether or not the desirer recognizes it as such. Therefore, full actualization is equivalent to final goodness, aimed at or desired by every thing.[12]

Finally, Aquinas argues that every action is ordered toward being, toward preserving or enhancing being in some respect either in the individual or in its species: in acting all things aim at being. Therefore, again, being is what all desire; and so being is goodness.[13]

On Aquinas's view, these various arguments show that when the terms 'being' and 'goodness' are associated with any particular sort of thing, both terms refer to the actualization of the potentialities that specify that thing's nature. Generally, then, 'being' and 'goodness' have the same referent: the actualization of specifying potentialities. The actualization of a thing's specifying potentialities to at least some extent is, on the one hand, its existence as such a thing; it is in this sense that the thing is said to have *being*. But, on the other hand, the actualization of a thing's specifying potentialities is, to the extent of the actualization, that thing's being whole, complete, free from defect—the state all things naturally aim at; it is in this sense that the thing is said to have *goodness*. Like the designations 'morning star' and 'evening star', then, 'being' and 'goodness' refer to the same thing under two descriptions and so have different senses but the same referent.

This claim of Aquinas's about being and goodness, his central metaethical thesis, is bound to give rise to several objections. But since effective replies to such objections depend on certain elements of Aquinas's metaphysics, we'll postpone considering them until we've presented those elements.

---

[10]See, e.g., *ST* IaIIae q. 1, a. 5.

[11]As we have already suggested (n. 8 above), when the thing described is a rational being, the object of its aim will include its *conception* of the fulfillment of its nature, which can be more or less mistaken. Objectively evil objects of desire are desired because they are perceived as good for the desirer to have.

[12]What is meant by 'equivalent' here is spelled out in our discussion of supervenience in sec. 5.

[13]*SCG* III 3.4 (n. 1881).

3 Full Actuality and Substantial Form

On Aquinas's view, every thing has a substantial form.[14] The substantial form of any thing is the set of characteristics that place that thing in its species and that are thus essential to it in Aquinas's sense of 'essential'.[15] Some of these essential characteristics determine the genus within which the thing's species belongs; the others differentiate the thing's species from other species of that genus. The thing's genus-determining characteristics (or simply its genus) and differentiating characteristics (or simply its differentia) together comprise its substantial form or specific essence, what is essential to it as a member of its species. All the characteristics making up the thing's substantial form are essential to it as an individual, but if there are individual essences as well, they will include characteristics over and above those constituting the substantial form.[16]

The substantial form as a set of essential characteristics invariably includes at least one power, capacity, or potentiality, because every form (any set of real rather than merely conceptual characteristics) is a source of some activity or operation.[17] Among the essential characteristics, the thing's differentia is a characteristic peculiar to and constitutive of the thing's species, the characteristic that can be identified as the thing's specifying potentiality (or potentialities). The differentia is thus the source of an activity or operation (or set of them) peculiar to that species and essential to every member of the species. As Aquinas puts it, the thing's specific nature includes the power to engage in a specific operation determining of and essential to that thing as a member of that species.[18]

---

[14]T. H. Irwin's "The Metaphysical and Psychological Basis of Aristotle's Ethics," in *Essays on Aristotle's Ethics*, ed. A. Rorty, (Berkeley: University of California Press, 1980) pp. 35–53, is particularly useful for our purposes here because of Aquinas's dependence on Aristotle. On the relevant role of substantial form in particular, see esp. pp. 37–39 of Irwin's article.

[15]See p. 282 above.

[16]See, e.g., *ST* Ia q. 5, a. 5; IaIIae q. 85, a. 4; *Quaestiones disputatae de veritate (DV)*, q. 21, a. 6.

[17]See, e.g., *SCG* III 7.7 (n. 1916); *ST* IaIIae q. 55, a. 2. A contemporary counterpart of this view of forms might be seen in Sydney Shoemaker's "Causality and Properties," in *Time and Cause*, ed. Peter van Inwagen (Dordrecht: Reidel, 1980), pp. 109–135; reprinted in Shoemaker, *Identity, Cause, and Mind* (Cambridge: Cambridge University Press, 1984), pp. 206–233.

[18]See, e.g., *SCG* I 42.10 (n. 343): "The differentia that specifies a genus does not

It follows that a thing's form is perfected when and to the extent to which the thing performs an instance of its specific operation, actualizing its specifying potentiality.[19] A thing's operation in accord with its specific power brings into actuality what was not actual but merely potential in that thing's form. So in Aquinas's basic, metaphysical sense of 'perfect', a thing is perfect of its kind to the extent to which it actualizes the specifying potentiality in its form.[20] The derivative, evaluative sense of 'perfect' is explained by the connection between actuality and goodness: for something to be actual is for it to be in being, and 'being' and 'goodness' are the same in reference. Therefore, a thing is good of its kind to the extent to which it is actual.[21] Or, putting it another way, a thing is good of its kind (or perfect) to the extent to which its specifying potentiality is actualized, and bad of its kind (or imperfect) to the extent to which its specifying potentiality remains unactualized.[22]

4 From Metaethics to Normative Ethics

The specifying potentialities of a human being are in the cognitive and appetitive rational powers, intellect and will, which comprise its differentia, reason.[23] Although endowed with freedom of choice, a human will in association with its intellect is inclined toward goodness not just naturally (like the appetitive aspect of every other being) but also "along with an awareness of the nature of the good—a condition that is a distinguishing characteristic of intellect."[24] Rational beings are "inclined toward goodness itself considered universally" rather than naturally directed toward one particular sort of goodness.[25] The operation deriving directly from the human essence, then, is acting in accordance

---

complete the nature (*rationem*) of the genus; instead, it is through the differentia that the genus acquires its being in actuality."

[19]See, e.g., *ST* IaIIae q. 49, a. 4, esp. ad 1.

[20]*ST* IaIIae q. 3, a. 2: "Anything whatever is perfect to the extent to which it is in actuality, since potentiality without actuality is imperfect."

[21]See, e.g., *SCG* III 16.3, 4 (nn. 1987 & 1988).

[22]See, e.g., *ST* IaIIae q. 18, a. 1.

[23]See, e.g., ibid., q. 55, aa. 1, 2; q. 63, a. 1.

[24]*ST* Ia q. 59, a. 1. As we've pointed out (nn. 8 and 11), the awareness concomitant with a rational appetite can be distorted.

[25]Ibid.; cf. *SCG* II 47 and *DV* q. 23, a. 1. See also our discussion in "Absolute Simplicity" sec. 5, 359–362.

with rationality, and actions of that sort actualize the specifying potentiality of human beings. A human being acting in accordance with rationality makes actual what would otherwise have been merely potential in his or her substantial form. By converting humanly specific potentiality into actuality, an agent's actions in accordance with rationality increase the extent to which the agent has being as a human being; and so, given the connection between being and goodness, such actions increase the extent to which the agent has goodness as a human being. Human goodness, like any other goodness appropriate to one species, is acquired in performing instances of the operation specific to that species, which in the case of humanity is the rational employment of the rational powers. The actions that contribute to a human agent's moral goodness will be acts of will in accordance with rationality.[26]

A thing's substantial form, the set of essential characteristics determining the thing's species, constitutes the nature of the thing. And so whatever actualizes a thing's specifying potentiality thereby also perfects the nature of the thing. Given what else we have seen of Aquinas's theory, it follows that in his view what is good for a thing is what is natural to it, and what is unnatural to a thing is bad for it. So, he says, the good is what is according to nature, and evil is what is against nature;[27] in fact, what is evil cannot be natural to anything.[28] As for human nature, since it is characterized essentially by a capacity for rationality, what is irrational is contrary to nature where human beings are concerned.[29]

Habits that dispose a person to act in accordance with nature—i.e., rationally—are good habits, or virtues.[30] Vices, on the other hand, are

---

[26]See, e.g., SCG III 9.1 (n. 1928); ST IaIIae q. 18, a. 5.

[27]ST IaIIae q. 18, a. 5, ad 1.

[28]SCG III 7.6 (n. 1915): "Therefore, since badness or evil is a privation of that which is natural, it cannot be natural to anything."

[29]See, e.g., ST IaIIae q. 71, a. 1.

[30]See, e.g., ST IaIIae q. 55, aa. 1–4. For human beings, acting in accordance with rationality is their second actuality (as Aquinas says, following Aristotle). A newborn human being is only potentially a reasoning being. A mature human being acting in accordance with rationality, such as Aquinas when he is writing on ethics, is rationally exercising his rational powers; and that actual exercise of the specifying potentiality for human beings is their second, or more fully complete, actuality. But there is a state intermediate between the newborn's and that of the fully active mature human being— e.g., the state of Aquinas when he is asleep or in some other way not then actualizing his specifying potentiality. The sleeping Aquinas, unlike the philosophizing Aquinas, lacks the second actuality appropriate to human nature; but even the sleeping Aquinas

habits disposing a person to irrationality and are therefore discordant with human nature.[31] Aquinas quotes with approval Augustine's appraisal of a vice as bad or evil to the extent to which it diminishes the integrity or wholeness of the agent's nature.[32]

It is an important consequence of this account of goodness and badness that no thing that exists or can exist is completely without goodness. This consequence can be inferred directly from the central thesis about being and goodness,[33] but some of its moral and theological implications are worth pointing out. Evil is always and only a defect in some respect to some extent; evil can have no essence of its own. Nor can there be a highest evil, an ultimate source of all other evils, because a *summum malum*, an evil devoid of all good, would be nothing at all.[34] A human being is defective, bad, or evil not because of certain positive attributes but because of privations of various forms of being appropriate to his or her nature.[35] And, in general, the extent to which a thing is not good of its kind is the extent to which it has not actualized, or cultivated dispositions for actualizing, the potentialities associated with its nature.[36] Every form of privation is covered by that observation—from physical or mental subnormality, through ineptitude and inattention, to debauchery and depravity. In each case some form of being theoretically available to the thing because of its nature is lacking.

These considerations put us in a better position to assess Aquinas's understanding of the difference in sense between 'being' and 'good-

---

has something the newborn infant lacks—an acquired disposition or habit to exercise his rational powers in certain ways. That is, the sleeping Aquinas has the being appropriate to human beings, but incompletely, in the condition picked out as first actuality (see, e.g., *ST* IaIIae q. 49, aa. 3, 4). Virtues are instances of first actuality relative to certain actions in accordance with rationality. Perfection as a human being (in this life) must include first actualities in part because the freedom associated with rational powers ranges over more alternatives than can be sorted out rationally and expeditiously on an occasion of action unless some disposition to respond in one way rather than another is part of the agent's character. That's one reason virtues are essential ingredients in human goodness. (See, e.g., *ST* IaIIae q. 49, a. 4; q. 55, a. 1.)

[31]*ST* IaIIae q. 54, a. 3: "And in this way good and bad habits are specifically distinct. For a habit that disposes [the agent] toward an action that is suited to the agent's nature is called good, while a habit that disposes [him] toward an action that is not suited to his nature is called bad."

[32]*ST* IaIIae q. 73, a. 8, s.c.

[33]See, e.g., *SCG* III 7, passim.

[34]*SCG* III 15, passim.

[35]See, e.g., *ST* Ia q. 5, a. 3, ad 2: "No being can be called bad or evil insofar as it is a being, but insofar as it lacks some sort of being—as a human being is called evil insofar as it lacks the being of virtue and an eye is called bad insofar as it lacks clarity of sight."

[36]See, e.g., *SCG* III 20, 22.

ness'. It should be clear by now that being is to be considered both absolutely and in a certain respect. Considered *absolutely*, being is the instantiation of a certain substantial form, the mere existence of a thing of some sort. But since each substantial form also includes a specifying potentiality, when that potentiality is actualized, the thing actualizing it is more fully a thing of that sort, a better specimen. When being is considered in this second way, it is correct to say that *in a certain respect* there is an increase of being for that thing. The ordinary sense of 'being' is being considered absolutely, that is, a thing's mere existence as the instantiation of some substantial form. But since to be is to be something or other, even being considered absolutely entails the actualization to *some* extent of *some* specifying potentiality, and in this way everything that is is good (in some respect and to some extent).

5 Supervenience

Aquinas, then, may be added to the lengthening list of those who think that goodness supervenes on some natural property.[37] As we've seen, Aquinas would say in general that an object a has goodness (to any extent) as an A if and only if a has the property of having actualized its specifying potentiality (to that extent). In particular, moral goodness supervenes on rationality in such a way that if any human being is morally good (to any extent), that person has the property of having actualized his or her capacity for rationality (to that extent); and if any human being has that property (to any extent), he or she is morally good (to that extent). Goodness supervenes on actualization of specifying potentialities; human moral goodness supervenes on actualization of rationality.

The relationship Aquinas sees between goodness and natural properties is complex and can be shown most easily by analogy. Fragility supervenes on certain natural properties without being reducible to any one of them, as Campbell and Pargetter have recently argued.[38]

---

[37] For a helpful survey, examples, and much else of relevance, see Jaegwon Kim, "Concepts of Supervenience," *Philosophy and Phenomenological Research* 45 (1984), 153–177.

[38] John Campbell and Robert Pargetter, "Goodness and Fragility," *American Philosophical Quarterly* 23 (1986), 155–165. "The relationship between fragility, fragility phenomena and the basis of the fragility is given by two identities. (1) being fragile = having some property which is responsible for being such that ⟨X is dropped, X breaks⟩, etc. and (2)

In line with their argument we might say that x is fragile in virtue of chemical bonding A, y in virtue of B, and z in virtue of C. Fragility cannot be reduced to or identified with bonding A, or B, or C, but it supervenes on each of them. It may be that what is common to x, y, and z is that each has weak chemical bonds in crucial spots, but those weak bonds are chemically quite distinct in connection with A, B, and C. In that case it can be said that the characteristic of being fragile and the characteristic of having weak chemical bonds in crucial spots are coextensive, and that fragility supervenes on natural characteristics, and yet it must also be denied that fragility can be identified with any one of those characteristics.

The relationship between fragility and other characteristics in that analysis is like the relationship between goodness and natural characteristics in Aquinas's ethical naturalism. A thing's goodness and the actualization of the thing's specifying potentiality are coextensive. Goodness in general is not to be identified with a particular natural characteristic, however, because the natural characteristic that is the actualization of a specifying potentiality will vary from one species of things to another. And the same observation holds regarding being: what is required to be a fully actualized member of species X is different from what is required to be a fully actualized member of species Y. The degree of actualization of the specifying potentialities for an X is the degree of being as an X, and this is also the degree of goodness as an X. But the specifying potentialities for an X differ from the specifying potentialities for a Y. So being and goodness are identical, but neither is to be identified with any one particular natural characteristic on which it supervenes.

But is moral goodness in particular identical with the natural characteristic of actualized rationality? Since human beings are essentially rational animals, human moral goodness is coextensive with actualized rationality. But moral goodness (or badness) is a characteristic of all beings whose nature involves freedom of choice, whether or not they are human. And so not even moral goodness is necessarily coextensive with the actualization of rationality, the specifying potentiality for human beings in the actual world. Goodness as an X will, for every X,

---

The property which is responsible for object O's being such that ⟨O is dropped, O breaks⟩, etc. = having chemical bonding B. This explicates the 'because' relation for fragility, i.e., it tells us what is meant when we say that O is fragile because it has bonding B. And when we say that object N is fragile because it has bonding A, clause (1) remains unchanged and clause (2) is changed in the obvious way" (p. 161).

be identical with the actualization of an X's specifying potentialities, but there is no natural characteristic such that goodness (or even moral goodness) is identical with it (where identity of properties is taken to require at least necessary coextension).

6 Objections to the Central Thesis

On the basis of this exposition of Aquinas's central thesis against its metaphysical background we can reply to objections the thesis is almost certain to generate. (The first two of those we consider are in fact considered and rebutted by Aquinas himself.)

Objection 1: A thing's being and its being good are clearly not the same—many things that are, aren't good—and so being and goodness are clearly not coextensive. But if the terms are identical in reference, as Aquinas claims they are, being and goodness would have to be coextensive.[39]

This first objection trades on the counterintuitive character of a corollary of the central thesis—viz., everything is good insofar as it is in being. Aquinas accepts that corollary, associating it particularly with Augustine.[40] But the corollary cannot be reduced to an absurdity simply by observing that there are things that aren't good. In accordance with the central thesis, a thing has goodness in a certain respect and to a certain extent simply by virtue of possessing a substantial form and thus existing as a thing of a certain sort. As we've seen, however, the sense of 'goodness' is not simply the possession of some substantial form but, in particular, the actualization of the specifying potentiality inherent in that form. Only to the extent to which a thing has actualized that potentiality is it true to say unqualifiedly that the thing is good. For instance, to call Hitler good (without identifying some special respect, such as demagoguery) is to imply that he is good as a human being, or as a moral agent, which is false in ways that Aquinas's practical morality could detail by indicating how this or that action or decree of Hitler's fails to actualize rationality.

Objection 2: Goodness admits of degrees, but being is all or nothing. No rock, desk, or dog is in being just a little; no dog is in being more than another dog. On the other hand, things clearly can increase or

---

[39]*ST* Ia q. 5, a. 1, obj. 1.
[40]*ST* Ia q. 5, a. 1, s.c. (Augustine, *De doctrina christiana* I 32).

decrease in goodness, and one thing can be better or worse than another thing of the same kind. Therefore, 'goodness' and 'being' can't have the same referent.[41]

It may be right to say of existence, at least abstractly, that it's all or nothing. But since every instance of existence is existence *as* something or other, and since existence as something or other typically admits of degrees—being a more or less fully developed actualized specimen—it is by no means clear that being is all or nothing. Making the same observation from Aquinas's point of view, we might say that there's more to being than just existence. Where contingent beings are concerned, potentiality for existing in a certain respect is a state of being that is intermediate between actually existing in that respect and not existing at all in that respect, as we've seen.[42] Furthermore, the actualization of potentialities is often gradual, so that the being of the thing whose specifying potentiality is being actualized admits of degrees. Stages in the actualization of a thing's specifying potentiality certainly can be and often are described in terms of goodness rather than being. All the same, the degrees of goodness picked out in such ordinary descriptions are supervenient on degrees of being.

Objection 3: According to Aquinas's central thesis, the more being, the more goodness. In that case unrestrained procreation, for example, would be a clear instance of promoting goodness, since the increase of the human population is an increase of being and consequently of goodness. But that consequence is absurd.

Human beings who bring another human being into existence have not in virtue of that fact alone produced any goodness in any ordinary sense. If with Aquinas we take the basic sense of 'goodness' to be the actualization of a thing's specifying potentiality, then a human being produces goodness to the extent to which it actualizes its own or something else's specifying potentiality. Considered in itself, bringing children into the world does nothing to actualize any human being's specifying potentiality.[43] On the contrary, a man who fathered very many children would probably contribute to a *decrease* of goodness. He would be unable to have much parenting influence on the lives of his children or to give them the care they needed just because there were

---

[41]*ST* Ia q. 5, a. 1, obj. 3.
[42]N. 30 above.
[43]The capacity for reproduction is a potentiality human beings share with all living things.

so many of them, and so it is at least a probable consequence of his unrestrained procreation that there would be more people whose chances of actualizing their specifying potentialities were unnaturally low.

But objection 3 is more complicated than the preceding objections just because goodness does supervene on being (in the way described in section 5 above). Consequently, whenever a thing has being in any respect, it also has goodness in some respect to some extent. If Ahasuerus, with his many wives and concubines, fathered, say, 150 children, he was partially responsible for the existence of 150 human beings and, consequently, for the goodness supervening on the being that constituted their existence. But neither we nor Aquinas would count Ahasuerus as a moral hero or even morally praiseworthy just because he fathered all those children.

Our rejoinder to objection 1 will help here. The small amount of goodness that must supervene on even the mere existence of a thing is not enough to call that thing good. In fact, if the thing falls too far short of the full actualization of its specifying potentiality, it is bad (or evil) considered as an instance of its kind, even though there is goodness in it. So insofar as Ahasuerus couldn't do what he ought to have done to help his children develop into good human beings, his unrestrained procreation couldn't count as the production of goodness; and to the extent to which his fathering so many children would be a factor in diminishing or preventing his care of them, it could count as producing badness.

Objection 4: According to Aquinas, loss of being is loss of goodness: badness (or evil) is the privation of goodness, which is a privation of being. In that case taking penicillin to cure strep throat would be a bad thing to do, since it would result in the destruction of countless bacteria. But that consequence is absurd.

Objection 4 gains a special strength from the fact that it forces a defender of Aquinas's position to take on the task of ranking natural kinds. The task may seem not just uncongenial but impossible for anyone who understands goodness as supervenient on being itself. In Jack London's story "To Build a Fire" either a man will save his life by killing his dog or the dog will continue to live but the man will die. Since in either case one being is left, it may look as if Aquinas's theory must be neutral on the question of which of those beings should survive. But a moral intuition that is at least widely shared would consider the case in which the dog dies and the man survives to be preferable.

Far from offending that intuition, Aquinas's theory can explain and support it because his metaphysics provides a systematic basis on which to rank natural kinds: the Porphyrian Tree, a standard device of medieval metaphysics inherited from Hellenistic philosophy. A Porphyrian Tree begins with an Aristotelian category (*substance* is the standard medieval example) and moves via a series of dichotomies from that most general genus through at least some of its species. (In theory, all its possible species can be uncovered by this means.) The dichotomies produce progressively more specific species by the application of a pair of complementary properties (differentiae) to a less specific species (a genus) already in the tree. In this way, for example, *substance* yields *corporeal substance* and *incorporeal substance* to begin the tree. Corporeal substances can in turn be divided into those capable and those incapable of growth and reproduction and other life processes; and corporeal substances capable of life processes can be divided into those capable and those incapable of perception—animals and plants, roughly speaking. Finally, those capable of perception can be divided into those capable and those incapable of rationality—human beings and other animals. In this schema, then, human beings are corporeal substances capable of life processes, perception, and rationality.

Since each dichotomy in the tree is generated by the application of complementary characteristics, and since (setting aside the complicated case of the first dichotomy) all the characteristics applied involve capacities, one of the species (or genera) encountered in any pair after the first is characterized by a capacity its counterpart lacks. But, given Aquinas's views on being and actuality, an increment in capacity (or potentiality) constitutes an increment in being; and, because of the supervenience of goodness on being, a species (or genus) with more capacities of the sort that show up in the differentiae will have potentially more goodness than one with fewer. So, other things being equal, the goodness of a human life is greater than that of a dog's just because of rationality, the incremental capacity.[44]

---

[44] The *ceteris paribus* clause in this claim is important. Even though species *A* outranks species *B* in the way described, it is theoretically possible that a particular individual of species *B* might outrank an individual of species *A*. Suppose that there are angels, that angels constitute a species as human beings do, that the species *angel* outranks the species *human being*, and that Satan is a fallen angel. It is theoretically possible that Mother Theresa outranks Satan in the relevant sense even though the amount of being available to an angel is greater than that available to any human being. For if Mother Theresa has actualized virtually all of her specifying potentialities and Satan very few

We don't have to accept the universal applicability of the Porphyrian Tree in order to see that in it Aquinas does have a method for ranking at least some natural kinds relative to one another, and that the method is entirely consistent with his central thesis. Moreover, the method yields results that elucidate and support the intuitive reaction to the Jack London story: other things being equal, we value a human being more than a dog (or a colony of bacteria) because there's more to a human being than there is to a dog (or a colony of bacteria). Finally, although Aquinas subordinates all other species of animal to the human species, this feature of his theory cannot be interpreted as sanctioning wanton cruelty toward nonhuman animals or their gratuitous destruction. It is another corollary of his central thesis that any destruction of being is always prima facie bad in some respect and to some extent. Because some destruction may often be less bad than the only available alternative, it may often be rationally chosen. But unless there is some greater good (some enhancement of being) that can be achieved only by means of destruction, an agent who chooses to destroy will choose irrationally.

In expounding and defending Aquinas's metaethics we have been moving toward a consideration of his normative ethics, to which we now turn.

7 The Evaluation of Actions

Aquinas's normative ethics is constructed around a theory of virtues and vices, which are conceived of as habitual inclinations, or dispositions toward certain sorts of actions. It will be helpful, therefore, to begin this consideration by looking briefly at his analysis and evaluation of human actions.[45]

A human action, strictly speaking, is one in which a human agent exercises the specifically human rational faculties of intellect and will.[46] (Absentminded gestures, consequently, are not human actions even

---

of his, it will be possible to ascribe more being and hence more goodness to Mother Theresa than to Satan.

[45]For a clear, succinct presentation of some of this material in more detail, see Alan Donagan, "Aquinas on Human Action," in *The Cambridge History of Later Medieval Philosophy*, ed. N. Kretzmann, A. Kenny, and J. Pinborg (Cambridge: Cambridge University Press, 1982), pp. 642–654.

[46]Aquinas's "Treatise on Action" is contained in *ST* IaIIae qq. 6–17; qq. 18–21 are concerned with the evaluation of actions.

though they are "actions associated with a human being."[47]) Every human action has an object, an end, and certain circumstances in which it is done.

An action's object, as Aquinas conceives of it, is fundamentally the state of affairs the agent intends to bring about as a direct effect of the action.[48] We might characterize the object as the immediate aim or purpose of the action. When Esther goes uninvited into the court of King Ahasuerus's palace, for instance, the object of her action is an audience with the king.

But in Aquinas's analysis of action, an action's object is distinguished from the action's end.[49] We might provisionally think of an action's end as the agent's motive for performing the action. So the end of Esther's action of coming to the palace is to persuade Ahasuerus to rescind his decree mandating the death of all the Jews in his kingdom.

Seen in this way, the *object* of an action is *what* the agent intends to accomplish as a direct result of her action, while its *end* is *why* she intends to accomplish it. Both the object and the end of an action are taken into account in determining the action's species, in determining what the action essentially *is*.[50] Given Aquinas's central thesis regarding being and goodness, then, it is not surprising to find him maintaining that the goodness or badness of any action is to be decided on the basis of an assessment of the action's object and end. If the contemplated states of affairs that the action aims at and that motivate the agent are good, the action is good; if either the object or the end is not good, the action is not good.

So far, this account of the goodness of actions seems to ignore the fact that certain types of actions are morally neutral. The object of pitching horseshoes is to get them to fall around a stake, a state of affairs that certainly seems to be neither morally good nor morally bad. Suppose the end of such an action on a particular occasion is to entertain a sick child, which we may suppose is morally good. Then it might seem that the action itself, pitching horseshoes to entertain a sick child, would have to be evaluated by Aquinas as not good; for although its end is good, its object is not.

[47]For this distinction, see *ST* IaIIae q. 1, a. 1.

[48]On the object of an action, see, e.g., *ST* IaIIae q. 10, a. 2; q. 18, a. 2.

[49]On the end of an action, see, e.g., *ST* IaIIae q. 1, aa. 1–3; q. 18, aa. 4–6. For our purposes here we are omitting some of the details of Aquinas's complex distinction between the object and the end of an action; for some of the complications see, e.g., *ST* IaIIae q. 18, a. 7.

[50]On specifying an action, see, e.g., *ST* IaIIae q. 1, a. 3; q. 18, aa. 2, 5, 7.

This counterintuitive evaluation can be dispelled by taking into account Aquinas's concept of the *circumstances* of an action: When was the action done? Where? By whom? How? etc.[51] An action's circumstances are obviously not essential features of a type of action, but they are what might be called *particularizing* accidents, because any broadly conceived type of action is particularized or recognized as the particular action it is by attending to its circumstances. So, for example, part of what makes Esther's action the particular action it is, is its circumstances. She comes uninvited to the court of the king's palace at a time when Ahasuerus has decreed death for anyone who comes into the court of the palace without having been called by the king, unless the intruder "finds favor with the king." Furthermore, because it has been a month since the king last sent for her, Esther has reason to believe she is out of favor with the king. Finally, she comes there at a time when Ahasuerus has decreed the death of all the Jews in his kingdom, and Esther's intention is to speak for her people. It is on the basis of a consideration of these circumstances that the action of coming uninvited to the king, which seems morally neutral, is particularized as Esther's act of courage and altruism.[52]

The importance of a consideration of circumstances in Aquinas's evaluation of actions can be seen in the fact that he takes any and every action particularized by its circumstances to be either good or bad, even though the type of the action broadly conceived of may be morally neutral (his paradigms are picking a straw off the ground or taking a walk).[53]

Not all of an action's accidents are included among its circumstances. So, for example, Esther's action has the accidents of contributing to the death of Haman and of being commemorated in a book of the Bible. But on Aquinas's theory neither of those accidents can or should make any difference to an evaluation of Esther's action. An action's circumstances, he says, are those accidents of it that are related per se to the action being evaluated; all its other accidents are related to it only *per accidens*.[54]

By this distinction he seems to mean that the circumstances of Esther's particular action, the action being evaluated in our example, are features accidental to the *type* of action she performs, but not accidental

---

[51]On the circumstances of an action, see esp. *ST* IaIIae q. 7, passim.
[52]On the role of circumstances in the evaluation of actions, see, e.g., *ST* IaIIae q. 18, aa. 3, 10, 11.
[53]*ST* IaIIae q. 18, a. 8.
[54]See, e.g., *ST* IaIIae q. 7, a. 2, ad 2.

to her particular action on that particular occasion. On the contrary, even our understanding of the object and end of her particular action is heavily influenced by what we know of its circumstances. In light of that knowledge we might want to revise our original broad assessment and say, more precisely, that the object of her action is a *dangerous and difficult* audience with the king, and that its end is a *resolute and self-sacrificial* attempt to get the king to rescind his edict.

The action's circumstances may be called its *intrinsic* accidents, the others its *extrinsic* accidents. The intrinsic accidents of Esther's action clarify and redefine our understanding of *what she does*, what she is responsible for; its extrinsic accidents—such as its being commemorated in a book of the Bible—obviously contribute nothing to such an understanding. Even the extrinsically accidental fact that her action has some causal relationship with Haman's death is not in any way a feature of what *she* does, because the connection between her action and his death is an unforeseeable and partly fortuitous chain of events, something she could not be held responsible for.

So Aquinas's evaluation of actions is based entirely on a consideration of *what* those actions *are* and not at all on a consideration of their extrinsic accidents. In that way it is a natural outgrowth of his central metaethical thesis. The object and end of an action determine the action's type and so, broadly speaking, they determine the being of the action; the action's circumstances determine the being of the particular action that is actually performed, and in doing so they clarify and refine our understanding of the particular action's object and end. A particular (actually performed) action, then, is good only in case both its object and its end as informed by its circumstances are good; otherwise the particular action is bad. The goodness of the action's object or end depends, in turn, on whether the contemplated state of affairs motivating or aimed at by the agent is good, as judged by the central thesis.

The end of Esther's action, for example, is to persuade the king to rescind his decree of death for all the kingdom's Jews. But the king's decree was irrational, on Aquinas's view, since it would have resulted in a great loss of being and hence of goodness without any greater good to justify that loss. Helping to bring about the rescinding of an irrational decree, however, is rational, other things being equal, and therefore morally good.[55] (Analogous things can be said about the object of Esther's action.)

---

[55]On Aquinas's treatment of issues of this sort regarding decrees or laws see Norman

8 Problems for a Simpleminded Application of the Thesis

In the story of Esther, her attempt to save her people involves her knowingly risking her life: "and if I perish, I perish." How, if at all, is the evaluation of her action in terms of its object and end affected by that circumstance of the action? Aquinas would, not surprisingly, find that aspect of her action praiseworthy. In discussing courage, he praises risking one's life in the defense of the common good as a prime example of that virtue.[56] But suppose that Esther succeeds in saving her people and dies in the attempt. Would Aquinas's theory still evaluate her action as good in that case?

The simpleminded reply to that question is an emphatic affirmative: Of course Esther's action is good even if it costs her her life; it saves thousands of lives at the expense of one. On balance there is a great surplus of being and consequently of goodness.

Although the affirmative reply seems right, the reason given for it is repugnant. If this simpleminded bookkeeping approach were what Aquinas's thesis about being and goodness required, the thesis would lead to results that are egregiously inconsistent with the rest of Aquinas's moral theory as well as repugnant to moral intuitions shared by most people in his time and ours. We can show this by considering applications of the simpleminded approach to three cases more complicated than our revised version of Esther's story. The first of them is a version of one of Aquinas's own examples.

The heaven case: Johnson is a murderer, and Williams is his innocent victim. But when Johnson murders him, Williams (unbeknownst to Johnson) is in a state of grace, and so goes to heaven. The ultimate end of human existence is union with God in heaven, and so by bringing it about that Williams achieves the ultimate end, Johnson brings about an increase of being (and consequently of goodness). In reality, then, Johnson's murder of Williams is morally justified.

Aquinas considers his version of the heaven case as an objection to his own claim that the deliberate killing of an innocent person is never morally justified.[57] His rejoinder to this objection is that the fact that

---

Kretzmann, "*Lex iniusta non est lex*: Laws on Trial in Aquinas's Court of Conscience," *American Journal of Jurisprudence*, forthcoming.
[56]See, e.g., *ST* IIaIIae q. 123, passim.
[57]*ST* IIaIIae q. 64, a. 6, obj. 2 and ad 2.

Williams goes to heaven, the good that is supposed to justify Johnson's murder of Williams, is an accident that is related to Johnson's action only *per accidens;* Williams's going to heaven is an extrinsic accident of Johnson's action. Aquinas is apparently thinking along this line: Williams's spiritual condition and not Johnson's action is what causes Williams to go to heaven, and it is an extrinsic accident of Johnson's action that Williams was in that condition at the time of the murder. Since it is a feature of Aquinas's theory that an action is to be evaluated solely on the basis of what it *is* and not on the basis of any of its extrinsic accidents, his evaluation of Johnson's action would not take any account of the fact that Williams goes to heaven. What Johnson's action *is*, as far as the story goes, is simply the murder of an innocent person, which is of course not morally justifiable in Aquinas's theory.

Aquinas's treatment of the heaven case strikes us as satisfactory, but his conclusion that sending Williams to heaven is only an extrinsic accident of Johnson's action seems to depend on the fact that Johnson does not (presumably cannot) know that Williams is in a state of grace. If Johnson knew that killing Williams would result in Williams's going to heaven, it would at least be harder to deny that achieving that result was part of the end of Johnson's action and thus part of what Johnson's action *was*. We want to consider some cases in which there is no relevant ignorance on the part of the agent.

The hostage case: A madman takes five people hostage and threatens to kill them all unless Brown kills Robinson, an innocent bystander. Brown decides that killing Robinson is morally justified by the surplus of being (and consequently of goodness) that will result from using Robinson's death to save the lives of the five hostages.

In the hostage case the object of Brown's action is Robinson's death, and its end appears to be the saving of five lives. Aquinas's way of dismissing the counterintuitive moral assessment in the heaven case is clearly unavailable as a way of dealing with the hostage case. The good that appears to justify Brown's action is the action's *end*, which *must* be taken into account in evaluating the action. In considering how Aquinas would deal with the hostage case, it will be helpful to look more closely at his conception of the end of an action.

Since it is Aquinas's view that actions should be evaluated only on the basis of what they are and not on the basis of their extrinsic accidents, and since it is also his view that actions are to be evaluated on the basis of their ends, the state of affairs sought after as the end of the action must be intrinsic to the action itself. For that reason it seems clear that the notion of motive, although it is in some respects close to Aquinas's notion of end, is not interchangeable with it. A state of affairs counts as the end of an action if and only if the agent performs the action for the sake of establishing that state of affairs, *and* the agent *can* in fact establish that state of affairs *solely by* performing that action.

In the hostage case the good that is supposed to justify Brown's killing the innocent Robinson is the saving of five lives. But that good cannot be the end of Brown's action because it is not a state of affairs he can establish by killing Robinson. The survival of the hostages depends not on Brown's action but on the action of the madman, who can of course kill them all even if Brown meets his demand. Therefore, the survival of the hostages is not a state of affairs Brown can be said to establish solely by killing Robinson. And once this more precise notion of the end of an action has been introduced, the hostage case can be assimilated to the heaven case after all. In both cases, the good that is supposed to justify the killing of an innocent person turns out not to be an intrinsic part of the action being evaluated but rather only an extrinsic acccident of it that is for that reason to be left out of account in the evaluation of the action. When Brown's action in the hostage case is evaluated in that way, it is evaluated simply as the deliberate killing of an innocent person; and since that state of affairs is unquestionably bad, the action itself is not morally justified.

But even if this attempt to defend Aquinas's evaluation of actions succeeds in the hostage case, it will apparently fail if we alter the form of the counterexample in one crucial respect.

The hospital case: Five patients in a hospital are waiting for donors to be found so that they can undergo transplant operations. One of them needs a heart; the second, a liver; the third, lungs; and the fourth and fifth each need a kidney. Every one of the five patients will be able to lead a normal life if, but only if, an organ donor can be found. Each of them will die very soon without a transplant operation. Jones, the skilled transplant specialist in charge of these patients, decides that killing Smith, a healthy, innocent person, is morally justified by the surplus of being (and consequently of goodness) that will result from using Smith's organs to save the five critically ill patients.[58]

---

[58]For a well-known form of the problem in the hospital case, see Philippa Foot, "The Problem of Abortion and the Doctrine of Double Effect," in her *Virtues and Vices* (Berkeley: University of California Press, 1978), pp. 19–32.

The end of Jones's action, even on the more precise interpretation of 'end', is the saving of five lives. In the hospital case, unlike the hostage case, no other agent's action is needed to establish the state of affairs Jones aims at establishing, because he is a relevantly skilled specialist in charge of the five patients. And if the saving of their lives can in this case count as the end of Jones's action, then it must be taken into account in evaluating the action. For that reason, the tactic that was effective in defending Aquinas's evaluation of actions against the hostage case won't work against the hospital case.

But Aquinas's evaluation of actions requires taking into account the action's object as well as its end. Since the object and the end together make the action what it *is*, and since the goodness of anything is a function of its being, both object and end must be good if the action is to be good. But the object of Jones's action in the hospital case is the death of the innocent Smith and the removal of his organs, which is unquestionably morally bad. Aquinas would, more specifically, condemn the object of Jones's action in the hospital case as *unjust* (as we will explain in the next section).

But the sacrifice of one to save many in the hospital case is formally like our revised version of Esther's story. In order to understand Aquinas's evaluation of the hospital case and to see whether it applies also to Esther's courageous act of altruism, we need to understand something of Aquinas's theory of the virtues in general and of justice in particular.

9 Justice and Its Place in the Scheme of the Virtues

Assuming for now the metaphysical underpinnings of Aquinas's theory of the virtues—his accounts of intellect and will, passion and operation, disposition and habit—we can begin this brief synopsis by saying that (human) moral goodness is a kind of goodness attainable only by rational beings and, as we've seen, a rational being is good to the extent to which it actualizes its capacity for rationality. Summarizing drastically, we can say that moral virtue is the will's habit of choosing rationally in controlling passions and directing actions.[59] Of the cardinal virtues, prudence is the habit of skil-

---

[59]See, e.g., *ST* IaIIae q. 60, passim. For a good discussion of the Aristotelian background, see L. A. Kosman, "Being Properly Affected: Virtues and Feelings in Aristotle's Ethics," in *Essays on Aristotle's Ethics*, ed. Rorty, pp. 103–116.

fully choosing means appropriate for the attaining of ends and so is concerned with directing actions; in this way prudence links intellectual and moral virtues.[60] As for the cardinal virtues concerned with controlling passions, if the passions are of a sort that need to be controlled in order to keep them from thwarting rationality, the relevant habit is temperance. And if the passions are the sort that need to be controlled in order to keep them from deterring the agent from an action to which reason prompts him, the relevant habit is courage.[61] Finally, if what is at stake is the exercise of rationality not in the agent's governance of himself but in his actions affecting other people, the relevant habit is justice.[62]

In Aquinas's view, a society has a being of its own. Some things contribute to the being of a society, and others to its dissolution. In accordance with Aquinas's metaethics, the things that contribute to a society's being are part of the society's good, and the virtue of justice generally in the members of the society is directed toward establishing and preserving that common good. Aquinas, who follows Aristotle closely here, distinguishes distributive from commutative justice in respect of the rational moral principles to which the virtue conforms. Distributive justice is the rational regulation of the distribution of the society's worldly goods, aiming at a rational relationship in that respect between the society as a whole and any individual member of it.[63] Commutative justice, on the other hand, is the rational regulation of relationships among individuals or subgroups within the society. The basis of commutative justice in Aquinas's treatment of it seems to be that human beings considered just as persons are equals, and that it is therefore rational for them, considered just as persons, to treat one another as equals, and irrational for them to treat one another unequally, considered just as persons.[64]

A used-car dealer and his customer, considered just as persons, are equals. If the dealer deceives the customer about the defects of a car and so cheats him out of much of the purchase price, then in that particular exchange of worldly goods the dealer gets a greater share than the customer gets—which is contrary to reason because the dealer and the customer are equals in all relevant respects. The inequality of

---

[60]See, e.g., ST IaIIae q. 57, a. 5; q. 58, a. 4; IIaIIae qq. 47–56.
[61]See, e.g., ST IaIIae q. 60, a. 4.
[62]See, e.g., ST IaIIae q. 61, a. 2; IIaIIae qq. 57–71.
[63]ST IIaIIae q. 61, a. 1.
[64]ST IIaIIae q. 61, a. 2.

the trade is part of what makes it an instance of cheating, and cheating is morally bad because it contravenes the principles of commutative justice.[65]

So, whenever one person takes another's worldly goods, the action will be just only if it is rational. A necessary (though not also sufficient) condition of its being rational is its involving an even trade. A slanderer, for instance, takes away the victim's reputation, one of the more important worldly goods, and gives nothing in return; slander is thus a gross injustice.[66] Murder is perhaps the grossest injustice of all, since in depriving the victim of life, the greatest of worldly goods, the murderer is not only providing no worldly compensation but also rendering the victim incapable of receiving any such compensation.[67]

In the hospital case the object of Dr. Jones's action is characterized by exactly that sort of injustice. His taking of Smith's life and vital organs involves considerable benefit for his five patients, but there can be no compensatory worldly good for Smith. The injustice in the object of Jones's action is a sufficient condition for evaluating the action as morally bad, regardless of the beneficial aspects of its end.

We began our investigation of the simpleminded application of Aquinas's central thesis by considering a revised version of the story of Esther, in which she loses her life in saving her people. It should now be clear that the intuitive positive evaluation of such an act of self-sacrifice is not affected by our negative evaluation of Jones's sacrifice of Smith in the hospital case. Esther would not be guilty of any injustice if she gave up her own life for her people, although of course Ahasuerus would be guilty of injustice if he took her life in those circumstances. In fact, according to Aquinas's account of commutative justice it is impossible for Esther to be unjust to herself, because a person cannot take *for* herself an unfair share of worldly goods *from* herself. The reasons for disapproving of Jones's action in the hospital case do not apply to Esther's hypothetical self-sacrifice, and approval of her self-sacrifice need not and should not be based on the simpleminded bookkeeping application of Aquinas's central thesis.

[65]See, e.g., *ST* IIaIIae q. 77, passim.
[66]See *ST* IIaIIae q. 73, passim; for comparisons of slander (or "backbiting") with theft or murder, see esp. a. 3.
[67]On murder as a vice in opposition to commutative justice and the vice "by which a man does the greatest harm to his neighbor," see *ST* IIaIIae q. 64, passim.

10 Agent-centered Restrictions in Aquinas's Ethics

These considerations give us reason to think that Aquinas's ethics is a deontological theory of morality that can handle the problem of agent-centered restrictions. Samuel Scheffler has recently described these restrictions as rendering "typical deontological views . . . apparently paradoxical."

> An agent-centred restriction is, roughly, a restriction which it is at least sometimes impermissible to violate in circumstances where a violation would serve to minimize total overall violations of the very same restriction, and would have no other morally relevant consequences. Thus, for example, a prohibition against killing one innocent person even in order to minimize the total number of innocent people killed would ordinarily count as an agent-centred restriction. The inclusion of agent-centred restrictions gives traditional deontological views considerable anti-consequentialist force, and also considerable intuitive appeal. Despite their congeniality to moral common sense, however, agent-centred restrictions are puzzling. For how can it be rational to forbid the performance of a morally objectionable action that would have the effect of minimizing the total number of comparably objectionable actions that were performed and would have no other morally relevant consequences? How can the minimization of morally objectionable conduct be morally unacceptable?[68]

While Aquinas's theory certainly endorses the truism that the good is to be maximized, it also interprets the nature of goodness in general and of good actions in particular in such a way that no action whose object is characterized by injustice can be rationally performed no matter how great a good is incorporated in the action's end. On this basis, a generalization of agent-centered restrictions can be endorsed and accommodated in Aquinas's teleological deontology.

The generalized version of Scheffler's example is a prohibition against perpetrating or permitting one injustice of uncompensatable suffering even in order to minimize the total number of injustices, and at this level of generality "the very same restriction" is the restriction against perpetrating or permitting injustice. Agent-centered restrictions that

---

[68]Samuel Scheffler, "Agent-Centred Restrictions, Rationality, and the Virtues," *Mind* 94 (1985), 409–419; 409. In this article Scheffler is commenting on Philippa Foot's "Utilitarianism and the Virtues," *Proceedings and Addresses of the American Philosophical Association* 57 (1983), 273–283; also (a revised version) *Mind* 94 (1985), 196–209. For Scheffler's own resolution of the puzzle of agent-centered restrictions, see his book *The Rejection of Consequentialism* (Oxford: Clarendon Press, 1982).

prohibit agents from perpetrating or permitting actions that constitute an injustice are rational for that very reason, regardless of the good to be achieved by performing those actions.

11 The Theological Interpretation of Aquinas's Central Thesis

Aquinas's central metaethical thesis has a theological interpretation more fundamental than any of its applications to morality. For since Aquinas takes God to be essentially and uniquely "being itself" (*ipsum esse*), it is God alone who is essentially goodness itself.[69] This theological interpretation of Aquinas's thesis regarding being and goodness entails a relationship between God and morality that avoids the embarrassments of both "theological subjectivism" and "theological objectivism"[70] and provides a basis for an account of religious morality preferable to any other we know of.[71]

The question "What has God to do with morality?" has typically been given either of two answers by those who think the answer isn't "Nothing."[72] God's will is sometimes taken to create morality in the sense that whatever God wills is good just because he wills it: consequently, right actions are right just because God approves of them and wrong actions are wrong just because God disapproves of them. This divine-command morality may be thought of as theological subjectivism (TS).[73] The second of these two typical answers takes morality to be grounded on principles transmitted by God but independent of him, so that a perfectly good God frames his will in accordance with those independent standards of goodness: consequently, God approves of

---

[69]See, e.g., *ST* Ia q. 2, a. 3 ("*Quarta via*"); q. 3, aa. 4, 7; q. 6, a. 3. Bonaventure, Aquinas's contemporary and colleague at the University of Paris, forthrightly identifies God as the single referent of 'being' and 'goodness' in his own version of the central thesis, interpreting the Old Testament as emphasizing being, the New Testament as emphasizing goodness (see, e.g., *Itinerarium mentis in deum*, V 2).

[70]See Norman Kretzmann, "Abraham, Isaac, and Euthyphro: God and the Basis of Morality," in *Hamartia: The Concept of Error in the Western Tradition*, ed. D. V. Stump, et al. (New York: Edwin Mellen Press, 1983), pp. 27–50.

[71]See our "Absolute Simplicity," 375–376.

[72]This brief discussion of religious morality is adapted from "Absolute Simplicity."

[73]For an interesting, sophisticated treatment of divine-command theories of morality, see, e.g., Philip Quinn, *Divine Commands and Moral Requirements* (Oxford: Clarendon Press, 1978).

right actions just because they are right and disapproves of wrong actions just because they are wrong (theological objectivism [TO]).

The trouble with TS is that by its lights apparently anything at all could be established as morally right or good by divine fiat. So, although TS makes a consideration of God's will essential to an evaluation of actions, it does so at the cost of depriving the evaluation of its moral character. Because it cannot rule out anything as absolutely immoral, TS seems to be a theory of religious morality that has dropped *morality* as commonly understood out of the theory. TO, on the other hand, obviously provides the basis for an objective morality, but it seems equally clearly not to be a theory of *religious* morality since it suggests no essential connection between God and the standards for evaluating actions. Furthermore, the status of the standards to which God looks for morality according to TO seems to impugn God's sovereignty.

So the familiar candidates for theories of religious morality seem either, like TS, to be repugnant to moral intuitions or, like TO, to presuppose moral standards apart from God, which God may promulgate but does not produce. For different reasons, then, both TS and TO seem inadequate as theories of religious morality; neither one provides both an objective moral standard and an essential connection between religion and morality.

On the conception of God as essentially goodness itself, however, there is an essential relationship between God and the standard by which he prescribes or judges. The goodness for the sake of which and in accordance with which he wills whatever he wills regarding human morality is identical with his nature. On the other hand, because it is God's very nature and not any arbitrary decision of his that thereby constitutes the standard for morality, only things consonant with God's nature could be morally good. The theological interpretation of the central thesis of Aquinas's ethical theory thus provides the basis for an objective religious morality.

12 Justice, Uncompensated Suffering, and the Problem of Evil

But a more pointed theological application of Aquinas's central thesis can be developed by combining the conception of God as perfect goodness itself with the impermissibility of certain actions as brought out in our generalized account of agent-centered restrictions. The rationality of agent-centered restrictions is a consequence of the irrationality of treating the victim of the initial action unjustly in such a way that even achieving that action's laudable end leaves the victim uncompensated, and it is the injustice of the uncompensated suffering that makes the action impermissible.[74] It follows that it is impossible that a perfectly good God would permit, much less perform, any action whose object involves a victim who is treated unjustly and left uncompensated, no matter how much other evil might be prevented thereby.

Nevertheless, many, perhaps most, attempts to solve the problem of evil portray God as permitting or even performing actions that appear to be impermissible in just that way. For instance, Richard Swinburne's "argument from the need for knowledge," which is certainly not idiosyncratic in its attempt to provide a morally sufficient reason for God's permitting natural evil, takes the initially attractive line that many natural evils "are necessary if agents are to have the *knowledge* of how to bring about evil or prevent its occurrence, knowledge which they must have if they are to have a genuine choice between bringing about evil and bringing about good."[75] But as this line is developed it turns out, not surprisingly, that in very many cases God must be portrayed as allowing some innocent person or persons to suffer without compensation so that others may learn to avoid or to prevent or mitigate such suffering on other occasions; "If God normally helps those who cannot help themselves when others do not help, others will not take the trouble to help the helpless next time."[76] Even if we suppose, as Swinburne does, that the knowledge gained in such a way cannot be gained otherwise, at least not efficaciously, God's role in this arrangement seems morally on a par with that of Dr. Jones in the hospital case—or worse, since the end of Jones's action is the preven-

---

[74]Dostoevsky presents the classic case of this sort of acknowledgement near the conclusion of Ivan's harangue of Alyosha over the problem of evil: " 'Imagine that you are creating a fabric of human destiny with the object of making men happy in the end, giving them peace and rest at last, but that it was essential and inevitable to torture to death only one tiny creature—that baby beating its breast with its fist, for instance—and to found that edifice on its unavenged tears, would you consent to be the architect on those conditions? Tell me, and tell the truth.' 'No, I wouldn't consent,' said Alyosha softly" (*The Brothers Karamazov*, Bk. V, chap. 4).

[75]Richard Swinburne, *The Existence of God* (Oxford: Clarendon Press, 1979), pp. 202–203.

[76]Ibid., p. 210.

tion of death while the end of God's nonintervention is the alleviation of ignorance.

Swinburne deals with difficulties of this sort by stressing God's right to treat us as we have no right to treat one another.[77] But to say in this context that God has such a right is to imply that there would be no injustice on God's part if he exercised the right. Swinburne's claim, then, comes to this: if God were to do something that would be unjust by human standards, it would not count as unjust simply because God was its perpetrator. If this claim is not to convey the morally repulsive suggestion that anything whatever that God might do would count as good solely because God did it (including, e.g., breaking his promise to save those who put their trust in him), then there must be morally relevant features of God's nature and action for which there are no counterparts in human nature and action.

Swinburne sometimes suggests that God's being the creator of the world is just such a feature. This seems to be the most promising line to take in support of Swinburne's claim about God's rights, but we do not think it succeeds. A mother is also in a sense the creator of her child. While that relationship gives her rights over the child that others do not have, it is not nearly enough to justify her if she inflicts uncompensated suffering on her unwilling child. If she were to deny her daughter any college education in order to have money enough to send her son to Harvard, when her daughter also wants an education and receives no compensating benefits for failing to get one, the mother would be outrageously unfair. That she was in some sense the creator of the children would in no way lessen the unfairness. Of course, God is the creator of human beings in a much more radical sense than a mother is the creator of her children. But would the assessment of the mother's unfairness be at all softened if it turned out that she had built these children from scratch in a laboratory? We see no respect in which the degree of radicalness in the claim that one person created another could be a morally relevant consideration in evaluating the justice of the creator's treatment of his creatures.

Similarly, Plantinga has suggested that natural evils might be perpetrated by fallen angels, and that the good there is in the exercise of free will on their part might provide a morally sufficient reason for God to allow instances of natural evil, if, and only if, the world char-

[77]Ibid., pp. 216–218.

acterized by such an arrangement is one in which there is more good than evil.[78] On this view, an omniscient, omnipotent, perfectly good God might permit the inhabitants of Mexico City to suffer in an earthquake so that the good of freedom might thereby be achieved in the earthquake-causing activity of fallen angels, as long as the general preponderance of good over evil was not thereby destroyed.[79] Plantinga's Free Will Defense (FWD) has sometimes been challenged because it has been thought to impugn God's omnipotence, but as far as we know, the literature on FWD has not so far addressed the challenge that arises from Aquinas's sort of ethical theory, which provides grounds for doubting whether FWD preserves God's perfect goodness. As our earthquake example suggests, FWD does not explicitly rule out attributing to God an action Aquinas would consider unjust and hence immoral. If it does not, then, on Aquinas's view, the reason FWD assigns to God for permitting some instances of evil (especially natural, but also some kinds of moral evil) is not a *morally* sufficient reason.

But the issue should not be construed as tied particularly to Aquinas's ethics. If moral goodness includes agent-centered restrictions, both general and particular, then God's justice and individual human rights must be taken into account in any attempt to explain God's permitting moral or natural evil. And it may be more effective to raise the issue in terms of agent-centered restrictions, which have a "considerable intuitive appeal" and "congeniality to moral common sense" quite independently of their involvement in Aquinas's or any other ethical theory. Putting the matter in those terms, if a proposed solution to the problem of evil depends on implicitly rejecting generalized agent-centered restrictions as having no application to God, it will be important to ask what sort of ethical theory is presupposed by the proposal and to consider whether such a theory is consistent with whatever else is held to be true about God by the defender of theism against the argument from evil.

In correspondence with us Plantinga has said of FWD that agent-centered restrictions and the requirements of justice

> clearly are not excluded; they just aren't explicitly mentioned. If you
> are right (and I'm not convinced you aren't) in thinking that God

[78]See, e.g., Alvin Plantinga, *The Nature of Necessity* (Oxford: Oxford University Press, 1974), pp. 192–193.

[79]Something similar can be said about cases in which the justification for God's allowing one human being to treat another in a flagrantly unjust way (as occurs in murder or rape, for instance) is basically the freedom of the perpetrator.

couldn't permit an innocent to suffer without some compensating good (accruing to that very person), then a world in which innocents suffer without such compensation won't be a very good world. In fact, if such a state of affairs is so evil that no amount of good can outweigh it, then *no* good possible world would be one in which there is such uncompensated suffering of innocents. . . . But can't we mend matters simply enough, just by adding . . . that *a* [the possible world God actualizes in FWD] meets the agent-centered restrictions: that *a* contains no instances of uncompensated suffering of innocents . . . [?]

Plantinga is plainly right to insist that FWD doesn't explicitly rule out agent-centered restrictions, but adding them successfully requires saying more about the nature of the world in which innocents suffer but are compensated.

Worries raised by consideration of agent-centered restrictions are not allayed simply by stipulating compensation for the suffering of innocent victims, as can be seen by considering an adaptation of an episode from Dickens's *Tale of Two Cities*. An enormously rich French aristocrat habitually has his carriage driven at high speeds through the streets of Paris and is contemptuously indifferent to the suffering thereby inflicted on the lower classes. One day his carriage cripples a child. Seeing that the child has been seriously hurt, the aristocrat flings several gold coins to the grieving family. The family, to whom the coins represent a fortune, are entirely satisfied; but no one would suppose that the aristocrat has thereby exonerated himself. It's easy to find circumstances of this sort, in which victims may consider themselves compensated even though the perpetrator (or permitter) remains unjustified.

Insisting on an essential rather than a merely accidental connection between the suffering and the compensation will not guarantee justification. If a mother forces her son into months of semistarvation and sensory deprivation in order to impress on him the blessings of ordinary life, he will no doubt find intense pleasure in ordinary experiences thereafter. Here the compensation is essentially connected with the suffering. But even if the pleasure is so intense as to outweigh all the pains of the deprivation, the mother is not thereby justified.

What else is required can be seen in a slight variation on our hostage case. Even if a madman were threatening to cut off five other children's fingers unless you cut off your child's fingers, you would not have a morally sufficient reason to do so. Our claim is based, as before, on considerations of the injustice in the object of the action demanded of you. Rational agent-centered restrictions make that action impermissible. And yet it's not difficult to describe circumstances in which you would have a morally sufficient reason for acting in that way, in which you would be not only not blamed but even praised for it. If your daughter's fingers were caught in machinery in such a way that she would die horribly unless they were amputated at once, and no one but you could perform the action, goodness would require it of you. It seems clear that all that accounts for the difference in the moral status of the act of amputation in these latter circumstances is that it is now the indispensable (or best possible) means to *preventing a greater evil* for the child herself.

Given the constraints raised by considerations of agent-centered restrictions, then, if an agent is to be justified in allowing the suffering of an innocent victim, he must (among other conditions) believe (reasonably) that without such suffering greater harm would come to the victim. Analogously, the strictures we have derived from the central thesis of Aquinas's metaethics preclude only such solutions to the problem of evil as fail to show how God's permitting innocent suffering can be the indispensable (or best possible) means of (at least) preventing greater harm to the victim.[80]

[80]For a recent attempt at a solution that sets out to avoid that sort of failure, see Eleonore Stump, "The Problem of Evil," *Faith and Philosophy* 2 (1985), 392–423. Ralph McInerny's "Naturalism and Thomistic Ethics" (*The Thomist* 40 [1976], 222–242) provides corrections of some misinterpretations of Aquinas's ethical naturalism. We are grateful for comments on earlier drafts of this paper by Richard Creel, James Keller, James Klagge, Scott MacDonald, Alvin Plantinga, Bruce Russell, Nicholas Sturgeon, Richard Swinburne, and Edward Wierenga.

11

Divine Necessity and
Divine Goodness

Keith E. Yandell

In contrast to the atheist, who denies, and the agnostic, who suspends judgment, the theist believes that *God exists* expresses a truth. Not every theist views that truth in just the same way. In particular, some view it as a necessary truth—a proposition whose denial is contradictory—and some view it as a contingent truth—a true proposition whose denial is not a contradiction. Call the view that *God exists* expresses a contingent truth *plain theism*—PT for short—and the view that *God exists* expresses a necessary truth *Anselmian theism*—AT for short. It seems highly plausible that propositions bear their modality with necessity— that if *p* is necessarily true, it is logically impossible that it not be necessarily true; that if *p* is contingent, it is logically impossible that it be other than contingent; and that if *p* is contradictory, it is logically impossible that it be other than contradictory. Its modality seems an essential feature of a proposition, as opposed to such contingent properties as what English or Sanscrit sentences happen to express it or (in the case of contingent propositions) whether they are true or false. Call the view that propositions possess their modality with necessity *the modality thesis*—MT for short. If MT is true, then either PT or AT must be necessarily false.[1]

---

[1] *Both* are necessarily false if *MT* is true and *God exists* expresses a contradiction.

Plain Theism

PT is sometimes expressed along these lines. The term *God* is not so much a proper name as a description of office that describes the being, if any, who holds the office in question. "God" is short for "that being who is the omnicompetent Creator and Providence" (or the like) as "president of the United States" is short for "that natural-born U.S. citizen of thirty-five or more years who was elected by the Electoral College and sworn in by the Supreme Court chief justice and is commander in chief" (or the like). Should God sin, in so doing He would resign the office of deity. This possibility can be expressed without appearance of contradiction in some such sentence as "Jehovah (or Jahweh), having sinned, is no longer God; though he retains omnipotence and omniscience, he no longer possesses omnibenevolence or moral perfection." For PT, that some such sentence be true is a logical possibility, but one whose truth is prevented by Jehovah being trustworthy. For AT, its truth is not a logical possibility.

But PT can be expressed in a quite different way that is more in accord with the Christian tradition and with some contemporary currents (themselves revitalizations of traditional themes) in metaphysics. The rough content of these currents goes as follows. Some properties are had by at least some of their possessors accidentally or contingently or nonessentially. A friend and I once painted our old blue house beige; it was the same house beige as blue. Other properties seem more plausibly viewed as being essential to whatever has them; *being mental* and *being physical* are classical examples, as are *being capable of consciousness* and *being spatially located*. Of the four properties just mentioned, the third and fourth partially comprise the more complex first and second, respectively. *Being capable of consciousness* partly comprises *being mental* and *being spatially located* partly comprises *being physical*, at least on standard accounts of these properties. The former member of each pair seems plausibly viewed as essential to what has it because the latter member of each pair seems to be a kind-characterizing property— seems to define an essence—that includes the former member. *Being chartreuse with brown stripes* and *being four and one-half feet long* seem neither to be themselves kind-characterizing properties nor to be included in any kind-characterizing properties. *Being a cat* and *being a human being* seem to be kind-characterizing properties, and *being mammalian* is included in both.

Kind theory or a doctrine of essences of course quickly becomes complex, and questions arise as to what comprises a basic kind and whether a noncomposite thing can belong to more than one basic kind and so on. The relevant point here is that *being divine* seems kind-characterizing or essence-defining; as standardly characterized in philosophical theology, it seems likely to characterize a kind that has very limited membership (*one* and *three* naming its most popular positive cardinalities). It seems implausible that an individual be divine, but only accidentally or contingently or nonessentially so.

Being divine, Judeo-Christianly construed, includes being omnipotent and omniscient and morally perfect. *Being the Creator* is standardly viewed as a property attaching to God only because He freely chose to create, so on that view *being the Creator* is not part of God's essence. On a minority view, it is part of God's essence, though *having created this world rather than another* is not. *Being providential* presupposes *being the Creator* and shares its status regarding essentiality.

PT, then, need not be construed along the lines described above. It can view *being divine* as an essence-defining property—can hold that anyone who has it has it as his nature. AT can hold the same. Wherein, then, does their difference lie? Essentially in this: that even on a version of PT in which "God" is the proper name of the being that possesses the essence *being divine*, it remains true that *God exists* is a logically contingent truth. On this view, if God should sin, He would not resign his high office, but commit deicide—cease to be altogether. On the standard theistic view that God and creation are related by an asymeterical dependence relation, this would have most unfortunate results for the rest of reality. For AT, the being that possesses the essence *being divine* is such as to exist with logical necessity. Deicide is hence logically impossible. One need not trust that God will not commit it; God could not commit it if He wished, and He could not wish to commit it.

For all that, if PT is true, deicide is not something to worry about. For if God can know the future—in particular, can know His own future choices—He can know whether He will ever choose to sin or not. Suppose He knows He will not. Then He will not. So deicide will not occur. Suppose He knows He will. Then He now knows that He will sin in the future, and does nothing now to prevent that inelegance, and so is not morally perfect even now, and so has committed deicide already. So if God exists at all, and deicide is a sin, then deicide will never occur.[2] Whatever reason we have to think that God does exist, we have the same reason to think that He will not self-destruct, whether or not AT is true.[3]

Omnipotence is an accidental or nonessential property of any being that has it but could exist without it; a being is necessarily omnipotent if it is omnipotent but not accidentally or nonessentially so. If PT is stated along the lines of *the essence thesis*—that if a being is divine, it is essentially divine, or divine by very nature—and *the omnicompetence thesis*—that divinity, Judeo-Christianly construed, is comprised by *being omnipotent, being omniscient*, and *being morally perfect*—then for PT God is necessarily omnipotent and of course necessarily omniscient and necessarily morally perfect as well.

We noted that what God lacks, on such a PT construal, is logically necessary existence. As this runs counter to a hoary tradition in which God is conceived as having all perfections, necessary existence among them, PT may seem suspect. Whether it is depends on the strength of the tradition at the point at which PT departs from it. Roughly—and it is very hard to be precise about the notion—*being a perfection* is *being the logically maximal degree of a property that has degrees and is better to have than to lack*. Existence, if it has degrees, is short on them; logically contingent and logically necessary existence exhaust the varieties. Beyond this, talk of degrees of existence is either incoherent or else is a misleading way of talking about degrees of complexity or wealth of properties or relative security of existence, or the like. I know of no good reason to suppose that the notion of logically necessary existence is the nonsense that some take it to be. It does seem implausible, however, that logically necessary existence is a *degree* of a property that logically contingent existence is a lower or lesser degree of.

Some hold that to be a property an item must be *individuating*—that it must be possible that having that item individuate its possessor from other things; they hold that *being a possibly individuating property* or *being a property possession of which might individuate its owner from all other things* are pleonastic for *being a property*. If so, existence, construed as a property of which necessary existence and contingent existence are degrees,

---

[2]I here adapt an argument of W. R. Carter, "Omniscience and Sin," *Analysis* 43 (March 1983). Of course, if *God exists* is false, deicide will not occur either. The argument holds, even if God is eternal.

[3]Provided deicide would be wrong—but that seems a necessary truth.

will not be a property; but then neither will *being self-identical* nor *having only consistent properties* be properties, which seems harsh.

If existence, for any reason, is not a property, then necessary existence cannot be a perfection construed along the lines indicated above. To include it, we will need some such recharacterization as *a perfection is the logically maximal degree of a property that has degrees and is better to have than to lack or else an undegreed property it is better to have than to lack.* On either account of *being a perfection*, the notion must have as its extension only the desired theistic properties; *being material*, for example, presumably cannot found among them.

Being a property it is better to have than lack cries out for elucidation, and I suppose its full articulation will include a considerable excursus into moral philosophy.

Those embracing AT tend to hold that it is a necessary truth that if a being has any perfection, then it has them all. This is certainly not obvious; it seems to me perfectly possible that something be omniscient but not omnipotent, though this will include knowing how to do things one in fact cannot do (as in "I know how to fix a bike, but I need my tools" or "I know how to bench lift five-hundred pounds—it is just like bench lifting four-hundred—but I'm not strong enough to do it").

These comments serve as no more than brief suggestions of issues that arise once one begins to think about the hoary tradition mentioned above. The questions raised may all have elegant and plainly justified answers that rejoice an *AT* supporter's heart, but that they do is not so obvious that to disagree with the tradition is irrational.

Suppose, contrary to AT expectations, that *existing with logical necessity—being N*, for short— and *being omnipotent, omniscient, and morally perfect—being O*, for short—are such that *being O* entails *being a moral agent* and *being a moral agent* entails *not being N*. Suppose also that *being O but not N* is better to possess than *being N but not O*. Then there will be a conflict among the perfections proposed on standard AT terms— it will be logically impossible that a being have every one of the properties that AT regards as perfections. Or suppose that *being a Redeemer* entails *not being N*, and *being a Redeemer but not being N* is better than *being N and not being a Redeemer*. Then similar results follow.

We have, then, two types of theism. Both, we shall suppose, embrace:[4]

---

[4]Of course one could explore varieties of theism that rejected one or more of these theses, but that is not part of our task here.

(1) *The Modality Thesis*: A proposition possesses its modality with necessity.

(2) *The Essence Thesis*: If a being is divine, then it is essentially divine.

(3) *The Omnicompetence Thesis: Being divine* is comprised (at least in part) of *being omnipotent, being omniscient, and being morally perfect.*

AT supposes *logically necessary existence* to also be part of God's essence, and PT does not.

It should not be thought that PT gives no sense to divine necessary existence or something like it. *For PT*, it is logically impossible that anyone or anything cause God to begin to exist or to cease to exist. If God exists at all, His existence is entirely secure from external threat. But it is not logically necessary existence.

Simplicity

Alvin Plantinga writes: "When Thomas Aquinas embarks on the task of characterizing God's attributes, simplicity is the first item on his list. He is quite clear, furthermore, as to his reasons for holding this doctrine; the fundamental reason is to accommodate God's aseity and sovereignty. Aquinas believes that if God had a nature and properties distinct from him, then there would be beings distinct from him to which he is subsequent and on which he depends; this would compromise his aseity and ill befits the status of the First Being."[5]

As Thomas Morris puts it: "Alvin Plantinga has suggested that a major reason theists historically adopted a doctrine of divine simplicity was to accommodate what he calls a 'sovereignty—aseity intuition,' a fundamental conviction that God must be such as to depend on nothing distinct from himself for what he is, and such that he has everything distinct from himself within his absolute control."[6]

This, clearly enough, is a crucial part of what leads to simplicity doctrine generally. Another concern (also suggested in the worry that God's nature and properties might "be distinct from him") is that God, so to say, not fall apart from inside. Such concern predates Christian thought. It is found regarding human nature in the Platonic dialogue

[5]Alvin Plantinga, *Does God Have a Nature?* (Milwaukee: Marquette University Press, 1980), p. 29.

[6]Thomas Morris, *Anselmian Explorations* (Notre Dame, Ind.: University of Notre Dame Press, 1987), p. 101.

Phaedo. Socrates is in prison about to receive hemlock. His friends Simmias and Cebes fear his death, for they fear that physical death ends all. (To put it anachronistically, they are concerned that Michael Scriven is right when he says "We die, then we rot.") Their worries have different sources deriving from different views of the soul. Simmias thinks of the soul as an "attunement" of the body: just as violins, well tuned, can produce music, so bodies, as physical particles organized into living organisms, can produce thought. Thus, Socrates notes: "Simmias is troubled with doubts. He is afraid that, even if the soul is more divine and a higher being than the body it may be destroyed first, as a kind of attunement."[7]

Cebes thinks of the soul as an enduring entity, related to the body as a tailor is to his coats: when one coat wears out, he puts on another. But, as Socrates again notes: "Cebes on the other hand appeared to agree with me that the soul is more enduring than the body, but to maintain that no one can be sure that, after repeatedly wearing out a great many bodies, it does not at last perish itself, leaving the last body behind; and he thinks that death may be precisely this, the destruction of the soul." (91d).

Simmias as an early functionalist agrees that Socrates and Socrates' body are nonidentical, for *having a mind* is essential to *being Socrates* and Socrates' mind is not identical to his body. Nothing that has capacities is identical to the capacities that it has. But Socrates' mind is comprised of various sophisticated capacities that his body possesses, and when it ceases to possess them, Socrates will cease to exist. Simmias fears that organic disintegration is sufficient for the soul's demise.

Cebes, as an early mind-body dualist (a substance-dualist, no mere property-dualist), holds that Socrates' mind differs from Socrates' body by way of being a different entity. Thus, no body that Socrates has is ever such that its organic disintegration is sufficient to erase Socrates' mind, and Socrates' mind *is* Socrates. But Cebes worries that minds, like bodies, suffer cosmic erosion, though it takes a mind longer than a body to wear down. Cebes fears that in the long run—and who can tell how far eroded one currently is?—mental dissolution is sufficient for the soul's demise.

The worry here, in part, concerns internal collapse. Either the mind vanishes as the body ceases to function or it wears out on its own. The

[7]*Phaedo*, 91d, in *Plato*, ed. Edith Hamilton and Huntington Cairns (New York: Pantheon, 1961).

former possibility, of course, concerns dependence on something 'external' to the mind, but the latter does not.

The Socratic reply to these concerns is that the soul is a substance on its own, and a substance of a sort that cannot erode or decompose. The soul governs the body (a nobler task requiring a nobler status, and so also requiring substantival status for the mind) and preexists the body in order for a priori knowledge to be explicable. And, more relevant to our concerns, the body is composed of parts but the soul is not.

To the second concern, then, Socrates responds:

> We ought, I think . . . to ask ourselves this. What sort of thing is it that would naturally suffer the fate of being dispersed? For what sort of thing should we fear this fate, and for what should we not? . . . Would you not expect a composite object or a natural compound to be liable to break up where it was put together? And ought not anything which is really incomposite to be the one thing of all others which is not affected in this way? (78 B) . . .
>
> The soul is most like that which is divine, immortal, intelligible, uniform, indissoluble, and ever self-consistent and invariable, whereas body is most like that which is human, mortal, multiform, unintelligible, dissoluble, and never self-consistent. . . . In that case is it not natural for body to disintegrate rapidly, but for soul to be quite or very nearly indissoluble? (80 B)

The soul as incomposite cannot fall apart or erode, and "soul resembles the divine" (80 A). God, then, is incomposite or simple, and as such cannot suffer internal dissolution. At least latent here is the concern that if God has multiple properties, they could separate, and that even if God is distinct from His one property (or, perhaps, from His having His one property) He could go one way and it (or His having it) another. So God, the reasoning goes, must be identical to each of His properties (or, perhaps, to His having each of the properties He has).[8] An intuition that internal composition is incompatible with necessity also lies behind the drive toward a doctrine of divine simplicity.

Among the many problems of wedding a doctrine of divine simplicity to traditional theism is one concerning contingent properties of God. Traditionally, Christian theology has held that *being Incarnate in Christ*

---

[8] For evidence of influence of this sort of reasoning on the Christian tradition, see Harry Austryn Wolfson, *Studies in the History of Philosophy and Religion*, vols. 1 and 2 (Cambridge: Harvard University Press, 1973 and 1977).

is a property that God freely chose to have, and hence has nonessentially. But if for any property *P* that God has, God is identical to *P* (or to *God's having P*) then if God has any property nonessentially, His existence will be logically contingent existence; if it is logically contingent that *God has P*, then if *God's having P* and *God's existing* are identical, *God exists* is logically contingent. As defenders of divine simplicity have tended to hold that God has logically necessary existence, this consequence will tend not to be welcomed.

Traditionally, Jewish and Islamic theology have held that *having created the world* is a property God contingently or nonessentially has, for He could have chosen not to create or not have chosen to create. Then similar problems will arise for those who wish to hold both that *God exists* is a necessary truth and that God is simple in the sense of being identical to each property He has (or to His having each such property). The same will hold if one thinks that *God creates a world* is a necessary truth but it is up to God what world He creates, and then goes on to hold that God has logically necessary existence and simplicity. A standard response to such considerations by defenders of simplicity has been to view such properties as *creating the world* (and, at least by extension, *being incarnate in Christ*) as items expressed by relational predicates that are grounded in no complexity in the referent of the subject of those predicates. I do not find such analyses sufficiently plausible to regard them as providing part of a version of AT that should be preferred to either a version of AT that does not embrace simplicity or to PT.

The Importance of Necessity

Christian theology assigns to God the metaphysical feature of being so related to the world that its existence depends on His maintaining it in existence without His depending for His own existence on anything. It assigns Him the religious function of being our only hope—our inexorable Judge if we remain in our sins and our Savior if we repent and make Him Lord. Given God's metaphysical and religious centrality, it is of concern to the believer that His character be reliable and His existence be secure.

Secure existence is *necessary* existence. No existence, of course, is more secure than logically necessary existence. But PT has its own version of existential security. Suppose that a person is omnipotent, omniscient, and morally perfect. As we have seen, such a being would not commit deicide. Being all-knowing, none could surprise Him; being all-powerful, none could overcome Him. So if He ever exists, He always does; an omnipotent, omniscient, and morally perfect being is also an everlasting being. He is threatened by nothing, internal or external. If such a being ever exists, He always exists, even though His existence is logically contingent. If we call the property *existing always if at all* the property of *existential continuity* it is a necessary truth that God has existential continuity. That is, (i) *If God ever exists, He always exists* and (ii) *God's existence is logically contingent* are, for *PT*, necessary truths. The apparent insecurity that attaches to God's existence, given (ii), is rendered only apparent, given (i).

The Anselmian Argument

According to Thomas Morris,[9] the Anselmian Christian theist will hold that:

(A1) Jesus Christ is God the Son.
(A2) An individual is God only if he is necessarily good.
(A3) God the Son is God.

From (A1) and (A3) it follows that:

(A4) Jesus Christ is God.

From (A2) and (A4) it follows that:

(A5) Jesus Christ is necessarily good.

Both of these claims seem to me to be necessary truths:

(T) An individual can be tempted only if it is possible that he sin.
(N) An individual cannot sin if he is necessarily good.

From (T) and (N) it follows that:

(TN) An individual cannot be tempted if he is necessarily good.

[9]Thomas Morris, *The Logic of God Incarnate* (Ithaca: Cornell University Press, 1987).

From (A5 and (TN) it follows that:

(A*) Jesus Christ cannot be tempted.

(A*) is not the sort of proposition that anyone who is a Christian in some nonfanciful sense of the term will rush to embrace, since the New Testament plainly says that Jesus was tempted. One alternative for an Anselmian theist is a priori New Testament criticism, not an altogether unknown phenomenon but not an attractive one either. Another alternative is to see whether some mistake may not have been made in the argument. (A*) follows from (A5) and (TN). (A5) is part of Anselmian orthodoxy, so an Anselmian will understandably pursue (TN). (TN) follows from (T) and (N). (N), I suggest, is simply true; its denial is tantamount to *It is logically impossible that S be other than perfectly good and it is wrong to sin and no one who does wrong is perfectly good and it is logically possible that S sin and so it is logically possible that S not be perfectly good*. That is, S is, and also is not, necessarily good. So much for denying (N). Perhaps (T) is more promising. Perhaps an individual can be tempted even though he cannot sin. But how so? Morris writes: "How can it be the case that Jesus was necessarily good and yet was tempted to sin? We have said that it seems to be a conceptual truth that, in some sense, temptation requires the possibility of sinning. On reflection, we can see that it is the *epistemic* possibility of sinning rather than a broadly logical, or metaphysical, or even physical possibility that is conceptually linked to temptation" (147).

What is the *epistemic* possibility of sinning? "Some proposition P is epistemically possible for some subject S at t just in case it is epistemically possible relative to a full accessible belief-set B of S at t" (147).

That, in turn, is glossed as: "P is epistemically possible for S relative to a full accessible belief-set B of S at t if and only if B neither contains nor self-evidently entails the denial of P, nor does B contain or self-evidently entail propositions which seem to S to show P to be either false or impossible. A full accessible belief-set of a person at a time consists in all and only those beliefs which are accessible to a range of conscious thought and deliberation of that person at that time sufficient to support the initiation of action" (147).

The general idea, then, seems to be that Jesus can be tempted so long as He does not know that He cannot sin. The necessary truth is not that an individual can be tempted only if he can sin, but rather that an individual can be tempted only if either he can sin or else he cannot sin but does not know that he cannot.

Ignorance by no means is always culpable. Further, one who says, "Thank God I didn't know how long the torture would last; if I had known, I'd have broken down and given them the names of all of our people" says nothing that need puzzle anyone. Being ignorant does not make a person evil and ignorance can be a good thing. So two barriers that might be thought to pose a problem for the notion of epistemic temptation do not do so.

The middle of the passages just cited speaks of various sorts of possibility—logical, metaphysical, and physical. I am not sure how to understand the last two sorts of possibility; perhaps Q is a metaphysically possible proposition if and only if there is no proposition P that is metaphysical and true such that Q's truth is incompatible with P's (perhaps Q too must be a metaphysical proposition), and perhaps R is a physically possible proposition if and only if there is no proposition P such that P belongs to physics and is true such that R's truth is incompatible with P's (perhaps R too must fall within physics). I think that the following sketch will serve the purpose of defining *possibility* relevantly for understanding *epistemic possibility* as this notion in turn is relevant to temptability.

No one (I suppose) can bench press half a ton all at once, though perhaps setting this as a goal (analogous to running 3.5-minute mile) makes gymnastic sense; this, I suppose, is de facto beyond the prowess of most people, though its being done perhaps would falsify no proposition of physics. Traveling to Mars simply by wiggling one's ears, I suspect, is such that its being done would falsify some proposition of physics. Squaring the circle, I take it, is logically impossible. We might, then, speak of prowess impossibilities, physical impossibilities, and logical impossibilities (though prowess possibility and physical possibility are to be understood in terms of consistency with truths about prowess or physics). If an action is always such as to exceed my prowess possibilities, or to be physically impossible, or to be logically impossible, I can attempt to perform it but I shall fail. I cannot know that an action A exceeds my prowess, or is physically or logically impossible, be clear about what I know, not forget what I know, and then go on to have a shot at doing A anyway—not in the sense of doing, or even trying to do, A rather than trying to convince someone that I am trying to do A or persuade them that I do not know that A is beyond me, or the like. But if I do not know that doing A exceeds my prowess, or is physically or logically impossible, then I can try to do *A*. It is such considerations as these, I gather, that lead up to or provide a setting for these remarks: "Jesus could be tempted to sin just in case it was epistemically possible for him that he sin. If at the times of his reported temptations [and, presumably, any unrecorded temptations], the full accessible belief-set of his earthly mind did not rule out the possibility of his sinning, he could be genuinely tempted, in that range of consciousness, to sin. But this could be so only if that belief-set did not contain the information that he is necessarily good. In order that he suffer real temptation, then, it is not necessary that sinning be a broadly logical or metaphysical possibility for Jesus; it is only necessary that it be an epistemic possibility for him" (148). Jesus need not believe that He is *not* necessarily good; He can hold no view at all on the matter, having never considered it, or suspend judgment.

Presumably, then, the idea of epistemically possible sinning can be captured somewhat along these lines. If performing action *A* at time *t* is beyond *S*'s prowess, or is physically impossible, or is logically impossible, then let us say that *A* at *t* is *inaccessible* to *S*. *S*, of course, cannot perform actions that are inaccessible to *S*. But that an action *A* is inaccessible to *S* at *t* will not preclude *S*'s being tempted to perform *A* at *t*—provided that *S* is unaware of *A*'s inaccessibility. Presumably if *S* is convinced that *A* is inaccessible to *S* at *t*, then *S* cannot be tempted at *t* to do *A*, even if *S* is wrong about *A*'s being inaccessible; but I will not pursue this wrinkle here.

Morris concludes his remarks concerning the Anselmian temptation of Jesus as follows:

> If we hold that Jesus was necessarily good, then does that mean that we must devalue his resisting of temptation? Can he be held responsible as a man for what he did? Was his choosing rightly a free act of his? Well, it must be admitted from the outset that he could not have chosen otherwise. His divine nature would have prevented it. But I think that, in order to avoid the heresy of monotheletism condemned at the Third Council of Constantinople—the view that every act of Christ was divinely accomplished, done only in virtue of his divinity, and never a properly human act—orthodox theologians must hold that the divinity of Christ, the modal properties which were his in virtue of being divine, played no actual causal role in his rightly resisting temptation. The decision arrived at in his earthly consciousness not to sin was not causally imposed on him by his divine nature. And in the sense of being both intentional and bereft of any such causal determination, it was free. (150)

If it is logically impossible that S do A, than plainly doing A is not within the physical or prowess possibilities of S. For AT, it is logically impossible that Jesus sin. So if AT is true, sinning was not within the physical or prowess possibilities of Jesus. It is true that sinning does not require that others have more physical strength or more intelligence than Jesus possessed. That one has the physical strength or intellectual capacity to sin does not make one physically stronger or intellectually more acute than Jesus. Even omnipotence and omniscience will not, for AT, place sinning within the physical or prowess possibilities of Jesus.

Compatibilism

If determinism is true, then at some time t before any human being existed, there obtained a complex state of affairs SA^t, and a set SL of natural laws obtained. No human choice or action affected either the content of SA^t or of SL. SA^{t+1} succeeded SA^t in such a manner that, given SA^t obtains and SL is true, it follows that SA^{t+1} obtains. Between SA^{t+1} and the time t^* of any choice or action of any person—say, Jane Doe's action a—there is a succession of states SA^{t+2} through SA^{t^*-1} such that each preceding state and SL are related to each following state as are SA^t and SL to SA^{t+1}. Thus, given SA^{t^*+1} obtains and SL is true, it follows that SA^{t^*} obtains, where *Jane Doe does a at t^** is included in SA^{t^*}.

If no one ever has any choice about whether SA^t obtains or SL is true obtains, and no one ever has any choice about whether (SA^t obtains and SL is true) entail (SA^{t+1} obtains), then no one ever has any choice about whether SA^{t+1} obtains. By a series of applications of this reasoning, no one ever has any choice as to whether SA^{t^*-1} obtains. If no one ever has any choice as to whether SA^{t^*-1} obtains, then no one ever has any choice about whether SA^{t^*} (and so its components) obtains. So no one (Jane Doe included) ever has any choice as to whether *Jane Doe does A at t^** obtains. *Jane Doe* being any person, and *doing A at t^** being any choice or any action at any time, that you like, if determinism is true, no one ever has any choice about the choices or actions he makes. If no one ever has any choice about the choice or action he makes, then libertarianism is false. So if determinism is true, libertarianism is false. By reversing the argument, beginning with the proposition that *libertarianism is true*, one can arrive at the conclusion that *determinism is false*. Putting the relevant conditionals together, one gets the result that determinism is true if and only if libertarianism is false. But then compatibilism is false.[10]

In its Morrisean form, AT includes libertarianism. I agree that Christianity is most plausibly understood as containing libertarianism, or best interpreted as compatible with libertarianism and strongly suggesting it, or the like. While this view is sometimes contested, I shall not defend it here. It is important, however, to note that in rejecting T, Morris is not intentionally embracing compatibilism. AT, as here understood, is to be interpreted as being fully compatible with libertarianism, and able to embrace both the argument against compatibilism presented above, and its conclusion.

Suppose it is the case that:

> (F) For every person S and any choice or action A of S at t, it is false that S can refrain from doing A at t.

Or to put the point another way:

> (F') For no choice or action A at any time t that any person S performs is it the case that S could do other than A at t.

Whereas (F) or (F') may not entail determinism, determinism entails (F) and (F'). Further, it is at least worth asking whether libertarianism is compatible with (F) or (F'). If (as seems true) compatibilism is false, the question is hardly empty.

If libertarianism is compatible with (F')—to take that expression of the claim that (F) and (F') both express—presumably this is so only because (sometimes, at least) what makes it the case that no one can ever choose or act other than as they do plays no causal role in bringing it about that people act as they do.

The Principle of Alternate Possibilities

The *locus classicus* of discussion that supports Morris in his rejection or revision of T is a 1969 article by Harry Frankfurt, the purpose of which is to challenge what Frankfurt calls *the principle of alternate pos-*

---

[10]For a detailed and sophisticated argument for this conclusion, which the argument here but echoes, see Peter van Inwagen, *An Essay on Free Will* (Oxford: Clarendon Press, 1983).

sibilities: "A person is morally responsible for what he has done only if he could have done otherwise."

The key to that challenge is this suggestion: "A person may do something in circumstances that leave him no alternative to doing it, without these circumstances actually moving him or leading him to do it—without them playing any role, indeed, in bringing it about that he does what he does."[11]

The general idea is this: There are cases in which an agent performs an action that she falsely believes she could refrain from performing and she performs it freely, and cases in which an agent refrains from performing an action that she falsely believes she could perform and she freely refrains. Consider these examples:

Case One

John sits down to his lunch of carrot sticks, broccoli stalks, cauliflower chunks, and lettuce leaves, topped with alfalfa sprouts. Having promised his wife to stick to his diet, he is sheepish as the thought strikes him that there are a cheeseburger, fries, and a shake available just next door at the local fast-food establishment, and that on his hedonic scale the latter trio rank several leagues above his salad. He barely manages to return to his healthful repast. He does not know that he has been programmed while he slept by a tape featuring his beloved mother's voice so that if he decides to go for fast food, he will be struck with an attack of desperate anxiety and realize that only partaking of carrot sticks, broccoli stalks, cauliflower chunks, and lettuce leaves, topped with alfalfa sprouts, will relieve the anxiety. But, given his faithfulness to his promise, the program never kicks in.

The moral: John is responsible for having stuck to his diet, even though he could not have forsaken it.

Case Two

Cheryl has written out a message that, relayed to her great-aunt in California, will yield sweet revenge. It is cast in just the right terms to devastate the sharp-tongued old tartar who has recently driven Cheryl's mother, sister, and daughter to tears by insults, and made her father, brother, and son weep by the misplaced guilt she has created. The message manages to denigrate astrology, Jerry Brown, and southern California at the same time as it puts down her aunt's most recent cult, and her aunt is ripe for devastation. Still, Cheryl

---

[11]Harry Frankfurt, "Alternate Possibilities and Moral Responsibility," *Journal of Philosophy* 66 (1969), 829–839.

decides that taking revenge is wrong, and that pleasure at the price of evil is purchased at too high a price. Very reluctantly she decides not to wire the message to her aunt, who in fact, unknown to Cheryl, died yesterday.

The moral: Cheryl is responsible for having refrained from doing an evil that in fact, unknown to her, she could not have accomplished.

Obviously, such cases could be multiplied indefinitely. Their purport is to show that:

1. It is false that S is responsible for doing A at time t only if S could have refrained from doing A at t.
2. It is false that S is responsible for refraining from doing A at t only if S could have done A at t.

The objection to cases one and two is obvious. What John is responsible for is *choosing* to stay on his diet, not for not going off it (which he could *not* do), and what Cheryl is responsible for is *choosing* to refrain from taking revenge, not for not having taken revenge (which she could *not* take). Each could have *chosen* otherwise. Insofar as John and Cheryl are responsible for actions that are not choices, they are responsible for not having *tried* to procure fast food and for not having *sent* a useless wire, and these are actions they both refrained from and could have performed. So the relevant principle is perfectly safe.

In fact, what is the case is that examples of sufficient subtlety remain to be formulated. In case one, what is needed is the revision that John cannot decide to seek fast food; he is programmed in such a manner that this faithless decision will not form itself. In case two, what is requisite is that Cheryl be so overpowered by her great-aunt that she could not bring herself to decide to take revenge. But John must be ignorant of his programming, and Cheryl must not know of her aunt's overpowering influence, and—what counts most—the programming has no causal role in John's decision to remain on his diet and the aunt's overpowering influence has no causal role in Cheryl's decision to forsake revenge. Discovering that this was so about John or Cheryl might be difficult or worse, but Frankfurt's point is one of metaphysics, not epistemology; this might be the truth about John and Cheryl, however hard it might be to discover it. Morris, then, rejects T. He believes that he does so with impunity, even as a libertarian, because while the

Principle of Alternative Possibilities is false, libertarianism does not require it.

In some ways, at least, the issues Frankfurt raises are not new. If William is unable to stop his car before it hits the child because he is stewed to the gills, he is responsible for hitting the child even though in the circumstances he cannot do otherwise, for it is his fault that he cannot do otherwise. It is not the principle of possible alternatives, exactly, that libertarianism favors, but something more along the lines of:

> (P*) S is responsible for doing A at t only if either S can refrain from doing A at t or S cannot refrain from doing A at t because S did something else that S could have refrained from doing such that S's doing that made it the case that S cannot refrain from doing A at t.

Familiar considerations of the problem of evil have raised the issue as to whether it is not possible, even assuming incompatibilism and libertarianism, that an agent be free and yet be such that she can only exercise her freedom in a morally positive manner—i.e., whether an agent cannot have only the making of right choices within her prowess, though which choice is made among morally happy alternatives is up to her. Wouldn't it be better that there be agents whose freedom was thusly restricted than that there be agents who can do wrong?[12] It was recognized that such an agent would be responsible for which morally happy choice she made, but theists who were also libertarians have generally denied that such an agent would be a moral agent in a full-blooded sense. The suggestion was that the goodness of such an agent, among whose prowess wrong basic and nonbasic actions would not be included, would be guaranteed, not earned; what such a person could earn is at most some particular modality of goodness rather than another, or perhaps a goodness caused by one set of good choices rather than another, but not a good moral character that was earned in a context in which *not* having a good moral character was an option, since no choices or actions that would lead to a bad character could be performed by such an agent. Programmed for goodness, it was standardly held, her freedom would range over too little territory to make her a moral agent.

---

[12]That such an agent could do no wrong would be built into the agent by God. I shall not discuss the logical status of the claim that such an agent can do no wrong.

Grant at the outset that such a moral heroine may exercise massive freedom regarding the modality of her goodness—all sorts of free choices between good alternatives may be hers. The question remains as to whether her goodness, whatever its modality, is hers through free choice, or is something that she is responsible for. Call an agent who cannot do wrong a *moralist*. How, exactly, are we to conceive of the conditions under which her sterling character allegedly is earned?

Suppose Joe knows of a lecture on Kant's ethics to be given a block away an hour hence. Relative to *attending* the lecture, Joe's alternatives are two: *attending the lecture* and *not attending the lecture*, or L and NL. Relative to *choosing* regarding the lecture, Joe's alternatives seem to be three: *choosing to attend the lecture, choosing not to attend the lecture*, and *making no choice regarding the lecture*, or C, CN, and NC. If Joe simply forgets the lecture, Joe does not attend the lecture—NL rather than L— but makes no choice regarding it—NC rather than C or CN.

Suppose that, for some reason, NL is morally wrong. If Joe is a *moralist* agent in the sense defined above, NL is not within Joe's prowess, and Joe will do L. Since choosing not to do what is right is itself wrong, CN is not in within Joe's prowess either. For Joe to intentionally make no choice about the lecture is tantamount to his making CN; NC is within his prowess only insofar as it results from nonculpable forget-fulness (or the like), and even then Joe, as a *moralist* agent, will end up going to the lecture.

Presumably we need to distinguish between persons who, so to say, are so *built* as to be unable to make wrong choices or perform wrong actions (*moralists*), and those who in fact *make* no wrong choices and perform no wrong actions, though they *could* do so (call these *saints*). But it seems possible that there be agents who cannot ever choose or act wrongly, though they are not so built or created. Perhaps, in the light of this possibility, we should distinguish between:

(1) *internal moralists*: agents so built or created (or, for present purposes, produced by purely mechanistic or by probabilistic or by random causes) that their nature precludes their choosing or acting wrongly;

(2) *external moralists*: agents who are such that they are actually prevented by external circumstances, on each case of morally relevant choice or action, from choosing or doing anything but what is right;

(3) *mixed moralists*: persons prevented sometimes by their nature

and sometimes by their circumstances, but always by one or the other, from doing anything but what is right.

Now Frankfurtian responsible agents are *not* moralists of any of these kinds. For while they cannot act other than rightly, what makes it impossible that they act other than rightly plays no causal role in their acting rightly. Always made incapable by some x or other (not necessarily always the same thing) from going wrong, what makes Frankfurtian agents incapable of doing wrong is not what leads them to do what is right.

What *does* lead a Frankfurtian agent to do what is right? The impression we are given is that it may be any of a vast number of things, and in particular anything a libertarian would like. One is tempted to think that this is perfectly in order: Joe in fact cannot do *NL*, but freely opts for *L*, ignorant of *NL* being outside his prowess. But is *CN* in his prowess? The same Frankfurtian analysis should work here. Joe cannot make choice *CN* (choose not to go to the lecture, assuming that to be a wrong choice) but can make *C* (can choose to go). Save for cases of inculpable ignorance (or the like) where Joe goes to the lecture anyway, *NC* is not available. But then why suppose that Joe is free concerning *C* or *L*? So long as we allow an agent the actual and exercisable capacity to *try* to act wrongly, or to *choose* wrongly, or to *try* to choose wrongly, it remains plausible to think of the agent as responsible; remove this actual and exercisable capacity and the plausibility goes as well.

Perhaps one can save Frankfurt's suggestion in the following manner. Suppose that Suzy, unknown to herself, has been hypnotized not to lie to her mother, but not hypnotized not to lie to anyone else. She is known for her honesty, having freely chosen to speak the truth under a variety of circumstances that have provided duress to prevaricate or promised reward for lying. So when she tells her mother the truth, those who know Suzy best find this altogether in character, and although they know she has been hypnotized, believe that she would have told her mother the truth even if she had not been hypnotized.

The plausibility of the Frankfurt cases can be put this way. The idea is that there is something that will "kick in" if one, in choice or in basic or nonbasic action other than choice, is about to go wrong. If Suzy begins to warm toward a sinful choice or other wrong basic or nonbasic action, a quick-freeze mechanism will come on and cool her off toward sin; but if she simply warms to righteousness, and remains cool to sin, on her own, then the mechanism never kicks in and her virtue is her own. The kicking in of the mechanism is itself the sign of sin in her members, but if it never kicks in over a lifetime of decisions and actions, she is sinless. All of this, however, will require that Suzy has among her repertoire of basic actions—within her prowess—choices and actions that if made or performed *would* bring the mechanism into action.

The problem is that Jesus, according to Morris, has no basic actions— no choices or overt behaviors—within His prowess that ever would cause it to be the case that He acts wrongly. He does not so act, but He also cannot so act. *Being necessarily good* precludes any such scope of freedom, any such repertoire of basic actions, any such prowess. If He *can* do something that would kick in the mechanism of His necessary goodness, and does not, He is responsible, on libertarian terms, for not so doing. But Jesus, for Morris can do nothing that would cause the mechanism of His necessary goodness to kick in. But then He is moralist after all, and not a saint. But the matter is difficult. Let us approach it another way.

Choices and Actions

Sometimes the choice/action distinction is clear. If Ruth decides to square the circle, fly to Venus by waving her arms, or to bench press a ton, since she will not be able to do these things, the choice (which she can make) is one thing and the action (which will not be forthcoming) is another. (Thus I shall not use "choice" as a 'success term' here; I shall not use it in a sense in which a choice to do x is made only if one does x.)

Choosing to marry Mary is one thing; marrying her is another. Deciding to catch the biggest goldfish in the aquarium is one thing; catching it is another. But choosing to avoid the oncoming car may be simply a matter of swerving out of its path and deciding to leave the meeting may be identical to walking out of it. Here, there may be nothing that corresponds to the choice/action distinction, for no reflection may precede the overt behavior and there may be no choice distinct from the intentional (deliberate, but not deliberated about) movement. Even where the choice/action distinction plainly applies, there need be no deliberation that leads to a choice. Choices themselves are plausibly viewed as actions, and perhaps the choice/action distinction is tantamount to a covert action/overt action, or a private action/public action distinction. A *basic action A* by S is an action A such that S can perform A without there being any action B such that B is distinct from A and that *S* must perform *B* in order to perform *A*. Presumably choices are basic actions, but are not our only basic actions.

Making a wrong choice, according to Morris, is not among Jesus' possible basic actions. His prowess does not extend to choosing or acting wrongly—His intelligence and strength are enough for His so choosing or acting, but due to His nature he cannot so act. On libertarian terms, then, He is—on a Morrisean construal—a moralist (an *inherent* moralist) rather than a saint (as defined above). A saint can be tempted. An inherent moralist cannot. So a Morrisean Jesus cannot be tempted. He can consider sinning, if that is not itself a sin. But He cannot choose to sin, or try to sin, or choose to try to sin, or the like—for these are sins. Whether He *knows* this or not is irrelevant, but assume that He does not. His nature, on Morris's account, prevents him from ever beginning to choose wrongly, or choosing wrongly insofar as he can. There is no "insofar as He can," only *not at all*.

Suzy, who *can* sin, always chooses rightly. Her nature does not make her a saint; her choices do. Jesus' choices do not make him a moralist; His nature does. Suzy, who could so act as to kick in her mechanism that prevents her from wrong action, is responsible for her choices and actions. A Morrisean Jesus, who cannot so act as to kick in His mechanism of necessary goodness, is not responsible for His. So Suzy is a saint, and Jesus a moralist.

The point here is subtle and difficult. I will argue it in another way.

Frankfurtian Circumstances and Temptability

Consider the little argument:

(1) If *P*'s truth is sufficient for *Q*'s truth, and *P* is true, then *that P is true* explains *that Q is true*.

(2) That *S cannot do A* is true is sufficient for the truth of *S does not do A*.

(3) If it is true that *S* cannot do *A*, then that *S* cannot do *A* explains that *S* does not do *A*. [from (1) and (2)]

Premise (2), I take it, is a necessary truth. (3) follows from (1) and (2). (1) seems plausible. Yet it sanctions the view that whatever truth *A* entails another truth *B* also explains *B*. Even when one requires that $A \neq B$, this seems false. It is true that Jon Moline is a dean, and true that Eric Davis is the Cincinnati Reds' young star, so it is true that *if*

Eric Davis is the Reds' young star then Jon Moline is a dean, and that, together with *Eric Davis is the Reds' young star*, entails *Jon Moline is a dean*; and yet we remain a bit short on explanation of Jon's elevation. One can raise the standards of entailment, in intent at least, by reverting to a 'relevance logic' that requires that some relevance relationship hold between antecedent and consequent of a true conditional, and it is notoriously hard to provide a plainly correct version of such a logic. Or one can otherwise try to specify what, besides *that A obtains* entails *that B obtains*, that *A obtains* explaining *that B obtains* involves. *Explanation* being an epistemic notion, it is not surprising that *entailment* does not exhaust it.

Still, (3) seems true. It does so because *S cannot do A* by itself both entails and explains *S does not do A*. One might, of course, want to know why *S* cannot do *A*; it is often true that *that A obtains* explains *that B obtains* and we want to know why *A obtains* is true. But between *S cannot do A* and *S does not do A* there is obvious relevance of content— enough, one would think, to satisfy any legitimate demand that an entailment relationship be fattened up before it counts as an explanation as well. (3), in sum, is plainly true on its own, and is all the more so once we see that, and why, the little argument fails—namely, that (1) is false for reasons that do not also infect (3).

If it is logically impossible that *S* do *A*, that is why *S* did not do *A*. The reason that *S* did not do *A*, if it is logically impossible that *S* do *A*, is not that *S* did not want to do *A*, or think of doing *A*, or found doing *A* repulsive, or had promised not to do *A*, or the like, because *S*'s wanting to do *A*, or thinking of doing *A*, or finding doing *A* attractive or at least not unattractive, or promising to do *A* or at least not having promised not to do *A*, or the like, would make no difference whatever to *S*'s not doing *A*. These things may be relevant to *S*'s choosing to do *A*, or trying to do *A*, or wishing *S* could do *A*, or the like, insofar as these things are things that it is not logically impossible that *S* do.

Similarly, if it is physically impossible that *S* do *A*, and if what is physically possible is not up to *S*, *that* is why *S* does not do *A*, and if *S* lacks the prowess to do *A*, and if what is in *S*'s prowess is not up to *S*, *that* is why *S* does not do *A*. Only if, and insofar as, what is physically possible—or what is in *S*'s prowess—is up to *S* is there any reason to say anything different about what is physically impossible for *S*—or not in *S*'s prowess—than what we have said about what it is logically impossible that *S* do. If *S can't* do *A*, *that* is why *S* doesn't do *A*, even in cases in which it is true (for reasons other than a self-contradictory antecedent) that S wouldn't do A even if S could. If A becomes physically possible, or comes to be within S's prowess, whereas before it was not, then if S under these new circumstances does not do A, it is no longer the case that S does not do A because S *cannot* do A. But so long as S can't do A, that is why S does not do A.

If this is right, then that S cannot do A is always relevant (and at least if the reason that S cannot do A is that doing A is physically impossible or is not within S's prowess, then that S cannot do A is always *causally* relevant) to S's not doing A. But, if this is so, then S's not being able to refrain from doing A—S's not being able not to do A—is what causes S to do A. Then Frankfurt's conditions are not satisfied.

If we consider both:

> (a) S is responsible for doing A at t even if S cannot refrain from doing A at t so long as what makes it impossible that S refrain from doing A at t plays no causal role in S's doing A at t

and

> (b) If S cannot refrain from doing A at t then that is why S does A at t

we seem forced to the conclusion that:

> (c) If S cannot refrain from doing A at t, then S is not responsible for doing A at t, because its being impossible for S not to do A at t is always why S does A at t.

("Why S does A at t" waffles between "the *explanation* of S's doing A at t" and "the *cause* of S's doing A at t." I shall address this waffling shortly.)

One can object that this does not capture Frankfurt's position, which is not strictly (A) but:

> (A') S is responsible for doing A at t even if it *would be* impossible for S to refrain from doing A at t so long as what *would* make it impossible for S to refrain from doing A at t plays no causal role in S's doing A at t.

And while Frankfurt uses locutions resembling (A) to express his view, it does seem correct that (A') captures it better. But then S must be able to *choose* not to do *A* at *t*, or to *try* not do *A* at *t*, or to *choose to try* not to do *A* at *t*, or some such thing that activates whatever would make *S*'s non-*A*-doing impossible—must be able to do something that transforms the *would be* into *is* or triggers the relevant *A*-producing mechanism. Often, if refraining from doing *A* is wrong, choosing not to do *A*, or trying not to do *A*, or choosing to try not to do *A*, or the like, is also wrong. Whenever this is so, since what triggers the mechanism is to choose not to do *A* (or the like), what one does that triggers the mechanism is wrong, and one is responsible with respect to it. One is responsible in Frankfurtian circumstances for doing *A* because one can do *A* freely, and one does *A* freely only if one does not do anything to trigger the mechanism although one could. At least ordinarily, what *S* does to trigger the mechanism will be something *S* ought not to do. Since ordinarily there is something that *S can* do that is something that *S* ought not to do, and this something is what will lead via the activated mechanism to *S*'s doing *A* after all, *S* is responsible in such cases, not for *doing A simpliciter*, but for *doing A freely* or for *doing A without being forced to do A*. Children are often responsible for such actions—for doing things on their own that they are going to have to do anyway, one way or the other; and what matters morally, then, is the way they are done—freely or forcedly. Remove, however, the capacity to so act as to trigger the mechanism, and you remove responsibility as well. What libertarianism would seem to require, in the light of reflection, on Frankfurt's concerns, is something like: "*S* is responsible with respect to doing *A* at *t* even though *S* would be made to do *A* were *S* to try not to do *A*, provided what makes it the case that *S* would be made to do *A* plays no causal role in *S*'s doing *A*, only if *S* can do, and can refrain from doing, what would bring into action that mechanism (or whatever) that would force *S* to do *A* even if *S*, unforced, would not do *A*."

It is, of course, logically impossible that a Morrisean Jesus do anything wrong—do anything, for example, that made it to be the case that He acted rightly only because forced to do so. So a Morrisean Jesus is not responsible for His acting rightly.

None of this denies that a Morrisean Jesus may choose among positive alternatives and pick His own route to sterling character (or to what would be sterling character had it been produced freely).

If *S* is (morally) tempted to do *A*, then doing *A* is wrong. Further, if *S* is tempted to do *A*, then *S* cannot know that *S* cannot do *A*. Further still, if *S* is tempted to do *A*, then *S* can choose to do *A*, or choose to try to do *A*, or can try to choose to do *A*, or can *want* to do *A* (or the like). But choosing to sin, or choosing to try to sin, or choosing to try to choose to sin, or wanting to sin, or even wanting to want to sin (and the like) are all themselves modalities of sinning. Jesus can no more do any of them than He can just outright perform an overt wrong action. So a Morrisean Jesus cannot be tempted after all. He can do nothing that would ever trigger a Frankfurtian mechanism. It is not merely that he *does* nothing that triggers such a mechanism, but that He *can* do nothing that would do so. But then he cannot be tempted. Let us look at this just one more way.

Action Biographies

An abstract description of an action—e.g., "drawing a sharp blade through a soft substance"—may describe what is in fact a right, a morally neutral, or a wrong action—e.g., part of a surgical operation, making a salad, or removing an honest judge who is in the Mafia's way. Let a *personalized tensed action description* be a description of an action that specifies it as performed by some particular person at some particular time and ascribes to the action each non-moral property that action has that is relevant to its being morally right or wrong. Consider, then, all the personalized, tensed action descriptions that Joe can ever make true. This will give us the raw materials for Joe's action biography; if determinism is true, it *gives* us Joe's action biography. If Joe is never able to do less than something right (if no morally evil actions are among the items to which Joe's action biography may refer) then Joe, in one sense, lacks the capacity to do evil. Evildoing does not fall within Joe's prowess, and—in Morris's terms—*being able to do evil* or *having doing evil within one's prowess* is common among human beings but not essential to *being human*. Let an action biography (which covers the choices and actions a person *can* make and perform, not merely those she *does* make or perform) that contains reference to no possible action that is other than morally right be a *necessarily morally impeccable* action biography.[13] For Morris, Jesus had such a biography. Let a person whose action biography is not necessarily morally impeccable, in that

---

[13]Since perhaps living requires that one function sometimes in morally neutral ways, perhaps it should contain reference to possible neutral choices and actions; perhaps it should contain no reference to a possible action that is not morally right *or neutral*.

it contains reference to wrong choices and actions, but who always chose and acted rightly, be such as to have a *contingently morally impeccable* action biography. Finally, let a person who chooses and acts always rightly have a *morally impeccable actual* biography. Orthodox Christianity insists that Jesus had a morally impeccable actual biography, and has been neutral about whether his action biography was necessarily or contingently impeccable (not, of course, that it has characteristically, or ever, put the issue in just these terms).

Temptation

Suppose, then, that Jesus is tempted to lie. For AT, it is logically impossible that He lie. But He does not know this, and He chooses not to lie, presumably without the fact that it is logically impossible that He lie playing any causal or explanatory role in His decision. But of course deciding to lie, or deciding to try to lie, or trying to lie, are also sins, and it thus logically impossible that Jesus decide to lie or that He decide to try to lie or that He try to lie; and even if Jesus does not know that it is logically impossible that He do any of these things, it surely is either false that the logical impossibility of His doing so plays no causal role in His not doing so or else false that this impossibility plays no sufficient explanatory role in His not doing so.

Consider the precise situation that Jesus was in, according to Morris, at any time t at which He chooses whether to lie:

(1) it is logically impossible that He lie at t
(2) He can be tempted to lie at t
(3) He does not know that (1) is true
(4) He chooses not to lie at t
(5) that (1) is true plays no causal role in producing (4).

Suppose that Ruth decides to square the circle; she makes the attempt at time t and fails. She will fail no matter how brilliant her mathematical skills, no matter how sincere and sustained her effort, no matter whatever you like. Perhaps her not knowing this is a necessary condition of her attempt, but it is in any case its being logically impossible to square the circle that explains her not succeeding.

It is tempting to try to avoid this conclusion—to say, for example, that Ruth is not paying attention to her task (she is thinking instead of her elegant simplification of the rule 'universal generalization'), or the problem is one of a class of problems such that any of them is beyond her skills, and squaring the circle thus would be beyond her even if it were logically possible. But inattention cannot be the explanation of failure if no amount of attention would help, and lack of skill cannot be the issue when no increase of skill would change things. The reason Ruth cannot square the circle is the same as the reason the Archangel Michael, or God Himself, cannot square the circle. It is logically impossible that it be done.

We can, then, allow that its being logically impossible to square the circle is (at least part of) the cause of Ruth's failure; perhaps this will be to allow that abstract and necessarily existent states of affairs can be causes. Or we can refuse to allow this but admit that the logical impossibility of squaring the circle is the *explanation* of her failure. Call the former *the causal alternative* (CA) and the latter *the explanatory alternative (EA)*. Either CA or else EA seems plainly correct, and we need not try here to decide between them.

Morris seems to hold some such principle as this:

> (M) S is responsible for doing A at t even though S could not refrain from doing A at t so long as what makes it impossible that S refrain from doing A at t played no causal role in S's doing A at t.

Exactly this sort of claim is explicitly crucial to Frankfurt's challenge. He writes:

> The fact that a person could not having avoided doing something is a sufficient[14] condition of his having done it. But, as some of my examples show, this fact may play no causal role whatever in the explanation of why he did it. It may not figure at all among the circumstances that actually brought it about that he did what he did, so that his action is to be accounted for on another basis entirely. Even though the person was able to do otherwise, that is to say, it may not be the case that he acted as he did *because* he could not have done otherwise. Now if someone has no alternative to performing a certain action but did not perform it because he was unable to do otherwise, then he would have

[14]Perhaps we could leave out the word *sufficient*, but since the relevant case of an action's not being performed involves it not being performed because it is logically impossible that it be performed, and the relevant case of an action's being performed is that it is performed because it is logically impossible that it not be, and its being logically impossible that p is always sufficient for the truth of not-p and its being logically impossible that not-p is always sufficient for the truth of p, I shall leave it in.

performed exactly the same action even if he *could* have done otherwise. The circumstances that made it impossible for him to do otherwise could have been subtracted from the situation without affecting what happened in any way. Whatever it was that actually led him to do what he did, or that made him do it, would have led him to do it even if it had been possible for him to do something else instead.[15]

Suppose one takes CA. Then perhaps (M) is true, but it does not apply to a case in which Jesus is tempted to sin, for that it is logically impossible that Jesus sin does, if we take CA, play a causal role in His not sinning.

Suppose instead that we take EA. Then, I suggest, (M) is inadequate; what Morris needs is something of this sort:

(M*) S is responsible for doing A at t even though S could not refrain from doing A at t so long as what makes it impossible that S refrain from doing A at t plays no sufficient explanatory role in S's doing A at t.

The necessary goodness of Jesus is always explanatorily sufficient for His making a right choice and refraining from making a wrong one, and always explanatorily sufficient for His performing a right action and refraining from performing a wrong one, though there may be explanatory slack, so to speak, regarding which right choice He makes or which right action He performs. Given (M*), Jesus is not responsible for always choosing or acting rightly.

The argument that is relevant here, then, can be put like this:

(1) What is or is not logically possible is not up to any agent.
(2) What is not up to any agent is not something any agent is responsible for or free concerning.
(3) What is or is not logically possible is not something any agent is responsible for or free concerning. [from (2) and (3)]
(4) Assume: it is not logically possible that S act other than rightly at t.
(5) S's not acting other than rightly at t is not something any agent (including S) is responsible for or free concerning. [from (3) and (4)]

According to Morris, it is not logically possible that Jesus ever act other than rightly. So if Morris is right about this, Jesus not acting other than

[15]Frankfurt, "Alternate Possibilities and Moral Responsibility," 836–837.

rightly is not something any agent (including Jesus) is responsible for or free concerning. But:

> (6) If S's not acting other than rightly is not something any agent (including S) is responsible for or free concerning, then S cannot be tempted to act other than rightly.
> (7) S cannot be tempted to act other than rightly. [from (5) and (6)]

So if Morris is right, Jesus cannot be tempted to act other than rightly. Behind (6), of course, is:

> (T*) An agent can be tempted not to act rightly only if the agent is responsible for or free concerning not acting rightly.[16]

So far as I can see, (T*) is a necessary truth.

The result of this line of reasoning is that a Morrisean Jesus cannot be tempted not to act rightly. But the New Testament says he was, and as Morris knows Jesus being "tempted in all points, even as we are, yet without sin" has theological relevance to both the atonement and the example that, according to orthodox Christian theology, Jesus provides.

Conclusion

I am not at all sure that I have gotten these matters right; Frankfurtian counterexamples, the principle of alternative possibilities and revision thereof, the conditions of temptability and the issues they raise are nothing if not complex. Still, it seems to me that at least somewhere in the philosophical neighborhood we have been visiting is a justification of (T)—of the claim that one can be tempted only if one can sin. If this is correct, since N is plainly true, we are back to TN, which T and N entail. Given (A*)—that Jesus was tempted—it follows, not that Jesus did sin, but that He could have sinned. If He could have sinned, He either lacks necessary goodness or else the result of His sinning would be deicide and so He lacks logically necessary existence. Assuming that there are not degrees of *being God* and that the existential status of each member of the Trinity is that of the others, if we retain

---

[16]Or, if you prefer, only if one can do wrong. Sin is evil or wrongdoing in a theistic world, or construed from a theistic perspective.

the omnicompetence thesis (that *being God* is at least partly comprised in *being omnipotent, omniscient, and morally perfect*) and *the essence thesis* (that nothing is divine that is not divine essentially), we can retain the necessary goodness of Jesus—His.essential moral perfection—compatibly with His being tempted only by denying that *God exists* is a logically necessary truth. *Jesus is necessarily good* will entail *Jesus would commit deicide by acting wrongly.*

If it is true that, existentially speaking, as one member of the Trinity goes, so go they all, it will follow both that:

(1) Had Jesus sinned, God would cease to exist

and (given the world's dependence on God)

(2) Had Jesus sinned, the world would cease to exist.

It does not follow, strictly speaking, that becoming incarnate was *risky* for God in the sense of His not knowing whether or not Jesus would sin, or of His being unsure whether the eventualities mentioned in (1) and (2) would come to pass. Being omniscient, God presumably knew that they would not.

Perhaps it is best to conclude by a summary of the argument of this essay. Theism comes in at least two varieties: *Anselmian* and *plain*. Plain theism itself comes in two varieties, one of which differs from Anselmian theism essentially at one point: for plain theism, *God exists* is a logically contingent, not a logically necessary, truth.

Anselmian theism, as Christian, embraces the doctrine that God became incarnate in Jesus Christ and accepts the New Testament claim that Jesus was tempted in all points as we are, yet without sin. It endeavors to deny that *S is tempted* entails *S can sin* by an ingenious strategic use of Frankfurtian counterexamples and a revision of the principle of alternate possibilities, while continuing (rightly, of course)[17] to embrace libertarianism. For all of its ingenuity, promise, and complexity, the strategy fails. It remains true that *S is tempted* entails *S can sin*. Compatibilism, being false, is no help here. So *Jesus did not sin* is best viewed by the Christian as a logically contingent truth. One alters Anselmian theism minimally by rejecting the claim that *God exists* is a

---

[17]See William Rowe's Central Division, APA Presidential Address, "Two Types of Freedom," *Proceedings of the American Philosophical Association* 60, no. 2 (1986).

logically necessary truth, i.e., by replacing Anselmian theism by the more promising and plausible version of plain theism. As deicide is no more to be feared by a plain than by an Anselmian theism, the importance of God's existence being secure from external threat and internal collapse—the intuition that if X is God, then X has a very secure existential status indeed—is provided for by plain theism (in the claim that God has *existential continuity*). Appeal to simplicity—that God is identical to each property (or to His having each property) that He has—is not necessary to provide a doctrine of divine existential security, nor—given that God has as contingent or nonessential properties *being incarnate* and *being the Creator of the actual world*—would it succeed in both accommodating standard theistic doctrine and providing God with logically necessary existence.

No doubt plain theism has its prices. A plain theist, I take it, cannot ground the truths of logic in God's thinking them, for they are necessarily true and it is not necessarily true that God exists to think them. Perhaps one could escape this consequence by rejecting the modality thesis, but it seems to me that that thesis should be retained. If the choice is between something like an a priori New Testament criticism that says that Jesus could not be tempted (so He wasn't) and an acceptance of the view that there are abstract objects that exist independent of God (assuming, what is after all challengeable, that the laws of logic require eternal objects of some sort as their truth conditions) it would be a fanciful Christianity that took the former route.

So far as I can see, then, it is plain theism that embraces as much of Anselmian theism as is defensible and that best captures Christianity, at least among the alternatives canvased here. And I, at least, know of no better alternatives.

12

How Does God Know
the Things He Knows?

George I. Mavrodes

This essay is an exercise in speculative epistemology. You may, if you wish, take the word 'speculative' in its philosophical sense, in which it means (I suppose) something like "theoretical." But I also intend it in its more ordinary sense, which is more like "conjectural." I hope to explore a certain suggestion about the epistemology of the divine knowledge. This proposal does not seem to have been very popular in the history of western philosophical theology. Perhaps, indeed, its unpopularity is well deserved. I shall try to say what I can in favor of it, and to defend it against certain objections and plausible (or possible) misunderstandings. But I do not think of myself as irrevocably committed to this conjecture, nor as having made it a really deep-rooted part of my own theistic belief. My intention here is primarily to *explore* this conjecture, and to reap some further understanding of it from a wider discussion.

1 The Divine Knowledge as Fully Inferential

The proposal to be explored is that God knows everything that He knows *by inference*. More explicitly the thesis at hand is

345

(T) For every proposition that God knows, He knows that proposition by inferring it from one or more other propositions that He knows.

This thesis really is intended here to apply to *everything* that God knows—including, for example, His knowledge of His own essence, His will, and so on. It can be taken, therefore, as denying that there is any such thing as privileged access in the divine epistemology (unless the divine inference is counted as a privileged access to everything). It can also be taken as asserting that there is a sense in which all of the divine knowledge is indirect, and that all of it is indirect in the same way. But more about that later.

As I said, this thesis has not been popular among Christian philosophers and theologians. I can think of no one who has positively defended this doctrine, and several seem to have explicitly denied it. Thomas, to take one example, asks "whether the knowledge of God is discursive."[1] And he replies that "in the divine knowledge there is no discursiveness." Thomas also gives an argument for this claim, to which I shall return. As a contemporary exponent of much the same view, Alvin Plantinga says: "Of course God neither needs nor uses logic; that is, he never comes to know a proposition A by inferring it from proposition B."[2] Plantinga makes this claim in a somewhat casual and offhand way, without suggestion of argument, as though he can assume that his audience and readers will accept it without question. Probably that assumption is, by and large, correct. But in this essay I explore a claim that is the contrary of that made by Thomas and Plantinga—the claim that the totality of the divine knowledge is discursive and inferential.

Before we speculate about *how* God has His knowledge, should we say something about *what* it is that God knows? Most orthodox Christian theologians, I think, have held that God is omniscient—that is, that He knows every truth. Perhaps that doctrine is a satisfactory account of the scope of the divine knowledge. At any rate, I have no critique of it here. Of course, this doctrine does not of itself determine just what is included within the domain of truth. But I do not explore that topic in any penetrating way either. Nothing that I argue here depends on any rather special view as to whether God knows future

---

[1] Thomas Aquinas, *Summa theologiae* (*ST*), Q. 14, A. 7.
[2] Alvin Plantinga, *Does God Have a Nature?* (Milwaukee: Marquette University Press, 1980), p. 144.

contingent propositions, for example, or the counterfactuals of freedom. But I assume that, at the very least, God knows many things, and a wide variety of things—many facts about the world of space and time, many facts about human actions, many truths of logic and mathematics, and many facts about God himself, His will, His desires, and His actions. In fact, my argument will require that God know an *infinity* of propositions, although this does not of itself entail that God knows *every* truth. If God does not know infinitely many truths, then (T) cannot be true.

2 Aristotle, Thomas, and the Divine Knowing

Speculation about the divine knowledge has had a long history in western philosophy, going back at least as far as Aristotle. In the *Metaphysics*, Aristotle has a well-known argument whose conclusion is that "it must be of itself that the divine thought thinks (since it is the most excellent of things), and its thinking is a thinking on thinking."[3] A paragraph later, Aristotle adds: "The divine thought and its object will be the same, i.e. the thinking will be one with the object of its thought."[4]

Not many of the Christian philosophers, even those who especially admired Aristotle, have followed him in this conclusion. It seems pretty clear from the discussion in these few paragraphs of the *Metaphysics* that Aristotle would not suppose that God knows, for example, what I am doing now. In fact, it appears that God would not know anything at all belonging to several of the categories that I mentioned above. God would not so much as *think* of such things. But the later Christian philosophers, no doubt driven (at least in part) by a desire to be faithful to the Christian tradition of God's love for the world and of His involvement in it by creation, revelation, and redemption, have generally maintained that God knows me, and everything else in the world, in all of our particularity. He knows what I have done, and what I am doing. And so, too, with all the facts of the world. So Thomas says, for example, that he will show "first, that the divine mind knows singulars; second, and things not yet actual; third, and future contingencies with infallible knowledge; fourth, and the motions of the will;

---

[3]Aristotle, *Metaphysics*, 1074b.
[4]Ibid., 1975a.

fifth, and infinities; sixth, and the humblest and vilest things; seventh, and all evils, deprivations, and defects."[5] Now, when Thomas says that God knows the humblest and vilest things, along with all evils and defects, he may well have been deliberately setting himself against the Aristotelian doctrine that a knower—and especially God, that most excellent of all knowers—ought to avoid knowing the worst things in the world, because "there are even some things which it is better not to see than to see."[6] There is, however, something more of interest, beyond this contrariety, in the relation between Aristotle's argument and that of Thomas. Why is it, according to Aristotle, that God's thought is simply a thinking on thinking? Well, here is what he says:

> The nature of the divine thought involves certain problems; for while thought is held to be the most divine of things observed by us, the question how it must be situated in order to have that character involves difficulties. For if it thinks of nothing, what is there here of dignity? It is just like one who sleeps. And if it thinks, but this depends on something else, then (since that which is its substance is not the act of thinking, but a potency) it cannot be the best substance; for it is through thinking that its value belongs to it. Further, whether its substance is the faculty of thought or the act of thinking, what does it think of? Either of itself or of something else; and if of something else, either of the same thing always or of something different. Does it matter, then, or not, whether it thinks of the good or of any chance thing? Are there not some things about which it is incredible that it should think? Evidently, then, it thinks of that which is most divine and precious, and it does not change; for change would be change for the worse, and this would be already a movement. First, then, if "thought" is not the act of thinking but a potency, it would be reasonable to suppose that the continuity of its thinking is wearisome to it. Secondly, there would evidently be something else more precious than thought, viz., that which is thought of. For both thinking and the act of thought will belong even to one who thinks of the worst thing in the world, so that if this ought to be avoided (and it ought, for there are even some things which it is better not to see than to see), the act of thinking cannot be the best of things. Therefore it must be of itself that the divine thought thinks (since it is the most excellent of things), and its thinking is a thinking on thinking.[7]

Now, ignoring the details of this argument for the moment, it seems clear that its general strategy consists of speculating about what sort

---

[5]Thomas Aquinas, *Summa contra Gentiles* 1, 63–64.
[6]Aristotle, *Metaphysics*, 1074b.
[7]Ibid.

of knowledge would be *appropriate* for God, given that God must be supreme in value and excellence. And while Thomas apparently rejected Aristotle's conclusion about the knowledge of the humblest and vilest things in the world, he does not reject the general strategy of Aristotle's argument. On the contrary, Thomas, along with others of the medievals, himself appeals to this pattern of argument. Discussing the question of "whether God has a speculative knowledge of things," for example, he says: "Whatever is the more excellent must be attributed to God. But *speculative knowledge is more excellent than practical knowledge*, as the Philosopher says in the beginning of the *Metaphysics*. Therefore God has a speculative knowledge of things."[8] And perhaps, at least for much of our thinking about the divine epistemology, we can do no better than this.

3 Inference and Infinite Knowledge

Let us turn more directly to a consideration of (T). What can we say about it? It is worth noting, to begin with, that the analogue of (T) cannot be true of a finite knower—of someone, that is, who knows only a finite number of propositions. At least, it cannot be true of such a knower if it is true (as I shall assume here) that circular patterns of inference are *epistemically* illegitimate. For if a noncircular chain of inferences is to be located within a finite domain of propositions, then the chain must somewhere come to an end in one or more premises that are not themselves inferred from antecedent premises within that domain. Perhaps the inferential chain is also an epistemic chain, in the sense that whatever is inferred from what is known is itself thereby legitimated as knowledge. But in that case, a finite knower, though he may know many things inferentially, must know something noninferentially. And this line of argument is, I think, the stock (and strongest) argument in favor of the most general form of foundationalism—i.e., the claim that the structure of human knowledge must terminate somewhere in items that are not derived from still further pieces of knowledge.

So far as the argument just sketched goes, it is possible that a finite knower has all of his knowledge noninferentially. And it is possible that his knowledge is epistemically mixed, some of it inferential and

---

[8]*ST*, Q. 14, A. 16.

some of it noninferential. But it is not possible that all of his knowledge is inferential. That argument seems to me to be correct, and I think that these conclusions are true. *But this line of argument does not apply to an infinite knower.*

Plato considers in the *Theatetus*, 201ff, the claim that knowledge consists of true belief accompanied by a *logos*. If having a *logos* consists of having some other piece of knowledge from which the first can be inferred, then no finite knower could satisfy that criterion. *But an infinite knower could satisfy it; such a knower might have a logos for every item in his knowledge.* For in an infinite domain of knowledge, a noncircular chain of inferences need never come to an end.

We should note, however, that the mere fact that someone is an infinite knower does not of itself guarantee that he is in a position to have a *logos* for every piece of his knowledge. (And, indeed, we should not be overly ready to assume that God is the only infinite knower.) Think, for example, of a knower who, for every integer, m, knows another integer, n, and knows that n is larger than m. He would be an infinite knower. Perhaps he also knows that I am revising a philosophical paper. But he might not know any truth at all from which it could be inferred, in a noncircular way, that this is what I am doing. If so, then despite the fact that he is an infinite knower, his knowledge of my actions cannot be inferential.

The fact, then, that someone is an infinite knower does not guarantee that all of his knowledge is inferential, and perhaps it does not even guarantee that it could be inferential. It does, however, block the foundationalist argument that I sketched above. If we are to have a reason for denying that all of his knowledge is inferential, then that reason must be something other than *that* argument.

Suppose, then, that I simply *postulate* the existence of an infinite knower—not necessarily God, and not necessarily an omniscient knower—but a knower in whom all knowledge is inferential. This knower, "K", knows an infinite set of truths, S. And for every proposition, p, which is a member of S, there is a set of propositions, S', all of which are also members of S, and which together entail p. Every member of S' must, of course, in its turn be entailed by other members of S in a similar way. But S is such that every member of S' has a full entailment "ancestry" within S that does not include p. That is, every proposition in S is the end of a beginningless and noncircular chain of entailments. And I postulate that K knows everything that he knows by inferring it in virtue of one of the entailments just mentioned.

With reference to this postulation we can ask three questions:

1. Do we have some reason to believe that K does not exist? I.e., is there reason to believe that there is no actual being who satisfies the description given in the preceding paragraph?

2. Do we have some reason to believe that K is not identical with God? I.e., is there some reason to think that God does not satisfy the description given above?

3. Do we have some reason to think that K *is* identical with God? I.e., is there some reason to think that God does satisfy the description given above?

The first of these questions is not very useful or illuminating. I can think of no very interesting reason for supposing that there is no such knower as K. The second question, however, invites us to consider several thorny objections, to which most of the remainder of this essay is devoted. And in response to the third question, I argue that there is at least one way, and perhaps two, in which the supposition that K is identical with God fits quite well with, and makes some sense out of, other things that many philosophical theologians have wanted to assert about God.

4 Objections and Replies

What reasons might there be for supposing that K cannot be God?

Objection 1. We have already seen that even an infinite knower need not be in a position to hold all of his knowledge by inference. Perhaps God, though He is an infinite knower, is not in that position.

What we saw earlier is that even an infinite set of propositions need not be "entailment-complete" in the way postulated in my description of K. That is quite true. But it is hard to see how any set of propositions that could plausibly be thought to be the content of *omniscience* could fail to be entailment-complete. Think, for example, of the series of propositions $1>0$, $2>1$, $3>2$, ... and so on through the set of integers. Presumably God, if He is omniscient, knows every member of this set. If so, then He knows an infinite set. And we can then add to this list any other propositions that God might be thought to know in virtue of His omniscience, such as *Mavrodes is revising a paper*. But for any two propositions, p and q, in this set there is also their conjunction, $p \& q$. And it seems implausible, to say the least, to hold that there is an infinite and omniscient being who knows a pair of propositions but does not know their conjunction. But if God knows the conjunction of every pair of propositions that He knows, and if He knows the series of propositions about the integers, then the *whole* set of propositions that He knows is entailment-complete. For any proposition, p, in that set, there is its conjunction, $p \& q$, with some other member. $p \& q$ entails p. But for $p \& q$ there is, in turn, the conjunction $(p \& q) \& r$, which entails $p \& q$, and in which r is a distinct proposition. Every member of this set, therefore, is the final member of a beginningless and noncircular series of entailments such as this.

What I have just given, of course, is an especially simple and trivial way in which the content of omniscience turns out to be entailment-complete. No doubt that same content is also entailment-complete by virtue of some more interesting logical relations among its members. But what is of importance to our discussion here is the *fact that* any plausible omniscience will have this property, not just *how* it happens to have it.

While it is true, therefore, that there might be an infinite knower who does not satisfy the description of K, it seems unlikely that the contents of omniscience could fail to have the logical relations that K requires.

Objection 2. It is not sufficient for K to know a set of propositions that is entailment-complete. K must also infer each piece of his knowledge in virtue of one of these beginningless and noncircular series. In the situation postulated above, for example, K might instead be inferring the conjunction $p \& q$ from its two constituents. And if that is so, then the entailments that are described above are irrelevant to the question of whether all of K's knowledge could be inferential.

All of this, while quite true, does not constitute a genuine objection to the thesis I am exploring. Certainly, if K were to infer $p \& q$ from its constituents, then the entailment series that I described above would be irrelevant to his knowledge. But what of that? Why should we not suppose in that case that there is another infinite knower, K', who knows the same set of propositions as K, but who knows them in a different inferential order? Of course the conjunction $p \& q$ can be inferred from the pair of propositions, p and q. But how can that fact serve to show that someone else could not infer that same conjunction from the larger conjunction $(p \& q) \& r$? So far as I can see, anyway, one of those entailments is just as good as the other, and I can think of no plausible reason for supposing that one or the other of these inferences is bound to be illegitimate. If it is not K, therefore, who is identical with God, then it may very well be somebody else, K', who fits the description given above and who is identical with God.

A somewhat related observation is this. No doubt the content of omniscience will include many logical relations besides the ones I described above. Very probably, for example, each element in that set of propositions will be part of a *circular* series of entailments. (There are many such circular series, for example, even in my own finite body of knowledge.) But that too seems to be irrelevant. For the knower we are interested in is the one who infers in virtue of the noncircular series. The existence of circular series within the same set could not prevent such inferences.

Objection 3. The supposition that God knows by inference imports an intolerable *temporality* into the divine nature. Therefore God has no inferential knowledge.

This is the argument that Thomas uses in the *Summa Theologica* when he discusses the question of the possible discursiveness of the divine knowledge. The *respondeo* of that discussion is as follows:

> In the divine knowledge there is no discursiveness; the proof of which is as follows. In our knowledge there is a twofold discursion. One is according to succession only, as when we have actually understood anything, we turn ourselves to understand something else; while the other mode of discursion is acccording to causality, as when through principles we arrive at the knowledge of conclusions. The first kind of discursion cannot belong to God. For many things, which we understand in succession if each is considered in itself, we understand simultaneously if we see them in some one thing; if, for instance, we understand the parts in the whole, or see different things in a mirror. Now God sees all things in one thing alone, which is Himself. Therefore God sees all things together, and not successively. Likewise the second mode of discursion cannot be applied to God. First, because this second mode of discursion presupposes the first, for whosoever proceeds from principles to conclusions does not consider both at once; secondly, because to advance thus is to proceed from the known to the unknown. Hence it is manifest that when the first is known, the second is still unknown; and thus the second is known not in the first, but from the first. Now the term of discursive reasoning is attained when the second is seen in the first, by resolving the effects into their causes; and then the discursion ceases. Hence as God sees His effects in Himself as in their cause, His knowledge is not discursive.[9]

The discussion of this topic must be complicated, I fear, by the distinction between time and eternity, a distinction that is none too clear. According to many Christian philosophers, both ancient and modern,

[9]Ibid., A. 7.

God is not really a temporal being at all. He is not, they say, "located in time." It is not entirely clear what this might mean, but presumably it implies at least that "really," "as He is in Himself," etc., God does not do one thing after another, He does not experience one thing after another, and one thing does not happen to Him after something else. So, although I am revising this paper some time after having written the first draft of it, God does not observe me doing the revising after observing me doing the initial writing. Sometimes it is said that in God all such things are simultaneous. It would seem, however, that simultaneity is just as much a temporal relation as is priority or posteriority. If it is really the case that temporal relations cannot apply to God, then simultaneity cannot be the truth about the divine experience. If eternity really is different from time, then eternity is not simultaneity. In that case, what is it? But this, I suppose, is essentially the problem of producing a positive characterization of eternity.

However that problem is solved, there is also another, at least for a philosopher who wants to retain some plausible connection with the usual Christian understanding of the world and God's relation to it. For that understanding seems to insist that God is related to temporal entities and processes, that the divine power is at work in many temporal events, and indeed that God's hand is present in some *special* way—in miracle, for example, or in revelation—in some temporal events. If that is so, then even if in God Himself no divine act comes before another, there must be a sort of shadow or effect or representation of those acts in the world, a representation to which temporal relations do apply. So however we understand the divine eternity, we must understand it in such a way as to allow for the truth of the fact that God raised Jesus from the dead many years after He delivered Israel from the bondage of Egypt.

Not all Christian philosophers, however, have held that God is eternal and "outside" of time. The view that God is a fully temporal being, although one Who is everlasting in the sense of having no beginning and no end, has recently been vigorously defended, for example, by Nicholas Wolterstorff.[10] Alvin Plantinga has also recently declared his own inclination to accept this view.[11] On this view, the temporal relations apply to God in a rather straightforward manner. God does

---

[10]Nicholas Wolterstorff, "God Everlasting," in *God and the Good*, ed. C. Orlebeke and L. Smedes (Grand Rapids: Eerdmans, 1975).

[11]Plantinga, *Does God Have a Nature?* pp. 44–46.

some things after He does others, and there would seem to be no general objection to supposing that He has some experiences after He has others.

Now, one can attempt to reply to Thomas's argument about the nondiscursiveness of the divine knowledge in terms of an understanding of God as eternal, or alternatively on the view that God is everlasting. The latter would seem to be easier, and I will try it first.

Thomas distinguishes two sorts of discursiveness in human knowledge. The first is simply temporal—having understood one thing, we turn our attention to another, and thus the second is known later than the first. The second sort of discursiveness, Thomas says, arises "when through principles we arrive at the knowledge of conclusions." I would call this a "logical" discursiveness, but Thomas prefers to say that it is "according to causality." In any case, it seems to be this second sort of case that is our primary concern here.

About the first sort of discursiveness, however, Thomas says that it cannot apply to God. Why not? Because "God sees all things together, and not successively." I am inclined to think that this is correct. Perhaps we could put the point as follows:

> (S) For any proposition, p, if there is a time at which God knows that p, then there is no time at which God does not know that p.

As I say, I am inclined to think that (S) is true. But what has that got to do with inference or discursiveness in the second sense?

Thomas says that the second mode of discursion "presupposes the first." Why? Because "whoever proceeds from principles to conclusions does not consider both at once." But this does not seem to be quite right. To whatever extent I can consider two propositions simultaneously, there seems to be no general barrier to my simultaneously considering two propositions that in fact have the logical relation of entailment between themselves. And if I have in fact proceeded from a principle to a conclusion why should I not now consider them both simultaneously? Indeed, how could the proceeding from a principle to a conclusion be brought to completion unless, when it succeeds, there is a simultaneous recognition of both the principle and the conclusion and of the logical relation between them?

It seems to me, therefore, that this first Thomistic reason is mistaken. It is, however, somewhat similar to a second reason that Thomas puts forward, though he does not appear to think that this second reason makes the second mode presuppose the first. The second reason for rejecting the discursiveness of the divine knowledge, Thomas says, is "because to advance thus is to proceed from the known to the unknown." And this, I think, is a more powerful reason.

Suppose that we reformulate the Thomistic claim as follows:

> (U)   For any propositions, p and q, and any knower, K, if K knows q by inference from p, then there is a time at which K knows p and does not know q.

If both (S) and (U) are true, then none of the divine knowledge can be inferential. As I have already said, I am inclined to accept (S). But what about (U)?

Well, what about it? I am inclined to think that (U) is false, and that its appeal probably depends upon a confusion between the *process* of inferring, as it occurs in ordinary human contexts, and the *result* of the inference. When I try to extend my knowledge by inferring a conclusion from a premise, then—usually, anyway—there is a time at which I know the premise and do not yet know the conclusion. I am indeed proceeding from the known to the unknown. But while I am engaged in that process the inference is not yet complete; for if it were complete I would know the conclusion too. Of course, if the process is actually successful, then there does come a time when the inference is completed. And at that time I cannot still be proceeding from the known to the unknown. For at that time, when the inference has been completed, neither the premise nor the conclusion is unknown. When I really do *know* something by inference, then I know that thing. There is indeed an asymmetrical relation between the premise and the conclusion, but it is not that one is known and the other unknown. It is rather that there are two pieces of knowledge, one of them depending on the other or based on the other. That relation remains when the process of inferring has terminated and ceased, but it is not a relation between what is known and what is unknown.

Now, the relation we are talking about is in part a matter of logic. That logical element in it consists of the logical relation between the premise and the conclusion. Presumably there is in it also something else—maybe it could be called an "epistemic" element. That element is whatever it is that makes it the case that my knowledge of q depends on my knowledge of p, and not on any of the other things that also entail q. I'm not sure how to characterize this element in any more illuminating way. But there seems to be such an element, and I will proceed here on that assumption.

Now, we can interpret thesis (T) as claiming that every piece of the divine knowledge is an element in a relation of this sort. It bears, of course, the logical element of that relation. That is, every piece of the divine knowledge is logically entailed by some other element in that body of knowledge. And it also bears the epistemic element of that relation. That is, every piece of the divine knowledge depends upon some other element in that body of knowledge. But perhaps it need not be interpreted as claiming that God's knowledge has involved the *process* of inferring. That is, the person who accepts (T) need not believe that there was once a time when God knew less than He knows now, and that He extended His knowledge by proceeding from the known to the unknown.

Still proceeding on the assumption that God is everlasting, however, we might consider yet another possibility. Suppose that, instead of denying that God engages in the process of inference, we were to say that He engages in it everlastingly? For every piece of His knowledge, that is, He everlastingly infers it from antecedents (and perhaps also everlastingly makes it the antecedent of another inference). We might note that, if God is both everlasting and essentially omniscient, then for every time at which He knows q there is a prior time at which He knew an antecedent of it, p. So perhaps in the divine consciousness the process of inference is everlastingly carried out, simultaneously completed and refreshed at every moment.

No doubt this possibility strikes one initially as strange. But is that because we think of it first in connection with ourselves? *There*, of course, it is impossible. I cannot complete again, in every moment, every inference that has been a part of my intellectual life. But is it a perfection in me, or instead a limitation, that I am not able now, in this moment, to complete again the inference of the Pythagorean theorem from Euclid's axioms? It is at least not clear that this inability is a perfection. Maybe, instead, its opposite is a perfection—maybe a perfection that God has.

In any case, I am inclined to believe that principle (U) is false, and that it does not provide us with a reason against (T).

If we turn now to the alternative supposition, that God is eternal instead of everlasting, we get initially a somewhat different result. (S) remains as a truth, and indeed becomes a triviality. (U) seems to me to remain at best doubtful in its fully generalized form. But the partially instantiated version of (U) that replaces 'K' with 'God' is more puzzling than before. Its consequent cannot be true, since on this hypothesis there is no time at all at which God knows p (or q), and indeed no time at all at which He does anything or is in any state or condition. If the antecedent of this partially instantiated (U) is false, then the whole thing may be true (interpreted as a truth function, it is certainly true). But if the antecedent is true, then the partially instantiated (U) is false.

Could that antecedent be true? Could a timeless, eternal being know something by inference? Perhaps such a being could not, strictly speaking, carry out a *process* of inference, because a process may be essentially temporal. But it looks as though we will have the same sort of difficulty with many other sorts of things that Christians have supposed that God does or has done. God will not, "really," be able to speak to Moses, for in speaking one word must come after another, and so on. This is one of the difficulties of thinking about eternity, but maybe it is not fatal. For it may be that God does an eternal, nontemporal, act, and the temporal representation or effect of that eternal act is that Moses hears a voice enunciating one word after another. Perhaps then we should say that, in the other case, God performs an eternal act (an eternal inference) whose temporal "shadow" appears as an everlasting process of inference.

But we also suggested earlier that, on the "everlasting" interpretation, God may not perform any process of inference. Perhaps, that is, His knowledge just is everlastingly in the inferential *state*, the state in which His knowledge of one thing is dependent on, or derived from, His knowledge of something else. But this suggestion seems to be transferable in a straightforward way to the "eternity" interpretation. On that interpretation it becomes the claim that God's knowledge is eternally and timelessly in the inferential state—i.e., that the elements of the divine knowledge bear these dependence relations to one another eternally and timelessly.

It seems to me, therefore, that on neither interpretation of God's relation to time does the Thomistic argument provide a persuasive objection to the conjecture that all of God's knowledge is inferential.

Objection 4. If (T) is true, then all of God's knowledge will be indirect. But it is better to know things directly than indirectly. God, as the greatest possible being, must have the very best version of every property, virtue, etc., that He has. He must, therefore, know everything directly, and (T) is not true.

This line of argument depends, I suppose, on the intuition that direct knowledge is in some important way superior to—perhaps nobler than—indirect knowledge. That intuition has appeal all right; I feel its tug myself. But it is not entirely unchallenged, even on its own ground. For sometimes we are inclined, I think, to the opposite intuition. In that mood, we think that the ideal of knowledge, the highest ideal, is that knowledge which is derived from a *logos*, the knowledge which has an explicit and statable reason. On this view it is a defect in human knowledge, an inescapable result of human finitude, that some of our knowledge must be without a *logos*. But the Divine Nature is not bound by finitude, and thesis (T) situates the divine knowledge within that alternative ideal.

Perhaps more important, however, is the fact that the intuition that elevates direct knowledge to the highest level of epistemic value threatens to conflict with another intuition about the divine greatness. And perhaps that is why some philosophers, such as Thomas, seem reluctant to make use of the argument from the preferability of direct knowledge.

The competing intuition that I have in mind is one to the effect that nothing about God, the supreme ruler of all, should depend upon anything other than God Himself. And so, for example, God's knowledge that I am working on a philosophical paper should not be derived from my present actions, as though God perceived me here, sitting in the library. It would be intolerable that anything in God Himself—in this case, an element in His knowledge—should depend upon a creature. Everything about God should be completely *independent* of the world of things that are not divine.

I said that Thomas is reluctant to appeal to the superiority of direct knowledge. This is not surprising, since his own views on the divine epistemology construe much of God's knowledge as being indirect. And it seems clear that what pushes Thomas in this direction is a conviction about the divine independence. What is in God should not be derived from what is not in God. So Thomas quotes Augustine as saying, "God does not behold anything out of Himself."[12] And he interprets this saying to refer not to the *objects* of the divine knowledge (which does include things that are outside of God) but rather to the *mode* of the divine knowledge—i.e., as claiming that "what is outside

---

[12]*ST*, Q. 14, A. 5.

Himself He does not see except in Himself."[13] And in the same article Thomas adds: "So we say that God sees Himself in Himself, because He sees Himself through His essence; and He sees other things, not in themselves, but in Himself, inasmuch as His essence contains the likeness of things other than himself."

Commenting on this aspect of Thomas's version of the divine epistemology, Etienne Gilson says:

> The only object which God knows by Himself and in an immediate manner is Himself. Indeed it is evident that in order to know immediately by Himself an object other than Himself, God would have to turn from His immediate object, which is Himself, in order to turn toward another object. But this other object could only be inferior to the first; and the divine knowledge would then lose some of its perfection, and this is impossible.
>
> God knows Himself perfectly and He knows only Himself immediately. . . .
>
> When we extend God's knowledge to all things, we do not make it dependent upon anything. God sees Himself in Himself, for He sees Himself by His essence. In what concerns other things, on the contrary, He does not see them in themselves but in Himself, in so far as his essence contains in itself the archetype of all that is not Himself. Knowledge, in God, is not specified by anything else than the very essence of God.[14]

It seems clear, then, that in Thomas's view God's knowledge of the world is indirect. He knows me by knowing something else. And that really is something *else*—something really other than me—since that thing is in the divine essence while I am not. Sometimes, as in the passages we have just been reading, that other thing is described as a "likeness" of the world, or (as by Gilson) as an "archetype." In some other places, I think, Thomas suggests that it is by knowing His own will and His causality that God knows the world. But in any case the knowledge of the world is indirect.

Now it would seem possible for knowledge to be indirect without being inferential. Perhaps much of my knowledge of other minds, etc., is of that sort. Perhaps, that is, I have a natural psychological "set" or readiness—a disposition—that generates in me the belief that other people are pleased or happy when I see them smiling, and so on. In

[13]Ibid., reply obj. 1.

[14]Etienne Gilson, *The Christian Philosophy of Thomas Aquinas*, trans. L. K. Shook (New York: Random House, 1956), pp. 111, 112.

that case I do not infer that they are happy, though my belief or knowledge that they are happy is derived from some other experience of mine, perhaps even from a recognition or knowledge in me.

Maybe we should construe the Thomistic view as invoking an analogue of that in God. There would be, that is, a divine disposition to generate in God the belief or knowledge that I am working on a paper on the occasion of God's knowing the relevant likeness or will or causality in Himself. Of course, the latter knowing is either eternal or everlasting, and so the indirect knowledge generated by the disposition would also be either eternal or everlasting.

The alternative I have suggested here is that we should construe the divine knowledge as having instead that other mode of indirectness, that of inference. But when I call it "that other" mode of indirectness I feel a twinge of doubt. Just how is it different? How is a disposition simply to believe q when I believe p different from a disposition to infer q from p? I don't know any deep and satisfying answer to that question. And if there is no important difference there, then maybe those who deny inferential knowledge in God and those who affirm it are not very far apart after all.

Even so, thesis (T) would continue to enshrine one difference. On the Thomistic view there is a sharp distinction between two modes of divine knowledge. Some things—at least one thing—God "sees" in itself. But other things He sees not in themselves but in something else. Some of His knowledge is direct, some of it is indirect. And this is the divine analogue of a similar distinction between two modes of human knowledge. (T), however, makes the divine knowledge all of one piece, a *single mode* operating everywhere. Would that itself be a mark of the divine perfection, that in God (unlike what is in finite creatures) there is only a single perfectly unified and all-encompassing mode of knowledge?

Contributors

WILLIAM P. ALSTON is Professor of Philosophy at Syracuse University.

JOHN MARTIN FISCHER is Associate Professor of Philosophy at Yale University.

THOMAS P. FLINT is Associate Professor of Philosophy at the University of Notre Dame.

ALFRED J. FREDDOSO is Associate Professor of Philosophy at the University of Notre Dame.

NORMAN KRETZMANN is the Susan Linn Sage Professor of Philosophy at Cornell University.

JONATHAN KVANVIG is Associate Professor of Philosophy at Texas A & M University.

HUGH McCANN is Professor of Philosophy at Texas A & M University.

WILLIAM E. MANN is Professor of Philosophy at the University of Vermont.

GEORGE I. MAVRODES is Professor of Philosophy at the University of Michigan.

THOMAS V. MORRIS is Associate Professor of Philosophy at the University of Notre Dame.

PHILIP L. QUINN is the John A. O'Brien Professor of Philosophy at the University of Notre Dame.

ELEONORE STUMP is Professor of Philosophy at the Virginia Polytechnic Institute and State University.

PETER VAN INWAGEN is Professor of Philosophy at Syracuse University.

KEITH YANDELL is Professor of Philosophy at the University of Wisconsin.

LINDA ZAGZEBSKI is Assistant Professor of Philosophy at Loyola Marymount University.

Index

Library of Congress Cataloging-in-Publication Data
Divine and human action.
    Includes index.
      1. Theism.   2. Providence and government of God.
  3. Philosophical theology.   I. Morris, Thomas V.
BD555.D58   1988   211'.3   88-47738
ISBN 0-8014-2197-7
ISBN 0-8014-9517-2 (pbk.)